CRITICAL ESSAYS OF THE EIGHTEENTH
CENTURY

CRITICAL ESSAYS OF THE EIGHTEENTH CENTURY

1700-1725

EDITED BY

WILLARD HIGLEY DURHAM, Ph.D.

New York

RUSSELL & RUSSELL

PR
74
. D8
1961

PREFACE

Much current misunderstanding of the theories about literature held by eighteenth century Englishmen is due to the fact that a large part of the criticism published in their time has been difficult of access. It is the purpose of this volume to lessen the difficulty by putting into the hands of the student a group of representative critical essays. Most of these have not been reprinted since the eighteenth century, and one of them has become really rare. To the less familiar work has been added a selection from the criticism of Steele, Addison, and Pope in order that the survey might be more nearly complete. Essays displaying general theories and tendencies have been chosen rather than those discussing only individual books or plays.

The volume aims to present, therefore, the more significant criticism published between 1700 and 1725. There are, however, two notable omissions. There is no representation either of Shaftesbury's criticism or of the several essays dealing with Shakespeare. The latter have been excluded on the ground that they are already easily accessible in D. Nichol Smith's *Eighteenth Century Essays on Shakespeare*. Shaftesbury has been excluded for reasons of space. It would have been impossible to represent him adequately without devoting to his work a disproportionate number of pages and consequently excluding other work of perhaps greater importance. This exclusion is the less to be regretted because the *Characteristics* have already been republished in an excellent modern edition.

In all cases the texts are exact reprints of original editions or of editions revised by the author. In the latter case the facts about the edition chosen have been stated in the notes. The notes also give more exact references to quotations vaguely indicated in the texts, and such necessary facts as might be unfamiliar to the reader of average information. Neither they nor the introduction pretend to be exhaustive. The latter aims merely to suggest certain points of view from which the texts may well be read. In both cases editorial matter has been sacrificed to a greater body of text.

It is intended that this volume shall be followed as soon as possible by a second which will cover the following quarter-century. This may later be supplemented by still another volume. It is also the editor's purpose to offer as a separate study a history of the development of literary criticism and popular taste in the eighteenth century.

W. H. D.

THE SHEFFIELD SCIENTIFIC SCHOOL,
March, 1915.

CONTENTS

INTRODUCTION

That period of English literature which is commonly styled—with more regard for alliteration than accuracy—the Age of Anne, is summarily dismissed by the average student of literary history. Here, if anywhere, he is undisturbed by critical doubts. He may question the absolute merit of the minor Elizabethans; he may have misgivings as to his estimate of the Victorians; but in dealing with the Augustans he is happily certain. Especially is this true of Augustan ideals and tendencies. There was the 'Classical School'; one can trace the 'beginnings of Romanticism'; the former is fortunately dead, the latter grown into something of much greater importance. It is all perfectly clear.

To the person, however, who takes pains to read what was written during this period, nothing is clearer than the falsity of such an opinion. The Age of Anne has suffered from adulation and from vituperation, from ignorant generalization and from scholarly misrepresentation, but from nothing so much as from being hastily pigeon-holed. It is possible to conceive how persons so unfortunate as to be blind to a certain type of literary merit might be eager to get this period off their hands. It is much more remarkable that they should suppose they had done so.

Such ungrounded assumption is largely the product of indifference, an indifference fortunately lessening. The mere passage of time is transferring it to the Victorian period. It begins to appear, for example, as if Tennyson were succeeding to Pope's position as a phenomenon sufficiently considered by English critics and now definitely disposed of and laid away. Cowley was similarly treated by the mid-eighteenth century. It is no new thing, this curt dismissal of our literary great-grandfathers; it is perhaps the original sin of criticism. The glory of the present or the immediate past has always cast a shadow backward. But, as the present becomes the past, the shadow moves.

If the early eighteenth century seems to have emerged somewhat slowly, the fact is due, in part at least, to two causes: to the character of the period and to the character of those who have written about it. The critics of the nineteenth century to whose lot fell the disposition of the 'classical period' were men of unusual ability, men who wrote with such force that it has often been easier to remember their criticisms than the work they criticized. The period, on the other hand, was of such a sort that it could not be completely forgotten. Its writers had a way of making phrases which became first proverbial and then banal, so that people became prematurely bored by men whom they had not read. "Fools rush in where angels fear to tread," "The proper study of mankind is man"—these, and a hundred others like them, are so familiar that it has been impossible to 'discover' Pope as the minor Elizabethans, for instance, were discovered.

Similarly, the critical theory of the period has been presented to us in compact, easily digested, and—to many minds—disagreeable doses, so that familiarity could easily breed ignorance. Queen Anne critics are believed to have cherished a pathetic devotion to 'the Rules' and the couplet. Some of their best-known work bears out this belief. We scorned the rules and were easily wearied by the couplet, and we accepted this as sufficient.

If we are to escape from this position into one from which we may estimate this period more justly, comprehend it more accurately, we shall not do so by means of new generalizations. Some very accurate generalizations about this period have already been made without much apparent effect. The one thing needful is that the student shall actually read what was then written, shall know in detail what these men thought they were doing. Then he will realize the variety of opinion which existed, and possibly come to feel that some of these opinions are not wholly without validity.

Believing this, I have not attempted to make this introduction in any sense a history of the critical theories championed between 1700 and 1725. I have attempted to point out certain fairly obvious facts concerning the real nature of some of these theories, to call attention to their variety—sometimes not superficially clear—and to indicate their general tendencies, their points of view, which are often quite other than what we should infer from isolated opinions and individual judgments.

Before attempting to determine what the critics of the time did do, it is necessary to emphasize one thing they did not do. There is an impression still at large that Alexander Pope, aided and abetted by servile followers, foisted upon the meek British public a hide-bound and pedantic theory of poetry commonly described as 'pseudo-classic'. Whatever Pope's faults may have been—and they were many—this was not one of them. He was neither the originator of this pseudo-classic theory nor its most extreme adherent. Nor was any other person in the eighteenth century. For the really thoroughgoing classicist or rationalist in criticism it is necessary to go to the preceding century. If by pseudo-classic is meant the type of mind which carries its admiration of the ancients to the point of idolatry, to the point of inculcating a slavish imitation of Greeks and Latins and of censuring departure from their methods, we can best find it in Thomas Rymer. In his *Short View of Tragedy,* which appeared in 1693, besides attacking Shakespeare with a virulence unparalleled in England until our own day, he strongly advised the use of the chorus in English tragedy. Admiration for the classics could scarcely carry one further. If, on the other hand, pseudo-classic be taken as referring to the theory that emotion in poetry should be kept in strict subjection to reason and common sense, we shall find the extreme position represented in D'Avenant's *Preface to Gondibert,* published in 1650. There, as a justification of his subject, he writes, "Truth operative, and by effects continually alive, is the Mistris of Poets, who hath not her existence in matter but in reason."[1] This insistence on reason to the neglect of feeling or imagination is characteristic of a critical temper which makes him look upon Spenser's *Fairy Queen* as a dream "such as Poets and Painters, by being overstudious, may have in the beginning of Feavers."[2] Neither Rymer nor D'Avenant is an isolated phenomenon. Opinions similar to theirs were repeatedly expressed in the third and fourth quarters of the seventeenth century. The eighteenth century cannot, therefore, be credited with either the invention or the most thoroughgoing application of pseudo-classic theory.

It is equally misleading to say that such theories as these were dominant in the period with which we are now concerned. In the first place a distinction should be made between the opinions of professional critics and men of letters and those of the reading and theater-going

[1]Spingarn, *Critical Essays of the XVII Century*, 2.11.
[2]*Ib.* 2.6.

public. The former are by no means homogeneous—
some of them show little trace of pseudo-classic influence.
The latter were commonly hostile to it. Dogmatic assertions about the popular taste of a bygone age require
considerable qualification, yet there is every reason to
believe that the great majority of the public regarded
the rules with suspicion and disfavor. There is, on the
one hand, the evidence supplied by the success of plays,
both old and new, written without regard for the rules,
and the failure of others which conformed to them.
There is also—more significant still—the admission by
critics who upheld the rules that their opinions were not
those generally prevalent. In the *Art of Poetry* Gildon
repeatedly asserts that his opinions are not those of the
crowd; and in his earlier *Essay on the Art, Rise, and
Progress of the Stage* he writes, "There is indeed a very
formidable Party among us, who are such Libertines in
all manner of Poetry, especially in the *Drama,* that they
think all regular Principles of Art an Imposition not to
be born." The author of *Cato Examin'd* (1713) gives
similar testimony: "For let the *ignorant Million* exclaim
as they please against the Rules, and Art, and make a
senseless Clamour about *Nature,* without giving us any
Account what they mean by the Word." From the
Harlequin Horace, published after the turn of the
quarter-century, we learn that

> "Most Readers like Romantick Flights alone,
> And scorn a Poem where Design is shewn."

Such quotations might be multiplied indefinitely. Moreover, the necessity of arguing in behalf of the rules shows
that the fight for them was far from won. The pseudo-
classic theory was by no means securely dominant.

Many writers and more readers were of quite another mind.

But popular taste is an indefinite and intangible thing. It is a composite of likings by no means feeble or without means of positive expression, yet inevitably unreasoned and unformulated. We are more immediately concerned with those likirgs which did find articulate expression, which were often only too well codified and reduced to neat formulas. We have to do, not with the taste that was necessarily dominant, but with that which wished to be dominant, that which men who had read and thought about matters critical felt ought properly to be dominant.

But before discussing individual critics of this period it may be well to summarize briefly the opinions which they inherited from a previous generation, to separate as clearly as may be the main currents of previous critical thought. Various such divisions have been made. One of the most useful is that of Hamelius,[1] who divides the critics of the later seventeenth century into four classes: the neo-classicists, the rationalists, the religionists, and the romanticists. We may pass over the religionists, if only because of the barbarity of the word. By these Hamelius means men who, like Milton, felt the importance to poetry of religion, especially the Christian religion, who insisted on the necessity of religious emotion as a vitalizing poetic force. Although Dennis, one of the most significant of eighteenth century critics, gave to this view its clearest and most definite expression, we may safely omit it from our classification on the ground that it is merely descriptive of an opinion of certain individuals, an opinion which was held as a

[1]*Die Kritik in der englischen Literatur des 17. und 18. Jahrhunderts.*

portion of a theory of poetry which otherwise falls in with one or more of the other three.

In defining classicist theories as they found expression in England it is important to remember that they manifest primarily an intense and justifiable admiration. They are often spoken of as though they expressed only an unjustifiable dislike for things not classic. Love for the classics needs no apology, and when lovers of the classics went astray it was primarily because they did not love enough. The faults of the school are most apparent in those who went, not to the classics, but to what later scholars had said about the classics.

In the classics men found a type of beauty rich without extravagance, simple without baldness, profound without obscurity. They learned from Aristotle that certain characteristics were common to the greater examples of this type. They found also that in much of modern poetry there was extravagance and obscurity, restlessness and confusion. They consequently urged the imitation of classical models, obedience to the laws of Aristotle, as a means of avoiding these faults. Many of them went too far in their admiration of a single type of beauty, but they did not—in England, at least—go so far as to suppose that mere imitation of the ancient authors would supply the lack of genius; they merely said that such imitation would lead genius into safer paths. Their theory had, therefore, the merits and defects which safe theories always have. Those who really follow them avoid great sins and great virtues. It must not be forgotten, however, that restraint is a virtue, and it should not be confounded with mere emptiness or mediocrity. In our condemnation of the namby-pamby we too often ignore the fact that the fault is not in restraint but in the lack of anything to restrain.

There is, however, in classical literature much that is freely imaginative. There are works in which the poet's imagination oversteps the bounds of prosaic reason. Consequently such critics as were most devoted to the white light of reason, those who were most offended by the extravagances of such writers as the 'metaphysicals', believed the classics somewhat lacking in qualities essential to a true literary guide. We find, therefore, among the critics of the seventeenth century, besides those who regarded the classics as infallible, others who wished a dual government of classics and reason, and a third class who felt that safety lay only in the constant restraint of the fancy by the judgment. These last cannot be called classicists without confusion of terms. It is simpler to label them rationalists.

The romanticists in criticism are easy to define for our purposes. The others are romanticists—the men who preferred Elizabethan to Greek or French drama—the men who saw possibilities in mediæval literature.

But all such division, as far as the first quarter of the eighteenth century is concerned, is of use solely as offering definitions of terms which are convenient to use. Practically no critic fits into one of these categories to the exclusion of the others. And no one—this cannot be too much emphasized—no one was the kind of classicist or rationalist that is to be found in some popular books and essays dealing with eighteenth century literature. The only appearance of this imaginary creature is among the straw figures which writers put together for purposes of demolition. That there was in this period any critic of importance who actually believed that one could make a poet by teaching rules, or that art could replace genius, or any such silly stuff, I emphatically deny. There were many shades of opinion, many opinions with which most of us would totally disagree, but none so patently absurd as they are often supposed to be, none that do not contain some truth—distorted, under or overstated, perhaps—but still truth.

The following discussions of individual men make no attempt, therefore, at any definite classification. They are neither pleas nor verdicts. They aim merely to point out such salient features as are especially significant for students of English criticism.

CHARLES If Charles Gildon occupies first place, it is
GILDON not because of his deserts. Whatever critical
ability he possessed best appears in the work he published before the beginning of the century, so that in fairness he had to be taken from the place in the second decade which his most pretentious work would have given him.

This duality of chronological position corresponds to a duality in character. As his life was divided between two centuries, so his opinions were divided between two extremes. Once a Catholic, he became a Deist; once a critic, he became a criticaster. It is not impossible that there was a connection between the two declensions, though they were not synchronous and though he partially recovered from the first. Certainly in both cases he substituted a barren and superficial rationalism for conceptions at once more fruitful and more profound.

In his earlier work, such as the attack on Rymer and the two essays here reprinted from the same Miscellany, he uses such authority as he has in defence of literary freedom, refusing to attribute universal validity to the opinions of Aristotle, and maintaining the principle that new times and new conditions demand new forms of literary expression. "And as in Physic, so in Poetry, there must be a regard had to the Clime, Nature, and Customs of the People."[1]   Such a dictum was by no means a critical commonplace in the seventeenth century. Apparently this young man—for he was not yet thirty— was in a fair way to become a critic of some ability.   If his enthusiasm for Dryden touched madness, it drove him at times to unusual sanity.

It is, therefore, with considerable surprise that one finds him publishing in 1710 an essay of a very different sort, that on the *Art, Rise, and Progress of the Stage.* This presents the same uncompromisingly rationalistic opinions as were later developed in the *Art of Poetry.* And here, as commonly elsewhere, rationalism is another name for crude dogmatism.   The *Art of Poetry* is almost devoid of real thinking.   It is an echo of echoes; for the sections that follow the one here reprinted are a cento of quotations from Roscommon, Mulgrave, and Boileau, with prose comments which are additions to the bulk rather than to the ideas of the work.   Obviously, then, the thought of the book is not of the eighteenth, but of the seventeenth century, and its positive value lies almost solely in the fact that it is the most complete statement which we have from this period of the point of view which is often supposed to have dominated it. The fact that such a statement found few purchasers is consequently significant.

Poor as the book is, it would be unfair to ignore its occasional flashes of insight.   Although the doctrine of 'English numbers' which forms the concluding section is mistaken, Gildon at any rate recognizes the existence of

[1]p. 4.

quantity in English verse. Unlike some modern theorists, he realized that even in English a pyrrhic and a spondee are not the same. He was able to perceive the genius of Milton and Shakespeare, although his praise is not ours; and in what he says of Shakespeare and Homer he shows a recognition of the fact that genius may come unconsciously and intuitively to the heights of art.

Despite such faint lights, however, our interest in the book is derived not from Gildon's opinions, but from those of his opponents. Whatever the cause of his change of front, it was certainly not the desire to be with the crowd. In presenting the views of Mrs. LaMode and her friends he shows that popular taste was against him. By ridiculing Pope under the name of Sawney Dapper, by attacking the *Tatler* and *Spectator,* he consciously ranges himself with the few against the many. Consequently we have here, as in no other single volume, evidence of the lack of unanimity among critics of the period, of the gulf fixed between the thought of the periodicals and that of the rationalists, and of the fact that the uncompromising defenders of the rules were fighting a losing battle. Whoever will read the book without prejudice will find the rigid neo-classical theory— even as Gildon presents it, with all his shallow thought and clumsy style—to be a point of view not without reason; but he will also find something of much greater significance, that most of the critics of the day, even those who thoroughly appreciated the worth of this point of view, were freeing the theory from its most glaring crudities, and were so altering it that from the standpoint of the stalwarts they seemed its enemies. Thus regarded the book becomes a valuable document, one indispensable to a real perception of critical conditions.

JOHN   To both Pope and Swift, John Hughes seemed
HUGHES   "among the mediocribus, in prose as well as
           verse."[1] Certainly there is nothing in the
Essay on Style to prove them wrong. But after the
straggling sentences of the *Art of Poetry* one turns with
relief even to mediocrity. Hughes, unlike some who
have written on style, practises his own precepts. These
precepts pretend to be nothing more than the simple rules
which are now the commonplaces of a thousand text-
books; but they have for us an interest as presenting
the point of view towards English prose—the principles
held and the men admired by the authors of the great
periodicals: for, next to Eustace Budgell, Hughes was
the most regular of the minor contributors to the
Spectator, and his intimate friendship with Addison is
well known. It would seem unnecessary to point out
that Hughes expressly asserts that genius is not commu-
nicable by rules, were it not for the delusion that eighteenth century critics denied this truism. Even today
long-suffering teachers of English composition are supposed to fail because they cannot make geniuses, a thing
which neither they nor John Hughes ever set out to do.

What Hughes has to say about Spenser is, however,
of much more interest than what he has to say about
style. That the edition of Spenser to which these essays
were prefaced was not reprinted for thirty years is
perhaps less symptomatic of popular taste than is sometimes supposed. If we except those who read Spenser
under compulsion in our schools and colleges and those
who read him because they wish to be 'cultured', we
should not find to-day a startlingly large number of
people whose familiarity with him went much beyond
hearsay. The important fact is that an edition with

[1]Pope's *Works*, ed. Elwin-Courthope, 7. 334, 335.

prefaces and glossary, an edition which presents himself as a labor of love, should have been put forth at all.

Similarly, the important aspect of Hughes' criticism of Spenser is not its weakness but its strength. If he devotes much space to the allegorical character of the *Fairy Queen,* he certainly lays no more stress upon it than Spenser laid; and if some modern critics deprecate this enthusiasm for allegory, they fault Spenser—and Dante—along with Hughes. But it is not the allegorical character of the poem which to Hughes constituted its chief merit; it is the character of the allegory—it is the "surprizing Vein of fabulous Invention, which . . . enriches it every where with Imagery and Descriptions more than we meet with in any other modern Poem."[1] It is the author's possession of a "kind of Poetical Magick."[1] With this view few would be disposed to quarrel, yet its expression then was no hackneyed critical tagging.

Nor would any save a Spenserian take violent exception to Hughes' charge that "Spenser's Abundance betrays him into Excess"[1] or to the statement that "the several Books appear rather like so many several Poems, than one entire Fable."[1] Even a criticism as obvious as this last and as axiomatic to the true classicist, is made with hesitation and qualification; for Hughes refuses to force the *Fairy Queen* into one of the fixed 'kinds' of poetry, and insists that it is not under laws which have power only over these 'kinds'. The comparison to the Gothic cathedral which follows by no means belittles either poem or building. Can the most passionate partizan of Gothic point to a great cathedral which is a perfectly unified whole? Or to one wholly free from "barbarism"? If not, the parallel holds, involving no blind disparagement, but rather an appre-

[1] p. 105.

ciation surprising to one who knows this period only from the hasty generalizations of historians.

Another significant feature of Hughes' criticism is his ungrudging recognition of individual temperament and its environment as valuable factors in poetic production. We may agree with him that Spenser might have formed a better plan when he questions whether Spenser would have executed any other so well. And we are far removed from the hidebound criticism which scorns all tastes save that of its own time, when we find a justification of Spenser's knights and tourneys on the ground that they reflect the taste of Spenser's age, that they are antiquated in the same way that the costumes of the Elizabethan court are antiquated, but not necessarily the worse for that.

Hughes' critical position, then, is neither one of blind adherence to the rules nor of blind opposition to them. He got at the principal merit of his author; he set forth that author's faults with discrimination and restraint; he showed that other features of the work apparently faulty could be accounted for and justified. He may not be a critic of extraordinary insight, he may even be a 'mediocrist'; but he has sympathy and sanity. On this score there is much to be said for mediocrity.

JOHN DENNIS Despite his plays and his poems, substantial and numerous as they were, John Dennis was known to his contemporaries not as playwright or poet, but as 'the critic'. This title is obviously a mark of distinction, not from other Dennises, but from other critics. No such title was given to Gildon or Hughes or Addison or Steele. Nor was it an ironical distinction—rather one given in recognition of serious purpose and solid attainment. For in bulk and solidity of performance Dennis was easily first among the English critics of his own time—and of earlier times. Not even Dryden—so much Dennis' superior in quality of criticism—went at his problems with the seriousness, with the consciousness of high function, that characterized 'the critic'.

Measured merely as quantity, Dennis' work was remarkable. Nowadays we have critics who put forth one or more volumes a year, but then little criticism was published save as prefaces, as occasional papers in periodicals, or as pamphlets. Yet Dennis' *Advancement and Reformation of Modern Poetry* is a considerable volume in itself, and the project of which the *Grounds of Criticism* was intended as a first instalment would, if completed, have covered several volumes. Add to these, prefaces and letters and pamphlets, and you have a quantity of work which leaves no doubt that Dennis went at criticism with great seriousness, with a sense of doing a really necessary work.

It cannot, unfortunately, be said that his achievement equalled his intention. At his best Dennis was unable to realize his ideals; at his worst the ideals were not worth realizing. And it is by his worst that he is commonly remembered. It is pitiful that this burly, independent theorist should have come down to us not as an original thinker, but as a victim of Alexander Pope. It is no wonder that Pope pilloried Dennis among the dunces, but it is painful to think of Dennis' suffering could he know that he owed his posthumous fame to the twisted poet he so thoroughly despised.

The pamphlet *On a certain Rhapsody entitled An Essay on Criticism* is typical of Dennis' share in the controversy. It shows clearly how a sense of personal injury, a feeling that he had been undeservedly ill-used, drove him to attacks which in later years became more bitter. It shows also how this personal grudge blinded him to Pope's merits, so that as a detailed review the pamphlet does not do the *Essay* justice. It is undoubtedly often carping and meticulous in its faultfinding. Yet many of Dennis' thrusts are as well-aimed as they are powerful. That they hit the mark is shown by the alterations Pope made in his poem. The text of the *Essay* as we have it to-day and the text as referred to in this pamphlet show important differences. The pamphlet has, therefore, a value not due solely to its rarity. It sheds light on Pope as well as on Dennis and Dennis' theories of criticism.

The *Large Account of Taste* may be read by the curious as revealing the point of view of a man who could alter Shakespeare's *Merry Wives* for the worse, as showing that such a man could still have a reasonable regard for Shakespeare's worth. It may be read by the historian of taste as giving some evidence, not entirely unbiased, concerning the way in which the political and social changes of the preceding seventeen years had affected the literary public. Of more general interest are the remarks on humor. Dennis uses the word in the Jonsonian sense, and in maintaining that for comedy humor is superior to wit he anticipated much that has since been said about Sheridan. Appended to this point is the shrewd observation, not without value for an estimate of 'sentimental comedy', that in comedy lowness, even obscenity, may be less harmful to morals than realistic representations of amorous passion—a truth still unheeded by our censors official and unofficial.

Of much greater value than either of these essays is that on the *Grounds of Criticism*. Much inferior in some ways to the *Advancement and Reformation of Modern Poetry,* it has the practical merit of presenting in a much more reasonable compass a point of view essentially the same. It is the sanity of this central thesis, the conviction and determination with which Dennis held to it, that arouses one's admiration for the man. Over and over again, in one work after another, he tells us that "Poetry then is an Art by which a Poet excites Passion."[1] Again, "Passion, then, is the characteristical Mark of Poetry. . . Every where a Discourse is not Pathetick, there it is Prosaick."[2] Unlike some critics, Dennis really knew poetry and loved it, and he was consequently unwaveringly certain that poetry must have some sort of emotional appeal—or it was a dead thing deserving to be cast out. To have held firmly such a simple doctrine as this, to have come to grips with it and beaten consequences out of it—untrue consequences, even—is to have done something if you live in an age of hyper-rationalism, if you are yourself a devotee of clear, dispassionate thought. And Dennis was this sort of man, despite his rages. It was his regard for pure reason that undid him. It was the broad road of logic which led him to critical destruction. Yet in spite of his time and himself, he never forgot the essential truth that poetry cannot be totally devoid of feeling, of some form or other of human emotion.

Out of this he developed his most original theory, the theory that the superiority of the ancients over the moderns lay not in their superior ability or training or environment, but in the fact that they filled their great poetry with religious emotion. From this judgment it is a natural inference that the secret of success for the

---

[1]p. 146.
[2]*Advancement and Reformation*, p. 46.

moderns, the means for the advancement and reformation of modern poetry, lies in the use of the Christian religion, in imbuing modern poetry with the highest and deepest emotions that Christianity can offer. The chain of reasoning by which Dennis arrives at this conclusion is neat. In substance it is something like this: The more sublime the subject, the greater and loftier the feelings aroused in the reader. Religious emotions, the feelings aroused by the contemplation of religious ideas, are the most profound, the most sublime of which man is capable. Ergo, religious poetry arouses the most profound and sublime emotions that poetry can arouse. Ergo, to make modern poetry great, make it religious.

Few have ever accepted this doctrine without reserve. In the first place, there is the question of the form in which the poet's conception is embodied. Dennis thought that the inward fire would necessarily produce an outward glory. But his own poems disprove this. They are lamentable evidence of the way in which a poet who is himself profoundly moved by a sublime idea may be incapable of moving his readers at all—unless to laughter. It is not enough to have a great subject. The thought of the Last Judgment inspired the *Dies Iræ,* but it also inspired some of the most irresistibly comic lines in literature. There are portions of Young's *Last Day* which are hopelessly ludicrous. On the other hand, some most affecting lines have been inspired by trifling subjects.

And yet Dennis' theory is not absurd. His completely logical proof of it, his thoroughly common sense application of it, his rigorous extension of it—these may be absurd; but the kernel of his thought is not absurd. It seems to have grown out of his admiration for Milton. We may not agree with Dennis that Milton is the greatest of poets, but we can hardly deny that *Paradise Lost* owes at least part of its sublimity to its theme. If we try to collect for ourselves the poems or portions of poems which are most irresistibly, profoundly moving, do we not find them filled with some form of religious or cosmic emotion—whether we think of the *Paradiso* or *Œdipus Rex* or *Job* or Lear on the heath or the *Lines written near Tintern Abbey*? The fact that Dennis mistook a half for a whole truth is no reason for ignoring the half.

One of Dennis' rigorously logical untruths is his deduction from the common theory that poetry, and all other art, should instruct. We need not debate this point. It would be difficult to prove that any art—that any external impression—can be without some effect upon personality. But when Dennis says that art instructs, he means that art should consciously instruct, and he makes the natural deduction that the lesson of the poet should be clearly expressed. Thence it naturally follows that a tragedy must show the guilty punished and the innocent rewarded. This is, of course, the familiar doctrine of poetical justice, the doctrine which Dennis defended again and again, especially in his remarks on Shakespeare. We find Addison denying it in a paper written for the *Spectator*.[1] We do not need to disprove it again; we need only note Dennis' advocacy of it against Shakespeare as a further instance of how his theories warred against his natural instincts, for he knew Shakespeare and loved him.

It would seem that a man who did not use classical practise as a norm, who denied the superiority of the ancients in many genres,[2] might have escaped the appella-

[1]pp. 306-8.
[2]cf. *Advancement and Reformation*, pp. 66-78.

tion of classicist. Yet Dennis is commonly so called.
The epithet is a convenient one when you happen to
dislike a critic. To be sure, Dennis emphatically dis-
approved of the tendency of poets to imitate the ancients;
he distinctly lamented that much of modern poetry was
a mere "copy of the ancient";[1] he ridiculed Addison for
servile obedience in *Cato* to the unity of place;[2] and he
began his critical career by an attack on Rymer's plea
for the restoration of the chorus in tragedy.[3] To my
mind this is not classicism, nor is a man a classicist who
maintains that Milton was the greatest of poets.[4] Yet
this Dennis firmly believed.

But, it is said, he upheld the rules. To be sure he
did, but not because they were ancient rules, but because
they were to him rational ones. If Dennis occasionally
uses the argument from authority, he puts it beside or
below the argument from reason. When, as in *Cato,* he
thought one of the rules led to absurdity, he opposed the
rules. If they were rational, well and good; if not, away
with them. Alas, he too often felt them to be rational.
Particularly as he grew older did his love for poetry
become more and more obscured by his love for a clear
and orderly theory, for a regular and rationalized
practise. The succession of enthymemes in his pages
make them perspicuous, but untrue. That poetry is an
art; that an art must have an end; that an end implies
a means; that this means must be discoverable—such a
series of unimportant or erroneous deductions appears
often in Dennis, but not in Dennis alone. Nor was this
manner of thinking confined to æsthetics. We find, for

[1]*Ib.*, pp. 28-29.
[2]*Remarks upon Cato.*
[3]*The Impartial Critick* (Spingarn, *Critical Essays of the XVII
Century*, 3. 148-197).
[4]cf. p. 172, and similar expressions elsewhere.

instance, many men of the time seriously maintaining by means of similar reasoning that true religion must be discoverable by the unaided reason of any man. If so, true religion is a strange, a varying, an extremely undesirable thing to have about. Such beliefs were, of course, the natural result of the trust in pure reason which grew up under the influence of Descartes and Locke—a pathetic trust only paralleled by the faith of the nineteenth century in the infallibility of natural science.

Of all the critics of the period, Dennis was the most philosophic, and consequently the one who suffered most from this trust in a frail reed. Naturally many of his conclusions are hopelessly inconclusive, much of his theory of poetry totally unpoetic. Yet one who reads Dennis instead of reading about him, continually feels behind the error a burly, sincere personality, that of a man devoted to the cause of good art, a man who felt truly, but whose vision was distorted by the superficial clarity of his thought.

GEORGE FARQUHAR   Farquhar is a totally different type. Never an abstract philosopher, he is only incidentally a critic. In his informal letter *On Comedy* he attempts to rationalize a practise which produced the *Trip to the Jubilee,* the *Beaux' Stratagem,* and the *Recruiting Officer.* It is, therefore, the by-product of successful comedy. It is, moreover, a theory which justifies comedy by its success. It presents the democratic theory of the drama, the theory which tests a play largely by the receipts of the box-office. A good play, says Farquhar, is one which can hold alike the wit, the courtier, the heavy citizen, the fine lady, and her footman—"and he that can do this best, and with most Applause, writes the best Comedy, let him do it by what Rules he pleases, so they be not offensive to Religion and good Manners."[1]

But Farquhar does not content himself with merely waving the rules aside. He first of all denies their validity on the ground that they are not the formulations of masters, but of observers, observers who may or may not have got at essential principles. One may note, for example, that all good plays are printed on paper without making any vital discovery. Furthermore, even if these principles were essential in Greece or Rome, they are very likely not so in England, where one writes for an audience different in race, in education, in custom, in temper. And finally he denies that the rules have the support of reason, ridiculing the statement that the compression of years of action into the space of three hours is absurd and improbable. It may be, in a sense, he says, but in that sense all drama is improbable. Is it any more impossible that three hours should contain twelve years than that they should contain twelve hours? Or is it any more impossible to move from Cairo to Astrachan between the acts than to move to Cairo at the rising of the first curtain?[2]

With such clear strokes Farquhar separates the rational from the rationalistic. It is the reasonable artist against the reasoning critic, and we are easily won. But the success is one of negation, and it leaves embarrassing problems unsolved. Is success the only test of good drama? Are all unsuccessful plays necessarily bad art? Would Farquhar's plays have been the worse if they had had a more unified structure? His essay lays in

[1]p. 277.
[2]p. 283.

ruins some jerry-built constructions, but leaves small shelter for our critical heads.

To the historian, at least, the essay has a positive value. It recalls the fact that *Cato* owed its success largely to extraneous conditions, and that the majority of plays successful at this time were not made in servile obedience to the rules. By its whole tone it shows that the opponents of free structure were in the minority, that they composed a complacent 'select circle', and that the popular taste of Queen Anne's time demanded from the drama essentially what we demand to-day. Consequently, if the drama of the period reached no very high level, the fact is not due to the stifling of dramatic ability by overbearing classical critics who damned everything that violated the strict French code.

ALEXANDER POPE   With the drama, save for his share in one ghastly failure, Pope had little to do; but he is commonly named as the greatest champion of the rules. This is partly due to the fact that as a critic he is best known and misjudged by his *Essay on Criticism*. It would have been too much to expect of even such a genius as Pope that he should produce before he was twenty-one a theory of poetry at once original and sound. The *Essay* is neither—it is not even a theory of poetry, despite Dennis and later critics. It is advice to critics, in matter now tritely right, now tritely wrong; but in manner brilliant, so brilliant that it makes an indelible impression on those who hate it most.

The next source of misinformation about Pope's mature critical attitude is to be found in his reported conversations with Spence. We need only ask ourselves

how we should feel if some of our remarks made in
casual conversation, remarks often made in rashness or
peevishness and remembered by chance, were preserved
for the delight of our enemies.   Such a collection is
likely to be as interesting as it is unfair.   The one thing
of which Spence's gossip makes us certain is that Pope
often contradicted himself, so that no conclusions can
be drawn from any one remark.

The only way of getting at Pope's ultimate attitude
toward poetry would be to consider a complete collection
of his critical remarks and writings in the light of his
poems; but in default of such a study, the best single
source is his preface to the translation of the *Iliad*.
Here he has given us his mature opinion of a great poet
with whose work he had busied himself for a period of
years, an opinion intended for publication and carefully
prepared for that purpose.

It is consequently significant to find that Pope here
insists from the beginning on the supreme importance
of poetic imagination, 'invention', its importance to the
whole and to the part.   To this essential quality all else
is subordinate.   Art is merely "a prudent Steward that
lives on managing the Riches of Nature.   Whatever
Praises may be given to Works of Judgment, there is not
even a single Beauty in them but is owing to the Invention."[1]   It is because of their extraordinary poetical
imagination, their 'invention', that Shakespeare and
Milton and Homer are great, because of his unsurpassed
invention that Homer is greatest.

It is this thesis, not profoundly original or daring, but
very far from what neo-classicism is often supposed to
have taught, that occupies the greater part of this
preface.   This thesis alone might relieve Pope from the

[1]p. 323.

charge of blindly doting on a mechanical correctness as
the be-all and end-all of poetry. But his enemies try to
explain this away. Leslie Stephen, for instance, insisted
that the use of the word invention implies that Pope
thought of Homer as working out his poem in some
such manner as a skilled mechanic works out some
problem which may lead to an improvement in an engine.[1]
That such an interpretation is strained and uncalled for
would make it only the more acceptable to many of the
moderns who have busied themselves with editing Pope
or writing his life. To admit the truth might weaken
their case against him. But the thesis remains, the
antithesis between invention and judgment stands, and
we perceive what we might have suspected all along, that
Pope knew what was the essential factor in the making
of good poetry. "A cooler Judgment may commit fewer
Faults, and be more approv'd in the Eyes of *One Sort* of
Criticks," he writes on a later page, "but that Warmth of
Fancy will carry the loudest and most universal Applauses
which holds the Heart of a Reader under the strongest
Enchantment."[2] This last phrase is not far removed from
one that latter-day critics are prone to overwork, one we
met before in Hughes, 'poetical magic'.

There can be no doubt that in this preface Pope occasionally lauds Homer for qualities which existed only
in the imagination of certain scholars. The glorification
and deification of Homer's learning, of his influence on
science and philosophy, were the extravagances of
scholarly fanatics. Pope knew too little about Homer to
deny such statements; he cared too little for such matters
to investigate them; so he includes them, but only as

[1]*History of English Thought*, 2, 356.
[2]p. 341.

further evidence, somewhat irrelevant, of his central thesis.

The rest of the preface is taken up with Pope's theory of translation, a theory presenting a middle ground between loose paraphrase and literal fidelity, the theory which is essentially that accepted by the best translators since Pope's day. Whatever we now think of Pope's application of this theory, we can hardly condemn the principle as it is here presented; and we may even question whether any translation since gives us as much of Homer's beauty and power as this gave to the audience for which it was designed.

RICHARD   An adequate representation of Dick Steele
STEELE   within the limits of this volume is even more
            difficult than that of Pope. Steele's criticism
is so informal, so occasional, that it never takes the form
of books or pamphlets, rarely of whole papers in the
Tatler, Spectator, or *Guardian.* Nowhere does he
formally enunciate a theory of poetry, nowhere set forth
his critical principles in due form and order. Here a
sentence, there a paragraph—perhaps a reference to
Shakespeare or Milton, perhaps to a contemporary like
Prior or Ambrose Philips, perhaps to the Bible or a
Lapland song—in any case a touch and go affair, sometimes trivial and worthless, sometimes illuminating and
suggestive.

The very fact that he thus approached criticism,
however, helps to place him, to show him for a man
impatient of formalism, impatient of elaborate parade of
knowledge, a critic satisfied to record the impression he
personally received from a work of art, and consequently
a critic whose words derive their weight from the fact
that Dick Steele's impressions are worth knowing.

Such a passage as that about Macduff represents the kind of criticism we know as 'impressionistic', a kind which at its best, as here, reveals beauty unnoticed by the casual reader or spectator.

When, as in the twelfth *Guardian,* Steele did attempt a more methodical setting forth of his views, he uses the tests of reason and good sense, the almost inevitable tests of the age; but he is still opposed to those critics who found good sense and the rules inseparable, or who demanded the support of ancient authority for their opinions. Steele, like other impressionistic critics, is at his weakest when he attempts to account for his likes and dislikes; at his best when he lets his taste be its own justification. But at all times he clearly belongs with the critics of the left wing, the free lances who refuse to be restrained by any formal critical code.

JOSEPH Addison, although intimately associated with ADDISON Steele, although lumped with him by Gildon and Dennis in their attacks on *Spectator* theories, although sharing much of Steele's general conception of poetical theory, was a critic of another type. His more pretentious series—such a series as Steele would never have attempted—are so familiar that it would have been labor lost to have reprinted them here. The papers on Milton, on *Chevy Chase,* on the Pleasures of the Imagination, are known to every student of criticism.

They are known, yes, but they are not always read without prepossession. How often has Addison been called a classicist for testing Milton by the rules of Aristotle, how often ridiculed as pedantic and uninspired. Yet what should he have done? Unless we are to content ourselves in criticism with a mere record of our feelings when reading a poem, or with a list of the purple passages it contains, or with a bio-genetic analysis dealing with heredity and environment, what are we to do? Is it absurd to ask whether a poem contains certain qualities which are to be found in other great poems of similar type? Is it pseudo-classicism to ask, for instance, whether *Lear* is a unit, and where that unity lies? Do we gain nothing from the attempt to discover whether the character of Hamlet is inconsistent with itself? There can be no doubt that by proposing and answering such questions we gain an insight otherwise unlikely. The absurdity begins only when we condemn a work of art because it does not meet all of a pre-established set of standards, not when we merely ask whether it does meet them or not. Addison, in the papers on Milton, analyzed a great poem in the light of others, assuming its greatness beforehand; and in so doing wrote a criticism which has for us little freshness and value merely because we are familiar with his opinions before we read his essays.

Similarly with the *Chevy Chase* papers. It is preposterous to assume that Addison admired *Chevy Chase* because he found that it would endure the application of some of the supposed principles of the epic. What really happened was, that he liked the poem and wanted to make others like it, and so tried to show them how it had in it some of the qualities they liked in poems with which they were already familiar. It must never be forgotten that the writers of the periodicals were pedagogues, that they wished to better the taste of the general public, and that they used devices not unlike those of the modern teacher. But where would many members of our English faculties be left were it assumed that their teaching devices represented accurately their own critical processes and theories?

By reason of his admiration for the Ballads, for Milton, and for Shakespeare, because of the stress he lays on novelty and curiosity in treating of the pleasures of the imagination, and because of his ungrudging recognition of a distinction between those geniuses which require the aid of conscious art and those which do not—because of these characteristics of his criticism it is fair to say that Addison stands close by Steele as an opponent of a narrow rationalism or classicism. Certainly Gildon recognized him as such an opponent. But his most important function was not as a champion of any principles, old or new; it was as a teacher and a popularizer. Thus it appears that the two Queen Anne critics who were most widely influential, the two who had a really considerable effect upon popular taste, were not on the neo-classic side at all—that in so far as they fit in any pigeon-holes they belong with the romanticists.

LEONARD WELSTED Welsted's *Dissertation* is that of a man influenced rather than influential. Coming as it did almost at the turn of the quarter-century, it serves to indicate something of the critical temper of that time. It touches on various matters—language, the rules, the usefulness of poetry, the state of prose—without making points extraordinarily true or untrue about any. It is precisely what one might expect from a somewhat supercilious mediocrity.

The point upon which he lays most stress, and that which, perhaps, most interests a student of criticism, is the uselessness of the rules. He sees no reason for accepting or rejecting them; for they are of no importance—they will neither make nor unmake a poet. Why, says he, quarrel about the great and fundamental rule of painting that a lady's face should be supplied with a nose? Or that commonly a head should be represented as crowned with hair? In so far as Welsted's attitude is typical, it shows that the rules were approaching the last stage of most dogmas, that at which they have less to fear from hostility than from indifference. This stage foreshadows a new difficulty, no longer that of guarding against their too autocratic sway, but that of getting men to remember that something may be said for some of them, that they really have some importance after all.

The one tenet of the old creed which still seems to have weight with Welsted is the assertion that poetry must instruct—through pleasure, of course, and indirectly—but still it must instruct. It is peculiarly unfortunate that the English, into whose keeping, as a nation, the dogma of the ethical value of art seems to have been entrusted, should usually hold this dogma in its crudest and most repellent form. By their manner of advocating this thesis the English have done more than any other race to make people believe that there is art which is devoid of ethical effect. Leonard Welsted is not peculiarly bad in this respect; he rather avoids the grosser form of statement; yet one feels sure that like Dennis he would have advocated the doctrine of poetical justice, had he ever written his promised treatise on the drama. To one unfamiliar with the precedent mental processes it is almost incredible that men should seriously have maintained that art to be true must lie about life.

When Welsted touches the question of the excellent in prose style, he is unhappily vague. One suspects that his purpose is chiefly to defend his own languid and trailing sentences feebly reminiscent of the stately, cadenced periods of seventeenth century prose. At any rate he censures Addison for the frequent recurrence of the full pause in his work, and regrets that Addison's manner is so easy to imitate. To-day the regret is rather that there were not more imitations. A flood of Addisonian sentences would have been vastly preferable to a flood of weak Popean couplets.

So Welsted ambles on, digressing here and there, and tempting the commentator to like sin. The curse of complacent mediocrity lies heavy upon the whole essay. One longs for a good, tough error of judgment like some of Dennis'. The remark that Milton's uncouth style prevents him from being the greatest of our poets, is too feeble to replace old Dennis' swashing blows. One would prefer even the violent classicism of Rymer's advocacy of the Greek chorus. One feels that Welsted didn't much care one way or the other; that, like many Englishmen, especially those of Georgian days, he felt that poetry was not a thing to get excited about, especially when writing to a lord.

ALLAN   There is nothing half-hearted or undecided
RAMSAY about Ramsay's preface. To be sure, Ramsay
         was Scottish, not English, and his few short
paragraphs are hardly criticism. But they are immensely
significant, and significant even more for what they
imply than for what they say. They imply a real demand
for what we call the romantic in literature. If Ramsay
was right, there was coming a real shift in the balance
of taste, not in an isolated individual here and there, but
in a growing body of readers. And that he was right
is abundantly shown both by the large sale of his books
and by subsequent literary history.

With such an essay as this the present volume properly
ends. The next quarter-century shows no more
unanimity of critical opinion than this; it marks evolution, not revolution. But the general tone of criticism

is different; the attitude toward the old problems is in
the main a new attitude. It would be pleasant to attempt
a characterization of this change, but it must be reserved,
for it properly demands the accompaniment of another
body of texts.

From even so cursory and superficial an examination
of these half-dozen critics must appear the fact, doubly
clear to one who actually reads their work, that none,
with the exception of Ramsay, can be neatly pigeon-
holed as a classicist or a romanticist or a rationalist or
an 'ist' of any sort. More accurately, each one has his
'ism'; but it is individual, not general. One, like Welsted,
scoffs at the rules, but scorns Miltonic diction; another,
like Dennis, deifies Milton, and defends the rules; a
third defends the rules and sniffs at Milton. Thus we
could continue to ring the changes and rearrange the
combinations, but to no useful purpose. To group them
is a help to memory, but a hindrance to accuracy.

Are there, then, no generalizations to make, no possible
conclusions as to the critical temper of this period? One
or two may possibly be hazarded, with the proviso that
they are intentionally vague and that they must constantly
be checked by reference to the actual opinions of
individual critics.

In the first place it is evident that criticism at this
time was not stagnant, that very few minds were content
to reiterate the old formulæ without limitation or alteration. Gildon alone, and he for only part of his life, was
content to quote without qualification the dicta of the
preceding period, and even he specifically recognizes the
fact that his system does not account for all the manifestations of real genius, that there is, at least, another

gate by which a few may enter the realm of art. The period is not, therefore, one in which tradition was blindly accepted; it is one in which men were working toward new points of view; in which theories, however narrow, were becoming more elastic, more capable of including the infinitely various manifestations of genius.

On the other hand, it would be a mistake, I believe, to say that these modifications of old formulæ, these attempts at a more accurate statement of critical truth, indicate a new 'critical movement'. A short time ago it seemed as if so much that could be called romantic was being discovered in this period that it could hardly be called a classical period at all. Hardly any piece of writing seemed incapable of being pressed into service as a 'beginning of the romantic movement'. That effort exhausted itself; its success showed its futility. It would certainly be a complete mistake to suppose that these critics were in a state of revolt, conscious or unconscious. They were not seeking to overturn the existing order, but to improve it.

But one word with regard to the supposed discovery of widespread romantic tendencies may still be in order. In all the arts, in philosophy, in politics, in practically all the activities of the human mind, two opposing tendencies are perceptible. In philosophy they appear as the sense of the one and the sense of the many. From the beginning of history there have been men who were profoundly impressed by the unity of the world, by its order and harmony; who have been fascinated by the possibility of an ultimate synthesis of all its elements. There have been others who were equally impressed by differences, by the variety of phenomena, by the strife and discord of the world, by its strangeness, mystery, and complexity. Such men have often completely lost sight of the conceivable unity. Philosophy has tried again and again to mediate between the two types, but they still exist in hostile camps. We still have monists and pluralists.

Theology has faced the same antipodal conceptions. It has had to deal with polytheists and unitarians, with all sorts and conditions of men between. Catholic theology, with its dogma of the Trinity, has boldly grasped both horns of the dilemma—God one and God many; but not even S. Thomas Aquinas succeeded in making the two points of view intellectually reconcilable.

Similarly in architecture. Given men who had a keen feeling for unity, simplicity, harmony, adaptation of the part to the whole, and they produce Greek temples. Given men with an overpowering sense of the mystery, the variety, the strangeness and occasional grotesqueness of life, and they may create a Gothic cathedral.

So in poetry. Given a man who loves above all things simplicity, obviousness, orderly beauty, and you will get what we call classic poetry. Given a man who finds strangeness, mystery, complexity in the simplest things, who regards those aspects of life as vital and essential, and you will get romantic poetry. And as in creation, so in appreciation, in criticism.

If, then, we use the words 'classic' and 'romantic' merely as convenient terms for two fundamental tendencies of human minds, they are serviceable. If for more, they are misleading. For the two classes of men exist always side by side; the two tendencies exist in the same men. Sometimes one is dominant, sometimes the other; but in greater or less degree both are there. It is merely a question of preponderance. The historian can only say which tendency is ascendant in the majority at a given moment. So in the England of this period what we have called the classic tendency—the monistic, the simplifying tendency—was dominant. But men were still conscious of the other point of view; some of them were trying to make their own broad enough to include it. But their basic attitude remained. Hence we may find romantic qualities by the score, both in production and in criticism; but we cannot, at this time, find a real romantic movement. The balance was not yet shaken.

It remains, in eighteenth century fashion, to point a moral. It is silly for those in either camp to curse their fellows across the way. The two points of view are both right. The world is one, it is simple; and it is many and complex. The greatness of the Iliad does not preclude that of the Paradiso. Until we can make a completely inclusive synthesis, we should beware lest our omissions be as great as those of our opponents. Modern criticism, which commonly stresses novelty and variety of emotional appeal, may be no nearer the whole truth than criticism of the Aristotelean sort. And unless modern criticism is striving with more and more success to equate the two opposing tendencies, it may in reality be less fruitful than that of those eighteenth century men who are to-day a hissing and a by-word.

There is, of course, a way out, that of shirking the whole problem. One may say of a new book, as of a new picture or a new piece of music, "It seems mad and ugly to me, but I am probably mistaken. It may be a masterpiece." To do that is to lay oneself open to the charge of cowardice, of unwillingness to risk possible ridicule from generations present or to come. To call indecision broadmindedness does not make it the less weak. Better to have scoffed at Shakespeare like Rymer, to have derided Wagner like Hanslick, to have insulted Whistler like Ruskin, than to be too feeble, too half-hearted to attack anything. Dennis and Gildon and

Hughes and Pope at least believed something. If they sometimes failed to distinguish correctly between good and bad in literature, they at any rate believed such a distinction could be made. Even if they had done no more than show that they had followed wrong roads, they would have assisted the discovery of the right one more than the men who dare try none.

CHARLES GILDON

CHARLES GILDON

I. AN ESSAY AT A VINDICATION OF THE
LOVE-VERSES OF COWLEY AND
WALLER, &c.

1694

In Answer to the Preface of a Book Intituled,
𝕷𝕰𝕿𝕿𝕰𝕽𝕾 and 𝖁𝕰𝕽𝕾𝕰𝕾 𝕬𝕸𝕺𝕽𝕺𝖀𝕾 and
𝕲𝕬𝕷𝕷𝕬𝕹𝕿.

Directed to
Mr. *CONGREVE.*

As in my two former Critical Discourses of this Book
against Mr. *Rymer's* 𝕾𝖍𝖔𝖗𝖙 𝖛𝖎𝖊𝖜 𝖔𝖋 𝕿𝖗𝖆𝖌𝖊𝖉𝖞, a Zeal for
the Honour of my Country in its greatest Ornaments,
her Poets, Engag'd me; so here I cannot help challeng-
ing the same Pretence, since I can't suppose them deficient in 𝕷𝖔𝖛𝖊, without derogating from the *Justness* of
their Characters.   But I must confess I have not the
same hopes of Success in this; for there I had to do with
an *impotent Opiniator*; but here with a Gentleman of a
great deal of *Wit* and fine *Sense*.   There I address'd to
Parties already sensible of the Justice of my Cause; here
to one who is prepossess'd of the contrary.   But on the
other hand I have the greater satisfaction here of being
Worsted by one whose *Wit* can better defend an *Error,*
than I the *Truth*; and I'm of Opinion, that 'tis a nobler
Fate to fall by the Hand of an Hero, than Conquer a

Dastard Pretender. And tho' my Prudence might be call'd in Question by this Attempt, yet my generous Ambition will merit a *Magnis tamen excidit Ausis.* One thing I must possess you of in my favour, that my unhappy Circumstances allow me not time to use all the Caution I ought, or search all the Reasons might be urg'd in this noble Cause! so that I am not only *Viribus,* but *Opibus impar*: However, I hope the Design will gain me the Opinion of a *Good English Man,* if my Performance shou'd not attain that of a *good Critic,* which will sufficiently compensate my trouble; for I shou'd be prouder to be thought a Zealot for the Glory as well as Interest of my Country, than the greatest Wit, and most Learned Arguer.

I shall never deny the Ancients their just Praise of the Invention of *Arts* and *Sciences*; but I cannot without contradicting my own Reason, allow them the Perfecters of 'em so far that they must be our uncontroverted Patterns and Standard: For our Physicians have found the Prescripts of *Hippocrates* very Defective: And as in Physic, so in Poetry, there must be a regard had to the Clime, Nature, and Customs of the People; for the Habits of the Mind as well as those of the Body, are influenc'd by them; and **Love** with the other Passions vary in their *Effects* as well as *Causes,* according to each Country and Age; nay, according to the very Constitution of each Person affected. This makes me hope, that the Ingenious Author of the *Letters and Verses Amorous and Gallant,* guides himself by a fallacious Rule, when he makes the Ancients the Standard of the Excellence of the Moderns (or indeed when by exalting *those,* he wholly deprives *these* of all Honour) in **Love-Verses.** His charge is reducible to these two Heads, *viz.* The *Occasions* and the *Performances.* He will have it, that *the*

Occasions on which their Poems are written are sought
out, and that none meet with 'em but themselves, whilst
those of the Ancients are such as happen almost to e'ry
Man in Love.   Next, *That the Verses of the Moderns,*
are filled with Thoughts that are indeed 𝖘𝖚𝖗𝖕𝖗𝖎𝖟𝖎𝖓𝖌 *and*
𝕲𝖑𝖎𝖙𝖙𝖊𝖗𝖎𝖓𝖌, *but not* 𝕿𝖊𝖓𝖉𝖊𝖗, 𝕻𝖆𝖘𝖘𝖎𝖔𝖓𝖆𝖙𝖊, *or* 𝕹𝖆𝖙𝖚𝖗𝖆𝖑 *for e'ry*
Man in 𝕷𝖔𝖛𝖊 *to think.*   This is the sum of his Charge
against 'em; of which in the Order I've plac'd 'em.
First, As for the *Occasions*; I cannot remember any
Subject chosen by either *Cowly* or *Waller,* (for we've
nothing to do here with *Petrarch* a Foreigner) that seems
to be sought out, or unnatural for a Man in Love to
choose; and if some of 'em do not happen to e'ry Man
in Love, they are yet on an equal Bottom with the
Ancients, many of whose *Subjects* or *Occasions,* are
far from happening to all Lovers, as none who can
pretend to any knowledge of their Writings can deny.
Corinna's Parrot dy'd, and *Ovid* writes its Funeral
Elegy; but sure none will contend that this is an
Accident common to all Ladies who have Lovers, and
those Poets too.   *Catullus* addresses one Copy of Verses
to the very Sparrow of *Lesbia,* and in another deplores
its Death.   A great many Lovers may have Mistresses
who never take a Voyage during their Amour, and yet
Ovid has an Elegy *ad Amicam Navigantem*; and so may
ten thousand true Lovers, especially such as are Poets,
never venture on any other Billows, but the Frown of
their Fair ones; and yet *Propertius* toss'd in another
Storm, Writes to *Cynthia* upon it.   And indeed to reduce
the *Subjects* or *Occasions* of 𝕷𝖔𝖛𝖊-𝖁𝖊𝖗𝖘𝖊𝖘 to any particular Standard, is highly Irrational, and must only be the
effect of want of Consideration, for the various Circumstances and Fortunes of the Lovers must diversifie and
alter the *Occasions* of writing to their Mistresses: So

that there is no Occasion that is General, and that can reach all Men in Love, but the Cruelty of their Mistresses on their first Addresses, (that is, their not immediate Compliance) for Jealousie is not· Universal, or at least to extend to the Beating of her a Man Loves; yet *Ovid* Writes *ad Amicam quam verberaverat.* I must confess, I can't see the least Reason why the *Name* and *Gloves* of a Mistress, with *the Place of her Birth,* are not as just *Occasions* to Write on as the Ring given to a Mistress, or her Parrot or Sparrow; or a great many more I might enumerate out of the Ancients. A true Lover thinks e'ry thing that belongs to her he Loves, worthy his Thoughts; and the more our Modern Poets extend their Reflections beyond the Ancients in this, so much the greater Lovers they shew themselves. But the *Place of one's Mistress's Birth* is not only worthy a Lover's Thoughts, but even an *Universal Occasion,* since no Lover but must meet with that Occurrence in whatever fair one he adores, among all the beauteous Daughters of *Eve.*

By what has been said, Sir, 'tis evident that our Moderns are not inferiour to the Ancients, in their judgment in chusing *Occasions* on which they write to their Mistresses: Or, That this Ingenious Gentleman has either through Want of Advertence, or out of Design expressed himself *ambiguously,* or at least not with that *Clearness* that is requisite to a conclusive Argument; which cannot be excused when the Honour and Merit of such great Men as *Cowley* and *Waller* is concerned; nay, the Honour of our Country.

I come now to the Second Accusation, which is, that *the Moderns fill their Verses with Thoughts* surprising *and* glittering, *but not natural for e'ry Man in Love to think.* This lies under the same Fault as the other does,

of being too general to be of any Force, it either condemns all that the Moderns have wrote, it casts off e'ry
Thought in their Love-Verses as not tender and passionate, or does nothing at all, for it instances no
particular. I'm confident the ingenious Gentleman will
have so much Candor, as to confess that there are a
great many very tender and soft Thoughts, and passionate
Expressions in *Cowley*'s 𝕸𝖎𝖘𝖙𝖗𝖊𝖘𝖘, as in this one, that
now occurrs to my Mind: *Then like some wealthy
Island thou shalt lie,* &c. but if there be some, nay, a
great many tender, soft, and passionate thoughts in our
Moderns, then is this general charge not at all conclusive
against 'em. Besides, *Thoughts natural to a Man in*
Love, is an obscure Expression, it conveys no clear Idea
of anything to the Mind; or, what is fully as erroneous,
it seems to level the Thoughts of all Mankind, but it
cannot be doubted, but that in the very same Circumstances the Thoughts of different Men will be various,
and more or less Excellent and Noble, as the Wit,
Judgment, Fancy, and the other Qualities of the Mind
of the Person affected, are more or less Excellent and
perfect: And I am confident your ingenious Friend
(whom I honour for his Wit, tho I differ from his
Opinion) will allow me, That one of Mr. *Cowley*'s
Genius wou'd no more have the Thoughts of a Fop, a
Beau, a Tinker, a Shepherd, or any other ignorant and
unelevated Mechanic, in Love, than out of it. *Again,*
Thoughts *surprizing,* and *glittering* without particular
Instances of 'em, as they prove nothing, so can they not
be well answer'd, for an Instance would have made us
apprehend what he takes for *surprizing* and *glittering*;
but without that, or any Definition, we wander in the
dark, and I can at best but only ghess at his meaning.
If by *Thoughts surprizing,* and *glittering* he means

extraordinary and *uncommon,* I'm apt to think he will allow them very natural to Mr. *Cowley* or Mr. *Waller* in any Circumstance. A Man that is us'd to a good Habit of thinking, cannot be without extraordinary Thoughts, on what concerns him so near as the Heart of his Mistress. *Lastly,* As to *far-fetch'd Similes,* 'tis an Expression very *obscure* and *ambiguous*; and I must acknowledge my self wholly to seek in his Meaning, if a *Simile* be just, and hold an exact Analogy to the thing 'tis applied to, and of the thing 'tis designed to heighten, I presume it cannot come into the Number of the *far-fetch'd,* and when-ever the Gentleman will please to instance in Particulars in either *Cowley* or *Waller,* I engage to fellow them with those that are full as faulty, even according to his own Definition, let that be what it will, (for I suppose it can't be much amiss from so accurate a Pen.) And till then I may supersede any particular Defence in this. Besides, 'tis not to be supposed, that the Verses written by Lovers are the *Extempore* Result of a sudden Gust of Passion, like the Inspirations of the *Delphic* Prophetess; for I'm confident he'll agree with me that the Excuse of Love will not free a Poet, that lets them pass so from the Censure of *Boileau*

> *Un sot en ecrivant, fait tout avec plaisir*
> *I'll na point en ses vers.l'ambarras de Choisir.*

A Poetizing Lover, must be allow'd not to be absolutely out of his Wits, and that 'tis possible for him to study, and consider what he says in so solemn a Manner to his Mistress.

After this bold Assertion without Proof, he advances to examine which are in the right, the Ancients or the

Moderns; the Rule of our Judgment in this, he justly makes the End the Poet aims at, *viz. The obtaining the Love of his Mistress,* tho I cannot see why he should suppose that contrary to, or inconsistent with getting *Fame* and *Admiration,* since Admiration is a certain Step to Love. When I read Mr. *Dryden's* Works, I cannot help Loving him. If I should not love and respect him and any other Poet that thinks well, and expresses his Thoughts nobly, I should sin against my Reason. *Ovid* urges his Fame and Reputation as a Motive for his Mistress's Love, and if that can move a Man of Sense, why should we think the Effect wou'd not be the same on a Woman of Sense, and Generosity? And indeed, in e'ry one but an absolute dull, insipid Fool, which no Lover can think his Mistress.

The End of Love-Verses being the gaining the fair ones Heart, he proceeds to the best means of obtaining that End. *viz. The convincing her that you love her.* I must deny this Assertion too, for tho *Love* in the Severity of Justice require *Love*; yet is that an Argument that ought not always to prevail, since 'tis a Plea that's common to a great many, for so the fair one ought to surrender to 'em all; a Liberty no Lover would willingly allow his Mistriss on any Consideration whatever. But how often does Experience tell us, that this *best Way* fails? Or indeed, how seldom does it hit? *Admiration* is the only just, and unquestioneable Parent of Love; for the Senses or the Mind must be first won with some Perfection, either real or imaginary. Whatever therefore can ravish Fame from the envious censorious World, may justly be suppos'd able to give *Admiration* to a Mistress. Nor is this inconsistent with the *true and lively Representation of the Pains, and Thoughts attending the Passion of Love*; for sure the

Advantage of *Art* in Poems cannot destroy the *End* which is not to be obtain'd in Painting without it, *viz.* a *lively Representation of Nature.* *Similes,* fine *Thoughts,* and *shining Points,* if they be just, and good, must certainly give a greater Idea of any Pain, than a bare and unpolished Rhime, without Beauty or Grace. *This* gives us a *weak,* a *faint,* an *unmoving* View of the Pain; *That* sets it close to us, magnifies and enlarges it: *This* gives it you as the reverse end of a Prospective Glass does Objects, *That* as the right end of it; so that if a Representation of our Pain be the Path to Success, *Art* will be no ill Help and guide in it; unless we'll suppose that our Mistress would be more sensibly touched with a *Grubstreet* Ballad, than a Copy of Verses by a *Cowley* or a *Waller.* But indeed, the Pain a Lover feels cannot be truely, and with Life represented without *Similes,* as is evident from the very Nature of the Mind, when in Pain: For 'tis an universal Measure of our Judgment of things to compare them with something else; and the Mind in expressing its Pains endeavours to make it known in its full Greatness: to give therefore the greater Image of it, it generally seeks out something by a Comparison of which it hopes to obtain that End; Comparison being the only Distinction of Degrees of things. This makes it narrowly in these Circumstances, regard and observe that Train of *Ideas* that continually pass before it, to call out such as are most proper for its purpose: For *'tis evident,* (as Mr. *Lock* remarks) *to any one that will but observe what passes in his own Mind, that there is a Train of Ideas constantly succeeding one another in his Understanding, as long as he's awake.* An Assertion therefore of an Ingenious Friend of mine, to the Prejudice of the Moderns, against *Similes* in the Expression of the Passions of Love and

Grief, is contrary to the very Nature of the Mind. For
let any Man endeavour to retain any particular Idea
firmly and without Alteration, he will find it not in his
Power to do it any considerable time, such a necessary
Succession and Variation of Ideas (the Origin of
Similes) is there in the human Mind. But because 'tis
said that *'tis the nature of Grief to confine the Soul,
straiten the Imagination, and extremely lessen the
Number of its Objects,* I shall only oppose the Assertion
of this Gentleman (whom I have always allow'd a Man
of great Wit and Sense) with an Observation of Mr.
Le Clerk, (whom I'm sure no Man that knows his Works,
will deny to be one of the best Philosophers of the Age)
in the *6th. Chapter* of his *Ontologie* and the *4th.
Paragraph,* he has to this purpose—"This being so, we
"observe that the time seems short to those who spend
"it in Mirth, or any Employment they perform with
"Pleasure and Desire; but on the contrary, Tedious and
"Irksome to the Unfortunate, and those that are in Pain,
"or to those that are against their Wills, oblig'd to some
"troublesome Business. For we keep the Idea that is
"Gratefull and Pleasant to us, as long without Variation
"as we are able, and thus by the viewing of the fewer
"Ideas, the time we spend in Pleasure and Content,
"seems the shorter; whilst on the contrary, our Minds
"endeavour to drive away a troublesome Idea, and strive
"to substitute some others in its room; Turning, Winding,
"Changing, Adding and Diminishing it, as the uneasie
"inquietude Prompts. Thus the time seems longer than
"it wou'd do else, by that vast and numerous Train of
"Ideas, which, as I may say, shew themselves *en passant*
"to the Mind, with an incredible Rapidity and Swiftness.
From this just and rational Observation of Mr. *Le Clerk*
'tis evident, That Similes are not so unnatural in expres-

sion of Grief or Pain, as some Ingenious Gentlemen contend: For the Mind (especially that which is us'd to an Expression of its self in Allegory and Similes) will easily in this Number of Ideas, meet with some that will answer the End, the Mind is born to with so much Impatience and Desire: For 'tis here also evident, That Grief multiplies nor lessens the Number of the Objects of the Mind.

From what has been said 'twill appear, That *Similes* cannot be an unnatural Expression of this Passion, or any Effects of it. I shall therefore proceed to those few particular Instances the Author of the *Preface* gives, by which he draws a short Parallel betwixt the Ancients and the Moderns. *I am pleas'd,* says he, *with* Tibullus, *when he says, he cou'd live in a Desart with his Mistress, where never any Humane Foot-steps appear'd, because I doubt not but he really thinks what he says: But I confess, I can hardly forbear Laughing, when* Petrarch *tells us he cou'd live without any other Sustenance than his Mistresses Looks.* I confess, I must ev'n here dissent from him too; for if you go to the Rigor or Severity of the Reason of both Expressions, they are equally impossible, and in Impossibilities as well as Infinites, there are no Degrees. For I can see no greater Probability of Living in a Desart where there were no Humane Foot-steps, than on the Looks of a Mistress only; unless like *Nebuchadnezzar,* he wou'd feed on the Leaves of the Trees, and Grass of the Ground if there were any; which is not very kind to hope his Mistress wou'd comply with. But supposing it impossible, is there any Necessity of a Lovers saying nothing that exceeds the Bounds of *Possibility*? especially in Poetry, where Hyperbole's are justifiable almost to Extravagance. That certainly wou'd be most unnatural of all, for the Thoughts of a Man really in Love, are naturally Extravagant ev'n to Impossibilities; tho *possunt quia posse videntur.* The very Definition of this Passion in Ethics, shews it violent and exorbitant. But we may in favour of *Petrarch* and Mr. *Cowley,* (who make use of the same Thought) say that they mean the Dyet of their Love, is a Look of their Mistress.

I must confess, I'm extremely surpriz'd to find your Ingenious Friend an Advocate for that which wou'd make all the Sir *Courtly*'s Compositions of the *Nation,* the Standard of good Verses; when he himself is really so well qualify'd to write like *Cowley* and *Waller,* and has by his own Practice in those Verses that are Publish'd, better confuted his Preface, than all I can pretend to say.

II. TO MY HONOURED AND INGENIOUS FRIEND MR. *HARRINGTON,* FOR THE MODERN POETS AGAINST THE ANCIENTS.

1694

As the Justice and Generosity of your Principle, the sweet Agreeableness of your Humor, the Vivacity of your Wit, and the strength and force of your Judgment and Penetration, justly endear you to all your Acquaintance, so they qualify you for a Judge of the present Controversie betwixt the Moderns and the Ancients, for the Prize of Glory in Learning and Poetry. Monsieur *Perault* (whom I have not yet had the Opportunity to Read) has given it to the Moderns, *Rapin* to the Ancients: Mr. *Rymer* has with abundance of Indignation appear'd on *Rapin's* side. I cannot determine whether Mr. *Perault* has been too partial to his own Countrymen, (an Error on the right side) but I'm sure Mr. *Rymer* has been extremely injurious to his; which has made me perhaps, too angry with him in my former Discourses. But I assure my self that you are too good an *Englishman,* to let Friendship to any Man, bribe you to condemn those rough Effects of my Zeal for the 𝕰𝖓𝖌𝖑𝖎𝖘𝖍 𝕹𝖆𝖙𝖎𝖔𝖓. I will be more just than my Adversary, I will yield that *Greece* had Great Poets, notwithstanding all those monstrous Faults and Absurdities they abound with; tho he will not allow the *English* any Honour, because they have been guilty of Errors. Nay, I'll say more, that the Poetry of *Greece* was her most valuable Learning, for that still maintains its Share of Glory and Esteem, whilst her Philosophy is now exploded by the Universal Reason of Mankind. *Homer, Pindar, Sophocles* and *Euripides,* will, as long as they are understood, preserve their Characters of Excellent Poets, tho the *Stagyrite* with all his Volumes, is now shrunk from his Ostentatious Title of the *Philosopher,* to that of a good *Critic,* or *Grammarian.*

Tho I grant the *Græcians* this, yet I cannot subscribe to the rest of the Hyperbolical Praises some of our Modern Critics give them. For I confess, I can discover no such *Universal Genius* in *Homer,* as they contend for, as that all Arts and Siences may be learn't from him: *Virgil* seems to me, more generally Learned by far; and Mr. *Cowley* among our *English* Poets, may without Partiality, be put up for his Rival in the Glory of Learning. As for the *Numbers* of *Homer, Rapin* vastly extols their Variety, and yet confesses that to be the Property of the *Greek* Language, which makes it the easier Task for *Homer t*o perform, and by consequence, lessens his Merit on that Account. But it cannot be deny'd that *Virgil* has as much Variety in this as the *Roman* Language wou'd allow; and as was necessary for the Beauty of his Poem; and they are in his Descriptions especially, so well chosen, that they extremely contribute to the Image of the thing describ'd; as *Gemitus dedere Cavernæ: præruptus aquæ Mons.* The sound of the first makes us as it were hear the hollow noise the Spear of *Lyacoon* made in the *Trojan* Horse; the other Places in our View such a watry Mountain. Among our *English* Poets, none can compare with Mr. *Dryden* for Numbers: His Descriptions are all very perfect in all things; but his Numbers contribute not a little to the force and life of the Representation, for they carry something in them distinct from the Expression and Thought; as in his Description of Night,

What an Image of a profound Stillness does this
following Verse set before us,

The Mountains seem to Nod their drousie Heads!

I have not room nor leisure at this time to make a
thorough parallel betwixt the *Ancients* and the *Moderns,*
and shall only cursorily run over the Heads. I have
touch'd the *Universality of Genius,* and the *variety of
Numbers* (this last being the Prerogative of the Language more than of the Poets.) *Judgment* I think is
apparently the due of the *Moderns,* who I'm confident
wou'd ne'er have been guilty of those Absurdities the
Ancients abound with. They seem to have been Masters
of but little Reason, when they made their Gods such
limited and *criminal Beings.* *Homer* often digresses
from the *Hero,* that is the Subject of his Poem, to
entertain us with other Objects too remote from
Achilles. You may, Sir, easily perceive that I press not
so hard as I might on the *Ancients*; that I omit abundance of *Improprieties,* and *Absurdities,* ridiculous even
to *Childishness,* because I wou'd not be thought to rob
the *Fathers* of Poetry of their just Value and Esteem;
tho I confess I am of Mr. St. *Euremont*'s Opinion, that
no Name can Privilege Nonsense or ill Conduct.

The Enemies of the Moderns will not deal so Civilly
with them. They deny them to be Poets because they
have not strictly observed the Rules laid down by
Aristotle, but by that they discover themselves either
ignorant or negligent of the most chief and important
end of Poetry, that is, Pleasure. Now, it cannot be
deny'd but he is the best Poet who takes the surest
means to obtain the end he aims at; in which, regard
must be had to the *Humour, Custom,* and *Inclination*
of the Auditory; but an *English* Audience will never

be pleas'd with a dry, Jejune and formal Method [that] excludes Variety as the Religious observation of the Rules of *Aristotle* does. And all those that exclaim against the Liberty some of our *English* Poets have taken, must grant that a *Variety* that contributes to the main Design, cannot divide our Concern: And if so, 'tis certainly an *Excellence* the *Moderns* have gain'd above the *Ancients*. This wou'd appear plainer if I had room and time to instance in Particulars. The Plays Mr. *Dryden* has bless'd the Age with will prove this; which is compar'd (as I hereafter intend) with those of *Sophocles* and *Euripides,* either for the Plot, Thought, or Expression, will gain him the Poets Garland from those two Hero's of Old *Greece*.

The *Plagiarism* objected to our Poets is common to the Ancients too; for *Virgil* took from *Homer, Theocritus,* and ev'n *Ennius;* and we are assur'd *Homer* himself built upon some Predecessors: And tho' their thoughts may be something a-kin, yet they alter their Dress, and in all other things we are satisfied with the *variety* of the outward visible Form, tho' the intrinsic value be the same, as Mr. *Congreve*'s Song has it, *Nothing new besides their Faces, e'ry Woman is the same.* In all things as well as Women the meer Variety of Appearance, whets our Desire and Curiosity. I am,

SIR,

Your Humble Servant,

CHARLES GILDON.

III. FROM *THE COMPLETE ART OF POETRY*.

1718

DIALOGUE II.

OF THE USE AND NECESSITY OF RULES IN POETRY.

I Have shewn you, *Crites,* in the former Dialogue, what past in our agreeable Company, on our first Meeting; and I am confident, that the Defence of that *noble Art,* in which you are so great a Master, and by Consequence, of which you are so great a Lover, can by no means be disagreeable to you; nay, I am well assured, that you will give the highest Approbation of what has been said on that Score, since it is founded on Justice and Reason.

I shall now proceed to let you know what pass'd in the second Day's Conversation, to prove a Point which, I am satisfy'd, you do allow to be Truth; and that is, the *Use* and *Necessity* of the *Rules of Art,* in *Poetry,* without which, all must be governed by *unruly Fancy,* and *Poetry* become the Land of *Confusion,* which is, in Reality, the Kingdom of *Beauty, Order,* and *Harmony.*

Laudon being thus enlarg'd from the Tyranny of *Business,* I could not deny my self the Pleasure of repeating my Visits as often as I could; and the more often I repeated them, the more my Appetite was raised for their Continuance; for I always came away with some Improvement of my Understanding, as well as a full Satisfaction for the Hours I spent in his Company.

A little before Dinner, *Laudon* was call'd down about Business; and in the mean while, happening to see a

Book lye in the Window, I took it up to pass the Time till his Return; but was not a little surpriz'd to find it to be, Bishe's *Art of* English *Poetry*; a very extraordinary Title, thought I, as if the *Art of Poetry* were not the same in all Languages.

I had not cast my Eye, in a cursory Manner, on many Pages, before *Laudon* return'd: Pray, Sir, said I, how came you by this worthy Author, who writing on the *Art of Poetry*, would perswade us, that there is no *Art* at all in it, and aims chiefly at the Knack of *Versifying*; and yet, even in that, is full of *gross Absurdities,* and *visible Contradictions?*

Why, Sir, reply'd *Laudon,* you must know, that the fine Mrs. *Lamode* was to pay my Wife a Visit yesterday, and brought this Book along with her; and I find, on her Departure, she forgot this noble Piece of *Criticism,* the infallible Director of her Speculations that Way. I would have sent it Home to her, but that she and her Husband, honest *Issachar,* are to dine with me to Day; for I would not bear the Scandal of having it thought Part of my own Collection.

It is impossible, my Friend, said I, that any one that knows you, should suspect you guilty of that Folly; and to cast an Eye upon a Book of so promising a Title, is justify'd by the Title. I have my self perus'd great Part of this ridiculous Author, and he had almost provok'd me into a *Writer,* to vindicate the Honour of the *Art* I admire, from the shameful Ignorance of a little *Pretender,* had not the Clamours of the *Traders* in Books deterr'd me, by asserting the Undertaking would be unfair, in not only interfering with the Sale of a Copy already receiv'd, but in all Probability, of transferring it from the Booksellers Shops, to those of the Pastry Cook and Grocer.

That Reason, in my Opinion, (interrupted *Laudon*) is too fallacious to influence so good a Judgment, to desist from a laudable Design, since it is drawn from private and particular Interest, against the publick and general Good; sacrificing the Improvement and Honour of Arts to the miserable Prospect of servile Gain. For this would be a certain and speedy Way of obstructing all Manner of Learning; since, had this been a Rule founded on general Consent (as, if it have any Validity, it must be) there never cou'd have been any Progress or Improvement in any Art or Science.

The Multiplicity of Books in other Arts, is no Objection to the Increasing the Number; and notwithstanding the present Perfection of the *Mathematics,* the Excellence of Sir *Isaac Newton*'s Discoveries, has not put an End to their *noble Enquiries.* And as no Man presumes to write in that Art, who is ignorant of its Principles, yet we see daily Improvements made in every Part of it.

I cannot therefore imagine why you, or any other Gentleman of your Knowledge, may not do the same Justice to *Poetry,* and vindicate that *divine Art,* which has been the *Glory of great Nations,* the *Favourite of great Monarchs,* the *illustrious Proof of a true and great Politeness,* in so many of the purer Ages, from the Abuses of a *Writer* that has discovered a most profound Ignorance of every Part of it (at least, as far as he has been pleased hitherto to attempt) and endeavours, by publishing his Absurdities, to promote them. For tho' he has ventur'd only on the inconsiderable *Knack of Versifying,* yet in that he is out in the very Fundamentals, which sufficiently betrays both the *Capacity* and the *Gusto* of the Person. But this is the hard Fate of *Poetry,* different from that of all other Arts and Sciences, that the Learned only write of those; but the

Rules and Theory of this falls often into as ignorant Hands, as the Practice generally does. For, as most commonly Men without *Genius* or *Skill* in the Art, set up for *Poets,* forgeting that of *Horace,*

> *Why is he honour'd with a Poet's Name,*
> *Who neither knows, nor wou'd observe a Rule.*   Rosc.

and would fain obtrude on the World, the *incoherent Libertinisms* of their own crude Fancies, for *Poetry*; so would this Author impose his shallow and *indigested Notions* (mostly borrow'd from the *Messrs. of the Port-Royal* on the *French* Versification) for the true and whole Art of *English Poetry.* The Plausibility of his Title has carried off so many Impressions, as have made it with the Ignorant, the *Standard* of Writing. So that the Reason is the stronger for a just *Criticism,* to destroy the ill Effects of this *false one.*

You must therefore find out some better Reason for your Silence on this Occasion, than what you have given, or plainly confess, that you sacrifice to *Idleness* more than to *Justice.*

I must own (reply'd I) that there is too much of that Allay in my Temper; and from that, it may be, these specious Scruples have had Power to deter me from this Task; yet assure your self, that I am not wholly without a reasonable Obstacle. I must tell you, that the Undertaking seems to me to be of no manner of *Use,* but lies under the forbidding and odious Imputation of *Ill-Nature.* The *Libertinism* of the *Age,* which makes *Scribbling* so very easy to every one who has the least Address at *Crambo,* will make the *Million* averse to all Regulations, which render Writing so very difficult; and this the *Poetasters* (much the Majority even of the

Writers in Vogue) at *Will*'s, do lay to the Charge of *Ill-Nature*.

All, therefore, that I can expect from such an Attempt, is to please a *very, very few, good Judges*, and Men of *true Sense,* and disoblige all the Ladies and the Beaux, by imposing Laws too severe on their *Sonnets* and *Madrigals*. And to deter us from all Rules, this *very Author* under our Consideration, this blind Guide to *Parnassus,* plainly tells us in the opening of his Preface, *That it is in vain to aim at a great Reputation on account of his poetical Performances, by barely following the Rules of others, and reducing their Speculations to Practice,* insinuating that the *Rules* of this *Art* are of little Consequence to a Perfection in it.

He seems (assum'd *Laudon*) very *obscure,* or very *false* in that po[s]ition. For if he mean, that the observing, that is, the coming up to the Rules of *Poetry* cannot produce any *great Reputation*; he is absolutely in the wrong, because, without this, no Man ever yet obtain'd any *considerable* or *lasting* Name in *Poetry*. If he mean not this, then he means nothing.

It has, I confess, been an old Dispute, whether *Art* or *Nature* made a *Poet,* but a Dispute, I think, like many more grounded on the not well understanding the *Terms*. For *Art* entirely includes *Nature,* that being no more, than *Nature reduc'd to Form*. However *Horace,* near the end of his Art of *Poetry,* seems long since to have decided this Question with great *Clearness* and *Brevity*.

> *Some think that* Poets *may be form'd by* Art.
> *Others maintain, that* Nature *makes them so:*
> *I neither see what* Art *without a Vein,*
> *Nor* Wit *without the Help of* Art *can do;*
> *But mutually* [they] *need each others Aid.*   Rosc.

This is the Opinion of *Horace* confirm'd by *Reason* and Experience. For without *Art,* there can be no Order, and without *Order, Harmony* is sought in vain, where nothing but shocking *Confusion* can be found. Those scatter'd Sparks of a great *Genius,* which shou'd shine with united Glory, are in the huddle of Ignorance or want of *Art,* so dissipated, and divided, and so blended with Contraries, that they are extreamly obscur'd, if not entirely extinguish'd. Thus the Particles and Seeds of Light in the Primocal Chaos strugled in vain to exert their true Lustre, till Matter was by *Art Divine* brought into order, and this *noble Poem* of the *Universe* compleated in *Number* and *Figures,* by the Almighty *Poet* or *Maker.*

But it has been the *Ignorance* of the Rules that has made the *Many* and their Advocates declaim with so much Vehemence against them, as Curbs to *Wit* and *Poetry*; for did they know them, they wou'd plainly see, that they do, in Reality, add to them the greatest Distinction and Honour they can hope for, by setting up a *true Standard,* by which the due Glory of *Wit* and *Poetry* may be paid to *Merit,* without so wretched a Fate, as to be oblig'd to share with *Poetasters, Versifyers,* and *worthless Pretenders*; which certainly cannot be look'd on, as an *ill-natur'd* Work; but the Effect of a *just* and *generous* Temper.

Thus (to instance in one sort of *Poetry*) the Enemies of *Art* wou'd fain persuade us, that no Play, in which the Rules of *Art* are observ'd, will please; whereas, indeed, no Play did ever please for any Time, but by those Parts of it, which were conformed to the Rules, which cannot really be reduc'd to Practice but by a Person of the greatest *Capacity* and *Genius.* For can there be any Creature, that pretends to the least Portion of a *rational Soul,* who is pleas'd with the Conduct of *Shakespear* (except in one or two Plays) in which there is nothing *curious,* nothing *great,* nothing *judicious.* No, it is the Excellence of that *Poet* in the *Expression* of the *Manners;* in the *Distinction* of the *Characters* and some of his Draughts of the *Passions,* added to *Prescription,* and the *Ignorance* of the Audience, that makes him please, in those of his Plays, which are fixt in the Esteem of the Town, to which the rest, though equally good, have often in vain endeavour'd to arise.

If some *Plays* have miss'd of Success, which were *call'd* regular, by those, who knew nothing of the *Rules,* I dare assert, that they were *only* call'd, but were not so in *Reality.* For it will be obvious to any Man, who is acquainted with them, that he, who comes up to them, must produce a *perfect Poem,* that must force it self, with a *resistless Pleasure* on all that hear it. To keep still to the *Dramma.* He must perfectly *know,* and form his *Design;* he must *know, distinguish,* and *preserve* the *Manners;* he must be throughly acquainted with all the *Springs, Motions, Degrees, Mixtures, Accesses,* and *Recesses* of every *Passion,* with their *Opposition,* and *Consistence.* He must be perfect in the *Sentiments,* and know their Propriety, and Agreeableness to the *Manners,* as those have to the *Action;* he must be skill'd, and practis'd in the *Diction,* which includes both *Numbers* and *Expression.* Who can do all this but a Man of a great *Capacity* of Soul (which we call *Genius*) a large and strong *Imagination* to receive and form the *Images* of Things, and a solid *Judgment* to reduce them to their *proper Order* and *Classes?* And this is writing *according to the Rules.*

But let the *Imagination* be never so strong, and fertile of *Ideas,* without the Assistance of Judgment (which can only be informed and directed by the Stated Rules) there can be nothing produc'd *entirely beautiful.* 'Tis all the rude Product of *uncultivated Wit.* There may be a great deal of rich Oar, but clogg'd with the dull and worthless *Sparr* and *indigested Earth.* But *Judgment,* like the Fire, can only separate the Parts, and draw thence an uniform and valuable Mass of Metal.

The Rules are a great Help to many a Man of *Genius*; for it is so far from probable, that it is scarce possible, that unassisted Nature, tho' never so vigorous, can find out and practise all the Parts necessary to the forming a compleat Poem. For as in Architecture, Painting, and Musick, no Man did give us any thing great and complete, without knowing, and long Practice of the Rules of those Arts; so in *Poetry,* nothing truly excellent was ever yet seen, without a Mastery in the *Poetic* Principles.

But (interrupted I) you forget, that *Homer* and the first Poets are objected against your Position; who, as they affirm, not only wrote before any Rules were form'd, but were the very Men from whom most of these were drawn by *Aristotle,* and the rest of the Critics.

I confess (reply'd *Laudon*) that I cannot tell you what Master's Instructions, or what Rules were regarded by *Homer*; or whether the Order and Conduct were the Business of *Lycurgus,* or *Pisistratus,* or any other who collected the scattered Books of that *Poet,* corrected, and first made an Edition of them entire; yet, from the Completeness of the Poem, as together, it is evident, that a certain Rule was propos'd by the *Composer* to himself (whether found out by *Homer* or *Lycurgus*) by which he form'd the most perfect *Poem* that any Age has yet produc'd. A short View of the Plan will put this beyond Question.

"The Love, Avarice, or Pride of *Agamemnon* made
"him deny the Restoration of *Chryseis,* which makes the
"angry God *Apollo* send the Plague into the *Grecian*
"Army, in the Cause of his injur'd Priest. This moves
"*Achilles* to oppose the arbitrary Will of this *King of*
"*Men,* so far, as to make him restore the Priest's
"Daughter, and seize on *Briseis.* This provokes *Achilles*
"to withdraw his *Myrmidons* from the Camp; which
"Retreat produc'd the Sufferings of the *Greeks,* and the
"Prevalence of the Army of *Troy.* That mov'd the
"Compassion of *Patroclus* for his Countrymen; and that
"generous, and publick-spirited *Pity* gave him his Death,
"after the Slaughter of many of the *Trojans.* His
"Death by *Hector* brings *Achilles* again into the Field,
"which was fatal to *Hector,* restor'd the Tranquillity of
"the *Greeks,* and so gave them a Possibility of Taking
"the Town.

This productive Chain of Incidents, in the *Ilias* could
not be formed without admirable Art and Design; and
consequently, by such Rules as no Man since has been
able to alter for the better. But whether these were
written, or traditionally taught by Professors of the
Art, or originally in the *Sovereign Genius* of *Homer*
himself, matters not in the least, since they are the same
that are now established both in the *Heroic Poem* and
the *Drama.*

It will be plain, that what I attribute to *Homer,* is not
because he was a *Greek* Poet, or one of such *venerable
Antiquity* (as by some to be made coeval with *David,*
which I do not think) but because it is from his *Poetry*
still extant, undeniably his Due; because I do here allow,
that the *Drama,* on its first Appearance in *Athens* it self,
was far from the Perfection it afterwards attain'd, tho'
the Idea of Tragedy was certainly taken from the *Heroic*

Poem; since we find it was in the Time of *Thespis,* almost as rude and inconsistent as our *Stage* is in our Days; that first Raiser of the *Athenian Theatre* bringing nothing to Perfection; that was only effected by the *Magistrates* Inspection of the Management, and the *gradual* Endeavours of *Æschylus, Sophocles, Euripides,* and others.

But my Friend (interrupted I) you know, that these Gentlemen urge, that *Shakespear* has appear'd in *England,* with the *highest Applause,* without the *Help of Art.*

But I must reply (said *Laudon*) first, that so did *Thespis,* and some others, in *Athens*; but their *Absurdities,* and *crude Entertainments* vanish'd on the Appearance of more *just* and *regular* Pieces. Next that (as I have already observ'd) *Shakespear* is great in nothing, but *what is according to the Rules of Art*; and where his Ignorance of them is not supply'd by his *Genius,* Men of *Judgment,* and *good Sense,* see such *monstrous Absurdities* in almost every Part of his Works, that nothing but his *uncommon* Excellencies in the other, cou'd ever prevail with us to suffer, and what he wou'd never have been guilty of, had his Judgment been but well inform'd by *Art.* He had a *Genius* indeed, capable of coming up to the *Rules,* but not sufficient to find them out himself, tho' it be plain from his own Words, he saw the *Absurdities* of his own conduct. And I must confess, when I find that Sir *Philip Sidney* before him has discover'd these Faults of the *English* Stage, and that he himself has written one or two Plays very near a *Regularity,* I am the less apt to pardon his Errors, that seem of choice, as agreeable to his *Lazyness* or *easie Gain,* by what he committed to the *Theatre.*

But *Rules* seem by so much the more necessary to

Poetry, than to any other *Art* or *Science,* by how much the more *common* the Invasions of this are, than of any other whatsoever. The *Love of Verse* seems to spread through all Mankind, while the Zeal of other Arts is confin'd to a particular *Clan* of Admirers. Thus every one is not ambitious to be thought a good *Mathematician,* or *Philosopher,* or *Divine,* or *Physician,* or *Painter,* or the like; yet almost every Man (as if Human Nature were imperfect without it) hopes, and courts *Admiration* and *Applause* from his Attempts on the *Muses.* This is not the Observation of a Day. *Horace* remark'd above 1700 Years ago something like it in his Epistle to *Augustus Cæsar.*

> *A Pilot only will a Vessel guide,*
> *And a* Physician *Medicines prescribe:*
> *And skilful Hands alone the Chizel use,*
> *But learned, and unlearned,* scribble *Verse,* &c.

The *Excellence* being, therefore, so confess'd, and the *Ambition* of it so general, the *Rules* that direct our Course to it, and distinguish the *right Road* from the various divious Paths, must certainly be agreeable to all, who have a Desire either of *reading* or *writing* with Satisfaction in this Way. For thus they may *judge* of, and *arrive* at *Excellence,* as being the only Proof of a *Genius,* and without which the most exalted (if any Copy of Verses can merit that Name without this Proof) is a rude and undigested Mass; the *greatest* Qualifications imperfect, and with which they can only shine in their *true Lustre.*

If, therefore, you cannot find a better Argument, than what you have produc'd, for not vindicating the *Art of Poetry* from the scandalous *Empericisms* of *Quacks,* you must own *Idleness* to be your Director.

I own, (returned I) that you have given sufficient Reasons to shew the *Necessity* of *Rules,* if we wou'd not still pass for *Barbarians,* with the *politer* Part of the World; yet I am afraid all you have said, *how rational* soever, will not satisfie too *Many* of our *Authors,* and most of our *courteous Readers,* nay even our *University Men,* who are, or are supposed to be bred in the very Presence of the *Muses,* that *Criticism* is not an *ill-natur'd* Thing. However I shall endeavour, at my Leisure to shew, the Prevalence of your Arguments by the Works of my Conviction. But as this Task is most necessary, so is it also attended with the greatest Difficulty, if I wou'd accomplish it with that easie Address, which a Discourse of this Nature requires to recommend it to the *Taste* of the *Town,* especially if I wou'd gratifie the *Goust* of the *Ladies,* who have no small Influence on the *Gentlemen* in this, as well as in most of our other Pleasures.

It is therefore, of the *last Importance,* to bring them over to the side of *Art,* and *good Sense*; and to do that, I must render the Discourse a little more *familiar,* than *Criticism* has generally been.

I agree perfectly with you (assum'd *Laudon*) and it were to be wish'd, that as Mr. *Fontinelle* has render'd the several Systems of *Ptolomy, Copernicus,* and *Tycho Brahe* intelligible, and obvious to a Lady's Capacity, some other Person, as great as he, wou'd attempt the same in *Criticism.*

Laudon had scarce done when Mrs. *Lamode,* her Husband, and the rest of the Company came in. She was no sooner got into the Dining-Room, and past some short Salutes to the Lady of the House, and the rest of the Company; but starting with an Air, peculiar to her self, to *Morisina.* - - - - Ah! my Dear (said she) I am

extreamly oblig'd to my good Stars, that I am come to
you; this may be of Consequence to my Cause, for if
your Husband shou'd not agree to my Opinion, I am sure
of your being of my Party.

Ah, Madam! (said *Morisina*) your Ladyship stands
in Need of no Second in any Cause you think fit to
espouse; so much *Wit,* and so much *Beauty* must always
be victorious; and while Mr. *Lamode,* and Mr. *Trifle*
(for *Tom Trifle* is a constant Attendant on Mrs.
Lamode) are here, your Party, Madam, will never need
a Reinforcement.

Alas, my Dear *Morisina* (reply'd Mr[s].*Lamode*) Mr.
Trifle declares against me, and *Issachar,* like a true
Husband, stands Neuter in his Wife's Quarrel.

Upon my Soul, Madam (cry'd out *Trifle,* with no
little Concern) your Ladyship does me an infinite deal
of Wrong; I cannot dissent from your Ladyship without
forfeiting all my Pretensions to a good Understanding.
I protest, Gentlemen and Ladies, I only said, I thought
the last new *Opera* miserably spoil'd by having so many
of the Words put into our *beastly, barbarous* Language;
and that if *Grimaldi,* and the other incomparable *Italians*
had not soften'd it with the gentle melodious Words of
the *Original,* it cou'd not have been borne by Ears of any
tolerable *Gusto.*

I protest my Love (assum'd *Issachar*) I think *Tom
Trifle* something in the right; for our Language is too
rough for *Harmony*; and in my Opinion, it would be
much better to have the *Opera*'s perform'd all in *Italian.*
For such a *Medly* of *English* and *Italian* renders the
Entertainment too obnoxious to the *Critics.*

Ah! Fie, Mr. *Lamode* (interrupted his Wife) don't
assume, don't assume so much, and set your Judgment
above the rest of the *Beau Monde,* who adorn the Boxes,

and fill the Theatre at these admirable Performances. For my Part, I am infinitely pleased with this pretty Variety of *Italian* and *English*; it looks like a Brocade of Silk in Cloth of Gold; nay, it transports me to *Italy,* and then removes me to *England,* as the divine Voice and Language succeeds our rough Tongue, and hoarse Voice. Pray, Mr. *Laudon,* what is your Opinion of this Matter? For ours is a rough ugly Language, not fit for the fine *Italian* Airs. I congratulate our *Manly* Tongue, assum'd *Laudon,* that cannot be debas'd to the Mouths of wretched *Eunuchs,* of the most corrupt and degenerate Nation in the World, entirely Slaves, and but half Men. And in my Opinion, a Man of *Sense* can have no excuse for seeing an *Opera,* after the new Mode. For this *Italian Opera,* so much cry'd up, seems to me, like the Puns and Jests of merry Fellows, that with the Help of the Warmth of the Bottle, and the Heat of Conversation, make us laugh in the unbending Hour, when severer Judgment is absent, but is scarce remember'd the next Day, but with Indignation, that it could surprise us into any Sort of Pleasure. They touch the Head by their Lightness, but never reach the Heart. But *Harry Purcel* seem'd to have the Genius of *Greek* Musick; he touch'd the Soul; he made his way to the Heart, and by that Means, left a Satisfaction in the Pleasure, when past. He had the Art of Painting in Musick, which *Aristotle* mentions of the *Greek* Musicians; witness his *Frost Scene,* where, by the admirable Conjunction of Flats and Sharps, he makes you almost shiver both with his Instrumental and Vocal Musick. So that, for my Part, Madam, I think, that if *Italian* Opera's are to be at all admitted, that they would be better in that Tongue, than in *English.* First, because the Musical Performances would be better; and next, because the Action of the

Performers might perswade the Imagination, that there is that in the Words which cou'd not be found there, if we understood them. But indeed we are not in Danger of understanding much when sung in *English,* by the admirable Management of those who sung in our Language. The *Recitativo* seems much like the Harmony of *Punch,* both as to the Sound and Manner, as well as Action; And I must needs say, that the worst Play of the worst Poet that ever writ, is a more rational Diversion than an *Opera,* after the Way of *Italy.* For indeed to me the Entertainment in it self seems so very insipid and absurd, that it is scarce possible to make any Addition of Absurdities to it.

Eh! Fie! (assum'd Mr[s]. *Lamode*) how can so well-bred a Gentleman be so singular in his Taste, as not to relish what all the Town admires? And not approve what both *France* and *Italy* are striving for the Pre-heminence in? Now if the Town should fancy a Mixture of three or four Languages, or more, I protest I verily believe, that I should not be so singular as to dislike it, What think you, Sir, said she to me?

Madam, (said I) 'tis a Dish I have the utmost Aversion to; it turns my Stomach. We have Trash enough of our own Growth, and we need not seek abroad for worse. The best Wits of *France* have declar'd against *Opera's:* *Rapin, Dacier, St. Everemont* and the rest, weigh more with me, than *Lullie, Louigi,* and the rest of the *Trilling Throng,* or all the Applauses of the *Parterre,* the *Amphitheatre,* or the *Lodges.* That Glory of your Sex, Madam *Dacier,* in her excellent Confutation of Mr. *La Mot,* attributes the Corruption of the Taste of the Age, to the Reception and Vogue of *Opera's.* A Man indeed may very well wonder how an *Opera,* and *Civil Reason,* should be the Growth of the same Climate.

Horace was angry at the empty Shows of the *Romans*; what would he then have said to this *vain Entertainment,* only directed to bewitch your Eyes and Ears; *Music* and *Machine,* the *Circe* and *Calipso,* in Conspiracy against *Nature* and *Good Sense.* 'Tis a Debauch the most insinuating, and the most pernicious. Tho' the *Grecians* were as much for *Singing* and *Dancing,* as any *French* or *Italian* whatever; yet their Music kept within Bounds, nor ever attempted to *metamorphose* the whole *Drama* into an *Opera.* The *Spectator* has been right in his Censure of this *monstrous Entertainment. It does not* (says he) *want any great Measure of Sense to see the Ridicule of this* monstrous *Practice* (*that is, of sing- ing partly* English, *and partly Italian*) ; *but it is not the Taste of the Rabble, but of the Persons of the greatest Politeness, which has establish'd it.*

He shou'd have said, Persons of the greatest *Quality*; for certainly *Politeness* cannot be the Share of those who indulge an *Absurdity,* which he confesses wants but a little Measure of Sense to discover.

But then I think nothing can be more absurd, than his preferring the ridiculous Qualities of an *Opera* after the *Italian,* to that after the Way of *Harry Purcel.* He laughs at the *Singing Superscriptions of Letters, Generals Singing the Word of Command*; *Ladies Delivering a Message* in *Music,* and the like, of which every *Italian Opera* is full. *But however* (says he) *this* Italian *Way of Acting in* Recitativo, *might appear at first Hearing, I cannot but think it much more just, than that which prevailed in our* English *Opera's before this Innovation. The Transition from the* Air *to the* Recitativo *Musick being more natural than the passing from a Song to plain and ordinary Speaking, which was the common Method in* Purcel's *Opera's.* This, to make Sense of it, and render it of a Piece with what went before, requires all the Art of the *Tatler, Spectator, Guardian*. For how can that be said to be more natural than any thing, which is in all its Parts entirely unnatural. Then what does he mean by the Transition from Speaking to Musick in *Harry Purcel*'s *Opera*'s? In them, what was proper for Musick, was sung, and the *Drama* performed as all other *Drama*'s were. The same might be said of the Tragedies of *Sophocles, Euripides,* and the rest of the Ancients; when the *Actors* came to a Pause, the *Chorus* sung, and when the *Chorus* had done singing, the *Actors* spoke again. And would this Author perswade any one in his Senses, that the *Modern Opera's* had a more natural Transition than the *Greek* Tragedies?

For my Part (interrupted Mrs. *Lamode*) I have so humble an Opinion of my self, as to think, that what pleases every Body, at least, the People of *Fashion,* ought to please me; and I have this Satisfaction, to find an Abundance of Pleasure in erring with all my Acquaintance. For that I may not be deceiv'd in my Opinion of a Play or an Opera, I never go to either, till I hear a Character of them from some of my Friends, and know how it takes with the Town. The Particulars sometimes the obliging Mr. *Trifle* does me the Favour of conveying to me, and sometimes my dear *Issachar*; and what pleases most, I always take to be best.

I profess (assum'd *Trifle*) I think your Ladyship infinitely in the Right. I always do the very same. I am content to leave the *Critics* the surly Satisfaction of being pleased with nothing that is not Two Thousand Years old; the regular, stiff Pieces of the *Ancients*; the Rules and Forms of an *old dull Philosopher,* who never understood Gayety and Gallantry; *Aristotle* with his *Sophocles,* and I know not what *Greek Bites* refuse me.

Admirably rally'd my Dear Mr. *Trifle* (assum'd Mrs. *Lamode* laughing) give me the *Wit* and *Poetry* of a fashionable Turn, *fine Things* and *fine Language.* For dear *Laudon,* there's a Mode of *Wit* and *Poetry,* as well as of *Cloaths*; and he or she, that is out of the *Fashion,* makes a very ridiculous Figure, and is very *scandalous Company.* Wou'd it not be a very pretty Sight to have a young Lady come into the Drawing-Room in a *Ruff,* and *Farthingal?* *London,* and *Athens,* are quite different Places, and the Modes, and Manners of the People differ so much, that what was bright, and pleasing in *Athens,* must be dull, and insipid in *London.*

Laudon (pursu'd *Issachar*) don't you think, that my Spouse has spoken like an Oracle? The *Critics* have not thought enough on this Point. I have been bred at the *University* my self, and I have read the Antients, and I profess, I can't discover those killing Beauties, which the Affectation of the *Critics* pretends to find in them. I vow I can't help thinking that *Cowley* is finer than *Ovid,* and the *Arthurs* as good as *Homer,* or *Virgil.* Nor can I see any Reason why our *Dramatic* Poets are not more valuable than *Sophocles,* or *Euripides.* All the Advantage these have, is, that they liv'd a great while ago, and that they writ in *Greek.* What say you, fair Lady (concluded he to *Morisina*) I am sure you can never admire those *Heathen Poets,* whom you do not understand, above our own *Countrymen,* whom you do.

I find so many Reasons (reply'd *Morisina*) to dislike those, whom I do understand, that I fancy I shou'd have as many to like those whom I do not understand; especially when I find the Accounts the Learned give of them (in the Language I know) and the Objections drawn from the *Antients* by them, against the *Absurdities* of our modern *Poets* so agreeable to *Nature* and

Reason. As for your Ladyship's *Mode* and *Fashion* of *Wit,* it may, perhaps, hold of the *Poems* of our Time; for we seldom find, that they keep up their easily acquir'd Reputation more than one Season. But as the present Duke of *Buckingham* has it in his admirable *Essay on Poetry.*

True Wit is everlasting like the Sun.

And to shew your Ladyship, that your Simile of *Ruffs,* and *Farthingal*'s, will be little Proof of what you urg'd it for; you must remember, that *Shakespear*'s Wit holds in Fashion still, though of the same Date with those Ornaments of Dress, which wou'd now appear so very ridiculous. Time, that has so often chang'd our Modes of Apparel, and made the same Things so often *modish* and *antiquated,* has only added Force, Respect, and Authority to the *true Wit* of One Hundred and Fifty Years standing. As we find this beyond Dispute in *Shakespear,* so the same will hold good of those great Masters of *Poetry* among the Antients of *Rome,* and *Athens*; who have in all Times, and all Nations (as soon as understood) kept up, nay encreas'd their Esteem, and Value, whilst every thing else chang'd: Imperial Families, Kingdoms, whole Nations, and People have perish'd or alter'd their *Modes, Forms,* and *Languages.*

And as for your Ladyship's *fine Things,* and *fine Language,* to prefer these to more charming, and more essential Excellencies, wou'd be as ridiculous, as to prefer your Ladyship's *Dress* to your *Person*: A Complement, I dare believe, that you wou'd not think so gallant, as the *Mode* and *Fashion* require. It is indeed, in some *Poems,* and some sort of *Poetry* the most valuable Part; but then that sort is of the most *inferiour* Rank, and full of the most base *Allay*; as perhaps the Men may really think *some Women* of *less* Value than their *Cloaths*.

Nor am I surpriz'd at the facetious Mr. *Trifle*'s humble Content in leaving the *Critics* the Satisfaction of being pleas'd with nothing but the regular Pieces of *Antiquity,* and *the Rules and Forms of an old doting Philosopher*; for I think that he ought to be consistent with himself, and no more approve of *Regularity* and *Order* in the Works of the *Poets,* than in his own Conduct, and Actions. Establish'd Customs, Habits, and Inclinations easily bribe a weak Judgment to their side; and render every thing agreeable, that carries any Resemblance to themselves.

As for Mr. *Lamode*'s putting modern *Authors* on a Foot with *Homer,* I am very confident, that the *admirable* Author of *the Creation,* has too much *Judgment,* and too much *Modesty,* to have any such Thought himself. Let it suffice, that the Author of the *Arthurs* has the Glory of excelling *Lucretius,* it is a Palm gain'd only by him; but leave the Soveraignty of *Homer* untouch'd even by *Milton* himself; who, I am afraid, in Justice with all his vast Imagination and Strength of Genius, will come in for no more than the *second Place.*

But, Madam, I wonder that your Ladyship, who value your self for the *grand Goust* in all the fine Pleasures above every one else, shou'd be for *levelling* your Understanding with the very *Canaille,* the Gross of the Readers and Spectators, who not only fill up the House, but like the Shoemaker of *Madrid* (as Madam *Dunois* tells you) dispos'd of the Fate of a Play. At this Rate you make your *Footman* in the upper Gallery, as good a Judge as your self. An Affront invented by the Malice of a half-witted Enemy, cou'd never be more reproachful than what you wou'd here put on your self.

But, dear Madam, I am so much your Friend, that I can never bear such an Indignity to your Sense, even from your own *fair Mouth*. Besides, if you allow the Applause of the Town to be the Test of what is *Good,* you must allow its *Neglect* or *Exploding* to be the Mark of the *Bad*; and then the very *same* thing must be *good* and *bad,* the *best,* and the *worst,* and the same Men in the *same* Poem the most *excellent,* and the most *execrable* of Poets. To avoid Instances of living Authors, the *Mamamouche* on its first Appearance, was acted a Month together, which must exalt it to the *highest Excellence*; but when it was reviv'd (as I am assur'd by those who were at it) it was *hiss'd* off the Stage; and so by the same Test became the *worst* of *Farces.* Thus you wou'd make the *Orphan* yield to the *Empress* of *Morocco,* and the *Plain-dealer* to the *Quixots,* yet, Madam, I am confident your Ladyship will never prefer the *last* to the *first*.

You must therefore, Madam, for your own sake, find out some surer Way of judging of the *lesser Poems,* as well as of *Plays,* than that *Run,* and *Reception,* they meet with from the *Town,* which is so uncertain, and varying in the frail Praise she bestows, that Poems have already lost their Glory, and are become as great Drugs as *Quar[l]e*'s and *Withers,* which for a while carry'd the Acclamations along with them: Nay, *Cowley* himself, so much ador'd for near Forty Years, loses every Day Ground with all those, who love *Nature,* and *Harmony,* which are Virtues not very common in that *learned* and *witty Person*.

Here the bright *Morisina* made an End, discovering as many Charms in her Soul, as Eyes. These may, perhaps, be equall'd by many of her Sex; but a Taste so *fine,* she enjoys almost without a Rival. Mrs. *Lamode* was confounded, and dismay'd, and cou'd scarce muster up Spirits enow to desire her to point out a better Method of judging, than the *Opinion* of the *Town*. But Dinner now coming in, suspended her Reply.

After our Repast was over, and the *Tea* on the Table, Mrs. *Lamode* renew'd her Request to *Morisina* to correct her Error, and give her a more infallible Method of judging justly of the *Poets Performance,* than the Applause they meet with from the *Town*.

Madam (answer'd *Morisina*) I know your Ladyship is an admirable Artist at your Needle, and I have with Wonder seen you rival *Nature,* when with that you paint the Flowers of the Field, the Branches of the Woods, the Birds of the Air, and the Beasts and Reptiles of the Earth. Now, Madam, wou'd you allow the Judgment of your *Groom,* your *Plowman,* or your *Cook-Maid,* or even of your Tenants in the Villages about you to decide the Merit of your Performance? Wou'd you not, on their Condemnation of your Work, appeal to those, who are skilful in the Art? And vindicate what you have done by shewing the several Stitches to be regular, and according to *Art*; that the Colours are justly mingled, insinuating themselves into each other with so nice a *Subtilty,* that it wou'd be a difficult Matter to point out their *Separation,* or say, where the Union begins, or where it ends? That the Disposition of the Parts is to the best Advantage, and *Nature* in the Whole, so well dissembled, that it must be a very curious Eye, that can distinguish the Copy from the Original? Such a Piece, Madam, as your Ladyship shew'd me, the last Time I did my self the Honour of waiting on you?

True (my dear *Morisina,* answer'd Mrs. *Lamode*) I had the Mortification to hear *Abigail* prefer an old, wild, antiquated Piece of Work of the Days of *good*

Queen *Bess* to that, which you so much admir'd. I ask'd
the *silly Creature,* how she cou'd like such *gouty*
Stitches, without Beauty, or Order, or prefer it to mine,
which was according to the nicest Samplars, and made
such near Approaches to Nature? The wretched
Creature reply'd, that there was *something,* she did *not
know what* of Antiquity in the other, that made it
venerable. That she did not know the *Art,* or the Nicety
of the Stitches, and happy Mixture of the Colours, and
the like; but her Eye was much more pleas'd with a
Je ne scay Quoyish Beauty of the old Piece without
Order, Beauty or Harmony of the Parts, than with all
the Correspondence and *Ordonance* of mine. I swear,
my dear, the dull Creature put me into a Passion, I cou'd
have almost have broken her Fingers with my Fan. I
am vext that the *insignificant* Thing cou'd ruffle me
so much.

Oh! my dear *Lamode* (cry'd *Morisina*) I have
surpriz'd you into my Party: For my Dear, you must
pardon me, you play the Part of *Abigail* your self, and
declaim against the *Rules* of *Art,* and cry up the wild and
confus'd Productions of *blind Fancy,* like *Abigail*'s
darling *Antique,* before a *beautiful Piece,* which like
your Ladyship's Work, derives an admirable *Order,* and
Harmony from the Observation of, and following the
Lineaments of *Nature,* taught by the *Rules* of the *Art*
of *Poetry.* For, Madam, *Poetry* in all its Parts, is an
Imitation: Proposing therefore a *certain End,* it must
have certain Means of attaining that End, which are the
Rules of *Art,* as your Ladyship observes in guiding your
curious Needle, through the Flowers, and Foliage of
your Work. The general *Judgment* of the *Town,* is like
your *Abigail*'s, made and form'd on *Je-ne-scay-Quoys,*
they *Know-not-what,* their *beautiful Extravagancies,*

and many such empty Sounds which have no manner of Idea fixt to them.

Well, well, fair *Morisina* (said Mrs. *Lamode*) if you have any better Way of judging, I beg you let us hear it; I vow I shall be surprisingly pleas'd with the instructing Amusement from so charming a Mouth.

Madam (assum'd *Tom Trifle* with a pert Insipidness) your Ladyship is infinitely in the Right, for Madam *Morisina*, I vow to Gad is the finest Amusement in the World.

That's a Task too difficult (return'd *Morisina*) for me to undertake, I shall leave that to my Spouse, and to his Friend *Gamaliel*.

No, no, my Dear (assum'd Mrs. *Lamode*) I never will consent to that, but as you have found Fault with my *Rule* of judging, pray do me the Justice to produce your own, *Laudon*, and his Friend will perfectly confound us with *Aristotle*, and a Thousand hard *Greek* Names. And for my Part, I have a mortal *Aversion* to all *Greeks*, and *Romans*, whom I do not understand. I may, perhaps, allow you something of the *French*, or the *Italian*, and in case of Necessity, perhaps, a *Spaniard:* But for your *Aristotle*, and your *Horace*'s, I know not what to say to them: They have reign'd long enough; it is Time to put an End to their Authority.

You must (assum'd *Laudon*) first put an End to *Nature*, and extinguish *all Sense* in Mankind. A new Model in *Poetry* must be monstrously absurd, and a wretched Refuge of ignorant *Poetasters* to shelter their own Follies from Censure. Thus *Lopez de Vega* undertook to write a New Art of *Poesie*, but he succeeded so ill in his Undertaking, that the Book has not been thought worthy to be Printed with the rest of his Works. *Cornielle* attempted the same in *France*, but what his

Success was, his own Countryman, the admirable *Dacier* (to say nothing of the *Academy of Sciences*) will discover by a Confutation of his Errors, with that Clearness, and good Judgment, that the Faults of *Corneilles* Plays (to remove which he set up those *New* Rules) remain, and *Aristotle* preserves his Reputation entire with all Men of *fine Sense,* and *sound Understanding.*

Horace first proposed this just Model (as a judicious *French* Author justly calls it) to the *Romans,* and the great Men of the Court of *Augustus* follow'd them as inviolable. After the taking of *Constantinople* by the *Turks,* many of the *Greek Authors* were transported to *Italy* by the Care, and Interest of *Cosmo* and *Lorenzo di Medici* (the great Restorers of ancient Learning, and Politeness after the long Night of *Gothick* and *Monkish* Ignorance and Barbarity) who were follow'd by several learned Men, who reviv'd and set up Schools of the then forgotten *Greek* Language. Hence soon arose a Multitude of Commentators on these admirable *Rules* of *Aristotle,* of whom *Piccolomini,* and *Casselvetro* had the best Success. Father *Rapin* building on them, excell'd the *Italians.* But Mr. *Dacier* has gone far beyond all others of any Nation in his Notes on this excellent Treatise of the *Philosopher*; *Laudon* had not quite done when *Tyro* came in with *Manilia.*

Ah! cry'd out Mrs. *Lamode,* my Dear *Manilia,* you are the most welcome Person alive; and you, Mr. *Tyro,* you come to the Relief of the distress'd *Damoisel*; I am besieg'd with *Giants,* and only your Prowess can bring me Relief.

The Matter, the Matter (said *Tyro*) I am always a Devote to the Ladies, especially when in Distress. But how can you be so in the Company of my Friend *Laudon,* I can't imagine, who is the most complaisant

Man in the World to the fair Sex. *Morisina* is such a B[r]ibe, that must always retain *Laudon* in the Ladies Cause.

Ah! Mr. *Tyro!* (cry'd Mrs. *Lamode*) *Laudon* has declar'd against me, and *Morisina* is the most violent Enemy I have. They have espous'd the Cause of the *Critics,* to whom I confess a mortal Aversion.

Nothing but a *Jeu de Esprit,* I dare be confident (assum'd *Tyro*) *Laudon* is a Man of too gay a Taste to espouse seriously the Cause of *Sowerness,* and ill *Nature.* It is a particular Observation I have always made, that of all Mortals, a Critic is the silliest.

That is (interrupted *Laudon*) of all Mortals, a Man of *Judgment* and *Skill* in *Art* is the silliest. For if you mean pretended *Criticks,* you shou'd have told us so. Now as to *Pretenders* to any *Art,* or *Thing,* without Foundation, they are equally silly, for it is want of Understanding in them all. The drawing a ridiculous Character, and the calling it a *Critic* is of no manner of Force against the *Thing.*

Ah! my Dear Friend *Laudon* (reply'd *Tyro*) you have intercepted what I had to say from the charming *Tatler* on this Head; for when he has told you that a *Critic* is the silliest of Mortals, he adds his Reason; *for* (says he) *by inuring himself to examine all Things, whether they are of Consequence or not, he never looks upon any thing, but with a Design of passing Sentence upon it; by which means he is never a Companion, but always a Censor. This makes him earnest upon Trifles, and Dispute on the most indifferent Occasions with Vehemence. If he offers to speak or write, that Talent, which shou'd approve the Work of the other Faculties prevents their Operation. He comes upon Action in*

Armour, but without Weapons; he stands in Safety, but can gain no Glory.

And a little after - - - - *A* thorough Critic *is a sort of* Puritan *in the* polite World. *As an* Enthusiast *in Religion stumbles at the ordinary Occurrences of Life, if he cannot quote Scripture Examples on the Occasion; so the* Critic *is never safe in his Speech or Writing, without he has among the celebrated Writers an Authority for the Truth of his Sentence.*

You need go no farther (said *Laudon*) 'tis only a very dry Ridicule on the Character, without the least Shadow of Reason. But Mr. *Isaac,* notwithstanding his Passion against *Critics,* has play'd the *Critic* himself not only in his eighth and ninth *Tatler,* but in several others; nay, indeed his whole Business seems to be a *Critic* on the Manners of Men; a harder Thing to determine than the *Rules* of *Art*; unless he wou'd shelter himself under the Name of *Censor,* which is one, who passes Judgment on something, and so comes to the same Point. But here I cannot omit one thing, which I find he attacks more than once in the Course of his Writings; and which I am afraid his enemies will say discovers him to be a most aband[on]ed *Pedant.* And this is that our *Critics* guide themselves by what they find in the *French* Writers, without being capable of going so high as the original *Greek* or *Latin* Masters. This I am sorry I must allow to be a sort of Refuge of *Pedantry,* as if there were really any *singular* Merit, as to the *Art* to understand *Greek* or *Latin.* No Man certainly can condemn the Reason of what we find in *French*; and yet it is the *Reason* of the Thing, and not the Language it is written in, that makes it valuable. But in opposition to the *Spectators,* and *Tatlers,* frequent Censure of the *French Critics.* I must observe first, that so great a Poet, and Judge of Poetry, as my Lord *Roscommon* had no such Opinion of the *French* Writers, in his Essay on translated Verse.

When France *had breath'd after intestine Broils,*
And Peace, and Conquest, crown'd her foreign Toils:
There (cultivated by a Royal Hand)
Learning grew fast, and spread, and blest the Land.
The choicest Books, that Rome *or* Greece *have known,*
Her excellent Translators made their own.
And Europe *must acknowledge that she Gains,*
Both by their good Example, and their Pains.

I must secondly remark, that they have preserv'd Politeness in all their Learning. *Bossu,* and *Dacier* write like Gentlemen, and Men of a *fine Taste,* tho' perfectly skill'd in all the necessary *Criticisms* of the *Greek* and *Roman* Language; whereas *Vossius,* (I mean *Gerrard,* not *Isaac,* who is much more polite) *Scaliger,* and many of our *English* Men of Learning, have so far lost themselves in *verbal Criticisms,* or in mere Collections of Opinions, that they never distinguish *finely,* and seldom observe further; but give us Authority on Authority, in a stiff, dry, jujune Manner, without drawing any valuable Doctrine from what they have taken the Pains to give from the Antients. The *French,* on the contrary, burthen not our *Memories,* nor confound our *Judgments,* by Multiplicity of Quotations, but give us the solid Doctrine they have drawn from them, and the insuperable Reasons on which they are founded. They dwell not on the meer *grammatical Criticisms* on Words, but penetrate farther into the *Reasons,* and *Sense,* and *Judgment* of the Authors; and give us Light out of Obscurity, which some have involv'd the Antients in. What Reason therefore has any Man to object, as an

Odium, our consulting the *French* Authors, when he, or his Colleagues, shall write like them: I dare engage the Ingenious will be oblig'd to them, and consult them without the *French.* There is nothing so trifling and ridiculous as the Praises given *Homer, Virgil,* &c. By the *Dutch,* most of the *Italian,* and *English* Writers; but *Bossu* and *Dacier,* to the Honour of their Country, enter'd into the true Merits of those great Poets in their Design, *&c. Dionysius Halicarnasseus* indeed, so long ago has hit right in praising *Homer*'s Contrivance, and Design, as well as the Greatness, and Majesty, of his Expression, and the lively and passionate Motions of the Sentiments. But I think you *Ladies* ought to declare against them, and all others, when they are for depriving you of all Resource, by confining all Knowledge to *Greek* and *Latin,* Languages you are not so familiar with as *French.*

Nay, I confess (said Mrs. *Lamode*) I am not of his Party in that, I am a profess'd admirer of the *French Tongue,* and whoever runs that down, I shall declare against him.

As for what Tongue it is in (assum'd *Manilia*) it matters not, but *Criticism* it self is the thing that the *Tatler* falls upon; and good Lord, indeed, what a Figure does Sir *Timothy Tittle* make in the *Tatlers?* One would think, that no Man of *Wit,* wou'd ever after that, have descended to own the Name of a *Critic.*

Oh! Madam (said *Laudon*) there is nothing more easie, than for a Grotesque Painter to clap Asses Ears on the Head of a *Socrates,* yet that wou'd betray the *Ignorance, Folly,* or *Impudence* of the Painter, but not any Defect in that wise *Athenian.* If the *Tatler* design'd by those, and some other Stroaks of the like Nature, to ridicule *Criticasters,* and impudent Pretenders to *Judg-*

ment, he shou'd not have endeavour'd to affix the Infamy he design'd to the Name of *Critic,* but have plainly, and evidently distinguish'd between them; otherwise the Asses Ears will cleave to his own Head, for ridiculing *Judgment,* without which nothing ever was, or ever can be, well and justly perform'd either in *Painting* or *Poetry.*

Bless me! (cry'd *Manilia*) you infinitely surprize me to hear you oppose the Sentiments of a Paper that so ravish'd the Town, and almost reconcil'd *Parties* in its Praise, that were opposite in every thing else. How shall we, *poor Women,* direct our Judgments, if by such celebrated Guides, we are led astray?

By *Reason* and *Nature,* Madam (reply'd *Laudon*) for it is only when these Authors desert them, that they become contemptible to the *judicious.*

Well, but (said *Tyro*) if you will not allow the Authority of the *Tatlers, Spectators,* and the like, I hope you will yield to that of Sir *William Temple.*

For my Part (reply'd *Laudon*) I cannot allow any Man's *Authority* against *Reason* and *Truth;* and if Sir *William* has advanc'd any thing that is so, I shall make no Scruple in dissenting from him.

It is in his *Essay upon Poetry* (assum'd *Tyro*) and after he has given his Sentiments at large, he draws towards a Conclusion in these Words, against the *Rules,* on which your *Criticism* is built. *The Truth is* (says he) *there is something in the Genius of* Poetry *too libertine to be confin'd to so* many Rules, *and whoever goes about to subject it to such Constraints, loses both its* Spirit *and* Grace, *which are ever Native, and never learned out of the best Masters.* Then he concludes this Point against the *French,* and our *Critics,* in these Words. *It wou'd be too much Mortification to these great arbitrary Rulers among the* French *Writers, and our own,*

*to observe the worthy Productions, that have been form'd
by their* Rules; *the Honour they have receiv'd in the
World, or the Pleasure they have given Mankind. But
to comfort them, I do not know that there was any great
Poet in Greece, after the Rules of that Art laid down
by* Aristotle; *nor in* Rome, *after those by* Horace, *which
yet none of our Moderns pretend to have outdone.
Perhaps* Theocritus *and* Lucan *may be alledg'd against
this Assertion; but the first offer'd no further than his
Idyls or Eclogues, and the last, tho' he must be own'd
for a true and happy Genius, and to have made some very
high Flights, yet he is too unequal to himself, and his
Muse is too young, that his Faults are too noted to allow
his Pretences. - - - After all, the utmost that can be
achiev'd by any Rules* in this Art, *is but to hinder some
Men from being very ill Poets, but not to make any one
a very good one.*

I think, that what Sir *William* has here urg'd, is as
plain against your *Rules,* and *Criticisms,* as any thing in
the *Tatlers, Spectators,* or the rest.

I grant it (reply'd *Laudon*) but with no more *Reason,*
than those Authors have built on; nay, with this Disadvantage, that Sir *William* either grossly contradicts
himself, or makes use of Words, which have no manner
of Meaning at all, which alone wou'd be sufficient to
destroy his *Authority* with any indifferent Judge. Let
us therefore hear Sir *William* in his own proper Person,
and in the very same *Essay.*

But though Invention *be the Mother of* Poetry, *yet
this Child is like all others born naked, and must be
nourish'd with Care, cloath'd with Exactness, and
Elegance, educated with Industry,* instructed *with* Art,
improv'd by Application, corrected with Severity, *and
accomplish'd with Labour, and Time; before it arrives*

at any great Perfection or Growth, it is certain that no Composition requires so many several Ingredients, and of more different Sorts, than this: Nor that to excel in any Qualities, there are necessary so many Gifts of Nature, and so many Improvements of Learning *and* Art. Again ---- *Without the Force of* Wit, *all* Poetry *is flat, and languishing, without the Succours of* Judgment, *it is wild, and extravagant.*

Here you find Sir *William* denying Perfection to *Poetry,* without it be instructed by *Art;* but if he mean any thing by *Art,* he means what every Body in the World means by it, that ever made use of that Word on any Occasion. Now every *Art* in its very Constitution proposes some certain *End* to obtain, and some certain *Means* of obtaining that *End;* but the Means in the *Art* of *Poetry,* as well as in all others, are what we call the Rules of the *Art.* So that to talk of the Necessity of *Art,* and at the same Time disallow of its *Rules* is downright Nonsense; or the proposing an *End,* without any *Means* of attaining that *End,* which is equally absurd and ridiculous. If he wou'd ascribe all to *Fancy* in Poetry, to what Purpose all this Pomp of Expression, in the displaying the other necessary Qualities of a Poet to arrive at Perfection? What mean the nourishing it with *Care;* cloathing it with *Exactness* and *Elegance;* educating it with *Industry;* instructing it with *Art;* improving it with Application; but above all, *correcting* it with *Severity?* What must *Fancy* be severe on *Fancy?* Must the Heat of *Fancy* be accomplish'd with Labour and Time? What will *Fancy,* without *Judgment,* be wild and extravagant, and yet no *Rules* to direct this wild and extravagant Quality of *Wit?* But if all these Pains are to be taken to regulate the *Fancy,* or *Genius* of *Poetry;* is not this to confine it to *certain Rules?*

Or is it to be confin'd and not confin'd; regulated by *Judgment,* and yet free from that Curb? These are the Contradictions of the Enemies of the *Rules.* Or is the *Judgment* to be without any certain Direction, and only the effect of the particular Writer's Notion, who is correcting his own Work? But how will Sir *William,* or any Advocate of his, distinguish between *Fancy* and *Judgment* in this Matter, and shew where their Duties are bounded? What is their Distinction, and how we shall know the Acts of the one from the other without fixing some *Rules?* But if they find themselves reduc'd to a Necessity of making some Standard of *Judgment,* let them shew that the *Fancy* or *Genius* will be less confin'd by them, than by those already in Force, and acknowledge[d] by all the learned of all Nations these 2000 Years. I am afraid that his *Rules* which require so much *Application* and *Severity,* are as likely to make *Poetry* lose its *Spirit,* and *Grace,* as those of *Aristotle,* and the rest of the *Critics,* So that if the *Genius of the* Poetry *have something too libertine in it, to be confin'd to so* many Rules, *and that whoever goes about to subject it to such Constraints, loses both its* Spirit, *and* Grace, *which are ever Native, and never to be learned of any* [M]aster. Then what becomes of his *nourishing, cloathing, instructing, correcting,* and the like?

Thus you see by what *Contradictions* and *Absurdities* this worthy *Essayist* is embarass'd in his Declamation against the *Rules* of *Art. But the Champions of these Rules have given the World nothing* admirable *and* entertaining. That is false, if justly consider'd according to the *Genius* of the Nation, that have written regularly and irregularly. Let us take *France,* whom he attacks. Are the *regular* Pieces of that People more valuable than those which are *irregular,* and on the contrary? Are not *Boileau, Racine,* and the like, more entertaining to them than *Alexander Hardy, du Bartas,* or the like? I think all *France* will give the Prize to the former; and if so, how have the *Rules* injur'd the *Poetical Productions* of *France?* Nay, *Corneille* himself, when he began to write after the Model of *Hardy,* found by his own good Sense, that *Rules* were necessary; and before he had inform'd his Understanding, by the Study of *Aristotle,* he form'd some general Precepts to guide his *Fancy* from those *Absurdities,* into which his Predecessor fell for want of such Helps.

But no great Poet appeared in Greece *or* Rome, *after the Publication of the Rules of* Aristotle *and* Horace. This is begging the Question with a Vengeance; and I wonder that Sir *William,* who appeals to the 600000 Volumes lost in the *Ptolemaic* Library, against the *Moderns,* in his first Essay, should pronounce so dogmatically in this Point, since it is as certain, that many great Poets, as well as other Authors, perish'd either there, or in the Havock of Time. But what does he think of *Menander* and all the Authors of the *new Comedy,* given us, in some Measure, by *Plautus,* and by *Terence?* Or is it probable, that *Athens,* which ever encouraged *Tragedy* more than *Comedy,* had no *Tragic* Poets of Worth after *Euripides, Agatho, Polydes,* and the rest that preceded *Aristotle?* But the most unlucky thing that could befal this Instance of our *Essayer,* is that *Virgil, that supreme Genius,* was after *Aristotle,* cotemporary with *Horace,* and as well acquainted with the *Fountain* of *Criticism,* as *Horace* himself; nay, and has visibly observed the Rules of *Aristotle,* in his *Æneis.* After this, what need we look into a bare List of Names of several eminent *Poets* that liv'd after *Horace,* tho' their Works be lost? What may we think of *Varius*

and *Tucca,* to whom *Virgil* submitted his Works?
Were they ignorant of the Rules which *Virgil* follow'd?
Must we, because the Works of many more, and those
eminent in their Time, are perish'd, conclude they were
not good Poets? That wou'd prove that all those who
have reach'd our Days are good, and that would establish
Lucan in spite of what the Knight has said against him.
For if, in Reality, *Lucan* be not a good Poet, it is because
he has not follow'd the same Rules that *Virgil* did. The
same may be said of *Statius, Silius Italicus,* and some
other *Roman* Authors that are still extant, and yet never
thought good Poets by the judicious Part of the World,
in any Nation where they have found Readers.

Painting is an Art that requires a *Genius,* and yet
cannot be justly perform'd without the Rules of Art.
The Proportion of a Man standing upright, is eight
Times the Length of his Head: The Arms hanging
straight down, reach within a Span of the Knee: A Hand
must be the Length of the Face, and the Arms extended
make the just Length of the whole Body. These, and
an Hundred more Rules must be known to, and follow'd
by every Painter, tho' of never so exalted a *Genius,* or
Gusto, which can never justify him in breaking any of
the Rules; for those of Painting, as well as those of
Poetry, are Nature, and shew us its just Lineaments,
by which every Judge may know the *Excellence* or
Defect of the Performer.

Thus in *Landskip* the Painter ought to be skill'd in
Perspective, else can he never know the Proportions, in
regard of the Distances, and the like. The knowing of
those Rules alone will not make a Painter, without both
a Genius and Practice; and in the same Manner, the
Rules of Poetry are necessary to the forming all valuable

Poems, but they are not able to make a Poet without Genius and Practice too.

In all the fine Arts indeed, there has a *Grotesque* and *Gothique* Taste prevail'd, which relishes every thing that is not natural. Thus, in general, we prefer the *Japan* Pictures for the Furniture of our Rooms, to the fine Prints of the *Audrands, Simoneans, Edlinahs,* and the rest of the great Masters; and by the same abandon'd *Gusto,* we encourage *Opera's* and *Farces,* before *Comedies* and *Tragedies.*

A modern Wit has a very great Aversion to Arts and Sciences, and with an Air of Sufficience, avows his Zeal for *Ignorance.* But as his Fancy only governs him, so are his Productions most commonly sad, crude, indigested things, *like sick Mens Dreams,* without either Head or Tail. If you chance to mention *Art,* he cries out, you are a *Critic,* an *ill-natur'd Person*; that Nature is not to be ty'd up to *Order, Harmony, Beauty* of Design; as if *Confusion* were the only Perfection. When they speak of a *Play,* the highest Praise they give it, in their Approbation, is, that it is *fine Language,* like Mr. *Wycherly*'s Lover, that cou'd find nothing about his Mistress to praise, but the *Tip* of her Ear, and her *Elbow.* So that most of our successful *Poets* ought to be ashamed of the Applause they obtain, as *Lucian* was when he wrote his *Zeuxis,* finding it to be paid to the Novelty, and Neatness of the Expression, and not to the Judgment of his Method, and the like.

But our *Wits* and *Lucian* are not of a Piece. I wou'd fain know of them whether *Architecture, Statuary, Music,* can be excell'd in by any one who is not a perfect Master of the establish'd Rules of either of them? And then I will yield, that Perfection in *Poetry* may be attain'd without knowing any thing of the Art.

The *Tatler* has been pleased to call the *Critics, Puritans,* whereas they are of the established Church; but the Gentlemen that are against them, are the true Fanaticks in Poetry, against *Order* and *Decency,* the Effect of it.

It is, as I have observed, urged against Criticism, or the Rules of *Art,* that a too regular Adherence to the Forms and Measures of them, is a Restraint on a Writer's *Invention,* and does more Harm than Good in Composition. For that the Imagination cannot so freely diffuse and expand it self, when it is oblig'd to any Bounds or Limits whatever. This Argument is sometimes illustrated and supported by that famous Example of an ungovernable Genius in *Heroic* Virtue; I mean *Alexander* the *Great,* whose vast Ambition never fail'd to hurry him beyond the due Measures of Conduct, upon which very Account, say they, his Exploits had always in them something wonderfully surprizing and astonishing. Whereas, *Cæsar*'s Actions, that were more cool, deliberate, and proportion'd to the Rules of Prudence and Policy, never give us such a sublime, exalted Idea of his Fortitude, as we must necessarily entertain of the *Greek* Heroes. The Friends too of our great Dramatic Writer *Shakespear* will not be perswaded, but that even his monstrous Irregularities were conducive to those shining Beauties which abound in most of his Plays: And that if he had been more a Critic, he had been less a Poet; that is, if he had known more of Nature (which only the Rules teach) he would have touch'd her less. But I say, that notwithstanding this Pleasure given by *Alexander*'s Deeds, good Conduct in War is no Hindrance to the boldest Undertakings. For any one that knows History, knows, that without it, *Cæsar*'s Atchievements had never been so glorious, nor most of *Alexander*'s too. These astonishing (I might call them accidental) Victories gain'd by the latter, betray'd (many of them at least) more of Foolhardiness than Valour. And a due Observation of natural Rules, that is, a strict Attendance to the *Rules* of *Nature* and Reason, can never embarrass or clogg an Author's Fancy, but rather enlarge and extend it. They might as well urge, that good and wholesome Laws that enjoin nothing but what a rational Nature would otherwise oblige us to, take away the Liberty of Mankind, whereas they are the very Life and Security of it.

But against Sir *William Temple,* the *Tatlers,* and other Enemies to the Rules, I shall give you the Opinion of a much greater Man, in his Way, I mean my Lord *Roscommon,* not only by his giving us a Version of the Art of Poetry of *Horace,* but from his *Essay on Translated Verse,* in the very first Lines.

> *Happy that Author whose correct Essay*
> *Revives so well our old* Horatian *Way;*
> *And happy those who (if concurring Stars*
> *Predestinate them to Poetic Wars)*
> *With Pains and Leisure by* such Precepts write,
> *And learn to use their Arms before they fight.*

For this Introduction is not only a just Commendation of the *Essay on Poetry,* which contains admirable Rules in that Art, but a Recommendation of Rules in general. And Mr. *Waller,* in his Verses before his Lordship's Translation of *Horace*'s *Art of Poetry,* tells us,

> Britain *whose Genius is in Verse exprest,*
> *Bold and sublime, but negligently drest.*

Recommends the Study and Observation of the Rules to our Authors, which will shew the Art of *Criticism*

to be the Art of inducing *proportion'd Wonders,* as
Waller expresses it.

> *He that proportion'd Wonders can disclose,*
> *At once his Fancy and his Judgment shews.*

For Fancy and Judgment must join in every great Poet,
as Courage and Judgment in every great General; for
where either is wanting, the other is useless, or of small
Value. Fancy is what we generally call *Nature,* or a
Genius; Judgment is what we mean by Art, the Union
of which in one Man makes a complete Poet.

I hope therefore (concluded *Laudon* to *Tyro*) that
I have made a Convert of you from that Vague and
inconsistent Notion to Regularity, Form, and Order,
which is what the Rules pretend to teach, and not a
Genius, which must indeed be born with you, or you will
find but little Advantage from the Rules. Man might
perhaps live without the Rules and Maxims of Government, but under all those Inconveniences that must
render Life as unpleasant as unsecure, but by the Rules
of Art (as I may call them) Men live in Society, with
all the Harmony of Subordination; and every Part
contributes to the Beauty of the Whole: So in Poetry,
Nature may inform some one great *Genius* to give us
some *fine Things,* as she may inspire some few Men to
follow her Laws, in their wild, uncultivated Way of
Living, like some of the *West Indians;* but then even
that one great Genius will be apt to abound in *monstrous
Absurdities,* and *incongruous Extravagancies,* which can
only be avoided by the constant and unalterable Rules
of Reason.

Here *Laudon* gave over speaking, and after a little
Pause, *Tyro* made this Reply. I confess, that from what
you have urg'd, there seems to me a Necessity of the

Poet's proposing to himself some Measures or Rules of Conduct in what he performs, which is the proper Task of *Judgment*. But I cannot from thence conclude, that therefore the arbitrary Dictates of every sower Humour that usurps the Authority of a *Critic,* should be of any Force against a Poem that has receiv'd the general Applause of the World. When I hear of any Piece of *Criticism,* I generally enquire for the Author's Name; and if he have not perform'd any thing himself, or not any thing well, and with the publick Approbation, I never give my self the Trouble of reading him over.

And I (assum'd *Laudon*) when I find any Writing or Speaking against *Criticism,* presently examine whether he has not written something that, how successful soever, will not stand the Test of Reason and Art. And I never once fail'd in finding, that his refusing the Judgment of the Critic, was caus'd by the real Defect of his Writing, which was indeed qualify'd for the Vogue of the Town, but not for the Taste of the Judicious. And therefore he disown'd the Authority of the Court, because he was sure there to meet with Condemnation. The Rules of Criticism are known, and fixt by *Aristotle, Horace, Dacier, Bossu,* and others; and tho' a Man may not have perform'd himself, yet by them he may be a very good Judge of another's Performance. As in Painting there are a great many Gentlemen, and Persons of Distinction and Quality, who scarce ever drew a Stroke, who are very good Judges of the Performances of Painters, and can distinguish between the several Hands that have given us the noblest Pieces of Painting. So that I would never reject a Piece of Criticism for the Name of the Author, but for the Defect of what he advances; for if a new Author gives you Reason for what he says, you are obliged to submit to the Determination, or to be an enemy to Reason.

Another thing I must observe, is, that not one of these Gentlemen who profess their Emnity to, or Contempt of a true Critic, but has shewn himself a meer *Criticaster,* when he has fallen upon the Subject; a meer *Piece-Broker* of *Parnassus,* and reaches no farther than Words and Sentences; dealing in the very Scraps of Poetry; a Couplet, an Expression is the utmost he pretends to. But for a Design, or complete Poem, to meddle with it, he accounts Pedantry, or Imposition.

Gerhard Vossius, a Man of consummate Learning, and a very good *Critic,* is entirely against this Notion, in his Preface to his Poetical Institutions. *Some, perhaps* (says he) *would wish, that a Work of this Nature had been undertaken by some one that was admitted to the sacred Office by the Muses, who might before have been seen in their Temple inflam'd with the Poetical Enthusiasm. Had any one made this Objection to* Lilius Giraldus *of* Ferrara, *the most learned of the* Italians *of his Age, when he wrote some things of the Art of Poetry, and more on the Poets, he would have answer'd in the same Words, which we find in his first Dialogue of his History of the Poets.* "It is an old Opinion of "*Plato,* that those have likewise a Share in the Poetic "Fire, who interpret the Verses of the Poets, and may "therefore put in their Claim to the Title of Poets. For "*Panætus,* the Philosopher, for this Reason gave the "name of Prophet, or Poet, to *Aristarchus,* and *Athenæus* "says the same. *Yet would I not arrogate to my self, for this Reason, the Poetic Fury or Genius,* and a little more to the same Purpose. *But setting this aside, I shall rather say, that no one ought to write Poetically but Poets; but that the Subject of writing on the Nature and*

*Rules of that Art, is rather the Business of a Philosopher.
For this I might quote* Aristotle, *who, tho' he was not a
celebrated Poet, was, however, eminent for his Knowledge of all Arts and Sciences, and than whom no one
ever discover'd a greater Penetration and Accuracy in
the Nature of every Kind of Poesy. It is certain, that
he in those Discoveries left those great Poets* Horace
and Vida *much behind him in Excellence, tho' they gain'd
no small Help from the Works of* Aristotle *on this
Subject. Nor can I for the latter find a better Excuse
for their falling short of the Philosopher, than that*
Aristotle *almost exceeded the Bounds of human Capacity
in his Understanding and Learning of every Kind; and
that it is far more easy to write of the Rules of Art in
Prose, than in Verse: To say nothing of the different
Readers that they writ to, the Philosopher to the subtil
Wits of* Greece, *these to their Countrymen a little
elevated above the Vulgar. Farther, I must observe, that
the Judges who were instituted to decide of Poetical
Performances in* Athens, Alexandria, *and* Rome, *were
not so much eminent Poets, as Men who understood the
Nature and Genius of Poetry,* &c.

This I think sufficient to shew, on how false a Bottom
that Maxim is built, which you, *Tyro,* introduc'd, tho'
borrow'd from the *Spectators* or *Tatlers,* of reading, or
not reading a *Critic,* as you heard, whether he had, or
had not written any thing himself. For that Rule would
have rejected *Longinus* himself, on whom those Papers
seem to lay some Stress. It may, I confess, be answered
as to *Aristotle,* that he was a Poet as well as a Philosopher, there being a traditionary Account, that he writ
above 40000 Verses. But it will hold of *Longinus,* and
the Judges just quoted by *Vossius,* as of *Lilius Giraldus,*
and *Vossius, Dacier,* and *Bossu*; nay, and in some

Measure, of *Aristotle:* For tho' there may be a Fragment
of his Poetry yet extant, and tho' he might have written
many Odes, Elegies, or the like, yet we do not find that
ever he writ a *Tragedy,* or *Epic* Poem; and yet his
Criticisms are chiefly on those two Kinds of Poesy.
But then *Horace* himself is against this false Notion,
that none but a Poet should criticize on a Poet, in his
Art of *Poetry,* as Englished by the Lord *Roscommon.*

> *Yet without Writing I may teach to write,*
> *Tell what the Duty of a Poet is;*
> *Wherein his Wealth and Ornament confess,*
> *And how he may be form'd,* &c.

Allowing what you have urg'd (said *Tyro*) in the
main, yet I see no Reason why we should be wholly
guided by the *Ancients.* The Moderns have the Advantage of having the Works of the *Ancients,* and therefore
should excel them. The *English* have likewise another
Benefit, of having the Translations of all the Moderns
of any Value, of all other Nations where polite Learning
has flourish'd. Then I believe I may say, that our
Countrymen have shewn Wit and Genius equal to the
greatest of *Greece* and *Rome.* Those indeed were the
first Nurseries of Art and Wit. For my Part, I am not
convinced of that Divinity of those old Heroes in Poetry;
and I think that he who idolizes them to that Degree,
must be blinded by the Clouds of Incense that are offered
to them by the affected Bigotry of After-Ages. They
certainly were Men of great Genius, and perform'd
Wonders for the Times they writ in; but I think, if
they had done less, they would not have wanted Admiration in our Days. Yet I cannot bear it, that because they
were look'd on as the chief in their own Time, they
should be thought so of all the Ages to come. If a

Contempt of, and Irreverence to the Ancients, be thought injurious to their Merit, it cannot with Justice be thought just to discover a Neglect and Contempt of the Moderns; for that must make Men of admirable Parts chuse rather to be still and idle, and bury their Talents in Obscurity, than venture to come into the Light, where they are sure to have their Performances meet with open Injustice. This was the Case of the Authors in the Time of *Augustus,* of which *Horace* complains, when his Contemporaries were for condemning every thing, not because ill perform'd, but because it was Modern.

What you have urg'd (said I) Sir, seems to me out of the Question at this Time. We are not for excluding the Moderns from their Merits, but insist, that no *Modern* has any Merit but what he owes to the Rules and Precedents of the *Ancients:* We are asserting the Necessity and Use of the Rules of Art established by the Ancients; and till you have confuted them, what has been said remains in full Force.

If you have any modern *Critic* who has gone on a different Foot from the *Ancients,* you should produce him; and not only so, but justify those Parts in which he dissents from *Aristotle* or his best Commentators. We have had some Attempts made at Criticism in the *Spectators, Guardians,* &c. but they have proceeded no farther than Words, and the subservient Parts to Poetry, but never durst advance to the Disposition of the Parts, and an Œconomy of an entire Poem, except in the excellent Examination of *Milton,* which is every where directed by the Rules of *Aristotle,* and the receiv'd *Critics.*

As it is the last Perfection in Painting, rightly to order and dispose of things, so it is in Poetry. This

Order and Disposition must be observ'd as well in a
Picture of one Figure, as in one of many. The Nature
of Man, says *Xenophon,* can name nothing so fair and
useful as Order; a confus'd Piece of Work can never
deserve Admiration. Those things only affect us, in
which every Part is not only perfect in it self, but also
well disposed by a natural Connection. Nature it self
seems to be upheld by Order, and so are all things else
which are subject to the same Cause. The Sun, Moon,
and Stars have gone their eternal Rounds by Rule, and
in Order; and yet certainly they must be allow'd to be
beautiful, and more charming than they could have been
without it.

I confess (reply'd *Tyro*) I have not yet thought enough
of this Matter to establish our Rules. But I can't
perswade my self but that is a Work to be effected by
Pains and Leisure.

Since, then, Sir, (said I) you are not furnish'd with
a new System, give me Leave to urge from the admirable *Dacier* his Reasons why that of *Aristotle* is to be
admitted; and if you have any Objections to make upon
hearing that, I do not doubt that I shall be able to give
you a satisfactory Answer.

As the Injustice of Men gave Occasion for the making
of Laws; so the Decay of Arts, and the Faults committed
in them, brought in a Necessity of making of Rules, and
of reviving them. But to prevent the Objections of
some who disdain to be confin'd to any Rules, but those
of their own Fancy, it seems to me very necessary to
prove, not only, that Poetry is an Art, but that this Art
is known, and its Rules be certainly those of *Aristotle,*
that it is impossible to succeed in this Art by any other
Ways. Having prov'd this Point, I shall examine the
two Consequences which naturally follow. First, that

the Rules, and what pleases, are never contrary to one another, and that you can never obtain the latter, that is, you can never please, without the former, that is the Rules. Secondly, that Poesy being an Art can never be prejudicial to Mankind; and that it was invented and improv'd only for their Advantage.

This Method obliges me to trace Poetry from its Original, to shew, that it was the Daughter of Religion; that, in Process of time, it was debauch'd and vitiated; and lastly, that it was brought under the Rules of Art, which assisted in the Correcting the Failures of Nature.

God, touch'd with Compassion for the Misery of Men, who were oblig'd to toil and labour for their Subsistance, instituted Days of Festival to give them Rest and Cessation from their Work; ordaining the Offering Sacrifices to himself, as a just Thanksgiving for the Blessings receiv'd from his Bounty. This is a Truth which was, and is acknowledg'd by the Heathens themselves. For they not only imitated these Days of Festival and Rest, but always spoke of them as a Gift of the immortal Gods, who having granted a Time of Repose, requir'd some Testimony of their Gratitude for the Benefit.

The first *Festivals* of the *Antients* were in this Manner; they assembled at certain Times, especially in the *Autumn,* after the gathering in of the Fruits of the Earth, to rejoice, and offer the most valuable, and choice of them to God. And this was it, that first gave Birth to *Poetry.* For Men who are naturally enclin'd to the Imitation and *Music,* employ'd their Talents to sing the Praise of that particular God whom they worshipp'd, and to celebrate his most conspicuous, and remarkable Actions.

If they had always kept to that primitive Simplicity,

all the *Poetry* we shou'd have had, wou'd have only been Hymns and Songs of Thanksgiving and Praise, as we find among the *Israelites* and *Jews* in the Old Testament: But it was very difficult, or rather impossible, that Wisdom and Purity shou'd reign long in the Assemblies of the *Heathens*. They soon mingled the Praises of Men, with those of their Gods; and at last came to the filling of their Poems with biting *Satires,* which they flung to one another at their drunken Meetings. Thus *Poetry* was entirely corrupted, the present carrying very few Marks of Religion, e'en in our Age of *Christianity*.

The *Poets,* that follow'd, and who (properly speaking) were the *Philosophers,* and *Divines* of those early Times, observing the general and earnest Bent of the People for those *Festivals,* and *Shows,* and the Impossibility of recovering the first *Simplicity,* pursu'd another Way of giving a Remedy to this Disorder; and making an Advantage of the Peoples Inclinations, gave them Instructions disguis'd under the Charms of *Pleasure,* as Physicians gild or sweeten the Pills they administer to their Patients.

I will not here pretend to observe and give a History of all the Changes, that have happen'd in *Poetry,* or shew by what Degrees it is arriv'd to that Perfection, in which we now find it.

Homer was the first that either invented or render'd compleat the *Epic* or *Heroic Poem*; for he certainly found out the Unity of the *Subject,* the *Manners,* the *Characters,* and the *Fable*. But this Poem cou'd only affect Customs; and was not moving enough to correct the *Passions*. There was *wanting* a Poem, which by imitating our *Actions,* might work on our Spirits a more ready and sensible Effect: This gave Rise to *Tragedy,* and banish'd all *Satyrs,* by which Means *Poetry* was entirely purg'd from all the Disorders into which its Corruption had brought it.

This is no Place to shew, that Men, who are quickly weary of regulated Pleasures, labour'd, and took Pains to plunge themselves again into their firmer Licenciousness by the Invention of *Comedy*. I shall keep my self to *Tragedy,* which is the most noble *Imitation*; in which all the Parts of an *Heroic Poem* are compriz'd.

How short soever this Account may be, it is yet sufficient to let you see that *Poetry* is an Art; for since it has a certain *End,* there must be some certain Way of arriving at that *End.* No Body can doubt of so evident a Truth, that in all Things, where there may be a *Right,* and a *Wrong,* there is an *Art,* and sure Rules to lead you to the former, and direct you how to avoid the latter.

The Question therefore now is, Whether these Rules are known, and whether they are those which are given us by *Aristotle?* This Question is no less doubtful than the former; I must also confess, that this cannot be determin'd, but by the *Unlearned,* who, because they are the greater Number, I shall make my Examination in their Favour. To do this with some sort of Method, there are some Things to be consider'd, (1.) *Who gives the Rules?* (2.) *The Time when he gives them.* (3.) *The Manner, in which he gives them.* (4.) *And the Effects they have wrought in different Times on different People.* For I believe, from these four Circumstances, I can draw such Conclusions, as the most obstinate shall not be able to deny.

He, who gives these Rules, is one of the greatest *Philosophers,* that ever was in the World; his Genius was large, and of a vast Extent; the great Discoveries he made in all Sciences, particularly in the Knowledge of Man, are certain Signs, that he had sufficient Insight into our Passions, to discover the *Rules* of the *Art of Poetry,* which is founded on them. But I shall suspend my Judgment, and pass on *to the Time in which* he gave these *Rules.*

I find, that he was born in the Age, in which *Tragedy* first appear'd, or at least made its first Advances towards Perfection. For he liv'd with the Disciples of *Æschylus,* who brought it out of *Confusion,* and he had the same Masters, that *Sophocles* and *Euripides* had, who carry'd it to its utmost Perfection. Besides, he was Witness of the Opinion, that the most nice, and knowing People of the World had of this Poem. 'Tis therefore impossible, that *Aristotle* shou'd be ignorant of the *Origin, Progress, Design,* and Effects of this *Art*; and consequently even before I examine these *Rules,* I am perfectly assur'd, on his Account, who gives them, that they have all the Certainty and Authority, that Rules can possibly have.

But when I come to examine the Manner in which *Aristotle* delivers them, I find them so evident, and so conformable to Nature, that I cannot but be sensible, they are true. For *Aristotle* gives not his *Rules* as *Legislators* do their Laws, without any other *Reason* than his Will; all that he advances is confirm'd by Reasons drawn from the common Sentiments of Mankind, so that Men themselves become the *Rule* and Measure of what he lays down. Thus, without considering, that the *Rules* are of almost equal Date with the *Art,* they teach, or any Prepossession in favour of *Aristotle*'s Name; (for 'tis the Work that ought to make the *Name* valuable, and not the Name the Work) I find my self oblig'd to submit to all his Decisions, the Truth of which I am convinc'd of in my self, and whose Certainty I discover by Reason, and Experience, which never yet deceiv'd any Body.

To this I shall add, *The Effects which these Rules have produc'd in all Ages, on different Sorts of People*; and I find, that as they made the Beauty of the Poems of *Homer, Sophocles,* and *Euripides* in *Greece,* from which they were drawn, so four or five Hundred Years after, they adorn'd the Poems of *Virgil,* and other famous *Latin Poets*; and that now after two Thousand Years, they make the best *Tragedies,* we have, in which *all* that pleases *only* does so as it is conformable to these *Rules* (and that too without one's being aware of it) and what is displeasing is such, because it is contrary to them: For *good Sense,* and *right Reason,* is of all Countries and Places; the same Subjects, which caus'd so many Tears to be shed in the *Roman Theatre,* produce the same Effect on ours; and those Things, that then gave Distaste do the same now. From whence I am convinc'd, that never any Laws had such Force and Authority. Humane Laws expire, or change very often after the Death of those, who enacted them, because Circumstances change, and the Interests of whom they are made to serve are different; but these still gain new Vigour, because they are the Laws of Nature, which always acts with Uniformity, renews them incessantly, and gives them a perpetuate Existence.

I won't pretend, however, that the *Rules* of this *Art* are so firmly establish'd, that it is impossible to add any thing to them; for tho' *Tragedy* has all its proper Parts, it is possible, that one of them may yet arrive at a greater Perfection. I am persuaded, that tho' we have been able to add nothing to the *Subject,* or Means, yet we have added something to the Manner. But all the new Discoveries are so far from destroying this Establishment, that they do nothing more than confirm it. For Nature is never contrary to it self; and we may

apply to the *Art* of *Poetry,* what *Hypocrates* says of
Physic. - - - Phisic (says he) *is of long standing, has
sure Principles, and a certain Way, by which in the
Course of many Ages, an Infinity of Things have been
discover'd, of which Experience confirms the Goodness.
All that is wanting for the Perfection of this Art, will,
without Doubt, be found out, by those ingenious Men,
who will search for it,* according to the Instructions and
Rules of the Antients, *and endeavour to arrive at what
is unknown, by what is already plain and evident. For
whoever shall boast, that he has obtain'd this Art by
rejecting the Ways of the* Antients, *and pursuing a quite
different Track, deceives others, and is himself deceiv'd;
because that is absolutely impossible.*

This Truth extends it self to all Arts and Sciences;
nor is it any difficult Matter to find a proper Example
in our Subject. There is no Want of *Tragedies,* where
the Management is directly opposite to that of the
Antients. According to the Rules of *Aristotle,* a *Tragedy*
is the Imitation of an Allegorical, and Universal Action,
which by the Means of *Terror* and *Compassion,* mod-
erates and corrects our Inclinations: But according to
these new *Tragedies,* it is an Imitation of some *particular
Action* (as in *England* of many Actions) which affects
no Body, and is only invented to amuse the Spectators
by the *Plot* or unravelling of a vain Intrigue tho' this
is far beyond our *English* Authors, who have not even
that to pretend to, which tends only to excite and satisfie
our Curiosity, and stir up our Passions, instead of
rendering them calm, and quiet. This is not only not
the *same Art,* but can be none at all, since it tends to no
Good, and is a pure Lye without any Mixture of Truth.
What Advantage can be drawn from this Falshood?
in short, it is not a *Fable,* and by Consequence is not at

all a *Tragedy,* for a *Tragedy* cannot subsist without a *Fable.*

We come now to the first Consequence, which we draw from what we have established, and shall endeavour to prove, that our *Laws,* and *what pleases,* can never be opposite, since the *Rules* were only made for that which does please, and are directed only to shew you, and point out the Way that you must walk in to do so. By this we shall destroy that false Maxim, *That all that pleases is good,* wou'd assert what we ought on the contrary to say that - - - *All that is good, pleases, or ought to please.* For the Goodness of any Work, whatever does not proceed from this, that it gives us Pleasure; but the Pleasure, that we have, proceeds from its Goodness, unless our deluded Eyes, and corrupt Imaginations, mislead us.

If the *Rules,* and *that which pleases,* were Things opposite, a Poet cou'd never arrive at giving Pleasure but by meer Chance, which is absurd. There must for that Reason be a certain Way that leads thither, and that Way is the *Rule,* which we ought to learn. But this *Rule* being drawn from the *Pleasant* and the *Profitable,* leads us to their very Source. The *Pleasant* and the *Profitable,* is that which pleases naturally; this it is that in all *Arts* we consult, and is the most sure and perfect Model that we can imitate. In it we find perfect *Unity* and *Order;* for it self is *Order,* or to speak more properly the Effect of *Order,* and the *Rules* which conducts us thither. There is but one Way to find *Order,* but a great many to fall into Confusion.

There wou'd be nothing bad in the World if all that *pleas'd* were *good;* for there is nothing so ridiculous, but what will have its Admirers. You may say indeed, that it is no truer, that what is *good pleases,* because we

every Day find Disputes of the *Good,* and the *Pleasant*;
that the same thing pleases some, and displeases others;
nay it pleases and displeases the very same Person at
different Times. From whence then proceeds this
Difference? It comes either from an absolute Ignorance
of the *Rules,* or that the Passions alter it. Rightly to
clear this Truth, I believe, I may lay down this Maxim,
that all sensible Objects are of two Sorts; some may be
judg'd of by Sense independently of Reason; (I call
Sense, that Impressions which the Animal Spirits make
on the Soul) others can't be judg'd of but by Reason
exercis'd in Science. Things simply agreeable, or disagreeable, are of the first Sort: All the World may judge
alike of these. For Example, the most ignorant in *Music*
observes very well when a *Lutinist* strikes one String
for another, especially if they strike out of Tune, because
he judges by his Sense, and that Sense is his *Rule.* On
such Occasions we may truly say, that what *pleases* is
good, because that which is *good* does please, or that
which is *bad* never fails to displease. For neither
Passions nor Ignorance dull the Senses; nay, on the
contrary, they sharpen them. But it is not the same
Things that spring from Reason. Passion and Ignorance
act very strongly on this, and very often check it; and
this is the Cause why we judge so indifferently of these
Things, of which Reason is the *Rule* and *Cause.* Why
what is *Bad* often *pleases,* and that which is *Good* does
not always do so, is not the fault of the Object, but of
him who judges. But what is *Good* will infallibly *please*
those who can judge, and that is sufficient. By this we
may see, that a Play, which shall bring those Things,
which are to be judged of by Reason within the *Rules,*
as also what is to be judg'd of by the Sense, shall never
fail to *please,* for that will please both the *Learned,* and

the *Ignorant.* Now this Conformity of Suffrages is the most sure, and according to *Aristotle,* the only Mark of the *Good,* and the *Pleasant.* Now these Suffrages are not obtain'd but by the Observation of the *Rules*; and consequently these *Rules* are the only Cause of the *Good,* and the *Pleasant*; whether they are follow'd methodically, or by Design, or by Accident only. For it is certain, that there are many Persons, who are entirely ignorant of these *Rules,* who do not however fail of Success in some Particular. But this is far from destroying the *Rules,* since it serves only to shew their Beauty, and proves how far they are conformable to *Nature,* since those often follow them who know nothing of them, as our *Shakespear.*

It is Time to come to the last Consequence, that *Poetry* is an *Art* invented for the Instruction of Mankind, and consequently must be *profitable.* 'Tis a general Truth, that every *Art* is a good Thing, because there is none whose End is not *good.* But as it is not less true, that Men often abuse the best Things, that which was design'd for a wholsome Remedy, may in Time become a very dangerous Poison. I speak not therefore (says *Dacier*) of corrupted *Tragedy*; for it is not in deprav'd Writers, that we must look for *Reason,* and the Intent of *Nature,* but in those, who are *sound* and *perfect.* I speak of the Ancient *Tragedy,* that which is conformable to *Aristote*'s *Rules,* and I dare say, that it is the most profitable and necessary of all Diversions.

If 'twas possible to oblige Men to follow the Precepts of the *Gospel,* nothing cou'd be more desir'd or happy in that they wou'd find true Peace and solid Pleasure, and a Remedy for all their Infirmities, and wou'd look on *Tragedy* as useless and below them. But as so much Corruption is inconsistent with so much Wisdom, the ancient Heathen Philosophers were forc'd to seek a Remedy to the Disorders of the Pleasures of Mankind. To this End they invented *Tragedy,* as a Means which was able to correct the Vices into which they plung'd themselves at their Festivals, and to render those Amusements *profitable,* which Custom, and their Infirmities, had made necessary, and their Corruption very dangerous.

Men are the same now that they were then; they have the same Passions, and run with the same Earnestness after Pleasures. To endeavour to reclaim them from that State by the Severity of *Precepts,* is no more than the attempting to put a Bridle on an unruly Horse in the midst of his Carreer. In the mean while there is no Medium, they run into the most criminal Excess, unless you afford them regular and sober Pleasures. 'Tis a great Happiness, that their remaining Reason enclines them to love Diversions, where there is *Order,* and Spectacles where *Truth* is to be found. Those People are distemper'd, and *Tragedy* is all the Remedy they are capable of receiving any Advantage from; for it is the only Recreation in which we can find the Agreeable and the Profitable.

But this is not in the common Scribbles of the Times, but in a perfect and general Fable, which only can give a general Instruction, and to form this Fable, and make it perfect in all its Parts; to attain this admirable End, Order, Harmony and Design must be fixt, and those are only to be found in the Rules laid down by *Aristotle.* The Excellence, of which I think I have made sufficiently evident from *Dacier.*

If, Sir, you have now any thing to object against what I have deliver'd, I should be glad to hear it.

I confess (said *Tyro*) I cannot deny the Reasons you

have urg'd from Mr. *Dacier,* and I believe, that if
Aristotle were a little more study'd by our *Tragedy
Writers,* we shou'd have their Works of a longer Life
than they now generally enjoy. But as *Tragedy* is not
the only Sort of *Poetry* that has appear'd in the World,
so I can't find but we shou'd be at a Loss in deciding the
Standard in several other Sorts of *Poetry.*

As for that (answer'd *Laudon*) we have *Reason,* and
Nature, and the *Practice* of the *Antients* in all the
valuable Parts of it. And as all *Poetry* is *Imitation,*
Aristotle will be no little Help to us in those very Parts,
which he has not professedly touch'd upon. It is sufficient, I think to the Point, that we have been arguing
upon, that it is evident, that as there is a *Right,* and a
Wrong, in all *Poetical* Performances, so there must be
a certain Way of knowing which is the *Right,* and which
the *Wrong,* else all must be *Confusion*; and every Man
being left Judge of these Qualities, there wou'd be no
such thing at last, if there were not *stated Rules* of
them; and I think it is as plain, that these *stated* Rules
are to be found in *Aristotle, Horace,* and their best
Commentators. And till some new Discoverer shall
arise, who shall shew us from a *farther Penetration* into
Nature, that our present Guides have mistaken her, we
ought to be directed by them.

For my Part (said *Manilia*) I have but few Objections
to make to what has been said, and as they come from a
Woman uninform'd by Learning, I hope they will meet
a favourable Hearing. The first is in the Behalf of
Opera's, that is in the Justification of *Music.* All that
can be said can never persuade our Ears, and Eyes, not
to be pleas'd with that which pleases them. And next,
though I shou'd own that it seems necessary, that there
should be *stated Rules* of *Right* and *Wrong* in *Poetry,* as

well as in all Things else; yet whilst you Men wrap up that Knowledge in such difficult and obscure Terms, that we *Women* cannot easily understand them; you labour at a Point which can never be obtain'd, for that wou'd exclude our Sex from the Prerogative we have of deciding on the *publick Diversions,* which we shall never willingly part with.

As for your first Objection (said *Laudon*) we do not endeavour to dissuade your Eyes and Ears, not to be pleas'd with what diverts them. All that we aim at is to persuade you not to be meer Sensualists, and pay more Deference to the Gratification of those two Senses, than to that of your *Reason,* and *Understanding*; nay, not to sacrifice your *Reason* and your *Understanding* to the Gratification of those two Senses. We wou'd not pretend to exclude the noble Entertainment of *Music,* we wou'd only have it reduc'd to its primitive Institution to be subservient to *Poetry,* and not to overwhelm it. We wou'd have it the *Servant,* and not the *Master,* as it originally was.

As for the latter, tho' my Friend *Gamaliel* designs a Piece for the Publick to render *Criticism* easy and familiar to the Ladies, yet if he, and this Company, think fit to humour me with two or three Meetings, I do not question but we may run through all the Parts of *Poetry* in such a Manner as may give a *Lady,* of your good Sense, a perfect View of the *Art* of *Poetry* in all its Parts.

Tyro and *Manilia* seem'd mightily pleas'd with the Proposal, and agreed to meet two Days after in order to begin the Disquisition. But Mrs. *Lamode, Issachar,* and *Tom Trifle,* made a Jest of it, and after Ceremonies past, took their Leave.

And this *Crites* was the Substance of our second Conversation, in which if I have done Justice to the Persons who made up the Discourse, and come up to your Notions of the Matter, I am satisfy'd that I am not far from the Truth.

The End of the Second Dialogue.

JOHN HUGHES

JOHN HUGHES

I. OF STYLE.

Written at the Request of a FRIEND, *in the Year*
MDCXCVIII.

WHEN, by the Help of Study, a sufficient Stock of
solid Learning is acquired, the next Business is to consider how to make use of it to the best Advantage. There
is nothing more necessary to this, than Good Sense and
Polite Learning; for as a Man may have the first without
the latter, so 'tis possible one may have the latter, and
yet be rather the worse than the better for it, at least to
others, if not to himself. A plain unletter'd Man is
always more agreeable Company, than a Fool in several
Languages. For a *Pedant,* tho' he may take himself for
a *Philosopher,* is far more prejudiced than an illiterate
Man; and *Sufficiency* (the chief Part of his Character,)
besides the Ill-manners of it, is really (as Sir *William
Temple* observes,) the worst Composition out of the
Pride and Ignorance of Mankind. Besides, *Affectation,*
its usual Attendant, is every Body's Aversion, from the
natural Hatred we have to all manner of Imposture.

So that if there was nothing else to recommend Polite
Learning, yet methinks this were enough, that it files off
the Rust of the Academy, and is the same to the Mind,
as Dancing to the Body, a Means of giving it a free Air
and genteel Motion. In a Word, it adds the Gentleman
to the Scholar, and when these two meet, they challenge
all Mens Respect and Love.

History and *Poetry* are the two chief Branches of those Studies, that are distinguish'd by the Name of *Polite.* But because, Sir, your Enquiry seems more particularly concerning *Language,* I shall confine my Discourse to the Style of *Prose,* as being that which is the most necessary. For *Poetry,* tho' it want not Arguments to recommend it, yet it may be dispensed with, and is either to be taken, or let alone at Pleasure.

All the Qualifications of a good Style I think may be reduced under these four Heads, *Propriety, Perspicuity, Elegance,* and *Cadence:* And each of these, except the last, has some relation to the Thoughts, as well as to the Words.

Propriety of Thoughts is two-fold; the first is when the Thoughts are proper in themselves, and so it is opposed to Nonsense; and the other when they are proper to the Occasion, and so it is opposed to Impertinence.

Propriety of Words, the first Qualification of a good Style, is when the Words do justly and exactly represent, or signify, the Thoughts which they stand for. The Knowledge of this is not to be sought for in Etymologies; for general Acceptation, which is the only Standard of Speech, has given many Words a quite different Sense from their Original. Your best Direction then will be a diligent and careful Perusal of the most correct Writers of the Language in their various Kinds, with the Conversation of People of Fashion, that speak well and without Affectation. The most correct Writers that I know, are Sir *William Temple,* Dr. *Sprat,* and Dr. *Tillotson* for Prose, and Mr. *Waller* for Verse. I mention the last, because Propriety both of Thoughts and Words is his chief Excellency, in which he has scarce any Equal. I have heard that Archbishop *Tillotson* took the pains to study all the synonymous Words of the Language, with

the nice Differences of them, which are commonly very
little observed, yet contribute very much to the Propriety
of Expression. There is another Particular which I shall
mention here, because I think it differs but little from
Propriety, and that is *Purity,* which I take more particularly to respect the Language, as it is now spoke or
written. The Rule of this is *modern Use,* according to
that of *Horace,*

> *Multa renascentur quæ jam cecidêre, cadentque*
> *Quæ nunc sunt in honore vocabula, si volet usus,*
> *Quem penes arbitrium est, & jus & norma loquendi.*

By this Rule, all obsolete Words are to be avoided.
But to a Man of long Practice and Reputation in the
Language, the Privilege may be allow'd sometimes of
reviving old, or bringing in new Words, where the
common ones are deficient. For this reason, we dare
not censure so great a Man as *Milton* for his antiquated
Words, which he took from *Spenser.* A good Instance,
in my Opinion, of a new Word is the Verb *falsify,* which
Mr. *Dryden* borrows from the *Italian,* to signify *not to
be of Proof.*

> ------------- *his Shield*
> *Is* falsify'd, *and round with Jav'lins fill'd.*

But this Liberty, tho' indulg'd to the Force and
Majesty of Verse, if it were made use of in Prose, which
is the Style of Business, wou'd be Affectation; and is
therefore, as was said before, carefully to be avoided.

Little need be said of the second Qualification, *viz.*
Perspicuity. If your Thoughts be not clear, 'tis impossible your Words shou'd, and consequently you can't be
understood: The chief Secret here is to express your
self in such a manner as to transfer your Ideas into the

Reader's Mind, and to set the thing before him in the very same Light, in which it appears to yourself. Here an Extreme is to be shunn'd, lest, while you aim to make your Meaning fully understood, you become Verbose. So that the Art lies in expressing your Thought clearly in as few Words as possible. Practice is the best way to attain this; and it may be useful to write some Essay, and lay it by, till you have forgot it; and then look it over as the Work of a Stranger. By this means you may discover a great many Faults which escaped you in the heat of Writing, and be able to correct them.

Elegance of *Thought* is what we commonly call *Wit,* which adds to Propriety, Beauty, and pleases our Fancy, while Propriety entertains our Judgment. This depends so much on Genius, that 'tis impossible to teach it by Rules. To the Elegance of Words, or Style, belong all the Figures of *Rhetorick,* and to use these to Advantage requires a Judgment well form'd by Observation. In this therefore, as in learning the Graces upon an Instrument of Musick, good Examples are the best Instruction. Thus a Man may write *Metaphors, Tropes, Hyperboles,* and all the other Figures, without the Trouble of studying a System of *Rhetorick;* and I believe better too, for to attend to a great many Rules whilst you are writing, is the way to make your Style stiff and constrain'd, whereas Elegance consists very much in a genteel Ease and Freedom of Expression; it is like a coy Mistress, of so nice a Humour, that to court her too much, is the surest way to lose her; and as Success in Love is owing to good Fortune, and the natural Happiness of pleasing, rather than to Fidelity and Attendance, so the Art of chusing, out of several Expressions equally proper, that which is the most graceful, is best call'd a *Curiosa*

Felicitas, which two Words seem to comprehend all that can be said upon this Head.

The last Qualification I mention'd is *Cadence,* in Poetry call'd *the Numbers.* It consists in a Disposing of the Words in such Order, and with such Variation of Periods, as may strike the Ear with a sort of musical Delight, which is a considerable Part of Eloquence. This is chiefly that which makes a Style smooth, and not merely the avoiding of harsh Words. The best way to attain it, is to prepare yourself, before you begin to write, by reading in some harmonious Style, that so you may get your Ear well in Tune.

Besides all these Qualifications, there is something in Language, which, to borrow a Word from Singing, may be call'd *a Manner.* This, like the Air of Faces, is a Mark of Distinction, by which every one has somewhat peculiar to it self from all others. For, besides the manifest Difference between Beauty and Deformity, there is a wonderful Variety even among good Faces, for which reason the Painters have learn'd, from many scatter'd Beauties, to collect one perfect Idea, which is hard to be found in any Individual.

To apply this; Sir *William Temple,* Sir *Roger L'Estrange,* and Dr. *Sprat* (to mention no more) are each of them allow'd Masters in the Tongue, and yet every one has a different Manner, as may be seen by a short Character of each.

The Style of Sir *William Temple* is very harmonious and sweet, full of Spirit, and *Raciness of Wit,* to use a Word of his own. His Similies are particularly fine, his Allusions graceful, his Words significant, and the whole has a kind of Charm, which amuses the Reader with serious Pleasure, puts him in a good Humour while he is reading, and leaves him thoughtful when he breaks off.

L'Estrange's Talent is Humour, in which his Vein flows very freely; agreeably to this he is a perfect Master of all the Idioms and Proverbial Expressions which are peculiar to our Tongue; these he often applies happily enough, tho' sometimes not without Affectation; yet, generally speaking, his Style is pleasant, smooth, and natural; and that Gaiety and seeming Negligence, which is peculiar to him, entertains you with a similar sort of Delight, like that of witty and facetious Company. There is the same Difference in the Styles of these two, as in those of *Cicero* and *Terence* in the *Latin*; in the first you find more of the *Orator,* and in the latter more of the *Englishman.*

The elegant Dr. *Sprat* is, in my Judgment, one of the most genteel and exact Writers we have. His Style is grave and manly, infinitely preferable to Sir *Roger*'s, and having all that is beautiful in Sir *William Temple,* only (if 'tis possible) with more Correctness and Decency. There appears in him all the Sweetness and Fluency, handsom Turns and apt Expressions, that can be desir'd. He has united the most charming Elegance to the strictest Propriety, and is witty without the least Shadow of Affectation. The soft Cadence of his Periods, methinks, resembles the Current of a pleasant Stream; It makes but little Noise, yet affects you with a calm Delight, which, if it were heard louder, wou'd be lost.

There are several other Writers, which may be read with great Profit; and above all, the Incomparable *Tillotson,* who always writes the best Sense, and in the best Manner. That which particularly recommends him is an Easiness and beautiful Simplicity in all his Expressions, which every one that reads him is apt to think may be imitated without much Difficulty, and yet nothing perhaps is so hard in the Experiment.

    - - - - - - - - - - - - *ut sibi quivis*
    Speret idem, sudet multum, frustraque laboret.
                                       Hor.

This brings to my mind what Monsieur *Le Clerc* says, that 'tis much easier to imitate the loftiest Flights in *Seneca*'s Tragedies, or *Lucan,* than the Simplicity of *Terence*.

After you have observed the different manner of Style amongst the best Writers, and collected a general Idea from them all, you are to consider next the different Manner to be us'd by the same Writer, according to the Subject he treats of. The Severity of *Philosophy* requires a grave *didactick* Style, agreeable to the Plainness and Simplicity of Truth and Reason. *Morality* and *Divinity* are capable of all the Ornaments of Wit and Fancy. *History* is content with a plainer Dress, as being a Relation of Matters of Fact, the Reflexions upon which are to be short and pertinent, and the rest left to the various Humour and Judgment of every Reader.

But of all sorts of Writing there is none has that Variety and Liberty as *Letters* and *Essays*; the former, especially, include all Subjects whatsoever, and are varied not only according to the Subject, but also according to the Person to whom you write, so that it wou'd be an endless Labour to give Rules about them. Yet this, being a way of writing in which every one is necessarily exercis'd more or less, it deserves a particular Regard; nor will it be a difficult thing, at the Expence of a little Thought and Observation, to furnish yourself with Rules sufficient to all the Variety of Occasions that may occur.

II. AN ESSAY ON ALLEGORICAL POETRY, &c.

1715

IT is a Misfortune, as Mr. *Waller* observes, which attends the Writers of *English* Poetry, that they can hardly expect their Works shou'd last long in a Tongue which is daily changing; that whilst they are new, Envy is apt to prevail against them; and as that wears off, our Language it self fails. Our Poets therefore, he says, shou'd imitate judicious Statuaries, that chuse the most durable Materials, and shou'd carve in *Latin* or *Greek,* if they wou'd have their Labours preserv'd for ever.

NOTWITHSTANDING the Disadvantage he has mention'd, we have two Antient *English* Poets, *Chaucer* and *Spenser,* who may perhaps be reckon'd as Exceptions to this Remark. These seem to have taken deep Root, like old *British* Oaks, and to flourish in defiance of all the Injuries of Time and Weather. The former is indeed much more obsolete in his Stile than the latter; but it is owing to an extraordinary native Strength in both, that they have been able thus far to survive amidst the Changes of our Tongue, and seem rather likely, among the Curious at least, to preserve the Knowledg of our Antient Language, than to be in danger of being destroy'd with it, and bury'd under its Ruins.

THO *Spenser*'s Affection to his Master *Chaucer* led him in many things to copy after him, yet those who have read both will easily observe that these two Genius's were of a very different kind. *Chaucer* excell'd in his Characters; *Spenser* in his Descriptions. The first study'd Humour, was an excellent Satirist, and a lively but rough

Painter of the Manners of that rude Age in which he liv'd: The latter was of the serious Turn, had an exalted and elegant Mind, a warm and boundless Fancy, and was an admirable Imager of Vertues and Vices, which was his particular Talent. The Embellishments of Description are rich and lavish in him beyond Comparison: and as this is the most striking part of Poetry, especially to young Readers, I take it to be the Reason that he has been the Father of more Poets among us, than any other of our Writers; Poetry being first kindled in the Imagination, which *Spenser* writes to, more than any one, and the Season of Youth being the most susceptible of the Impression. It will not seem strange therefore that *Cowley,* as himself tells us, first caught his Flame by reading *Spenser*; that our great *Milton* own'd him for his Original, as Mr. *Dryden* assures us; and that *Dryden* study'd him, and has bestow'd more frequent Commendations on him, than on any other *English* Poet.

THE most known and celebrated of his Works, tho I will not say the most perfect, is the *Fairy Queen.* It is conceiv'd, wrought up, and colour'd with a stronger Fancy, and discovers more the particular Genius of *Spenser,* than any of his other Writings. The Author, in a Letter to Sir *Walter Raleigh,* having call'd this Poem, *a continu'd Allegory, or dark Conceit,* it may not be improper to offer some Remarks on Allegorical Poetry in general; by which the Beauties of this Work may more easily be discover'd by ordinary Readers. I must at the same time beg the Indulgence of those who are conversant with Critical Discourses, to what I shall here propose; this being a Subject something out of the way, and not expresly treated upon by those who have laid down Rules for the Art of Poetry.

AN Allegory is a Fable or Story, in which, under imaginary Persons or Things, is shadow'd some real Action or instructive Moral; or, as I think it is somewhere very shortly defin'd by *Plutarch,* it is that *in which one thing is related, and another thing is understood.* It is a kind of Poetical Picture, or Hieroglyphick, which by its apt Resemblance conveys Instruction to the Mind by an Analogy to the Senses; and so amuses the Fancy, whilst it informs the Understanding. Every Allegory has therefore two Senses, the Literal and the Mystical; the literal Sense is like a Dream or Vision, of which the mystical Sense is the true Meaning or Interpretation.

THIS will be more clearly apprehended, by considering, that as a Simile is but a more extended Metaphor, so an Allegory is a kind of continu'd Simile, or an Assemblage of Similitudes drawn out at full length. Thus, when it is said, That *Death is the Offspring of Sin,* this is a Metaphor, to signify that the former is produc'd by the latter, as a Child is brought into the World by its Parent. Again, to compare Death to a meager and ghastly Apparition, starting out of the Ground, moving towards the Spectator with a menacing Air, and shaking in his Hand a bloody Dart, is a Representation of the Terrors which attend that great Enemy to Human Nature. But let the Reader observe, in *Milton*'s *Paradise Lost,* with what exquisite Fancy and Skill this common Metaphor and Simile, and the Moral contain'd in them, are extended and wrought up into one of the most beautiful Allegories in our Language.

THE Resemblance which has been so often observ'd in general between Poetry and Painting, is yet more particular in Allegory; which, as I said before, is a kind of Picture in Poetry. *Horace* has in one of his Odes pathetically describ'd the ruinous Condition of his

Country after the Civil Wars, and the Hazard of its being involv'd in new Dissensions, by the Emblem of a Ship shatter'd with Storms, and driven into Port with broken Masts, torn Sails, and disabled Rigging; and in danger of being forc'd by new Storms out to Sea again. There is nothing said in the whole Ode but what is literally applicable to a Ship; but it is generally agreed, that the Thing signify'd is the *Roman* State. Thus *Rubens,* who had a good Allegorical Genius in Painting, has, in his famous Work of the *Luxemburg* Gallery, figur'd the Government of *France,* on *Lewis* the Thirteenth's arriving at Age, by a Galley. The King stands at the Helm; *Mary* of *Medicis,* the Queen Mother and Regent, puts the Rudder in his Hand; Justice, Fortitude, Religion, and Publick Faith are seated at the Oars; and other Vertues have their proper Employments in managing the Sails and Tackle.

By this general Description of Allegory, it may easily be conceiv'd that in Works of this kind there is a large Field open to Invention, which among the Antients was universally look'd upon to be the principal Part of Poetry. The Power of raising Images or Resemblances of things, giving them Life and Action, and presenting them as it were before the Eyes, was thought to have something in it like Creation: And it was probably for this fabling Part, that the first Authors of such Works were call'd *Poets* or *Makers,* as the Word signifies, and as it is literally translated and used by *Spenser;* tho the learned *Gerard Vossius** is of opinion, that it was rather for the framing their Verses. However, by this Art of Fiction or Allegory, more than by the Structure of their Numbers, or what we now call *Versification,* the Poets

*De Arte Poetica, *Cap.* 3. §. 16.

were distinguish'd from Historians and Philosophers; tho the latter sometimes invaded the Province of the Poet, and deliver'd their Doctrines likewise in Allegories or Parables. And this, when they did not purposely make them obscure, in order to conceal them from the common People, was a plain Indication that they thought there was an Advantage in such Methods of conveying Instruction to the Mind; and that they serv'd for the more effectual engaging the Attention of the Hearers, and for leaving deeper Impressions on their Memories.

PLUTARCH, in one of his Discourses, gives a very good Reason for the use of Fiction in Poetry, because *Truth of it self is rigid and austere, and cannot be moulded into such agreeable Forms as Fiction can.* "For neither "the Numbers, says he, nor the ranging of the Words, "nor the Elevation and Elegance of the Stile, have so "many Graces as the artful Contrivance and Disposition "of the Fable." For this Reason, as he relates it after *Plato,* when the Wise *Socrates* himself was prompted by a particular Impulse to the writing of Verses, being by his constant Employment in the Study of Truth, a Stranger to the Art of inventing, he chose for his Subject the Fables of *Æsop*; not thinking, says *Plutarch, That any thing cou'd be Poetry which was void of Fiction.* The same Author makes use of a Comparison in another place, which I think may be most properly apply'd to Allegorical Poetry in particular: That *as Grapes on a Vine are cover'd by the Leaves which grow about them, so under the pleasant Narrations and Fictions of the Poets, there are couch'd many useful Morals and Doctrines.*

IT is for this reason, that is to say, in regard to the moral Sense, that Allegory has a liberty indulg'd to it beyond any other fort of Writing whatsoever; that it often assembles things of the most contrary kinds in Nature, and supposes even Impossibilities; as that a Golden Bough shou'd grow among the common Branches of a Tree, as *Virgil* has describ'd it in the Sixth Book of his *Æneis*. Allegory is indeed the *Fairy Land* of Poetry, peopled by Imagination; its Inhabitants are so many Apparitions; its Woods, Caves, wild Beasts, Rivers, Mountains and Palaces, are produc'd by a kind of magical Power, and are all visionary and typical; and it abounds in such Licences as wou'd be shocking and monstrous, if the Mind did not attend to the mystick Sense contain'd under them. Thus in the Fables of *Æsop*, which are some of the most antient Allegories extant, the Author gives Reason and Speech to Beasts, Insects and Plants; and by that means covertly instructs Mankind in the most important Incidents and Concerns of their Lives.

I AM not insensible that the word *Allegory* has been sometimes us'd in a larger Sense than that to which I may seem here to have restrain'd it, and has been apply'd indifferently to any Poem which contains a cover'd Moral, tho the Story or Fable carries nothing in it that appears visionary or romantick. It may be necessary therefore to distinguish Allegory into the two following kinds.

THE first is that in which the Story is fram'd of real or historical Persons, and probable or possible Actions; by which however some other Persons and Actions are typify'd or represented. In this sense the whole *Æneis* of *Virgil* may be said to be an Allegory, if we consider *Æneas* as representing *Augustus Cæsar,* and his conducting the Remains of his Countrymen from the Ruins of *Troy*, to a new Settlement in *Italy,* as emblematical of *Augustus*'s modelling a new Government out of the

Ruins of the Aristocracy, and establishing the *Romans* after the Confusion of the Civil War, in a peaceable and flourishing Condition. It does not, I think, appear that *Homer* had any such Design in his Poems, or that he meant to delineate his Cotemporaries or their Actions under the chief Characters and Adventures of the *Trojan* War. And tho the Allusion I have mention'd in *Virgil* is a Circumstance, which the Author has finely contriv'd to be coincident to the general Frame of his Story, yet he has avoided the making it plain and particular, and has thrown if off in so many Instances from a direct Application, that his Poem is perfect without it. This then, for distinction, should, I think, rather be call'd a Parallel than an Allegory; at least in Allegories, fram'd after this manner, the literal Sense is sufficient to satisfy the Reader, tho he should look no further; and without being consider'd as emblematical of some other Persons or Action, may of it self exhibit very useful Morals and Instructions. Thus the Morals which may be drawn from the *Æneis* are equally noble and instructive, whether we suppose the real Hero to be *Æneas* or *Augustus Cæsar*.

THE second kind of Allegory, and which, I think, may more properly challenge the Name, is that in which the Fable or Story consists for the most part of fictitious Persons or Beings, Creatures of the Poet's Brain, and Actions surprising, and without the Bounds of Probability or Nature. In Works of this kind, it is impossible for the Reader to rest in the literal Sense, but he is of necessity driven to seek for another Meaning under these wild Types and Shadows. This Grotesque Invention claims, as I have observ'd, a Licence peculiar to it self, and is what I wou'd be understood in this Discourse more particularly to mean by the word Allegory. Thus

Milton has describ'd it in his Poem call'd *Il Penseroso,* where he alludes to the Squire's Tale in *Chaucer:*

> *Or call up him that left half told*
> *The Story of* Cambuscan *bold,*
> *Of* Cambal *and of* Algarsife,
> *And who had* Canace *to Wife:*
> *That own'd the virtuous Ring and Glass,*
> *And of the wondrous Horse of Brass,*
> *On which the* Tartar *King did ride;*
> *And if ought else great Bards beside*
> *In sage and solemn Tunes have sung*
> *Of Turneys and of Trophies hung,*
> *Of Forrests and Enchantments drear,*
> *Where more is meant than meets the Ear.*

It may be proper to give an Instance or two, by which the Distinction of this last kind of Allegory may more plainly appear.

THE Story of *Circe* in the *Odysses* is an Allegorical Fable, of which there are perhaps more Copies and Imitations than of any other whatever. Her offering a Cup, fill'd with intoxicating Liquor, to her Guests; her mingling Poison with their Food, and then by magical Arts turning them into the Shapes of Swine; and *Ulysses* resisting her Charms by the Virtue of an Herb call'd *Moly,* which he had receiv'd from the God *Mercury,* and restoring his Companions to their true Persons, are all Fictions of the last kind I have mention'd. The Person of the Goddess is likewise fictitious, and out of the Circle of the *Grecian* Divinities; and the Adventures are not to be understood but in a mystical Sense. The Episode of *Calypso,* tho somewhat of the same kind, approaches nearer to Nature and Probability: But the

Story of *Dido* in the *Æneis,* tho copy'd from the *Circe* and *Calypso,* and form'd on the same Moral, namely, to represent a Hero obstructed by the Allurements of Pleasure, and at last breaking from them; and tho *Mercury* likewise assists in it to dissolve the Charm, yet is not necessarily to be look'd upon as an Allegory; the Fable does not appear merely imaginary or emblematical: the Persons are natural, and, excepting the Distance of Time which the Criticks have noted between the real *Æneas* and *Dido,* (a Circumstance which *Virgil,* not being bound to Historical Truth, wilfully neglected) there is nothing which might not really have happen'd. *Ariosto*'s *Alcina,* and the *Armida* of *Tasso,* are Copies from the same Original: These again are plainly Allegorical. The whole literal Sense of the latter is a kind of Vision, or a Scene of Imagination, and is every where transparent, to shew the moral Sense which is under it. The Bower of Bliss, in the Second Book of the *Fairy Queen,* is in like manner a Copy from *Tasso*; but the Ornaments of Description, which *Spenser* has transplanted out of the *Italian* Poem, are more proper in his Work, which was design'd to be wholly Allegorical, than in an Epick Poem, which is superior in its Nature to such lavish Embellishments. There is another Copy of the *Circe,* in the Dramatick way, in a Mask, by our famous *Milton*; the whole Plan of which is Allegorical, and is written with a very Poetical Spirit on the same Moral, tho with different Characters.

I Have here instanc'd in one of the most antient and best-imagin'd Allegories extant. *Scilla, Charibdis,* and the *Syrens,* in the same Poem, are of the same Nature, and are Creatures purely Allegorical: But the *Harpies* in *Virgil,* which disturb'd *Æneas* and his Followers at their Banquet, as they do not seem to exhibit any certain

Moral, may probably have been thrown in by the Poet only as an Omen, and to raise what is commonly call'd *the Wonderful*; which is a Property as essential to Epick Poetry, as Probability. *Homer*'s giving Speech to the River *Xanthus* in the Iliad, and to the Horses of *Achilles,* seem to be Inventions of the same kind, and might be design'd to fill the Reader with Astonishment and Concern, and with an Apprehension of the Greatness of an Occasion, which by a bold Fiction of the Poet is suppos'd to have produc'd such extraordinary Effects.

As Allegory sometimes, for the sake of the moral Sense couch'd under its Fictions, gives Speech to Brutes, and sometimes introduces Creatures which are out of Nature, as Goblins, Chimæra's, Fairies, and the like; so it frequently gives Life to Virtues and Vices, Passions and Diseases, to natural and moral Qualities; and repre-sents them acting as divine, human, or infernal Persons. A very ingenious Writer calls these Characters *shadowy Beings,** and has with good reason censur'd the employing them in just Epick Poems: of this kind are Sin and Death, which I mention'd before in *Milton*; and Fame in *Virgil*. We find likewise a large Groupe of these shadowy Figures plac'd in the Sixth Book of the *Æneis,* at the Entrance into the infernal Regions; but as they are only shewn there, and have no share in the Action of the Poem, the Description of them is a fine Allegory, and extremely proper to the Place where they appear.

Vestibulum ante ipsum, primisq; in Faucibus Orci
Luctus & ultrices posuere cubilia *Curæ,*
Pallentesq; habitant *Morbi,* tristisq; *Senectus,*
Et *Metus,* & malesuada *Fames,* ac turpis *Ægestas,*
Terribiles visu Formæ; *Lethumq; Labosq;*

**Spectator*, Vol. IV. N⁰ 273.

Tum consanguineus Lethi *Sopor,* & mala Mentis
Gaudia, Mortiferumq; adverso in limite *Bellum*;
Ferreiq; Eumenidum Thalami, & *Discordia* demens,
Vipereum crinem vittis innixa cruentis.
In medio ramos annosaq; brachia pandit
Ulmus opaca, ingens; quam sedem *Somnia* vulgo
Vana tenere ferunt, foliisq; sub omnibus hærent.

Just in the Gate, and in the Jaws of Hell
Revengeful Cares, *and fullen* Sorrows *dwell,*
And pale Diseases, *and repining* Age,
Want, Fear, *and* Famine'*s unresisted Rage;*
Here Toils *and* Death, *and Death's Half-Brother,* Sleep,
Forms terrible to view, their Centry keep;
With anxious Pleasures *of a guilty Mind;*
Deep Frauds *before, and open* Force *behind:*
The Furies Iron Beds, and Strife *that shakes*
Her hissing Tresses, and unfolds her Snakes.
Full in the midst of this infernal Road
An Elm displays its dusky Arms abroad;
The God of Sleep here hides his heavy Head,
And empty Dreams *on every Leaf are spread.*
Dryden.

As Persons of this imaginary Life are to be excluded
from any share of Action in Epick Poems, they are yet
less to be endur'd in the *Drama*; yet we find they have
sometimes made their Appearance on the antient Stage.
Thus in a Tragedy of *Æschylus, Strength* is introduc'd
assisting *Vulcan* to bind *Prometheus* to a Rock; and in
one of *Euripides, Death* comes to the House of *Admetus*
to demand *Alcestis,* who had offer'd her self to die to
save her Husband's Life.   But what I have here said

of Epick and Dramatick Poems does not extend to such Writings, the very Frame and Model of which is design'd to be Allegorical; in which therefore, as I said before, such unsubstantial and symbolical Actors may be very properly admitted.

Every Book of the *Fairy Queen* is fruitful of these visionary Beings, which are invented and drawn with a surprizing Strength of Imagination. I shall produce but one Instance here, which the Reader may compare with that just mention'd in *Virgil,* to which it is no way inferior: It is in the Second Book, where *Mammon* conducts *Guyon* thro a Cave under Ground to shew him his Treasure.

> At length they came into a larger *Space,*
> That stretch'd it self into an ample *Plain,*
> Thro which a beaten broad *High-way* did trace,
> That straight did lead to Pluto's grisly *Reign:*
> By that *Way's* side there sate infernal *Pain,*
> And fast beside him sat tumultuous *Strife*;
> The one in hand an *Iron Whip* did strain,
> The other brandished a bloody *Knife,*
> And both did gnash their *Teeth,* and both did threaten *Life.*

> On th' other side in one *Consort* there sate
> *Cruel* Revenge, *and rancorous* Despight,
> *Disloyal* Treason, *and Heart-burning* Hate;
> *But gnawing* Jealousy, *out of their sight*
> *Sitting alone, his bitter Lips did bite;*
> *And trembling* Fear *still to and fro did fly,*
> *And found no Place where safe he shroud him might.*
> *Lamenting* Sorrow *did in Darkness lie,*
> *And* Shame *his ugly Face did hide from living Eye.*

And over them sad Horror, *with grim Hue,*
Did always soar, beating his Iron Wings;
And after him Owls and Night-Ravens flew,
The hateful Messengers of heavy things,
Of Death and Dolour telling sad Tidings;
Whilst sad Celeno, *sitting on a Clift,*
A Song of Bale and bitter Sorrow sings,
  That Heart of Flint *asunder would have rift;*
Which having ended, after him she flyeth swift.

All these before the Gates of Pluto *lay,* &c.

The Posture of Jealousy, and the Motion of Fear in this
Description, are particularly fine. These are Instances
of Allegorical Persons, which are shewn only in one
transient View. The Reader will every where meet with
others in this Author, which are employ'd in the Action
of the Poem, and which need not be mention'd here.

HAVING thus endeavour'd to give a general Idea of
what is meant by Allegory in Poetry, and shewn what
kind of Persons are frequently employ'd in it; I shall
proceed to mention some Properties which seem requisite
in all well-invented Fables of this kind.

THERE is no doubt, but Men of Critical Learning, if
they had thought fit, might have given us Rules about
Allegorical Writing, as they have done about Epick,
and other kinds of Poetry; but they have rather chosen
to let this Forest remain wild, as if they thought there
was something in the Nature of the Soil, which cou'd not
so well be restrain'd and cultivated in Inclosures. What
Sir *William Temple* observes about Rules in general, may
perhaps be more particularly applicable to this; that
they may possibly hinder some from being very bad
Poets, but are not capable of making any very good one.

Notwithstanding this, they are useful to help our Observation in distinguishing the Beauties and the Blemishes, in such Works as have been already produc'd. I shall therefore beg leave to mention four Qualities, which I think are essential to every good Allegory: the three first of which relate to the Fable, and the last to the Moral.

THE first is, that it be lively, and surprizing. The Fable, or literal Sense, being that which most immediately offers it self to the Reader's Observation, must have this Property, in order to raise and entertain his Curiosity. As there is therefore more Invention employ'd in a Work of this kind, than in meer Narration, or Description, or in general Amplifications on any Subject, it consequently requires a more than ordinary Heat of Fancy in its first Production. If the Fable, on the contrary, is flat, spiritless, or barren of Invention, the Reader's Imagination is not affected, nor his Attention engag'd, tho the Instruction convey'd under it be ever so useful or important.

THE second Qualification I shall mention is Elegance, or a beautiful Propriety, and Aptness in the Fable to the Subject on which it is employ'd. By this Quality the Invention of the Poet is restrain'd from taking too great a Compass, or losing it self in a Confusion of ill-sorted Ideas; such Representations as that mention'd by *Horace,* of *Dolphins in a Wood,* or *Boars in the Sea,* being fit only to surprize the Imagination, without pleasing the Judgment. The same Moral may likewise be express'd in different Fables, all of which may be lively and full of Spirit, yet not equally elegant; as various Dresses may be made for the same Body, yet not equally becoming. As it therefore requires a Heat of Fancy to raise Images and Resemblances, it requires a good

Taste to distinguish and range them, and to chuse the most proper and beautiful, where there appears an almost distracting Variety. I may compare this to *Æneas* searching in the Wood for the Golden Bough; he was at a loss where to lay his Hand, till his Mother's Doves, descending in his sight, flew before him, and pearch'd on the Tree where it was to be found.

ANOTHER essential Property is, That the Fable be every where consistent with it self. As licentious as Allegorical Fiction may seem in some Respects, it is nevertheless subject to this Restraint. The Poet is indeed at liberty in chusing his Story, and inventing his Persons; but after he has introduc'd them, he is oblig'd to sustain them in their proper Characters, as well as in more regular kinds of Writing. It is difficult to give particular Rules under this Head; it may suffice to say that this wild Nature is however subject to an Oeconomy proper to it self, and tho it may sometimes seem extravagant, ought never to be absurd. Most of the Allegories in the *Fairy Queen* are agreeable to this Rule; but in one of his other Poems, the Author has manifestly transgress'd it: the Poem I mean, is that which is call'd *Prothalamion*. In this, the two Brides are figur'd by two beautiful Swans sailing down the River *Thames*. The Allegory breaks before the Reader is prepar'd for it; and we see them, at their landing, in their true Shapes, without knowing how this sudden Change is effected. If this had been only a Simile, the Poet might have dropp'd it at pleasure; but as it is an Allegory, he ought to have made it of a piece, or to have invented some probable means of coming out of it.

THE last Property I shall mention, is, That the Allegory be clear and intelligible: the Fable being design'd only to clothe and adorn the Moral, but not to hide it, should methinks resemble the Draperies we admire in some of the antient Statues; in which the Folds are not too many, nor too thick, but so judiciously order'd, that the Shape and Beauty of the Limbs may be seen thro them.

IT must be confess'd, that many of the antient Fables appear to us at this Distance of Time very perplex'd and dark; and if they had any Moral at all, it is so closely couch'd, that it is very difficult to discover it. Whoever reads the Lord *Bacon*'s *Wisdom of the Antients,* will be convinc'd of this. He has employ'd a more than ordinary Penetration to decypher the most known Traditions in the Heathen Mythology; but his Interpretations are often far fetch'd, and so much at random, that the Reader can have no Assurance of their Truth. It is not to be doubted that a great part of these Fables were Allegorical, but others might have been Stories design'd only to amuse, or to practise upon the Credulity of the Vulgar; or the Doctrines they contain'd might be purposely clouded, to conceal them from common Knowledge. But tho, as I hinted in the former part of this Discourse, this may have been a Reason among Philosophers, it ought not to be admitted among Poets. An Allegory, which is not clear, is a Riddle, and the Sense of it lies at the Mercy of every fanciful Interpreter.

THO the Epick Poets, as I have shewn, have sprinkled some Allegories thro their Poems, yet it wou'd be absurd to understand them every where in a mystical Sense. We are told of one *Metrodorus Lampsacenus,* whose Works are lost, that turn'd the whole Writings of *Homer* into an Allegory: it was doubtless by some such means that the Principles of all Arts and Sciences whatever were discover'd in that single Author; for nothing can escape an Expositor, who proceeds in his Operations like a *Rosycrucian,* and brings with him the Gold he pretends to find.

IT is surprizing that *Tasso,* whose *Jerusalem* was, at the time when he wrote, the best Plan of an Epick Poem after *Virgil,* shou'd be possess'd with this Affectation, and shou'd not believe his Work perfect till he had turn'd it into a Mystery. I cannot help thinking that *the Allegory,* as it is call'd, which he has printed with it, looks as if it were invented after the Poem was finish'd. He tells us, that the Christian Army represents Man; the City of *Jerusalem,* Civil Happiness; *Godfrey,* the Understanding; *Rinaldo* and *Tancred,* the other Powers of the Soul; and that the Body is typify'd by the common Soldiers; with a great deal more that carries in it a strong Cast of Enthusiasm. He is indeed much more intelligible, when he explains the Flowers, the Fountains, the Nymphs, and the musical Instruments, to figure to us sensual Pleasures, under the false Appearance of Good: But for the rest, I appeal to any one who is acquainted with that Poem, whether he wou'd ever have discover'd these Mysteries, if the Poet had not let him into them; or whether even after this, he can keep them long in his Mind while he is reading it.

SPENSER's Conduct is much more reasonable; as he design'd his Poem upon the Plan of the Vertues by which he has entitled his several Books, he scarce ever loses sight of this Design, but has almost every where taken care to let it appear. Sir *William Temple* indeed censures this as a Fault, and says, That tho his Flights of Fancy were very noble and high, yet his Moral lay so bare, that it lost the Effect: But I confess I do not understand this. A Moral which is not clear, is in my Apprehension next to no Moral at all.

IT wou'd be easy to enumerate other Properties, which

are various, according to the different kinds of Allegory, or its different Degrees of Perfection. Sometimes we are surpriz'd with an uncommon Moral, which ennobles the Fable that conveys it; and at other times we meet with a known and obvious Truth, plac'd in some new and beautiful Point of Light, and made surprizing by the Fiction under which it is exhibited. I have thought it sufficient to touch upon such Properties only as seem to be the most essential; and perhaps many more might be reduc'd under one or other of these general Heads.

I MIGHT here give Examples of this noble and antient kind of Writing, out of the Books of Holy Writ, and especially the *Jewish* Prophets, in which we find a Spirit of Poetry surprizingly sublime and majestick: But these are obvious to every one's reading. The East seems indeed to have been principally the Region of these figurative and emblematical Writings. Sir *John Chardin* in his Travels has given us a Translation of several Pieces of modern *Persian* Poetry; which shew that there are Traces of the same Genius remaining among the present Inhabitants of those Countries. But, not to prolong this Discourse, I shall only add one Instance of a very antient Allegory, which has all the Properties in it I have mention'd: I mean that in *Xenophon,* of the Choice of *Hercules* when he is courted by Virtue and Pleasure, which is said to have been the Invention of *Prodicus.* This Fable is full of Spirit and Elegance; the Characters are finely drawn, and consistent; and the Moral is clear. I shall not need to say any thing more of it, but refer the Reader to the Second Volume of the *Tatler,* where he will find it very beautifully translated.

AFTER what has been said, it must be confess'd, that, excepting *Spenser,* there are few extraordinary Instances

of this kind of Writing among the Moderns. The great
Mines of Invention have open'd long ago, and little new
Oar seems to have been discover'd or brought to light
by latter Ages. With us the Art of framing Fables,
Apologues and Allegories, which was so frequent among
the Writers of Antiquity, seems to be, like the Art of
Painting upon Glass, but little practis'd, and in a great
measure lost. Our Colours are not so rich and transparent, and are either so ill prepar'd, or so unskilfully
laid on, that they often sully the Light which is to pass
thro them, rather than agreeably tincture and beautify
it. *Boccalini* must be reckon'd one of the chief modern
Masters of Allegory; yet his Fables are often flat and
ill chosen, and his Invention seems to have been rather
fruitful than elegant. I cannot however conclude this
Essay on Allegory without observing, that we have had
the satisfaction to see this kind of Writing very lately
reviv'd by an excellent Genius among our selves, in the
true Spirit of the Antients. I need only mention the
Visions in the *Tatler* and *Spectator,* by Mr. *Addison,* to
convince every one of this. The Table of Fame, the
Vision of Justice; that of the different Pursuits of Love,
Ambition, and Avarice; the Vision of *Mirza,* and several
others; and especially that admirable Fable of the two
Families of Pain and Pleasure, which are all imagin'd,
and writ with the greatest Strength and Delicacy, may
give the Reader an Idea more than any thing I can say of
the Perfection to which this kind of Writing is capable
of being rais'd. We have likewise in the Second Volume
of the *Guardian* a very good Example given us by the
same Hand, of an Allegory, in the particular manner
of *Spenser.*

III.   REMARKS ON THE *FAIRY QUEEN*

By what has been offer'd in the foregoing Discourse on *Allegorical Poetry,* we may be able, not only to discover many Beauties in the *Fairy Queen,* but likewise to excuse some of its Irregularities.   The chief Merit of this Poem consists in that surprizing Vein of fabulous Invention, which runs thro it, and enriches it every where with Imagery and Descriptions more than we meet with in any other modern Poem.   The Author seems to be possess'd of a kind of Poetical Magick; and the Figures he calls up to our View rise so thick upon us, that we are at once pleased and distracted by the exhaustless Variety of them; so that his Faults may in a manner be imputed to his Excellencies: His Abundance betrays him into Excess, and his Judgment is overborne by the Torrent of his Imagination.

That which seems the most liable to Exception in this Work, is the Model of it, and the Choice the Author has made of so romantick a Story.   The several Books appear rather like so many several Poems, than one entire Fable: Each of them has its peculiar Knight, and is independent of the rest; and tho some of the Persons make their Appearance in different Books, yet this has very little Effect in connecting them.   Prince *Arthur* is indeed the principal Person, and has therefore a share given him in every Legend; but his Part is not considerable enough in any one of them: He appears and vanishes again like a Spirit; and we lose sight of him too soon, to consider him as the Hero of the Poem.

These are the most obvious Defects in the Fable of the *Fairy Queen.*   The want of Unity in the Story makes it difficult for the Reader to carry it in his Mind, and distracts too much his Attention to the several Parts of it; and indeed the whole Frame of it wou'd appear monstrous, if it were to be examin'd by the Rules of Epick Poetry, as they have been drawn from the Practice of *Homer* and *Virgil*. But as it is plain the Author never design'd it by those Rules, I think it ought rather to be consider'd as a Poem of a particular kind, describing in a Series of Allegorical Adventures or Episodes the most noted Virtues and Vices: to compare it therefore with the Models of Antiquity, wou'd be like drawing a Parallel between the *Roman* and the *Gothick* Architecture. In the first there is doubtless a more natural Grandeur and Simplicity: in the latter, we find great Mixtures of Beauty and Barbarism, yet assisted by the Invention of a Variety of inferior Ornaments; and tho the former is more majestick in the whole, the latter may be very surprizing and agreeable in its Parts.

It may seem strange indeed, since *Spenser* appears to have been well acquainted with the best Writers of Antiquity, that he has not imitated them in the Structure of his Story. Two Reasons may be given for this: The first is, That at the time when he wrote, the *Italian* Poets, whom he has chiefly imitated, and who were the first Revivers of this Art among the Moderns, were in the highest vogue, and were universally read and admir'd. But the chief Reason was probably, that he chose to frame his Fable after a Model which might give the greatest Scope to that Range of Fancy which was so remarkably his Talent. There is a Bent in Nature, which is apt to determine Men that particular way in which they are most capable of excelling; and tho it is certain he might have form'd a better Plan, it is to be question'd whether he cou'd have executed any other so well.

It is probably for the same reason, that among the

Italian Poets, he rather follow'd *Ariosto,* whom he found more agreeable to his Genius, than *Tasso,* who had form'd a better Plan, and from whom he has only borrow'd some particular Ornaments; yet it is but Justice to say, that his Plan is much more regular than that of *Ariosto.* In the *Orlando Furioso,* we every where meet with an exuberant Invention, join'd with great Liveliness and Facility of Description, yet debas'd by frequent Mixtures of the comick Genius, as well as many shocking Indecorums. Besides, in the Huddle and Distraction of the Adventures, we are for the most part only amus'd with extravagant Stories, without being instructed in any Moral. On the other hand, *Spenser*'s Fable, tho often wild, is, as I have observ'd, always emblematical: And this may very much excuse likewise that Air of Romance in which he has follow'd the *Italian* Author. The perpetual Stories of Knights, Giants, Castles, and Enchantments, and all that Train of Legendary Adventures, wou'd indeed appear very trifling, if *Spenser* had not found a way to turn them all into Allegory, or if a less masterly Hand had fill'd up his Draught. But it is surprizing to observe how much the Strength of the Painting is superior to the Design. It ought to be consider'd too, that at the time when our Author wrote, the Remains of the old *Gothick* Chivalry were not quite abolish'd: It was not many Years before, that the famous Earl of *Surry,* remarkable for his Wit and Poetry in the Reign of King *Henry* the Eighth, took a romantick Journey to *Florence,* the Place of his Mistress's Birth, and publish'd there a Challenge against all Nations in Defence of her Beauty. Justs and Turnaments were held in *England* in the Time of Queen *Elizabeth.* Sir *Philip Sidney* tilted at one of these Enter- tainments, which was made for the *French* Ambassador,

when the Treaty of Marriage was on foot with the Duke
of *Anjou:* and some of our Historians have given us a
very particular and formal Account of Preparations, by
marking out Lists, and appointing Judges, for a Tryal
by Combat, in the same Reign, which was to have decided
the Title to a considerable Estate; and in which the whole
Ceremony was perfectly agreeable to the fabulous
Descriptions in Books of Knight-Errantry. This might
render his Story more familiar to his first Readers; tho
Knights in Armour, and Ladies Errant are as antiquated
Figures to us, as the Court of that time wou'd appear,
if we cou'd see them now in their Ruffs and Fardingales.

THERE are two other Objections to the Plan of the
Fairy Queen, which, I confess, I am more at a loss to
answer. I need not, I think, be scrupulous in mentioning
freely the Defects of a Poem, which, tho it was never
suppos'd to be perfect, has always been allow'd to be
admirable.

THE first is, that the Scene is laid in *Fairy-Land,* and
the chief Actors are *Fairies.* The Reader may see their
imaginary Race and History in the Second Book, at the
end of the Tenth Canto: but if he is not prepar'd beforehand, he may expect to find them acting agreeably to the
common Stories and Traditions about such fancy'd
Beings. Thus *Shakespear,* who has introduc'd them in
his *Midsummer-Night's Dream,* has made them speak
and act in a manner perfectly adapted to their suppos'd
Characters; but the *Fairies* in this Poem are not
distinguish'd from other Persons. There is this Misfortune likewise attends the Choice of such Actors, that
having been accustom'd to conceive of them in a diminu-
tive way, we find it difficult to raise our Ideas, and to
imagine a *Fairy* encountring with a Monster or a Giant.
Homer has pursu'd a contrary Method, and represented

his Heroes above the Size and Strength of ordinary Men; and it is certain that the Actions of the Iliad wou'd have appear'd but ill proportion'd to the Characters, if we were to have imagin'd them all perform'd by Pigmies.

BUT as the Actors our Author has chosen, are only fancy'd Beings, he might possibly think himself at liberty to give them what Stature, Customs and Manners he pleas'd. I will not say he was in the right in this: but it is plain that by the literal Sense of *Fairy-Land,* he only design'd an *Utopia,* an imaginary Place; and by his *Fairies,* Persons of whom he might invent any Action proper to human Kind, without being restrain'd, as he must have been, if he had chosen a real Scene and historical Characters. As for the mystical Sense, it appears both by the Work it self, and by the Author's* Explanation of it, that his *Fairy-Land* is *England,* and his *Fairy-Queen,* Queen *Elizabeth*; at whose Command the Adventure of every Legend is suppos'd to be undertaken.

THE other Objection is, that having chosen an historical Person, Prince *Arthur,* for his principal Hero; who is no *Fairy,* yet is mingled with them: he has not however represented any part of his History. He appears here indeed only in his Minority, and performs his Exercises in *Fairy-Land,* as a private Gentleman; but we might at least have expected, that the fabulous Accounts of him, and of his Victories over the *Saxons,* shou'd have been work'd into some beautiful Vision or Prophecy: and I cannot think *Spenser* wou'd wholly omit this, but am apt to believe he had done it in some of the following Books which were lost.

*Vid. *Letter to Sir* W. Raleigh.

In the moral Introductions to every Book, many of which have a great Propriety and Elegance, the Author has follow'd the Example of *Ariosto*. I will only beg leave to point out some of the principal Beauties in each Book, which may yet more particularly discover the Genius of the Author. . .

JOHN DENNIS

JOHN DENNIS

I. A LARGE ACCOUNT OF THE TASTE IN POETRY

1702

To the Honourable
GEORGE GRANVILLE, Esq;

SIR,

I Know that a great many Persons in the World would take it for an affront, to have a Play addressed to them, which had been unfortunate in the Representation. But you, Sir, have discernment enough to be of another opinion; for a Poet, who Dedicates a Play that has not been successful, will, if he takes care of his Reputation, choose a powerful Patron, who is every way qualified to defend it. One who is generous enough to support whatever he can justly excuse, and who with a piercing Eye can reach to his Beauties, while others stop at his Faults.

When I first communicated the design which I had of altering this Comedy of *Shakespear,* I found that I should have two sorts of People to deal with, who would equally endeavour to obstruct my success. The one believed it to be so admirable, that nothing ought to be added to it; the others fancied it to be so despicable, that any ones time would be lost upon it.

That this Comedy was not despicable, I guess'd for several Reasons: First, I knew very well, that it had pleas'd one of the greatest Queens that ever was in the World, great not only for her Wisdom in the Arts of

Government, but for her knowledge of Polite Learning, and her nice taste of the Drama, for such a taste we may be sure she had, by the relish which she had of the Ancients. This Comedy was written at her Command, and by her direction, and she was so eager to see it Acted, that she commanded it to be finished in fourteen days; and was afterwards, as Tradition tells us, very well pleas'd at the Representation. In the second place, in the Reign of King *Charles* the Second, when People had an admirable taste of Comedy, all those men of extraordinary parts, who were the Ornaments of that Court; as the late Duke of *Buckingham,* my Lord *Normandy,* my Lord *Dorset,* my late Lord *Rochester,* Sir *Charles Sidley,* Dr *Frazer,* Mr *Savil,* Mr *Buckley,* were in Love with the Beauties of this Comedy. In the third place, I thought that after so long an acquaintance as I had with the best Comick Poets, among the Antients and Moderns, I might depend in some measure upon my own Judgment, and I thought I found here three or four extraordinary Characters, that were exactly drawn, and truly Comical; and that I saw besides in it some as happy touches as ever were in Comedy: Besides I had observed what success the Character of *Falstaffe* had had, in the first part of *Harry* the Fourth. And as the *Falstaffe* in the Merry Wives is certainly superiour to that of the second part of *Harry* the Fourth, so it can hardly be said to be inferior to that of the first.

For in the second part of *Harry* the Fourth, *Falstaffe* does nothing but talk, as indeed he does nothing else in the third and fourth Acts of the first part. Whereas in the Merry Wives, he every where Acts, and that action is more Regular, and more in compass than it is in the first part of *Harry* the Fourth. 'Tis true, what he says in *Harry* the Fourth is admirable; but action at last is the business of the Stage. The Drama is action itself, and it is action alone that is able to excite in any extraordinary manner the curiosity of mankind. What News, is the Question now adays ev'ry moment, but people by that question demand what is done, and not what is said upon the Great Stage of the World. In short, I defie any man to name me a Play that has ever succeeded without some sort of action or another. But I could if I pleased mention more than one, that has succeeded barely by the force of Action, without almost any thing else.

It was for the above-named reasons, that I thought this by no means a despicable Comedy. And it was for the Reasons which follow, that I believed it not so admirable, but that it might receive improvement. First, I knew very well, that in so short a time as this Play was writ, nothing could be done that is perfect. Secondly, I knew very well, that this Comedy had never upon Revivals had any great success, and that particularly when it was Revived in King *Charles* the Seconds time, the only Character that pleased to a height was *Slender* acted by *Wintershal*. And that tho something like this may very well happen to a living Author without any just Cause, yet that there must be reason for it, when it happens to an Author who has a long time been dead, and whose Reputation has been long established. And indeed the *Merry Wives of Windsor,* as it has great Beauties, so it has strange Defects, which tho they past at first for the sake of the Beauties, yet will come to be less endured as the Stage grows more Regular. For there are no less than three Actions in it that are independant one of another, which divide and distract the minds of an Audience, there is more than one insignificant Scene, which has nothing to do with any other part of the Play, which is enough to obstruct and stifle the Action. The Style in some places is stiff and forced and affected, whereas the Dialogue in Comedy ought to be as free as the air. This affectation is particularly remarkable in some part of the first Scene between the Wives, and in all *Ford*'s part of the first Scene between him and *Falstaffe*. This is not said in the least with a design to derogate from *Shakespear*'s merit, who performed more than any one else could have done in so short a time. In the alteration I have endeavoured to Correct the foresaid Errours.

I have made every thing Instrumental to *Fenton*'s Marriage, and the whole to depend on one common Center, which I believe was hardly in the power of every Writer to perform. I have added to some of the parts in order to heighten the Characters, and make them show the better. I have above all things endeavoured to make the Dialogue as easie and free as I could. For in Comedy, which is an Image of common Life, every thing which is forc'd is abominable. In short, I have alter'd every thing which I disliked, and retain'd every thing which I or my Friends approved of, excepting something of Justice *Shallow* in the first Scene of the Play, which I omitted for two Reasons, the one was because I could not bring it into the same design with the rest, the second because I knew no body who would be capable of Acting that Character, unless those who would be otherwise employed.

Thus, Sir, I have endeavoured to convey two things by you to the General Reader, the one, that this Comedy is not so Despicable as to be Incapable of Improvement; the other, that it is not so admirable, as not to stand in need of any. Whether, Sir, I have improv'd it or no I leave it to you to determine, whether the Scene between the Wives in the first Act be alter'd for the better or the worse, whether that between *Falstaffe* and *Ford* in the second Act is aptly contriv'd to give occasion to an excellent Actor to shew himself; whether that between *Falstaffe* and the Wives in the third Act be wholly without art, and whether that between *Falstaffe* and *Ford* in the fourth Act, may be said to be truly Comical.

But before it comes to that, Sir, I who am resolved to have you fully informed before you come to give sentence, and who am ignorant whether you were in Town when this Play was Acted or no, think my self obliged to make you acquainted, that *Falstaffe*'s part, which you know to be the principal one of the Play, and that on which all the rest depends, was by no means acted to the satisfaction of the Audience, upon which several fell from disliking the Action to disapproving the Play, which will be always very natural upon such occasions, tho sometimes not very reasonable, and divers objections were immediately made, which if the Play had succeeded, had perhaps never been thought of. I desire that you would give me leave to lay them and their answers before you, and so leave the whole to your impartial decision.

The first is, that the Characters in this Comedy are very low, and that there is neither much Wit, nor Love nor Gallantry in it. To which I answer first, that tho the Characters are low they are true and good, that there is as perfect a Plot as I was able to build upon another mans Foundation; and that the lowness of the Characters derogates not a jot from the perfection of the Fable; that in all Fables all Characters are Universal and Allegorical, and that it signifies nothing to the Beauty of the Fiction, or the importance of the Moral, whether we bring in Kings or Shepherds, so they are

introduced aptly.   In the next place, there is Humour
every where in this Comedy.   And Humour after the
Plot is what is most valuable in Comedy.   I desire then,
Sir, that I may have leave to prove two things: First,
that Humour is more the business of Comedy than Wit:
And secondly, that Humour is more to be found in low
Characters, than among Persons of a higher Rank, and
consequently that low Characters are more proper for
Comedy than high, and that low Comedy is to be preferred to the high.   And when I have done this, I desire
to speak a word of Love and Gallantry, of the want of
which this Play is accus'd.

First then, Humour is the business in Comedy, and
not Wit.   The business of a Comick Poet is to shew his
Characters and not himself, to make ev'ry one of them
speak and act, as such a person in such circumstances
would probably act and speak.   Comedy, is an Image
of common Life, and in Life, a Man, who has discerning
Eyes, may find something ridiculous in most People, but
something that is witty in very few.   And a Comick Poet
may be certain of this, that the grossest touches which
are in nature, will please the men of sense, more than
the most delicate strokes which are out of it.   Now that
which is truly ridiculous in any man is chiefly Humour,
or the effect of Humour.   It is plain too for the following Reasons, that Humour is more proper for Comedy
than Wit.   First, because it is harder to write, for the
writing Wit is the effect of the Fancy, and the writing
Humour the work of the Judgment.   'Tis observation
alone that can qualify a man for it, and observation is
the business of the Judgment.   Now tho a fine Imagination is to be met with in few, Judgment is to be found
in fewer.   Humour then is harder to be Written than
Wit, and that which in any kind of Writing is the hardest

to be attaind, makes the principal Beauty of that kind
of Writing: But secondly Humour is more proper for
Comedy than Wit; because it gives a necessary occasion
for Action, which Wit does not, and Action after all is
the very Life and Soul of the Theatre. Now that
Humour gives a necessary occasion for Action is plain,
because Humour is Passion, as I have shewn in another
place,* and nothing but Action is
able to express Passion, as nothing
but Passion can give an occasion for
Action: But thirdly, Humour in
Comedy is to be preferr'd to Wit,
because it distinguishes the Characters better. For Wit
very often destroys and confounds them, whereas
Humour if it be true and good must always maintain
and preserve them, as we shall prove more evidently,
when we come to shew that Humour is chiefly to be
found in low Characters, and therefore since Humour
distinguishes the Characters, it must be always agreeable
to men of Sense, whereas Wit must be often shocking
and nauseous to them, because it destroys and confounds
the Characters, which is a fourth reason for giving
Humour the preference; because it is plain that what is
always agreeable in any kind of Writing must be preferable to that which is sometimes shocking. But fifthly
and lastly, if Comedy is Poetry, 'tis Humour chiefly
which makes it so, for that which Characteristically
distinguishes Poetry from Prose is Passion, as I have
prov'd in another place,* and Humour
is subordinate Passion. You know
very well, Sir, that what I have said
here is exactly agreeable to the sentiments of a great† Critick, who speaking of Comedy tells us.

*Advancement
and Reformation
of Modern Poetry.*

*Advancement
and Reformation
of Modern Poetry.*

†*Lord Marquess
of* Normanby.

> *A fault which often does befal,*
> *Is when the Wit of some great Poet shall*
> *So overflow, that is be none at all;*
> *That all his Fools speak sense, as if possest,*
> *And each by Inspiration breaks his jest.*
> *If once the Justness of each part be lost;*
> *Well we may laugh, but at the Poets cost.*

How fine an observation is this, Sir? For the different Characters in Comedy, like the several parts in Musick, make up the consort of the Play, and as soon as one Character says any thing which does not belong to it, there is a string which is out of Tune, and the Harmony of the whole is destroy'd. But that Noble Critick goes on.

> *That silly thing men call sheer Wit avoid,*
> *With which our Age so nauseously is cloy'd;*
> *Humour is all, Wit should be only brought*
> *To turn agreeably some proper thought.*

Thus, Sir, having shewn that Humour is more properly the business of Comedy than Wit, I come now to shew in the second place, that Humour is chiefly to be found in the lower sort of People. For Reason in one Man is the same with Reason in another man, excepting the differences of more or less. But Passion and Humour, which is a sort of Passion, are very different according to their different subjects in their kinds, as well as their degrees. For every man shews his Anger and his Joy, his Peevishness and his Jollity a different way from another. Reason is a calm and quiet thing, and has nothing to do with the Body, only Passion and Humour can reach the Body, and by the influence which they have upon the voice, and the Gestures, sensibly distin-

guish one Character from another. So that 'tis Passion
and Humour which is subordinate Passion, which distinguish Man from Man. Now the more education a
Man has, the more he is capable of subduing, or at least
of hiding his Passions and his Humours. And that
which we call good Breeding, is, or should be nothing
else but a Habit and Custom of doing things, which
reas[o]n has dictated for the convenience, and ease, and
good of Society. From which it follows, that among
People of condition, there is more Resemblance, and a
greater appearance of Reason. And 'tis among People
of the lower sort, that by the means of Passion and
Humour, Nature appears so admirably conspicuous in
all her Charming diversities: Since therefore Humour
is the chief business in Comedy after the Fable, and
Humour is more to be found among those of the lower
sort, than among those of a higher Rank, it is very plain
that low Characters are more proper for Comedy than
high ones, and that low Comedy is to be preferred to
the high.

Not but that high Characters are very good sometimes for the sake of variety, and consequently Wit is
very good, when it is so writ, that it falls within the
compass of the Characters which speak it. But by Wit
here I by no means intend point, the excess of which is
always despicable, but such fine Observation and fine
Satyr as my Lord *Normanby* means, and as is to be found
in Mr *Wycherley's* Writings; who since he comes in
my way, must have justice done him; and be allowed
to be almost the only person, who has given the World
a Master-piece, in which a great deal of Humour is
shewn in high Characters. But that is not to be done
every day; and we are treating here of such Comedy
as is usually writ. But to return from whence we

digress'd. As Wit in Comedy, where it is proper, is very good and diverting, so is Gallantry and Courtly Love, for it is now time to speak a word of them too; but Humour is to be preferr'd before either of them, and for most of the very same Reasons, for which it is to be preferred before Wit. For Humour is harder to write than Love; because every body has something of Love in him, and is help'd in writing it, by the present influence which that Passion has upon him; whereas writing Humour must be chiefly the effect of his past observation. But secondly, Humour distinguishes the Characters better, and gives an occasion for a greater variety of Action. For tho the Love of one man must be allow'd to be very different from the Love of another man, yet Love is but a single Passion, and Humour comprehends them all. For to every Passion there is a Humour which answers to it, which Humour is nothing but a less degree of that Passion. As for example, Anger is a Passion, Peevishness and Moroseness are Humours, Joy when it is great is a Passion, Jollity and Gayety perhaps may be said to be Humours, so that if any man asks for a description of Humour, I answer that 'tis the expression of some subordinate Passion. But if he asks for a full definition of it, by which we may distinguish Humour in one man from Humour in another man; I answer that Humour is subordinate Passion expressed in a particular manner. Fear is a Passion, Timerousness is a Humour. Now since Humour comprehends all Passions, it must have infinitely more variety than a single Passion.

But further, without the *Ridiculum* Comedy cannot subsist, for the design of Comedy is to amend the follies of Mankind, by exposing them. But the *Ridiculum* is a great deal more to be found in Humour, than it is in

Love. For Love is so agreeable in its own nature, that it can never be made to appear Ridiculous, unless it is joyned with an Humour. Besides, Humour, if it is well writ, is always both delightful and instructive, it entertains and does good at the same time; whereas Love is very often agreeable without being instructive; nay, it very often gives a pernicious pleasure. For after all, it is a very great error in some Persons at present, to be so shy of Bawdy, and so fond of Love. For Obscenity cannot be very dangerous, because it is rude and shocking; but Love is a Passion; which is so agreeable to the movements of corrupted Nature, that by seeing it livelily touched and often represented, an Amorous disposition insensibly insinuates itself into the chastest Breast. Now as the design of every Art is to instruct and delight, it must be the design of Comedy; and therefore Humour which always both instructs and delights, must be more proper for Comedy than Love, which sometimes only barely delights, and sometimes is so far from instructing, that it insensibly corrupts an Audience.

After all, I was so willing to comply with Custom, that this Play has more of Love in it than the Original Comedy. But I desire People to consider, that *Moliere* got a great deal of Reputation in *France* by Comedies, in which there is very little or no Love, and that by those Comedies he very agreeably entertain'd the finest Ladies of the Court of *France*; that Madam *de Montausier* highly approved of the *Precieuses Ridicules,* tho there was not one jot of Love in it, that those Ladies were too proud to be thought to have Souls that were incapable of being pleased with an exact Imitation of Nature, tho that Imitation had nothing in it of the business to which they were bred; that those Persons who are for nothing but perpetual Love in our Plays, would do well to consider, whether they do not give others an occasion to think, that this error in them, proceeds either from the narrowness of their capacities, or the corruptness of their desires; that Humour, which was a diversion to Queen *Elizabeth,* and the Ladies of the Court of *France,* may not be thought a very improper one, for the most delicate Persons of the present Age; that *Shakespear* had little Love in the very best of his Plays, and *Johnson* less in his, and yet that this last was one of the best Comick Poets that ever was in the World; that he was so sensible, that the *Ridiculum* was the chief thing in Comedy, that he has always in his chief Comedies joyn'd his Love with Humour, and so made it ridiculous.

Another Objection is, that several Characters of this Comedy are obsolete and quite out of date. The matter of Fact indeed cannot be denied, and the Objection has some force. For if there is any thing resembling in Poetry and Painting, as the Sisters are certainly like, then Heroick and Tragick Poetry may be compar'd to History Painting; and Comedy, to Drawing after the Life. Now the Pictures which are done after the Life, if they are drawn by Masters, will certainly please Masters, and all who are able to judge of the boldness and the delicacy of the strokes: but the People who judge only of the resemblance, are most delighted with the Pictures of their acquaintance. Thus any Characters in Comedy, which are finely drawn, will please those who can judge; but a Poet to please the generality, must Copy the present Age. Thus, Sir, have I fairly stated the objection in its utmost force; and now I shall answer two things to it, first, that I never made it my chief aim to please the generality, and a little lower shall give my Reasons for it. Secondly, that supposing I had, tho several of the Characters of this Play are indeed obsolete, yet that of *Falstaffe* will always be new, and whenever it comes to be Acted to the satisfaction of an Audience, will infallibly fill the Stage better than a great many Characters.

These, Sir, are the two general Objections, but there are two particular ones. The first is, that I have introduc'd an unnecessary Character in the Host of the *Bull*. But I believe, Sir, that I have consider'd of this matter with a little more attention than they who made the Objection, and I know, that that Character is absolutely necessary for the carrying on the Action probably, which in the original Play is by no means probable. For it is not likely, that *Falstaffe* would suffer himself to be carried in the Basket, as far as *Datchet Mead,* which is half a Mile from *Windsor*; and it is plain, that they could not carry him, if he made any resistance. Nor is it likely, that he would defer his reflections upon his adventure, till he came back to *Windsor*. So that the Soliloquies which he makes in the fourth Act before *Ford*'s entrance, are not design'd for himself, but apparently address'd to the Audience, which is the greatest fault that can possibly be in the *Drama*.

The last Objection is, that the forementioned Scene in the fourth Act, which is very long, is nothing but a discovery of what the Audience had been Eye-Witnesses of before. But this objection is unreasonable with Relation to the original Play, and more unreasonable with Relation to the altered one. For in the original Play, *Falstaffe* makes a Relation to *Ford* not so much of his being put into the Buck Basket, as of the circumstances which attended it; of what he suffer'd while he was in it, and upon his coming out of it. And in this lyes the excellency of that Scene, that it gives an occasion for a great Actor to shew himself. For all the while *Falstaffe* is making this Relation, *Ford* at the same time, that in dumb acting, he shews a concern, and a fellow-feeling to the Knight, shews a great deal of Joy and Satisfaction to the Audience.

Thus in the original Scene *Falstaffe* makes a relation of what had happened to him, since he left the Stage last, and that Relation must be Comical, by Reason of the occasion that it gives for an excellent Actor to shew himself. But for the Alter'd Scene there is something more to be said. For after that *Falstaffe* has rais'd *Ford*'s Joy for the others disappointment, which yet he was forced to screen and shelter from the Knight with a dissembled sorrow, *Falstaffe* by making a discovery of something which had not happened, and strangely altering the Adventure of Mrs *Page,* which he thought himself obliged to do for the sake of his Credit, gives his jealous Coxcomb a fresh alarm, and throws him into real Convulsions.

Thus, Sir, have I laid before you the objections and the answers to them, and leave it to you to judge, whether the last are satisfactory, and whether the first had ever been made, if the Play had succeeded on the Stage; for you know, Sir, that Plays are like Men, the successful are sure to find Friends enough, let them be never so worthless, while ev'ry Maggot will be censuring the conduct of the deserving unfortunate. For so fantastick a composition is Man, that tho of all the Creatures which the Sun illuminates, he is at once the vainest and most miserable, at the same time so vain and so miserable, that Nature seems to have given him Vanity as a support, and a counterballance for Misery; yet he is often so very unthinking, and so foolishly severe against himself, as

to affirm that there can be no Merit, where there is no
Success.

Thus Fortune enslaves ev'n the Souls of men to
opinion; but she has never been able to reach yours.
You have been so far from thinking the better of others
for their enjoying her, that you have yourself refused
her favours, and disdained the allurements of a Mistress,
in whom you would have so many worthless persons
your Rivals. You look upon things as you see them
yourself, and not as the World mistakes them. You
know that success can at the best but illustrate merit,
and that it never gives it. That good Sence like Virtue
is not always prosperous at first, while Folly like Vice
triumphs. That it is unreasonable to believe that any
thing that is writ, should be better for succeeding, any
more than any thing that is done. That if an Action
may succeed because it is base and villanous, a Play may
well be supposed to take because it is very foolish.

But that as an action that pleases good men, must be
in itself good, the Play must certainly be well writ, which
pleases those who have taste. That as the a[c]tion
which pleases none but Villains, must in itself be hor-
ribly villainous, the Play which satisfies only those
persons who are not able to judge, must in itself be
extreamly ridiculous.

In short, Sir, that you might always pass a true judgment on the productions of the mind, you have Reli-
giously observed the beautiful directions of a Modern
Critick. From hence it comes that you have
*St Evre-
mont*
neither shown an unjust aversion for the
Living, nor a fantastick veneration for the
Dead, that you reject what's trifling in the last, while you
esteem what's valuable in the first. That as Novelty has
no allurements for you, you have no aversion for that, but

embrace or reject the works of an Author according to their real merit, and the Impression which they ought truly to make upon you; and that your decisions are as just and reasonable, and as free from whimsey as they are impartial.

To conclude that a Play is good because Mr *Granville* is pleased by it, is but a reasonable way of arguing. But to say, that it is good because it pleases the generality of an Audience is a very absurd one. For ev'ry man has, and will have his different pleasure. Wise men will be sure to be pleased with things that are wise, and Fools will be inclined to be pleased with things that are foolish. *Montagn* was pleased with playing with his Cat; but at the same time he does her and himself the Justice to believe she thought him an Ass for it. Would to Heaven that some part of our Audiences were but as just as the *Frenchman,* and some part of our Authors but as reasonable as the Beast. Before a Play can be concluded to be good because it pleases, we ought to consider who are pleased by it, they who understand, or they who do not. They who understand? Alas, they are but few, and are seldom pleas'd there of late. They who do not? That methinks is odd. Suppose a man should tell an Author he never so much as heard of his Play, and should the very moment following tell him he liked it. Would he be satisfied with this approbation? Would he not be really mortified at it? Now ev'ry one who talks like an Ass tells the World, tho against his will, that he does not understand one word of a Play; and is not he who never heard a word of a Cause as justly qualified to determine it, as he who never understood a word of it.

'Tis for this Reason, Sir, that when-ever I write I make it my business to please such men as you are. As

very well knowing that whatever is writ has its immediate success from Fortune, but its lasting one from
Art and Nature. That the People are always uncertain
and fluctuating, and guided by Opinion, and not by
Judgment, that the surest way to arrive at Reputation
is to please the knowing few, for that they at last must
draw in the multitude, but are never to be drawn in by
them.

I have been already tedious, or it would be an easie
matter to shew, that they who in all Ages have appeared
at once good Poets and good Criticks have writ to a
few Persons, I mean to a few at present. For he who
writes to the many at present writes only to them, and
his works are sure never to survive their admirers; but
he who writes to the knowing few at present, writes to
the Race of mankind in all succeeding ages. But I am
glad that this is addrest to a Gentleman, who needs only
be put in mind of this, who is perfectly well acquainted
with *Horace* and *Boileau,* and who has often read the
Satyrs and the Epistles of both; and who consequently
is able to inform others, that those two celebrated Poets
directed their writings to the knowing few, and were
neither exalted by the approbation, nor dejected by the
censure of the rest, and that by such a proceeding they
came to please universally: That some of the most agreeable parts of those Satyrs and those Epistles, are those
in which they laugh at the taste of the Vulgar, and that
among the vulgar they reckoned not only a great many
who were distinguished by their Rank from others, but
several whom the World called Wits and Poets; and
that they had a greater Contempt for those Wits and
Poets, than they had for any sort of People whatever,
unless for those who admired them.

Ainsi qu'en sots Auteurs
Notre siecle est fertile en sots admirateurs
Et sans ceux qui fournit la ville et la Province
Il en est chez le Duc, Il en est chez le prince
L'ouvrage le plus plat, a chez les courtesans
Detout temps recontrez des Zeles partisans,
Et pour finir enfin par un trait de Satyre
Un sot trouve toujours un plus sot qui l'admire

Boileau lart. Poe tique Cant.

As th' Age produces shoals of scribbling
  Fools,
'Tis full as fertile in admiring Tools;
Besides whole swarms in Country and in
  Town,
Versailles *has some of Lustre and Renown.*
Th' Absurdest Ass that e're made Reader
  sport,
Has in all times found zealous Friends at
  Court,
No scribbling Fool so much a Fool can be,
But finds to admire him greater Sots than he.

They were perfectly satisfied that your ill Poets, and
your Would-be-Wits have in all ages been the most
undiscerning and most injudicious absurd People upon
Earth even in their own business. That it is not Wit,
but Reason and Judgment, which distinguish a man of
Sense from a Fool. That as nothing but Reason distinguishes Man from Beast, he who in his writings
frequently shocks Reason infallibly shews himself an
Ass; and that tho he may impose upon Fools for a time,
by a wretched glimmering of Fancy, and a contemptible
clink of Verse, as Woodcocks and Widgeons are caught
by a lowd Bell and by a greasie Light, yet whenever he

comes to write in Prose, where Reason is plainly to appear, he plainly appears to have none.

I could have said a great deal to have shewn, that the most judicious of the Ancient *Romans,* and the Modern *French* have been out of Humour with the taste of the People, if I had not writ to a Gentleman, who is perfectly satisfied about the matter. But now, if *Horace* was justly out of Humour with the taste of the *Roman* People in the time of *Augustus Cæsar,* I believe no reasonable man will wonder if an *English* Writer is dissatisfied with the taste of the *English* at this present conjuncture. For you know very well, Sir, that let us flatter ourselves as long as we please, there is no manner of comparison between the *Roman* People and ours. And the *English* were never sunk so miserably low in their taste, as they are at present. If then the advice that *Horace* gave in the tenth Satyr of the first Book was good at that time, when directed to *Roman* Authors,

> *Neque te ut miretur Turba labores*
> *Contentus paucis lectoribus.*

It certainly must be much better now, when address'd to our *English* Writers. I will not now pretend to determine whether the general taste of *England* ever was good or no. This we know very well, that several Plays have been indifferently received at first, which have succeeded very well afterwards. The only Play that ever Mr *Cowley* writ, was barbarously treated the first night, as the late Mr *Dryden* has more than once informed me, who has told me that he went to see it with the famous Mr *Sprat,* now Bishop of *Rochester,* and that after the Play was done, they both made a visit to Mr *Cowley,* whom the Death of his Brother had obliged to keep the House, and that Mr *Cowley* received the news of his ill success, not with so much firmness, as might have been expected from so great a man.

But to return from whence I digressed, *She wou'd if she cou'd* met with no better usage from the People at first, tho at the same time it was esteem'd by the Men of Sense, for the trueness of some of its Characters, and the purity and freeness and easie grace of its Dialogue. I need not say, that both those Plays have been since acted with a general applause; and it wou'd be as needless to shew on the other side, that a thousand Plays which were extravagantly applauded at first, are now sunk to the very last degree of Contempt.

But, Sir, whether the general taste of *England* ever was good or no, this I think cannot be controverted, that the taste of *England* for Comedy, which ought to be the thing in question now, was certainly much better in the Reign of King *Charles* the Second, than it is at present. For it was then extreamly good, and is now excessively bad. The occasion, Sir, is fair, and nothing in this sort of Criticism could be more curious or more important than to enquire into the causes of this degeneracy of taste. Notwithstanding that I have already detained you too long, I flatter myself so far as to fancy, that the handling a Subject so very new, may prove entertaining to you, and therefore I will venture to treat of it.

Give me leave then, Sir, to lay down the following Maxims, as things that are self-evident, and require no proof.

First, That then there is among any People a good taste for Comedy, when a very considerable part of an Audience are qualified to judge for themselves, and when they who are not qualified to judge for themselves, are influenced by the authority of those who are rightly qualified. Secondly, that then there is among any

People a bad taste for Comedy, when very few of an Audience are qualify'd to judge for themselves, and when the rest are influenced by the authority of those who are not rightly qualified.

And now having laid down these two Maxims, I shall shew as briefly as I can,

First, That in the Reign of King *Charles* the Second, a considerable part of an Audience were qualified to judge for themselves, and that they who were not qualified, were influenced by the authority of those who were.

Secondly, That in the present Reign a very inconsiderable part of an Audience are qualified to judge for themselves, and that the rest are not influenced by the authority of those, who are rightly qualified; but in order to the doing this, it will be requisite to declare what qualifications are necessary for the judging of Comedy.

This, I think, Sir, need not be disputed, that for the judging of any sort of Writings, those talents are in some measure requisite, which were necessary to produce them. As for example, there are two things absolutely required for the succeeding in Polemical Divinity; the one is a reasonable Head, and the second an acquaintance with the Scriptures, Fathers and Councils; and it is plain, that a proportionable share of Reason, and an acquaintance with the same Learning, are absolutely necessary to judge of the goodness or badness of such controversies. Now there are three things required for the succeeding in Poetry. 1. Great parts. 2. A generous Education. 3. A due Application.

First, There are required great Parts. I suppose, Sir, this need not be proved, because it has been sufficiently proved by experience. For whenever a good Poet has laid aside Poetry for any other employment, he has seldom failed of succeeding in that employment, tho it has been of never so great importance; but here by great parts is meant chiefly a lively, and a warm, and a strong imagination, and a solid and piercing judgment; for the production of a Reasonable Creature, must derive its chief advantage from Reason, which gave occasion for that precept of *Boileau* in the first *Canto* of his Art of Poetry.

> *Aimez donc la Raison que tou jours vos Ecrits*
> *Empruntent d'elle seule et leur lustre et leur prix.*

But Secondly, for the succeeding in Comedy, there is required a generous Education, which comprehends; 1. Learning. 2. A knowledge of Mankind and the World. 1. Learning, for tho it may be pretended, that some have succeeded in Comedy, without the least knowledge of the Learned Languages; yet here by Learning I mean the knowledge of things, and not that of words, which knowledge is absolutely necessary, because the ultimate end of Comedy is to instruct, and to instruct all; and it is impossible that the Learned should be instructed by the Ignorant. But secondly, a knowledge of the World and of Mankind, are necessary for succeeding in Comedy. For since Comedy is drawing after the Life, and a Comick Poet is obliged to Copy the Age to which he writes, how should he possibly draw them like, without knowing the persons.

But the third thing requisite for the succeeding in Comedy is a due Application, and that likewise includes two things, the one of which is Leisure, and the other Serenity. First, Leisure, for Poetry is of that Dignity, that it requires the whole man. And never any man writ any thing that was admirable, who had any avocations at the time that he writ it. But secondly, to succeed in Comedy requires Serenity. For a Comick Poet is obliged to put off himself, and transform himself into his several Characters; to enter into the Foibles of his several persons, and all the Recesses and secret turns of their minds, and to make their Passions, their Interests, and their Concern his own. Now how should he possibly do this, unless he is absolutely free, and undisturbed by tormenting Passions, which bind him, as it were, and if I may use that expression, chain him fast to himself.

But now, as Parts, Education and Application are necessary to succeed in the writing Poetry, they are requisite in some degree for the forming a true judgment of it. No man can judge of a Beautiful imagination in another, without some degree of it in himself. And as for the judging rightly of any thing without Judgment, that is a contradiction in terms. And if Philosophy and a knowledge of the World are necessary to a Comick Poet, for his forming his Characters; if an acquaintance with the best Authors among the Antient and Moderns, be requisite for the attaining the Vivacity and Grace of the Dialogue; why, then for the forming a true judgment of these, the same Learning and the same Experience are necessary. And lastly, if a Poet had need to have his mind free, that he may the more thoroughly enter into the concerns of the Theatre, and put on the Passions and Humours of his different Characters, so as to make them by turns his own; why the Spectator, that he may judge whether the Author does this or no, must enter into those Passions and Humours in some proportionable degree, and consequently ought to have his mind free from all avocations of Business, and from all real vexatious Passions.

Having premis'd all this, we shall now come to shew: First, that in the reign of King *Charles* the Second, a considerable part of an Audience had those Parts, that Education and that Application, which were requisit for the judging of Poetry, and that they who had not, were influenced by the authority of those who had; and Secondly, that in the present Reign very few in an Audience have the forementioned qualifications; and that those who have them not, have not the advantage to be influenced by the authority of those who have.

First then, in the Reign of King *Charles* the Second, a considerable part of an Audience had those parts, which were requisite for the judging of Comedy. And we have shewn above that those parts comprehend principally a fine Imagination and a sound Judgment. Well, but says an Objector; Are not the Imaginations and Judgments of Mankind the same that they were then, or is Humane Nature decay'd since the Reign of *Charles* the Second? To which I answer, That the capacity of imagining and of judging have been in all Ages equal in Mankind. But then this is certain, that the faculties of the Soul, like the parts of the Body, receive nourishment from use, and derive skill as well as they do force and vigour from exercise. Now I leave to any one to judge whether the imaginative faculty of the Soul, must be more exercised in a Reign of Poetry and of Pleasure, or in a Reign of Politicks and of Business. Besides, as an Artist may have that sort of Beauty of Imagination, which is sufficient for the succeeding in Painting and Carving, and may at the same time be not one jot the more qualified for the succeeding in Poetry; so a man may have that sort of Imagination, which is necessary for the judging of Painting and Carving, and yet may not be at all Capacitated to give his judgment of Poetry; and this, if we will believe the Testimony of *Horace,* was the case of the great *Alexander.*

Idem rex ille Poema
Qui tam ridiculum tam care prodigus emit
Edicto vetuit nequis se præter Apellem
Pingeret aut alius Lysippo duceret æra.
Fortis Alexandri vultum simulantia quod si,
Judicium subtile videndis artibus illud,
Ad libros & ad hæc Musarum dona vocares
Bæotum in Crasso Jurares aere natum.

We may say the very same thing of Judgment, a man may be well qualify'd to judge of Fortifications, or the Interest of Princes, and yet may show himself to be very weak, when he comes to judge of Poetry (not that I think that either a Statesman or an Ingineer is obliged to understand Poetry; but he who pretends to judge of any thing which he does not understand is certainly so far weak.) So that 'tis Education and Application, which qualify the Imagination and the Judgment for the passing a right Judgment on Poetry; and therefore 'tis time to proceed to the consideration of those two Heads.

Secondly, then in the Reign of King *Charles* the Second, a considerable part of an Audience had such an Education as qualified them to judge of Comedy. That Reign was a Reign of Pleasure, even the entertainments of their Closet were all delightful. Poetry and Eloquence were then their Studies, and that human, gay, and sprightly Philosophy, which qualify'd them to relish the only reasonable pleasures which man can have in the World, and those are Conversation and Dramatick Poetry. In their Closets they cultivated at once their Imaginations and Judgments, to make themselves the fitter for conversation, which requires them both. And the Conversation of those times was so different from what it is now, that it let them as much into that particular knowledge of Mankind, which is requisite for the judging of Comedy, as the present Conversation removes us from it. The discourse, which now every where turns upon Interest, rolled then upon the Manners and Humours of Men. For let us take a little view of the state of the Nation, during the Reign of that Prince, from the year Sixty to Eighty. They were overjoy'd to find themselves delivered from the apprehensions of another Civil War, and not only in quiet, but as they thought, in profound security. They were at the same time free from Fears and Taxes, and by reason of that plenty which overflowed among them, they were in the happiest condition in the World, to attain to that knowledge of Mankind, which is requisite for the judging of Comedy. For while some were dissolv'd in the wantonness of ease, and grown careless how they exposed themselves, others were at leisure to observe their frailties; to watch the turns and counterturns of their Humours, and trace the windings of them up to their very springs. All the sheer Originals in Town were known, and in some measure copied. But now the case is vastly different. For all those great and numerous Originals are reduced to one single Coxcomb, and that is the foolish false Politician. For from *Westminster* to *Wapping,* go where you will, the conversation turns upon Politicks. Where-ever you go, you find Atheists and Rakes standing up for the Protestant Religion, Fellows who never saw a Groat in their Lives, vehemently maintaining Property, and People that are in the *Fleet* and the *Kings Bench* upon execution for their Lives, going together by the ears about the Liberty of the Subject. There is not the emptyest Coxcomb in Town, but has got his Politick Shake and his Shrug, and is pretending to wisdom by Gestures, while his Tongue,

the surest Index of his Soul, declares him a very Ass.
Go among either the Lame or the Blind, and you shall
find them intercepting the Plate Fleet, or sending Forces
into *Italy*. For all Men are alarmed by the present
posture of affairs, because all men believe they are concerned, which universal alarm has reduced those
Characters which were so various before, to a dull
uniformity. For great Fools, like great Wits, require
leisure and ease to shew themselves. And as this
uniformity of Characters has directly done a great deal
of harm to Comedy, because our Poets, for want of
Originals are forced to bring Copies, or else to draw
after their own Imagination, rather than after the Life,
so it has hurt it too indirectly, by the harm which it has
done to Playing. For observation is necessary to our
Comedians as well as our Comick Poets. And I verily
believe, that the want of Originals has been one great
cause of the decay of acting. And the decay of this is
the cause that when a good Comedy does come to be
writ, it can never be lik'd because it can never be Acted,
for the better a Play is acted, the better it is sure to
succeed. Now an empty trifling Play can better be
Acted by ill or indifferent Actors, than one that is
strongly writ in Nature, because the last requires
Masters.

Besides, there are three sorts of People now in our
Audiences, who have had no education at all; and who
were unheard of in the Reign of King *Charles* the Second.
A great many younger Br[o]thers, Gentlemen born, who
have been kept at home, by reason of the pressure of
the Taxes. Several People, who made their Fortunes
in the late War, and who from a state of obscurity, and
perhaps of misery, have risen to a condition of distinction
and plenty. I believe that no man will wonder, if these

People, who in their original obscurity, could never attain to any higher entertainment than Tumbling and Vaulting and Ladder Dancing, and the delightful diversions of *Jack Pudding,* should still be in Love with their old sports, and encourage these noble Pastimes still upon the Stage. But a 3d sort of People, who may be said to have had no education at all in relation to us and our Plays, is that considerable number of Foreigners, which within these last twenty years have been introduc'd among us; some of whom not being acquainted with our Language, and consequently with the sense of our Plays, and others disgusted with our extravagant, exorbitant Rambles, have been Instrumental in introducing Sound and Show, where the business of the Theatre does not require it, and particularly a sort of a soft and wanton Musick, which has used the People to a delight which is independant of Reason, a delight that has gone a very great way towards the enervating and dissolving their minds.

But thirdly, in the Reign of King *Charles* the Second, a considerable part of an Audience had that due application, which is requisite for the judging of Comedy. They had first of all leisure to attend to it. For that was an age of Pleasure, and not of Business. They were serene enough to receive its impressions: For they were in Ease and Plenty. But in the present Reign, a great part of the Gentlemen have not leisure, because want throws them upon employments, and there are ten times more Gentlemen now in business, than there were in King *Charles* his Reign. Nor have they serenity, by Reason of a War, in which all are concerned, by reason of the Taxes which make them uneasie. By reason that they are attentive to the events of affairs, and too full of great and real events, to receive due impressions from the imaginary ones of the Theatre. They come to a Playhouse full of some business which they have been solliciting, or of some Harrangue which they are to make the next day; so that they meerly come to unbend, and are utterly incapable of duly attending to the just and harmonious Symetry of a beautiful design. Besides, the Faction which has been so long in their Politicks is got into their Pleasures, and they refuse to be delighted with what some People write, not because they really dislike it, but only because others are pleased with it, as if any one should be such a Sot as to refuse Champaign, because his Enemy finds it delicious.

Thus, Sir, I have shewn, that in King *Charles* the Second's time, a considerable part of an Audience were qualified to judge for themselves, and that at present a considerable part of our Audiences are not qualify'd for it. But there is an important thing behind, which I have only time to hint at. That they who were not qualified to judge in King *Charles* his Reign, were influenced by the authority of those who were; and that is of the Court, which always in a peculiar manner influences the pleasures of the Gentry. And some of the most eminent young Courtiers had then an admirable taste of Comedy, as it must always happen in a Court where the Prince delights in it. But the Court of *England* at present has other things to mind than to take care of Comedy. 'Tis true, there may be several Gentlemen in it who are capable of setting others right, but neither have they leisure to do it, nor have others time to attend to them.

Thus, Sir, have I endeavour'd to shew the causes of the degeneracy of taste in Comedy; which is every day more and more declining. I might perhaps say the same thing concerning Tragedy: For, in short, Sir, some of the best Tragedies which have been writ since *Shake-*

spear's time were writ in the Reign of *Charles* the Second. And you are almost the only Person alive, who are capable of Writing a true Tragedy. In that which you have already given us, you took the judicious advice of *Horace,* and chose a known subject from one of the noblest Poems in the World. Your incidents have both Art and Nature to maintain them, and are as probable as they are surprizing: Your Characters resembling your sentiments, easie, proper, great, elevated; your Expressions Strong without Constraint, Engaging without Artifice, Charming without Wantonness, and Majestick without Pride. These, Sir, together with that noble Fire which ev'ry where reigns in your Writings, are the qualities which make you a Poet, and so clearly distinguish you from the Common numerous Playwrights that pass upon the easie Town.

But 'tis high time to have done, for I am not guilty of a fault myself, but what is worse, making you guilty of a greater. For I am declaring what all the World is sensible of, and you are blushing only at hearing the truth.   I am,

SIR,

Your most Humble and most Obedient Servant,

JOHN DENNIS.

II. THE GROUNDS OF CRITICISM IN POETRY

1704

Chapter I.

*The Design of the following Treatise, is the
Re-establishment of Poetry.*

THE Design of the ensuing Treatise, whether we consider the Importance or the Extent of it, is perhaps the
greatest in this kind of Writing, that has been conceiv'd
by the Moderns; for 'tis no less than an Attempt to
restore and re-establish the noblest Art in every Branch
of it: an Art, that by the Barbarity of the Times, is
fallen and sunk in them all, and has been driven and
banish'd from every Country excepting *England* alone;
and is even here so miserably fallen for the most part by
the Extravagance of its Professors, and by the Unskilful-
ness of its Admirers, that we have reason to apprehend
it to be departing from hence too.

That Poetry is the noblest of all Arts, and by consequence the most instructive and most beneficial to Mankind, may be prov'd by the concording Testimony of the
greatest Men, who have liv'd in every Age; the greatest
Philosophers, the greatest Heroes, and the greatest
Statesmen, who have, as it were, unanimously cherish'd,
esteem'd, admir'd it: and never has it been disesteem'd
or neglected by any but some Pretenders to Wisdom, and
by some contemptible Politicasters, Persons who have
got into the Management of Affairs only by the Weakness
of those who have employ'd them, and who have utterly
wanted Capacity to know what a glorious Use may be

made of it, for the Benefit of Civil Society. But in the Sequel of this Discourse, by discovering the Nature of Poetry in general (which seems to me to have been hitherto but little understood) I shall clearly shew its Excellence, and the Importance of this Undertaking. And by laying down either the general Rules of it, or by tracing out that sublime Art, which to make use of *Milton*'s Expression, teaches what the Laws are of a true Epick Poem, what of a Dramatick, what of a Lyrick, what Decorum is, what is the grand Masterpiece to observe; I shall not only lay a good Foundation for the judging of the Performance of the several Poets, whose Works I have undertaken to examine, but shall, as *Milton* says in his Treatise of Education to Mr. *Hartlip,* soon make the World perceive what despicable Creatures our common Rhymers and Play-wrights are, and shew them what religious, what glorious, and magnificient Use may be made of Poetry, both in Divine and in Human Things.

Chapter II.

That Poetry is to be establish'd, by laying down the Rules.

THAT an Art, so Divine in its Institution, is sunk and profan'd, and miserably debas'd, is a thing that is confess'd by all. But since Poetry is fallen from the Excellence which it once attain'd to, it must be fallen either by the want of Parts, or want of Industry, or by the Errors of its Professors. But that it cannot be for want of Parts, we have shewn clearly in the Advancement of modern Poetry; nor can it be supposed to be for want of Industry, since so many of its Professors have no other Dependance. It remains then that it must have fallen by their Errors, and for want of being guided right. Since therefore 'tis for want of knowing by what Rules they ought to proceed, that Poetry is fallen so low, it follows then that it is the laying down of those Rules alone, that can re-establish it. In short, Poetry is either an Art, or Whimsy and Fanaticism. If it is an Art, it follows that it must propose an End to it self, and afterwards lay down proper Means for the attaining that End: For this is undeniable, that there are proper Means for the attaining of every End, and those proper Means in Poetry we call the Rules. Again, if the End of Poetry be to instruct and reform the World, that is, to bring Mankind from Irregularity, Extravagance, and Confusion, to Rule and Order, how this should be done by a thing that is in it self irregular and extravagant, is difficult to be conceiv'd. Besides, the Work of every reasonable Creature must derive its Beauty from Regularity; for Reason is Rule and Order, and nothing can be irregular either in our Conceptions or our Actions, any further than it swerves from Rule, that is, from Reason. As Man is the more perfect, the more he resembles his Creator; the Works of Man must needs be more perfect, the more they resemble his Maker's. Now the Works of God, tho infinitely various, are extremely regular.

The Universe is regular in all its Parts, and it is to that exact Regularity that it owes its admirable Beauty. The Microcosm owes the Beauty and Health both of its Body and Soul to Order, and the Deformity and Distempers of both to nothing but the want of Order. Man was created, like the rest of the Creatures, regular, and as long as he remain'd so, he continu'd happy; but as soon as he fell from his Primitive State, by transgressing Order, Weakness and Misery was the immediate Consequence of that universal Disorder that immediately follow'd in his Conceptions, in his Passions and Actions.

The great Design of Arts is to restore the Decays that happen'd to human Nature by the Fall, by restoring Order: The Design of Logick is to bring back Order, and Rule, and Method to our Conceptions, the want of which causes most of our Ignorance, and all our Errors. The Design of moral Philosophy is to cure the Disorder that is found in our Passions, from which proceeds all our Unhappiness, and all our Vice; as from the due Order that is seen in them, comes all our Virtue and all our Pleasure. But how should these Arts re-establish Order, unless they themselves were regular? Those Arts that make the Senses instrumental to the Pleasure of the Mind, as Painting and Musick, do it by a great deal of Rule and Order: Since therefore Poetry comprehends the Force of all these Arts of Logick, of Ethicks, of Eloquence, of Painting, of Musick; can any thing be more ridiculous than to imagine, that Poetry it self should be without Rule and Order?

Chapter III.

What Poetry is, and that it attains its End by exciting of Passion.

WE have said above, that as Poetry is an Art, it must have a certain End, and that there must be Means that are proper for the attaining that End, which Means are otherwise call'd the Rules: But that we may make this appear the more plainly, let us declare what Poetry is. Poetry then is an Art, by which a Poet excites Passion (and for that very Cause entertains Sense) in order to satisfy and improve, to delight and reform the Mind, and so to make Mankind happier and better: from which it appears that Poetry has two Ends, a subordinate, and a final one; the subordinate one is Pleasure, and the final one is Instruction.

First, The subordinate End of Poetry is to please, for that Pleasure is the Business and Design of Poetry is evident; because Poetry, unless it pleases, nay and pleases to a height, is the most contemptible thing in the World. Other things may be borne with if they are indifferent, but Poetry, unless it is transporting, is abominable: nay, it has only the name of Poetry, so inseparable is Pleasure from the very nature of the Thing.

But, *Secondly,* The final End of Poetry is to reform the Manners: As Poetry is an Art, Instruction must be its final End; but either that Instruction must consist in reforming the Manners, or it cannot instruct at all, and consequently be an Art; for Poetry pretends to no other Instruction as its final End. But since the final End of Poetry is to reform the Manners, nothing can be according to the true Art of it, which is against Religion, or which runs counter to moral Virtue, or to the true Politicks, and to the Liberty of Mankind: and every thing which is against the last, tends to the Corruption and Destruction of Mankind; and consequently every thing against the last, must be utterly inconsistent with the true Art of Poetry.

Now the proper Means for Poetry, to attain both its subordinate and final End, is by exciting Passion.

1st, The subordinate End of Poetry, which is to please, is attain'd by exciting Passion, because every one who is pleas'd is mov'd, and either desires, or rejoices, or admires, or hopes, or the like. As we are mov'd by Pleasure which is Happiness, to do every thing we do, we may find upon a little Reflection, that every Man is incited by some Passion or other, either to Action, or to Contemplation; and Passion is the Result either of Action or of Contemplation, as long as either of them please; and the more either of them pleases, the more they are attended with Passion. The Satisfaction that we receive from Geometry it self, comes from the Joy of having found out Truth, and the Desire of finding more. And the Satiety that seizes us upon too long a Lecture, proceeds from nothing but from the Weariness of our Spirits, and consequently from the Cessation or the Decay of those two pleasing Passions. But,

2dly, Poetry attains its final End, which is the reforming the Minds of Men, by exciting of Passion. And here I dare be bold to affirm, that all Instruction whatever depends upon Passion. The moral Philosophers themselves, even the dryest of them, can never instruct and reform, unless they move; for either they make Vice odious and Virtue lovely, or they deter you from one by the Apprehension of Misery, or they incite you to the other by the Happiness they make you expect from it; or they work upon your Shame, or upon your Pride, or upon your Indignation. And therefore Poetry instructs and reforms more powerfully than Philosophy can do, because it moves more powerfully: And therefore it instructs more easily too. For whereas all Men have Passions, and great Passions of one sort or another; and whereas those Passions will be employ'd, and whatever way they move, they that way draw the Man; it follows, that Philosophy can instruct but hardly, because it moves but gently: for the violent Passions not finding their account in those faint Emotions, begin to rebel and fly to their old Objects; whereas Poetry, at the same time that it instructs us powerfully, must reform us easily;

because it makes the very Violence of the Passions
contribute to our Reformation. For the Generality of
Mankind are apparently sway'd by their Passions, nay,
and perhaps the very best and wisest of them. The
greatest Philosophers and the greatest Princes are
influenc'd by their Favourites, and so are the wisest
Magistrates. And 'tis for this reason that not only the
Devil, who must be suppos'd to understand human
Nature, corrupts Mankind by their Passions; (for
Temptation is nothing but the inclining Men to such and
such Actions, by the raising such and such Passions in
them) but God himself, who made the Soul, and best
understands its Nature, converts it by its Passions. For
whereas Philosophy pretends to correct human Passions
by human Reason, that is, things that are strong and
ungovernable, by something that is feeble and weak;
Poetry by the force of the Passion, instructs and reforms
the Reason: which is the Design of the true Religion, as
we have shewn in another place. So that we have here
already laid down one great Rule, necessary for the succeeding in Poetry: for since it can attain neither its
subordinate nor its final End, without exciting of Passion,
it follows, That where there is nothing which directly
tends to the moving of that, there can be no Poetry; and
that consequently a Poet ought to contrive every thing in
order to the moving of Passion, that not only the Fable,
the Incidents and Characters, but the very Sentiments and
the Expressions, ought all to be design'd for that. For
since Poetry pleases and instructs us more even than
Philosophy it self, only because it moves us more, it
follows, That the more Poetry moves, the more it pleases
and instructs: and it is for this reason that Tragedy, to
those who have a Taste of it, is both more pleasing and

more instructing than Comedy. And this naturally brings us to the dividing Poetry into the greater and the less.

1. The greater Poetry is an Art by which a Poet justly and reasonably excites great Passion, that he may please and instruct; and comprehends Epick, Tragick, and the greater Lyrick Poetry.

2. The less Poetry is an Art by which a Poet excites less Passion for the foremention'd Ends; and includes in it Comedy and Satire, and the little Ode, and Elegiack and Pastoral Poems. But first we shall treat of the former.

Chapter IV.

What the greater Poetry is, what Enthusiasm is.

THE greater Poetry then, is an Art by which a Poet justly and reasonably excites great Passion, in order to please and instruct, and make Mankind better and happier; so that the first and grand Rule in the greater Poetry is, that a Poet must every where excite great Passion: but in some Branches of the greater Poetry, it is impossible for a Poet every where to excite in a very great degree, that which we vulgarly call Passion: as in the Ode, for example, and in the Narration of the Epick Poem. It follows then, that there must be two sorts of Passion: *First,* That which we call Vulgar Passion; and *Secondly,* Enthusiasm.

First, Vulgar Passion, or that which we commonly call Passion, is that which is moved by the Objects themselves, or by the Ideas in the ordinary Course of Life; I mean, that common Society which we find in the World. As for example, Anger is moved by an Affront that is offer'd us in our presence, or by the Relation of one;

Pity by the Sight of a mournful Object, or the Relation of one; Admiration or Wonder, (the common Passion, I mean; for there is an Enthusiastick Admiration, as we shall find anon) by the Sight of a strange Object, or the Relation of one. But,

Secondly, Enthusiastick Passion, or Enthusiasm, is a Passion which is moved by the Ideas in Contemplation, or the Meditation of things that belong not to common Life. Most of our Thoughts in Meditation are naturally attended with some sort and some degree of Passion; and this Passion, if it is strong, I call Enthusiasm. Now the Enthusiastick Passions are chiefly six, Admiration, Terror, Horror, Joy, Sadness, Desire, caus'd by Ideas occurring to us in Meditation, and producing the same Passions that the Objects of those Ideas would raise in us, if they were set before us in the same light that those Ideas give us of them. And here I desire the Reader to observe, that Ideas in Meditation are often very different from what Ideas of the same Objects are, in the course of common Conversation. As for example, the Sun mention'd in ordinary Conversation, gives the Idea of a round flat shining Body, of about two foot diameter. But the Sun occurring to us in Meditation, gives the Idea of a vast and glorious Body, and the top of all the visible Creation, and the brightest material Image of the Divinity. I leave the Reader therefore to judge, if this Idea must not necessarily be attended with Admiration; and that Admiration I call Enthusiasm. So Thunder mention'd in common Conversation, gives an Idea of a black Cloud, and a great Noise, which makes no great Impression upon us. But the Idea of it occurring in Meditation, sets before us the most forcible, most resistless, and consequently the most dreadful Phænomenon in Nature: So that this Idea must move a great deal of Terror in us, and 'tis this sort of Terror that I call Enthusiasm. And 'tis this sort of Terror, or Admiration, or Horror, and so of the rest, which express'd in Poetry make that Spirit, that Passion, and that Fire, which so wonderfully please.

Thus there are two sorts of Passions to be rais'd in Poetry, the Vulgar and the Enthusiastick; to which last, the Vulgar is preferable, because all Men are capable of being moved by the Vulgar, and a Poet writes to all: But the Enthusiastick are more subtle, and thousands have no feeling and no notion of them. But where the Vulgar cannot be moved in a great degree, there the Enthusiastick are to be rais'd. Therefore in those parts of Epick Poetry, where the Poet speaks himself, or the eldest of the Muses for him, the Enthusiastick Passions are to prevail, as likewise in the greater Ode. And the Vulgar Passions are to prevail in those parts of an Epick and Dramatick Poem, where the Poet introduces Persons holding Conversation together. And perhaps this might be one Reason, for which *Aristotle* might prefer Tragedy to Epick Poetry, because the Vulgar Passions prevail more in it, and are more violently moved in it; and therefore Tragedy must necessarily both please and instruct, more generally than Epick Poetry. We shall then treat of the Vulgar Passions when we come to speak of Tragedy, in which Poem they ought most to prevail: we shall then more particularly shew the surest and most powerful ways of raising Compassion and Terror, which are the true Tragical Passions.

We shall at present treat of the Enthusiastick Passions, and how they are to be rais'd. We have taken notice above, that they are to be mov'd by Ideas occurring in Contemplation; that they are to be mov'd in a great degree, and yet justly and reasonably. We shall now

shew, that the strongest Enthusiastick Passions, that are
justly and reasonably rais'd, must be rais'd by religious
Ideas; that is, by Ideas which either shew the Attributes
of the Divinity, or relate to his Worship. And this we
shall endeavour to prove, 1*st,* By Reason: 2*dly,* By
Authority: 3*dly,* By Examples.

1*st,* We shall endeavour to prove it by Reason. Since
the foresaid Passions are to be mov'd in a great degree,
and are to be mov'd by their Ideas, it follows, that to be
justly and reasonably mov'd, they must be mov'd by
great Ideas. And therefore the stronger the Enthusiasm
is, the greater must the Ideas be. Now those Ideas are
certainly the greatest, which are worthiest to move the
greatest and the wisest Men: for there the Enthusiastick
Passions in Poetry are truly admirable, when the greater
and more violent they are, the more they show the Largeness of Soul, and Greatness of Capacity of the Writer.
For Men are mov'd for two Reasons, either because they
have weak Minds and Souls, that are capable of being
mov'd by little Objects, and consequently by little and
ordinary Ideas; or because they have Greatness of Soul
and Capacity, to discern and feel the great ones: for the
Enthusiastick Passions being caus'd by the Ideas, it
follows, that the more the Soul is capable of receiving
Ideas whose Objects are truly great and wonderful, the
greater will the Enthusiasm be that is caus'd by those
Ideas. From whence it follows, that the greater the Soul
is, and the larger the Capacity, the more will it be mov'd
by religious Ideas; which are not only great and wonderful, but which almost alone are great and wonderful to
a great and wise Man; and which never fail to move
very strongly, unless it is for want of due Reflection, or
want of Capacity in the Subject.

Since therefore the Enthusiasm in the greater Poetry,

is to hold proportion with the Ideas; and those Ideas are certainly the greatest, which are worthiest to move the greatest and the wisest Men: and Divine Ideas, or Ideas which shew the Attributes of God, or relate to his Worship, are worthiest to move the greatest and the wisest Men; because such Ideas belong to Objects which are only truly above them, and consequently truly Admirable, Desirable, Joyful, Terrible, *&c.* it follows, That the greatest and strongest Enthusiasm that can be employ'd in Poetry, is only justly and reasonably to be deriv'd from Religious Ideas.

But here we desire the Reader's leave to make this Observation, That since Religious and Divine Ideas, or Ideas which shew the Attributes or relate to the Worship of the Divinity, are the worthiest to move the greatest and the wisest Men; and the greater and wiser the Men are, the more they must move and raise them; as for example, the greater and more comprehensive the Soul is, which reflects upon the Idea of God, the more that Idea must fill that Soul with Admiration: it follows, That as great Passion only is the adequate Language of the greater Poetry, so the greater Poetry is only the adequate Language of Religion; and that therefore the greatest Passion is the Language of that sort of Poetry, because that sort of Poetry is the worthiest Language of Religion.

But, *2dly,* We shall proceed to prove by Authority, That the strongest Enthusiastick Passions in Poetry are only justly and reasonably to be rais'd by religious Ideas: And this we shall show by the Authority of the greatest Criticks among the Antients, *Aristotle, Hermogenes,* and *Longinus.*

(1.) *Aristotle* says, in the third Book of his Rhetorick, *cap.* 2, & 3. That the frequent Use of Metaphors,

Dialects, Epithets, is a great deal fitter for Poetry than it is for Prose, because they are the Language of Passion; and Poetry is more Passionate or more Enthusiastick than Prose, for this Reason, because the Persons and the Things of which Poetry treats, are many degrees above those which are the Subjects of Prose. Now all the World knows, that the *Grecians* treated of the greatest human Persons and Things in their Prose, but that Poetry was a Language which they reserv'd for their Gods, and for the Things which related to them. And I am apt to believe, that Poetry from hence was call'd the Language of the Gods, because whenever the *Grecians* in the Poetical Times introduced their Gods speaking, they were sure to speak in Verse. But,

(2.) *Hermogenes,* in the sixth Chapter of the first Book of his Treatise, concerning the Forms of Speech, tells us, that there are four kinds of Thoughts or Ideas, or Conceptions, which were proper to give that Elevation and Gravity to a Discourse, which by their Union compose that Quality in Writing which we call Majesty.

1. The first and principal of them are all such Thoughts or Ideas of God, as are worthy of the Divinity; not like some of the *Homerical* Conceptions of *Jupiter,* which, says *Hermogenes,* being more Human than Divine, and unworthy of the Divinity, are contrary to true Majesty.

2. Next to these the Conceptions which give Elevation and Gravity, and consequently Majesty to a Discourse, are such Thoughts or Ideas concerning the Works of God, as are worthy the Divine Workmanship.

3. The third sort of Conceptions are, of such Things as are indeed themselves Divine, but they are such Emanations of Divinity, as are to be seen in Men; as

Justice, Temperance, Fortitude, Nature, Law, and the like; to which may be added, Number, Power and Might.

4. The fourth sort are, of Things that indeed are Human, but are reputed Great and Illustrious, as Conquest, Riches, Nobility, &c. But here I desire the Reader to observe, that *Hermogenes* is here speaking concerning Pieces of Eloquence, and such Discourses as are writ in Prose; for it is certain, that these last Ideas, as they are of Things that are merely Human, can never afford the greatest Spirit that can be employ'd in Poetry. For as the Objects themselves are not truly great, because, as *Longinus* says, a Man who has it in his power to possess them, shows himself great by contemning them; it is impossible that a Spirit that is very great, can flow from these Ideas, because the Spirit that is very great must hold proportion with its Ideas, as the Ideas must with their Objects: and therefore these Ideas cannot be great, because their Objects are not great.

We ought now, in the third place, to proceed to the Authority of *Longinus*. But that we may diversify this Treatise the more, and make it the more entertaining, we shall first shew Examples of the several Kinds of the foremention'd Thoughts, producing that sort of Spirit in Poetry which we call Enthusiastick Admiration: and that we may show the Reader more plainly how that Spirit is produc'd, we shall set before him as near as we can, such kind of Thoughts as inspire the Soul with Admiration alone, uncomplicated with Terror, or any other Passion.

These Thoughts, or Ideas, which produce that Enthusiasm which we call Admiration, are Thoughts or Ideas which hold some proportion with such Objects, as in their nature are truly admirable. Those Thoughts or Ideas are of two sorts, Ideas of Sounds, and Ideas of

Things. We shall then have occasion to treat of Ideas of Sounds, when we come to speak of Terror, and some of the other Enthusiastick Passions: we shall at present treat of such Ideas of Things, as are proper to excite Admiration.

We have shown that *Hermogenes,* in the first Rank of these, reckons those Thoughts and Ideas of God, that are worthy of the Creator: Such is the Invocation of *Milton,* in the beginning of *Paradise Lost.*

> And chiefly Thou, O Spirit! that dost prefer
> Before all Temples, th' upright Heart and pure,
> Instruct me, for Thou knowst, Thou from the first
> Wast present, and with mighty Wings o'erspread,
> Dove-like sat'st brooding on the vast Abyss,
> And mad'st it pregnant; what in me is dark,
> Illumine, what is low raise and support,
> That to the Height of this great Argument
> I may assert Eternal Providence,
> And justify the Ways of God to Men.

And that it was these Divine Ideas, that rais'd his Soul, and fill'd it with Admiration, and with a noble Greatness, (which Passion express'd, makes the Greatness of the Spirit) the Reader who goes back to the beginning of the Poem, will find no manner of room to doubt. For *Milton,* like a Master, begins with a gentle Spirit, which he continues for the twelve first Lines: In the thirteenth, where he speaks of the Boldness of his Attempt, he begins to rise; and in the nineteenth, where he talks of the Power of the Holy Ghost, he is quite upon the Wings.

Instruct me, for Thou know'st, Thou from the first.

And such are the Thoughts concerning God, which are spread thro that Divine Dialogue between God and *Adam,* in the eighth Book of the same Poem: I believe the Reader will pardon the length if I repeat it, which I am very much inclin'd to do, not only because I challenge the most zealous Admirers of Antiquity to produce any thing like it, from among all the Dialogues in *Homer* and *Virgil,* that are between either a God or a Man, or between one God and another; but because the Reader who sees the Inequalities in it, will easily see that it derives its Greatness and its Sublimity from the becoming Thoughts which it has of the Deity. That the Reader may thorowly understand it, without turning to the Book, the occasion of it is this: *Adam,* relating the History of the Creation to the Angel *Raphael,* tells him, how after he had given Names to the Birds and the Beasts, which God had brought before him for that purpose; he who understood their Natures, and saw none of them was fit for his Conversation, desir'd of God in the following Words a Partner fit for Human Society.

> Oh by what Name, for Thou above all these,
> Above Mankind, or ought than Mankind higher
> Surpassest far my naming, how may I
> Adore Thee? Author of this Universe,
> And all this Good to Man, for whose Well-being
> So amply, and with Hands so liberal,
> Thou hast provided all things. But with me
> I see not who partakes; in Solitude
> What Happiness? Who can enjoy alone?
> Or all enjoying, what Contentment find?
> Thus I presumptuous; and the Vision bright,
> As with a Smile more brightned, thus reply'd.

Here by the way I desire the Reader to observe, how
the Spirit of the Poem sinks, when *Adam* comes from
God to himself; and how it rises again, when he returns
to his Creator. But let us proceed to God's Reply.

> What call'st thou Solitude? Is not the Earth
> With various living Creatures, and the Air
> Replenish'd; and all these at thy Command,
> To come and play before thee? Know'st thou not
> Their Language and their Ways? They also know,
> And reason not contemptibly; with these
> Find Pastime, and bear Rule, thy Realm is large.
> So spake the Universal Lord, and seem'd
> So ordering: I with leave of Speech implor'd,
> And humble Deprecation, thus reply'd.

> Let not my Words offend Thee, Heavenly Power,
> My Maker be propitious while I speak:
> Hast not thou made me here thy Substitute,
> And these inferior far, beneath me set?
> Among Unequals what Society
> Can sort? What Harmony or true Delight,
> Which must be mutual in proportion due,
> Given and receiv'd; but in disparity
> The one intense, the other still remiss,
> Cannot well suit with either, but soon prove
> Tedious alike? Of Fellowship I speak,
> Such as I seek fit to participate
> All rational Delight; wherein the Brute
> Cannot be human Consort: They rejoice
> Each with their Kind, Lion with Lioness;
> So fitly them in Pairs thou hast combin'd:
> Much less can Bird with Beast, or Fish with Fowl

So well converse; nor with the Ox the Ape;
Worse then can Man with Beast, and least of all.

    Whereto the Almighty answer'd, not displeas'd;
A nice and subtle Happiness, I see,
Thou to thy self proposest, in the choice
Of thy Associates, *Adam,* and wilt taste
No Pleasure, tho in Pleasure solitary:
What think'st thou then of me, and this my State?
Seem I to thee sufficiently possest
Of Happiness or not, who am alone
From all Eternity?   For none I know
Second to me, or like, equal much less:
How have I then, with whom to hold Converse,
Save with the Creatures which I made, and those
To me inferior infinite Descents
Beneath what other Creatures are to thee?

The Reader may easily see, that here is all that is great
and sublime in Reason, express'd with the Spirit of that
just Admiration, with which such worthy Thoughts of
the Deity must naturally fill the Soul.   But now let us
see *Adam*'s Answer.

    He ceas'd.   I lowly answer'd, To attain
The Height and Depth of thy Eternal Ways,
All Human Thoughts come short: Supreme of Things,
Thou in thy self art perfect; and in Thee
Is no Deficience found: not so is Man,
But in degree, the Cause of his Desire
By Conversation with his Like to help
Or solace his Defects: no need that Thou
Shouldst propagate, already Infinite,
And thro all Numbers absolute, tho One:

But Man by Number is to manifest
His single Imperfection, and beget
Like of his Like, his Image multiply'd,
In Unity defective, which requires
Collateral Love and dearest Amity.
Thou in thy Secrecy altho alone,
Best with thy self accompany'd, seek'st not
Social Communication; yet so pleas'd,
Canst raise thy Creature to what height thou wilt,
Of Union, or Communion deify'd:
I by conversing cannot these erect
From prone, nor in their ways Complaisance find.

What *Milton* saith of the Son of God hymn'd by the
Angels, in the third Book of that Poem, is very lofty and
elevated.

Thee next they sang, of all Creation first
Begotten Son, Divine Similitude,
In whose conspicuous Countenance, without Cloud
Made visible, the Almighty Father shines,
Whom else no Creature can behold; on Thee
Impress'd th' Effulgence of his Glory abides,
Transfus'd on Thee his ample Spirit rests:
He Heaven of Heavens, and all the Powers therein,
By Thee created, and by Thee threw down
Th' aspiring Dominations; Thou that Day
Thy Father's dreadful Thunder didst not spare,
Nor stop thy flaming Chariot-Wheels that shook
Heaven's everlasting Frame, while o'er the Necks
Thou drov'st of warring Angels disarray'd.

I have the rather mention'd these Verses, to show that
Milton was a little tainted with Socinianism, for by the

first Verse 'tis evident, that he look'd upon the Son of
God as a created Being. The last thing that I shall
mention, is, what God says of Himself, in the Seventh
Book; for speaking of Chaos, he says, that is boundless
because He is infinite.

> Boundless the Deep, because I Am who fill
> Infinitude, nor vacuous the Space;
> Tho I uncircumscrib'd my self retire,
> And put not forth my Goodness, which is free
> To act or not; Necessity and Chance
> Approach not Me, and what I will is Fate.

I could add an infinite Number of Examples, if it
were not altogether needless; for what has been said may
suffice to show, that a Poet, who intends to give that
Elevation and that Gravity to his Poem, which compose
Majesty, can fetch his Ideas from no Object so proper
as from God. For as great Elevation must be produced
by a great Admiration, as every Passion which the Poet
excites ought to be just and reasonable, and adapted to
its Object, it is impossible that any one, who is not stupid,
can seriously contemplate his Maker, but that his Soul
must be exalted and lifted up towards its Primitive
Objects, and be fill'd and inspired with the highest
Admiration. For 'tis then that the Enthusiasm in Poetry
is wonderful and divine, when it shows the Excellence
of the Author's Discernment, and the Largeness of his
Soul: now all the Ideas of God are such, that the more
large and comprehensive the Soul of a Poet is, and the
more it is capable of receiving those Ideas, the more is
it sure to be raised, and filled, and lifted to the Skies
with Wonder: The Spirit or the Passion in Poetry ought

to be proportion'd to the Ideas, and the Ideas to the Object, and when it is not so, it is utterly false. And therefore whenever in Poetry there is a great Spirit which is derived from Ideas, whose Objects are unworthy to move the Soul of a great and a wise Man, there that Spirit is either false, or at least has nothing sublimely admirable in it. But nothing but God, and what relates to God, is worthy to move the Soul of a great and a wise Man. But let us proceed to consider the glorious Works of the Creator, which, next to Himself, are worthy to move with Admiration all who are worthy to be called wise; because these, when they are reflected upon by the Great and the Wise, never fail to declare his Eternal Power and Godhead. Our Religion tells us, that the first, the greatest, and most glorious of his Works, are the Angels; who whether we consider their Power, their Swiftness, their Science, or their Sanctity, are fit Objects of our Admiration, and consequently of lofty and elevated Poetry. Let us see then how *Tasso* describes the Angel *Gabriel,* and his Descent, in the first Canto of the *Hierusalemme.*

Stan. XIII.

Cosi parlogli, & Gabriel s' accinse
Veloce ad essequir l'imposte cose.
La sua forma inuissibil d' Aria cinse,
Et al senso mortal la sottopose.
Humane membra, aspetto human si sinse;
Ma di celeste maestà il compose,
Tra Giouane, e fanciullo et à confine
Prese, & ornò di raggi ill biondo crine.

Stan. XIV.

Ali bianche uesti, c'han d'or le cime
Infaticabilmente agili, e preste
Fende i uenti, e le nubi, e ua sublime
Soura la Terra, e soura il Mar con queste.
Cosi uestito indirizzossi a l' ime
Parti del mondo il Messaggier Celeste,
Pria sul Libano monte ei si ritenne,
E si libro su l' adeguate penne.

And thus it is translated by *Fairfax,* who tho he by no means sheweth all the Spirit and Beauty of the Original, yet even in his Antiquated Version he discovers something of them.

Stan. XIII.

This said, the Angel swift himself prepar'd
To execute the Charge impos'd aright,
In form of airy Members fair embar'd,
His Spirits pure were subject to our Sight;
Like to a Man in shew and shape he far'd,
But full of heavenly Majesty and Might,
A Stripling seem'd he thrice five Winters old,
And radiant Beams adorn'd his Locks of Gold.

Stan. XIV.

Of Silver Wings he took a shining Pair,
Fringed with Gold, unweary'd, nimble, swift,
With these he parts the Winds, the Clouds, the Air,
And over Seas and Earth himself doth lift:
Thus clad he cut the Spheres and Circles fair,
And the pure Skies with sacred Feathers cleft,
On *Libanon* at first his Foot he set,
And shook his Wings with roary *May*-Dews wet.

But let us now consider *Michael*'s Descent in the Night, in the ninth Canto of the *Hierusalemme*.

Stan. LXII.

Venia scotendo con l' eterne piume
La Caligine densa, e i cupi horrori;
S'indoraua la notte al diuin lume,
Che spargea scintillando it uolto fuori;
Tale il Sol ne le nubi ha per costume,
Spiegar dopo la pioggia i bei colori;
Tal fuol fendendo il liquido sereno
Stella cader de la gran madre in seno.

Which in *English* is as follows:

And as he flew, the Darkness of his way,
And the black Horrors of the dreary Sky,
He shaking his Eternal Wings, dispers'd;
Old Night illustrated her dusky Face
With Rays, which his Celestial Eyes diffus'd.
Thus breaking thro a Storm, the Lord of Day
The Clouds with Purple and with Gold adorns;
And thus a Star from the Nocturnal Heav'n,
Into the Lap of our great Mother falls.

Where the Reader may take notice, that the Comparison of the Sun to *Michael* the Prince of the Arch-Angels, is extremely Just and Noble, because the top of the visible is admirably liken'd to the top of the invisible Creation: But in the two last Verses, *Tasso* has injudiciously been guilty of an Anticlimax. But now let us see how *Milton* describes the Descent of *Raphael* to Paradise, in the fifth Book of *Paradise Lost.*

Down thither prone in Flight
He speeds, and thro the vast Etherial Sky
Sails between Worlds and Worlds, with steddy Wing;
Now on the Polar Winds, then with quick Fan
Winnows the buxom Air, till within Soar
Of tow'ring Eagles, to all the Fowls he seems
A Phoenix, gazed by all, as that sole Bird
When to enshrine his Relicks in the Sun's
Bright Temple, to *Egyptian Thebes* he flies.
At once on th' Eastern Cliff of Paradise
He lights, and to his proper Shape returns:
A seraph wing'd: six Wings he wore to shade
His Lineaments Divine; the Pair that clad
Each Shoulder broad came mantling o'er his Breast
With Regal Ornament; the middle Pair
Girt like a Starry Zone his Waist, and round
Skirted his Loins and Thighs with downy Gold,
And Colours dipt in Heaven; the third his Feet
Shadow'd from either Heel with feather'd Mail,
Sky-tinctured Grain: like *Maia*'s Son he stood,
And shook his Plumes, that heavenly Fragrance fill'd
The Circuit wide.

Thus the Reader may see, by what has been said, that
the Ideas of Angels are exceeding proper to raise
Enthusiastick Admiration, as being the most glorious
and admirable Beings of the Creation, and which lead
the Soul immediately to its Creator. Next to these come
the other Creatures of the immaterial World, as Demons,
Apparitions of all sorts, and more particularly the Spirits
of Men departed: then follow Prophecies, Visions,
Miracles, Enchantments, Prodigies, and all things which
have an immediate Relation to the Wonders of another

World; of most of which we shall give Examples, when we come to speak of Terror, because they are rather wonderful, than they are admirable. We name those things wonderful, which we admire with fear.

The next Ideas that are most proper to produce the Enthusiasm of Admiration, are the great Phænomena of the Material World; because they too lead the Soul to its Maker, and shew, as the Apostle says, his eternal Power and Godhead: As the Heavens and Heavenly Bodies, the Sun, the Moon, the Stars, and the Immensity of the Universe, and the Motions of the Heaven and Earth. Witness what *Milton* says of the Sun, when he describes the Descent of Satan from Heaven-Gates to Paradise, *lib.* 3.

> Above them all,
> The golden Sun, in Splendour likest Heaven,
> Allur'd his Eye; thither his Course he bends
> Thro the calm Firmament, but up or down
> By Center, or Eccentrick, hard to tell,
> Or Longitude, where the great Luminary
> Aloof, the vulgar Constellations thick,
> That from his lordly Eye keep Distance due,
> Dispenses Light from far; they as they move
> Their Starry Dance in Numbers, that compute
> Days, Months, and Years tow'rds his all-chearing Lamp,
> Turn swift their various Motions, or are turn'd
> By his magnetick Beam, that gently warms
> The Universe.

But to show how very much these fall short of the immaterial Creation, a Poet, that he may make them more admirable, contrives to give Spirit and Soul to them.

> Where the great Luminary
> Aloof, the vulgar Constellations thick,
> That from his lordly Eye keep Distance due,
> Dispenses Light from far.

And in that noble Apostrophe to the Sun, the Devil makes in the beginning of the third Book.

> O thou that with surpassing Glory crown'd,
> Look'st from thy sole Dominion like the God
> Of this new World, at whose sight all the Stars
> Hide their diminish'd Heads, *&c.*

And in that admirable Passage in the seventh Book, where *Adam* desires the Angel to give him an Account of the Creation.

> If unforbid thou mayst unfold
> What we, not to explore the Secrets, ask,
> Of his Eternal Empire; but the more
> To magnify his Works, the more we know:
> And the great Light of Day yet wants to run
> Much of his Race, tho steep, suspense in Heaven,
> Held by thy Voice, thy potent Voice he hears,
> And longer will delay to hear thee tell
> His Generation, and the rising Birth
> Of Nature, from the unapparent Deep.

And in the Apostrophe to the Sun in the fourth Æneid.

Sol, qui Terrarum Flammis Opera omnia lustras.

Which is in *English*:

> Great God of Day, that with thy flaming Beams
> View'st and illuminat'st at once a World.

And in what *Milton* says of the Moon, in the fourth
Book of *Paradise Lost.*

> *Hesperus,* that led
> The Starry Host, rode brightest, till the Moon,
> Rising in clouded Majesty, at length
> Apparent Queen unveil'd her peerless Light,
> And o'er the Dark her silver Mantle threw.

For the Stars, and the Immensity of the Universe, I
desire the Reader would give me leave to bring an
Example, from the Paraphrase upon the *Te Deum,* where
thus the Angel speaks to God.

> Where'er at utmost Stretch we cast our Eyes,
> Thro the vast frightful Spaces of the Skies,
> Ev'n there we find thy Glory, there we gaze
> On thy bright Majesty's unbounded Blaze:
> Ten thousand Suns, prodigious Globes of Light,
> At once in broad Dimensions strike our Sight;
> Millions behind, in the remoter Skies,
> Appear but Spangles to our weary'd Eyes:
> And when our weary'd Eyes want farther Strength
> To pierce the Void's immeasurable Length,
> Our vigorous tow'ring Thoughts still further fly,
> And still remoter flaming Worlds descry:
> But even an Angel's comprehensive Thought,
> Cannot extend so far as thou hast wrought;
> Our vast Conceptions are by swelling, brought,
> Swallow'd and lost in Infinite, to nought.

The Idea of the World's Immensity is very proper to
produce Admiration, as leading us to the Glory of the
Creator; the Use that *Milton* makes of it, in the eighth
Book of *Paradise Lost.*

And for the Heavens wide Circuit, let it speak
The Maker's high Magnificence, who built
So spacious, and his Line stretch'd out so far,
That Man may know he dwells not in his own;
An Edifice too large for him to fill,
Lodg'd in a small Partition, and the rest
Ordain'd for Uses to his Lord best known.

And *Tasso* finely makes use of that noble Idea, to
repress the Pride and Ambition of Man. 'Tis in the 14th
Canto of the *Hierusalemme*, where *Hugo* bids *Godfrey*,
who had been rapt up to Heaven in a Vision, look down
from the Firmament to the Earth

Stan. IX.

China, poi disse, e gli additò la Terra,
Gli occhi a ciò, che quel globo ultimo serra.

X.

Quanto e uil la cagion, ch'a la uirtude
Humana e cola giù premio, e contrasto:
In che picciolo cerchio, e fra che nude
Solitudini e stretto il uostro fasto.
Lei come Isola, il mare intorno chiude,
E lui, c' hor Ocean chiamat'e, hor uasto
Nulla eguale a tai nomi ha in se di magno,
Ma e bassa palude, e breue stagno.

Stan. XI.

Cosi l' un disse e l' altro in giuso i lumi
Volse, quasi sdegnoso, e ne sorrise;
Che uide un punto sol, mar, terre, e fiumi,
Che qui paion distinti in tante guise,
Et ammiro, che pur a l' ombre, a i fumi,

La nostra folle humanita s' affise,
Seruo Imperio cercando, e muta fama,
Ne miri il ciel, ch' a se n' inuita, e chiama.

The following Verses of *Milton,* in the eighth Book of *Paradise Lost,* concerning the Magnitude and the Motions of the Heavens and Earth, derive a lofty Spirit from their Subject; for there says *Adam,*

When I behold this goodly Frame, this World,
Of Heaven and Earth, consisting, and compute
Their Magnitudes, this Earth a Spot, a Grain,
An Atom with the Firmament compar'd
And all her numbred Stars, that seem to roll
Spaces incomprehensible (for such
Their Distance argues, and their swift Return
Diurnal)

I could here bring Examples of the same kind of Spirit, deriv'd in due Proportion from Ideas of Sublunary Things; as of the four Elements, Water, Earth, Air, Fire; Winds and Meteors of all sorts, Seas, Rivers, Mountains: but I am afraid of running into length, and heaping too many Citations one upon another. Besides, it will be very convenient to make two or three Remarks here.

First, That the Wonders of the Universe afford the more admirable Ideas, and a more admirable Spirit, the more they shew the Attributes of the Creator, or relate to his Worship. *Secondly,* That Natural Philosophy is absolutely necessary to a Poet, not only that he may adorn his Poem with the useful Knowledge it affords, but because the more he knows the immense Phænomena of the Universe, the more he will be sure to admire them. For the more we know of Things that are never to be comprehended by us, the more that Knowledge must make

them appear wonderful. The third Remark that I shall
make is this, That they to whom Nature has given that
happy Elevation of Thought, which alone can make a
great Poet, will often be directed by that Tendency to
Greatness, which they have within them to Ideas, from
which they may derive a lofty Spirit; yet I shall shew,
by the Example of *Milton,* that they may often very
grosly fail, for want of a certain Knowledge of the
Objects from which they are to draw their Ideas: for
'tis for want of that Knowledge that *Milton* has done
the most unartful thing that perhaps ever was done, in
the two or three last Books of the greatest Poem that
ever was written by Man. For whereas in the first
eight Books, he had by the Mouth of God or Angels,
or of Man the Companion of Angels, divinely entertain'd
us with the wondrous Works of God; in the latter end
of his Poem, and more particularly, in the last Book,
he makes an Angel entertain us with the Works of
corrupted Man. From which it is very plain, by what
has been deliver'd above, concerning the nature of
Enthusiastick Passion, that that Angel could draw no
sort of Enthusiasm, and least of all that of Admiration
and Terror, which give the principal Greatness and
Elevation to Poetry. For how flat, how low, and
unmusical is the Relation of the Actions of fallen Man,
in the tenth Book, tho deliver'd by the Voice of
Divinity?

> On *Adam* last thus Judgment he pronounc'd;
> Because thou hast hearkned to the Voice of thy Wife,
> And eaten of the Tree, concerning which
> I charg'd thee, saying, Thou shalt not eat thereof,
> Curs'd is the Ground for thy sake, thou in Sorrow
> Shalt eat thereof all the Days of thy Life;

Thorns also, and Thistles it shall bring thee forth
Untill'd, and thou shalt eat the Herb of the Field.
In the Sweat of thy Face shalt thou eat Bread,
Till thou return unto the Ground, for thou
Out of the Ground wast taken; know thy Birth,
For Dust thou art, and shalt to Dust return.

The late Mr. *Dryden,* with a great deal of Injustice, us'd to attribute the Flatness of *Milton,* in this and some other Passages, to his getting into a Track of Scripture, as he was pleas'd to express himself: Whereas the thing that made him sink, was plainly the Poorness and Lowness of the Ideas. For how could the Works of corrupted Man afford any other to God or Angels? But what lofty, what glorious Ideas does a religious Mention of the Works of God afford to Man in his Primitive State, in that incomparable Hymn in the fifth Book of the same *Paradise Lost?* A Hymn, which tho it is intirely taken from Scripture, for it is apparently the 148th Psalm, yet will always stand alone, the Phœnix of lofty Hymns; and nothing equal to it, no nor second to it, can ever be produc'd from the *Grecian* Writers of Hymns. It is impossible I can do a greater pleasure to the Reader, who either has not read or does not remember *Milton,* than to insert it here.

These are thy glorious Works, Parent of Good,
Almighty, thine this Universal Frame,
Thus wondrous fair, thy Self how wondrous then!
Unspeakable; who sit'st above these Heavens,
To us invisible, or dimly seen
In these thy lowest Works; yet these declare
Thy Goodness beyond Thought, and Power Divine.
Speak ye who best can tell, ye Sons of Light,
Angels, for ye behold him, and with Songs

And Choral Symphonies, Day without Night
Circle his Throne rejoicing, ye in Heaven
On Earth join all the Creatures, to extol
Him first, Him last, Him midst, and without end.
Fairest of Stars, last in the Train of Night,
If better thou belong not to the Dawn,
Sure Pledge of Day, that crown'st the smiling Morn
With thy bright Circlet, praise him in thy Sphere,
While Day arises, that sweet Hour of Prime.
Thou Sun, of this great World both Eye and Soul,
Acknowledge Him thy Greater, sound his Praise
In thy eternal Course, both when thou climb'st,
And when High-Noon hast gain'd, and when thou fall'st.
Moon, that now meets the Orient Sun, now fly'st
With the fix'd Stars, fix'd in their Orb that flies;
And ye five other wandring Fires, that move
In mystick Dance not without Song, resound
His Praise, who out of Darkness call'd up Light.
Air and ye Elements, the eldest Birth
Of Nature's Womb, that in Quaternion run
Perpetual Circle multiform, and mix
And nourish all things, let your ceaseless Change
Vary to our great Maker still new Praise.
Ye Mists and Exhalations that now rise,
From Hill or steaming Lake, dusky or grey,
Till the Sun paint your fleecy Skirts with Gold,
In honour to the World's great Author rise,
Whether to deck with Clouds th' uncolour'd Sky,
Or wet the thirsty Earth with falling Showers;
Rising or falling still advance his Praise.
His Praise, ye Winds, that from four Quarters blow.
Breathe soft or loud; and wave your tops, ye Pines,
With every Plant, in sign of Worship wave.
Fountains, and ye that warble as ye flow

Melodious Murmurs, warbling tune his Praise.
Join Voices all ye living Souls, ye Birds
That singing up to Heaven-Gates ascend,
Bear on your Wings, and in your Notes, his Praise.
Ye that in Waters glide, and ye that walk
The Earth, and stately tread, or lowly creep,
Witness if I be silent Morn or Even,
To Hill or Valley, Fountain or fresh Shades,
Made vocal by my Song, and taught his Praise.
Hail Universal Lord, be bounteous still,
To give us only Good; and if the Night
Have gather'd ought of Evil or conceal'd,
Disperse it, as now Light dispels the Dark.

'Tis easy to discern here, with how much more
Divinity *Milton* makes a Man speak concerning the
Works of God, than he makes even the Creator himself
speak concerning the Works of Man. But here if the
Reader will pardon a Digression, I shall make an
Observation which may not be disagreeable to him.
The Observation is this, That all the Passages in *Paradise
Lost,* where God is introduced speaking, are flat to the
reserve of those in which he speaks of himself. Upon
inquiring into the Reason of it, I found, that according
to the Account which I have given of Poetical Enthusiasm, or of the Spirit of Poetry, it is nothing but that
Admiration and Terror, and the rest of those Enthu-
siastical Passions which are produced by their proper
Ideas, and which are to hold proportion with their Ideas,
as their Ideas must with their Objects. Now nothing
is more impossible than that God should either fear or
admire his own Creatures. But where *Milton* makes
him speak concerning himself, or his infinite Power,

there he makes him speak with a great Spirit, as in that
Passage of the sixth Book where he speaks to his Son.

Go then thou mightiest in thy Father's Might,
Ascend my Chariot, guide the rapid Wheels,
That shake Heaven's Basis, bring forth all my War,
My Bow and Thunder, my Almighty Arms.

'Tis plain that here the Poet is guilty of a Mistake,
but indeed a Mistake that is almost unavoidable; for 'tis
the Admiration and Terror that make the Spirit in the
preceding Verses; and it is impossible to conceive the
Ideas without feeling the Passions: so that *Milton,* while
he was rapt with Admiration, and moved with Terror
by the Ideas which he had conceiv'd, shifts Persons
insensibly, and forgetting who speaks, expresses himself
with those Passions which indeed are proper enough in
the Poet, but never can be so in the Deity. For neither
his Bow, nor his Almighty Arms, his Thunder, nor the
rapid Wheels that shake Heaven's Basis, can be in the
least admirable or terrible to the Divinity; so that Mr.
Cowley is certainly in the right in his Notes upon his
Davideis, where he tells us, that God is to be introduced
speaking simply. And this puts me in mind of an
extraordinary Argument of Monsieur *Paschal,* proving
the Divinity of our Saviour by the Simplicity of his
Stile; for, says he, our Saviour speaks of the sublimest
Subjects, even the Glories of the Kingdom of Heaven,
without being moved at all, which shews that he was
really God: for suppose a Peasant, says he, or an
ordinary Man should be carry'd to the Court of some
Prince, as for example the Great Mogul, and there be
shewn all his Riches, his Pomp, and his Power; this
Peasant at his return would certainly speak of these

things in extravagant terms, in terms that would sufficiently declare his Transport. But if the Mogul himself
was to speak of them, he who had been always used to
them, would speak without any Emotion. So, says
Monsieur *Paschal,* if any one else had deliver'd any thing
concerning the Glories of the Kingdom of Heaven, he
would certainly have done it with Transport, nay tho
he had been a Fanatick or an Impostor: for let those
Divine Ideas come how they will, 'tis impossible for Man
to think of them without being ravish'd by them. But
our Saviour, who was God, and who consequently had
been used to them from all Eternity, spoke of them
unconcern'd.

But let us come to the third sort of Thoughts, which,
Hermogenes says, are proper to give Elevation and
Gravity to a Discourse; and those are things which
indeed are divine, says he, but are often beheld in Men.
These Emanations of Divinity are the Virtues, such as
Temperance, Justice, Fortitude, Magnanimity; or Nature,
Law, Power, and the like. And we should never make
an end, if we should give Examples of all the Passages,
whose Greatness of Spirit is deriv'd from these Ideas.
But for the Reader's Entertainment, we shall mention
a few.

The Power of ruling our own Minds, which may be
refer'd to Temperance, gives noble Ideas, and consequently a noble Spirit, as we may see by the second Ode
of the second Book of *Horace.*

> *Latius regnes avidum domando*
> *Spiritum, quam si Lybiam remotis*
> *Gadibus jungas, & uterque Pænus*
> > *Serviat uni.*

Which in *English* is thus:

> Thou a more absolute Command shalt gain,
> A larger nobler Empire shalt obtain,
> If thy wild Lust of Pow'r thou canst restrain;
> Than if to *Spain* thy conqu'ring Troops should join
> The *Moors,* that fry beneath the parching Line,
> And both the *Carthaginians* should be thine.

And the Idea of Fortitude affords too a noble Spirit, as we may see in the twelfth of the *Æneis,* where *Turnus* replies to *Æneas,* who upbraids him with Fear.

> ——*Non me tua fervida terrent*
> *Dicta ferox. Dii me terrent, & Jupiter hostis.*

> 'Tis true, I am afraid, but not of thee,
> Nor thy vain threatning Words, insulting Man:
> The Gods alone can frighten me, and *Jove*
> Who now declares against me.

And that is a very remarkable Passage in the fifteenth Stanza of the fourth Canto of the *Hierusalemme*; for after *Pluto* had demanded of the assembled Fiends, if they will stand idle and suffer the Christian Armies to throw down their Altars, and destroy their Worship; he adds,

> *Ah non fia uer, che non sono anco estinti*
> *Gli spirti in uoi di quel ualor primiero,*
> *Quando di ferro, e d'alte fiamme cinti*
> *Pugnammo gia contra il celeste Impero;*
> *Fummo (io no'l nego) in questo conflitto vinti,*
> *Pur non mancò uirtute al gran pensiero,*
> *Hebbero i piu felici al hor uittoria*
> *Rimase a noi d' inuitto ardir la gloria.*

Which in *English* is thus:

> Ah never let it be, ye assembled Gods!
> For still, we still th' unconquer'd Spirit feel
> Of that eternal Valour, when of old
> Begirt with shining Arms and brighter Flames,
> Against th' Omnipotent we daring fought.
> 'Tis true, we lost the Day, but not for want
> Of Valour equal to the vast Design;
> Fortune gave him the Field, th' immortal Fame
> Was ours of having made the brave Attempt:
> Th' immortal Fame was ours, who still retain'd
> That Fire invincible with which we fought,
> And dar'd what never Angels durst before.

From which *Milton* has apparently borrow'd part of *Lucifer*'s Speech in the first Book of *Paradise Lost*.

> What tho the Field be lost?
> All is not lost; th' unconquerable Will,
> And Study of Revenge, immortal Hate,
> And Courage never to submit or yield.

And in *Armida*'s Speech to *Godfrey,* Canto 4. Stan. 63. *Tasso* derives a noble Spirit from *Godfrey*'s Power and Justice.

> *Tu, cui cocesse il Cielo e dielti in fato*
> *Voler' il giusto, e poter cio, che uuoi.*

Which is in *English*;

> Then for whom dooming Heav'n has made it Fate,
> That thy Designs should still be just, and thou
> Shouldst ne'er want Power to act those vast Designs.

And from the Magnanimity of *Rinaldo,* in the fourteenth Stanza of the fifth Canto.

> *Onde cosi rispose, i primi gradi*
> *Piu meritar, che conseguir desio,*
> *Ne pur, che me la mia uirtu sublimi*
> *Di scettri altezza inuidiar degg'io.*

In *English*:

> *Rinaldo* answer'd thus, The foremost Rank
> I rather would deserve, than would obtain;
> And can contemn the Scepters held by all
> Whose Fame to my superiour Virtue yields.

The fourth sort of Thoughts which *Hermogenes* mentions, as Riches, Nobility, Place, Office, Rank, and the like; we shall purposely pass by, without giving Examples of them, because we shall have a particular occasion to do it hereafter. Let us now pass to the next Enthusiastick Passion, which is Terror; than which, if it is rightly managed, none is more capable of giving a great Spirit to Poetry. This Passion scarce ever goes by it self, but is always more or less complicated with Admiration. For every thing that is terrible, is great at least to him to whom it is terrible. 'Tis now our business to shew two things: First, what this Enthusiastick Terror is; and, Secondly, from what Ideas it is chiefly to be deriv'd.

First, let us show what this sort of Enthusiasm is; and in order to that, let us shew as briefly as we can, what the common Passion is, which we call Terror. Fear then, or Terror, is a Disturbance of Mind proceeding from an Apprehension of an approaching Evil, threatning Destruction or very great Trouble either to us or ours. And when the Disturbance comes suddenly with surprize, let us call it Terror; when gradually, Fear. Things then that are powerful, and likely to hurt, are the Causes of common Terror; and the more they are powerful and likely to hurt, the more they become the Causes of Terror: which Terror, the greater it is, the more it is join'd with Wonder, and the nearer it comes to Astonishment. Thus we have shewn what Objects of the Mind are the Causes of common Terror, and the Ideas of those Objects are the Causes of Enthusiastick Terror.

Let us now shew from what Ideas this Enthusiastick Terror is chiefly to be derived. The greatest Enthusiastick Terror then must needs be deriv'd from Religious Ideas: for since the more their Objects are powerful, and likely to hurt, the greater Terror their Ideas produce; what can produce a greater Terror, than the Idea of an angry God? Which puts me in mind of that admirable Passage of *Homer,* about the Fight of the Gods, in the twentieth of the Iliads, cited by *Longinus* in his Chapter of the Loftiness of the Conception.

Δεινὸν δ᾽ ἐβρόντησε πατὴρ ἀνδρῶν τε, θεῶν τε,
Ὑψόθεν · αὐτὰρ ἔνερθε Ποσειδάων ἐτίναξε
Γαῖαν ἀπειρετέην, ὀρέων τ᾽ αἰπεινὰ κάρηνα·
Πάντες δ᾽ εσσείοντο πόδες πολυπιδάκος Ιδης,
Καὶ κορυφαὶ. Τρώων τε πόλις, καὶ νῆες Αχαιῶν
Εδδεισεν δ᾽ ὑπένερθεν ἄναξ ἐνέρων Ἀϊδωνεὺς,
Δείσας δ᾽ εκ θρόνου ἆλτο, καὶ ἴαχε μὴ οἱ ὕπερθε
Γαῖαν ἀναῤῥήξει Ποσειδάων ἐνοσίχθων,
᾽Οικία δέ θνητοῖσι, καὶ ἀθανάτοισι φανείη,
Σμερδαλε, εὐρώεντα τὰ τε στυγέουσι θεοί περ.

Which in *English* is thus:

Jove flung his dreadful Thunder from on high,
Mean while Majestick *Neptune* from below

The reeling Globe with his huge Trident strook,
Shook its vast Plains, and made its Mountains smoke;
Mount *Ida* trembled from his hoary Top,
And from his nethermost Foundations shook,
Troubling a thousand Springs that from him flow:
Pluto, from lowest Hell both heard and felt,
And shivering started from his burning Throne;
Then striking his infernal Breast, cry'd out,
Lest wrathful *Neptune* with another Stroke
Of his dread Trident should the Globe divide,
Should too, to the gaping Center let in Light,
To Mortals and Immortals should display
The dreadful Secrets of his dire Domain;
At the bare Thought of which, ev'n Gods are wont to
  shake.

Behold here, says *Longinus,* the Earth laid open to the
very Center, and Hell about to be expos'd to view, and
all the vast Machine of the World demolish'd and
overturn'd, to shew that in that important Conflict both
Heaven and Hell, both mortal and immortal things, every
thing in nature engaged with the Gods, and nothing was
free from Danger.

And now I mention *Longinus,* this is the properest
place to shew, by his Authority, that Religious Ideas are
the most proper to give Greatness and Sublimity to a
Discourse.   And this I shall shew, First, by his
Examples; and, Secondly, by his Precepts.

First, by his Examples.   All the Examples which he
gives of Sublimity in his Chapter of the Loftiness of the
Conceptions, of which the above-mention'd Passage is
one, are taken from the *Grecian* Religion, as this.

Iliad V.

Οσσον δ' ἠεροειδὲς ἀνὴρ ἴδεν ὀφθαλμοῖσιν
Ἡμενος ἐν σκοπιῇ, λεύσσων ἐπι οἴνοπα πόντον.
Τόσσον ἐπιθρόσκουσι θεῶν ὑψηχέες ἵπποι.

Which in *English* is thus:

As far as one, who tow'rd the Ocean looks,
Can from some lofty Promontory spy
Through the vast Desarts of a cloudless Sky;
So far th' immortal Gods sonorous Steeds
Can at one Leap advance.

Where, says *Longinus,* he measures the Length of
their Leap by the Extent of the World. Who is it then,
says he, that might not with reason cry out, that if the
Horses of the Gods would take a second Leap, they
would not find Space enough in the Universe?

And what follows concerning *Neptune,* descending
from a Mountain in *Thrace,*

Iliad XIII

Τρέμε δ' οὔρεα μακρὰ καὶ ὕλη,
Ποσσὶν ὑπ' ἀθανατοῖσιν Ποσειδάωνος ἰόντος.

As from the shaggy Mountain he descends,
The Mountain trembles, and the Forest bends.

And a little beyond:

Ἑοῦ δ' ἐπεβήσετο δίφρου·
Βῆ δ' ἐλάαν ἐπὶ κύματ' · ἄταλλε δὲ κήτε ὑπ' αὐτῷ
Πάντοθεν ἐχ κευθμῶν, οὐδ' ἠγνοίησεν ἄνακτα·
Γηθοσύνῃ δὲ θάλασσα διίστατο.

In *English* thus:

His golden Chariot *Neptune* now ascends;
And as he drives along the watry Plain,
Huge Whales, and all the Monsters of the Main,
Wallowing around him with unwieldy Gate,
Tempest the Ocean to salute their King;
Ocean rejoicing, yawns before his March,
And lets him through a dreadful Chasm.

And it was from this Passage, I make no doubt, that *Spencer* drew his admirable Picture of *Neptune,* in the eleventh Canto of the third Book of his *Fairy Queen.*

Stan. XL.

Next unto him was *Neptune* pictured,
In his Divine Resemblance wondrous like;
His Face was rugged, and his hoary Head
Dropped with brackish Dew; his three-fork'd Pike
He sternly shook, and therewith fierce did strike
The raging Billows, that on ev'ry side
They trembling stood, and made a long broad Dyke,
That his swift Chariot might have Passage wide.
Which four great *Hippodames* did draw, in Teemwise
    ty'd.

Stan. XLI.

His Sea-Horses did seem to snort amain,
And from their Nostrils blow the briny Stream,
That made the sparkling Waves to smoke again,
And flame with Gold; but the white foamy Cream
Did shine with Silver, and shoot forth her Beam.

I now come to the Precepts of *Longinus,* and pretend
to shew from them, that the greatest Sublimity is to be
deriv'd from Religious Ideas. But why then, says the
Reader, has not *Longinus* plainly told us so? He was
not ignorant that he ought to make his Subject as plain
as he could. For he has told us in the beginning of his
Treatise, that every one who gives Instruction concerning an Art, ought to endeavour two things: The first is
to make his Reader clearly understand what that is which
he pretends to teach: The second is to shew him how it
may be attain'd. And he blames *Cecilius* very severely
for neglecting the last; how then, says the Objector,
comes he himself to have taken no care of the first?
Is it because *Cecilius* had done it before him? If so, it
was a very great Fault in *Longinus* to publish a Book
which could not be understood but by another Man's
Writings; especially when he saw that those Writings
were so very defective, that they would not probably
last. But what, continues the Objector, if *Cecilius* had
not done it before him? For *Longinus* tells us, that
Cecilius makes use of a multitude of Words to shew
what it is; now he who knows any thing clearly, may in
a few Words explain it clearly to others; and he who
does not, will make it obscure by many.

To this I answer, that tho *Longinus* did by long Study
and Habitude know the Sublime when he saw it, as well
as any Man, yet he had not so clear a Knowledge of the
nature of it, as to explain it clearly to others. For if he
had done that, as the Objector says, he would have
defin'd it, but he has been so far from defining it, that
in one place he has given an account of it that is contrary
to the true nature of it. For he tells us in that Chapter
which treats of the Fountains of Sublimity, that Loftiness is often without any Passion at all; which is contrary

to the true nature of it. The Sublime is indeed often without common Passion, as ordinary Passion is often without that. But then it is never without Enthusiastick Passion: For the Sublime is nothing else but a great Thought, or great Thoughts moving the Soul from its ordinary Situation by the Enthusiasm which naturally attends them. Now *Longinus* had a notion of Enthusiastick Passion, for he establishes it in that very Chapter for the second Source of Sublimity. Now *Longinus,* by affirming that the Sublime may be without not only that, but ordinary Passion, says a thing that is not only contrary to the true nature of it, but contradictory to himself. For he tells us in the beginning of the Treatise, that the Sublime does not so properly persuade us, as it ravishes and transports us, and produces in us a certain Admiration, mingled with Astonishment and with Surprize, which is quite another thing than the barely pleasing, or the barely persuading; that it gives a noble Vigour to a Discourse, an invincible Force, which commits a pleasing Rape upon the very Soul of the Reader; that whenever it breaks out where it ought to do, like the Artillery of *Jove,* it thunders, blazes, and strikes at once, and shews all the united Force of a Writer. Now I leave the Reader to judge, whether *Longinus* has not been saying here all along that Sublimity is never without Passion.

That the foremention'd Definition is just and good, I have reason to believe, because it takes in all the Sources of Sublimity which *Longinus* has establish'd. For, first, Greatness of Thought supposes Elevation, they being synonymous Terms: And, secondly, the Enthusiasm or the Pathetique, as *Longinus* calls it, follows of course; for if a Man is not strongly mov'd by great Thoughts, he does not sufficiently and effectually conceive them.

And, thirdly, the figurative Language is but a Consequence of the Enthusiasm, that being the natural Language of the Passions. And so is, fourthly, the Nobleness of the Expression, supposing a Man to be Master of the Language in which he writes. For as the Thoughts produce the Spirit or the Passion, the Spirit produces and makes the Expression, which is known by Experience to all who are Poets; for never any one, while he was wrapt with Enthusiasm or ordinary Passion, wanted either Words or Harmony, as is self-evident to all who consider that the Expression conveys and shows the Spirit, and consequently must be produc'd by it.

Thus the Definition which we have laid down being, according to *Longinus*'s own Doctrine, the true Definition of the Sublime, and shewing clearly the thing which he has not done, nor given any Definition at all of it; it seems plain to me, that he had no clear and distinct Idea of it; and consequently Religion might be the thing from which 'tis chiefly to be deriv'd, and he but obscurely know it: but that Religion is that thing from which the Sublime is chiefly to be deriv'd, let us shew by the Marks which he has given of the latter; which will further strengthen our Definition. 1. Says he, that which is truly Sublime has this peculiar to it, that it exalts the Soul, and makes it conceive a greater Idea of it self, filling it with Joy, and with a certain noble Pride, as if it self had produc'd what it but barely reads.

Now here it is plain, that the highest Ideas must most exalt the Soul, but Religious Ideas are the highest.

The more the Soul is moved by the greatest Ideas, the more it conceives them; but the more it conceives of the greatest Ideas, the greater Opinion it must have of its own Capacity. By consequence the more it is moved by the Wonders of Religion, the more it values it self upon its own Excellences. Again, the more the Soul sees its Excellence, the more it rejoices. Besides, Religious Ideas are the most admirable; and what is most admirable according to the Doctrine of *Aristotle,* is most delightful. Besides, Religious Ideas create Passion in such a manner, as to turn and incline the Soul to its primitive Object. So that Reason and Passion are of the same side, and this Peace between the Faculties causes the Soul to rejoice; of which we shall have occasion to say more anon.

2. The second Mark that *Longinus* gives of the Sublime, is, when a Discourse leaves a great deal for us to think. But now this is certain, that the Wonders of Religion are never to be exhausted; for they are always new, and the more you enter into them, the more they are sure to surprize.

3. The third Mark is, when it leaves in the Reader an Idea above its Expression. Now no Expressions can come up to the Ideas which we draw from the Attributes of God, or from his wondrous Works, which only the Author of them can comprehend.

4. The fourth Mark is, when it makes an Impression upon us, which it is impossible to resist.

God, who made Man for himself, and for his own Glory, and who requires chiefly his Heart, must by consequence have form'd him of such a nature, as to be most strongly moved with Religious Ideas, if once he enters into them. So that the Impressions which they make, are impossible to be resisted.

5. The fifth Mark is, when the Impression lasts, and is difficult to be defaced. Now that the Impressions which Religion makes upon us are difficult to be defaced, is plain from this, that they who think it their Interest to deface them, can never bring it about.

6. The sixth Mark is, when it pleases universally, People of different Humours, Inclinations, Sexes, Ages, Times, Climates. Now there is nothing so agreeable to the Soul, or that makes so universal an Impression, as the Wonders of Religion. Some Persons are moved by Love, and are not touch'd by Ambition; others are animated by Ambition, and only laugh at Love. Some are pleas'd with a brave Revenge, others with a generous Contempt of Injuries; but the Eternal Power, and the Infinite Knowledge of God, the Wonders of the Creation, and the beautiful Brightness of Virtue, make a powerful Impression on all.

I must confess I have wonder'd very much, upon Reflection, how it could happen that so great a Man as *Longinus,* who whenever he met a Passage in any Discourse that was lofty enough to please him, had Discernment enough to see that it had some of the preceding Marks, should miss of finding so easy a thing as this, that never any Passage had all these Marks, or so much as the Majority of them, unless it were Religious.

But to return to Terror, we may plainly see by the foregoing Precepts and Examples of *Longinus,* that this Enthusiastick Terror contributes extremely to the Sublime; and, secondly, that it is most produced by Religious Ideas.

First, Ideas producing Terror, contribute extremely to the Sublime. All the Examples that *Longinus* brings of the Loftiness of the Thought, consist of terrible Ideas. And they are principally such Ideas that work the Effects, which he takes notice of in the beginning of his Treatise, *viz.* that ravish and transport the Reader, and produce a certain Admiration, mingled with Astonishment and with Surprize. For the Ideas which produce Terror, are necessarily accompany'd with Admiration, because ev'ry thing that is terrible, is great to him to whom it is terrible; and with Surprize, without which Terror cannot subsist; and with Astonishment, because every thing which is very terrible, is wonderful and astonishing: and as Terror is perhaps the violentest of all the Passions, it consequently makes an Impression which we cannot resist, and which is hardly to be defaced: and no Passion is attended with greater Joy than Enthusiastick Terror, which proceeds from our reflecting that we are out of danger at the very time that we see it before us. And as Terror is one of the violentest of all Passions, if it is very great, and the hardest to be resisted, nothing gives more Force, nor more Vehemence to a Discourse.

But, secondly, it is plain from the same *Longinus,* that this Enthusiastick Terror is chiefly to be deriv'd from Religious Ideas. For all the Examples which he has brought of the Sublime, in his Chapter of the Sublimity of the Thoughts, consists of most terrible and most religious Ideas; and at the same time every Man's Reason will inform him, that every thing that is terrible in Religion, is the most terrible thing in the World.

But that we may set this in a clearer Light, let us lay before the Reader the several Ideas which are capable of producing this enthusiastick Terror; which seem to me to be those which follow, *viz.* Gods, Dæmons, Hell, Spirits and Souls of Men, Miracles, Prodigies, Enchantments, Witchcrafts, Thunder, Tempests, raging Seas, Inundations, Torrents, Earthquakes, Volcanos, Monsters, Serpents, Lions, Tygers, Fire, War, Pestilence, Famine, *&c.*

Now of all these Ideas none are so terrible as those which shew the Wrath and Vengeance of an angry God; for nothing is so wonderful in its Effects: and consequently the Images or Ideas of those Effects must carry a great deal of Terror with them, which we may see was *Longinus*'s Opinion, by the Examples which he brings in his Chapter of the Sublimity of the Thoughts. Now of things which are terrible, those are the most terrible which are the most wonderful; because that seeing them both threatning and powerful, and not being able to fathom the Greatness and Extent of their Power, we know not how far and how soon they may hurt us.

But further, nothing is so terrible as the Wrath of infinite Power, because nothing is so unavoidable as the Vengeance design'd by it. There is no flying nor lying hid from the great universal Monarch. He may deliver us from all other Terrors, but nothing can save and defend us from him. And therefore Reason, which serves to dissipate our Terrors in some other Dangers, serves but to augment them when we are threatned by infinite Power; and that Fortitude, which may be heroick at other times, is downright Madness then.

For the other Ideas, which we mention'd above, they will be found to be more terrible as they have more of Religion in them. But we shall have so many necessary Occasions of giving Examples of them, in the Sequel of this Treatise, that it will be altogether needless to do it now. But here it will be convenient to answer an Objection: For how come some of the foremention'd Ideas, which seem to have but little to do with Religion, to be terrible to great and to wise Men? as it is plain that such, when they read the Descriptions of them in *Homer* and *Virgil,* are terrify'd.

To which we answer, That the Care, which Nature has inrooted in all, of their own Preservation, is the Cause that Men are unavoidably terrify'd with any thing that threatens approaching Evil. 'Tis now our Business to shew how the Ideas of Serpents, Lions, Tygers, *&c.*

were made by the Art of those great Poets, to be terrible to their Readers, at the same time that we are secure from their Objects.

'Tis very plain that it is the Apprehension of Danger which causes that Emotion in us which we call Terror, and it signifies nothing at all to the purpose whether the Danger is real or imaginary; and 'tis as plain too, that the Soul never takes the Alarm from any thing so soon as it does from the Senses, especially those two noble ones of the Eye and the Ear, by reason of the strict Affinity which they have with the Imagination; and the Evil always seems to be very near, when those two Senses give notice of it; and the nearer the Evil is, the greater still is the Terror. But now let us see how those two Poets did, by virtue of their Ideas, bring even absent terrible Objects within the reach of those two noble Senses. First then, to bring an absent terrible Object before our Sight, they drew an Image or Picture of it; but to draw an Image or Picture of a terrible Object, so as to surprize and astonish the Soul by the Eye, they never fail'd to draw it in violent Action or Motion; and in order to that, they made choice of Words and Numbers, which might best express the Violence of that Action or Motion. For an absent Object can never be set before the Eye in a true Light, unless it be shewn in violent Action or Motion; because unless it is shewn so, the Soul has leisure to reflect upon the Deceit. But violent Motion can never be conceiv'd without a violent Agitation of Spirit, and that sudden Agitation surprizes the Soul, and gives it less time to reflect; and at the same time causes the Impressions that the Objects make to be so deep, and their Traces to be so profound, that it makes them in a manner as present to us, as if they were really before us. For the Spirits being set in a violent

Emotion, and the Imagination being fir'd by that Agitation; and the Brain being deeply penetrated by those Impressions, the very Objects themselves are set as it were before us, and consequently we are sensible of the same Passion that we should feel from the things themselves. For the warmer the Imagination is, the less able we are to reflect, and consequently the things are the more present to us of which we draw the Images; and therefore when the Imagination is so inflam'd, as to render the Soul utterly incapable of reflecting, there is no difference between the Images and the Things themselves; as we may see, for example, by Men in raging Fevers. But those two great Poets were not satisfy'd with setting absent Objects before our Eyes, by shewing them in violent Motion; but if their Motion occasion'd any extraordinary Sounds that were terrifying, they so contriv'd their Numbers and Expressions, as that they might be sure to ring those Sounds in the very Ears of their Readers.

We ought now to treat of the other Enthusiastick Passions, as Horror, Grief, Joy, and Desire: But to the end that we may diversify this Treatise as much as we can, and not tire out the Reader with too much Speculation at a time, we shall omit speaking of them till we come to the Epick Poets.

Chapter V.

Recapitulation; and that Religion is the Basis and Foundation of the greater Poetry.

BUT now let us recapitulate: We have shewn in the foregoing part of this Discourse, that Passion is the

Characteristical Mark of Poetry, and that all Poetry is pathetick; and then we divided it into two kinds, the greater and the less; and shew'd that the greater Poetry comprehends Epick, Tragick, and the greater Lyrick, and that our Design was in the first place to treat of it. Then we proceeded to shew, that as Passion is the Characteristical Mark of Poetry, great Passion must be the Characteristical Mark of the greater Poetry, and consequently that this last must have every where great Passion; but that since what we commonly call Passion cannot be every where, there must be something distinct from ordinary Passion, and that must be Enthusiasm. Then we endeavour'd to discover what Enthusiasm is, and how many several sorts there are of it; and that Admiration and Terror make the principal Greatness of Poetry, and are the chief of the Enthusiastick Passions; that those two Passions are to bear proportion with the Ideas from which they are deriv'd, and that consequently the greatest must flow from religious Ideas. We shall shew too in the Sequel of this Discourse, that not only the remaining Enthusiastick Passions, Horror, Sadness, Joy, and Desire; but that even the ordinary Passions, which contribute most to the Greatness of Poetry, as Admiration, Terror, and Pity, are chiefly to be deriv'd from Religion; but that the Passions of both sorts must, for the most part, flow greater from Revelation than from Natural Religion; because all Reveal'd Religion, whether true or pretended, speaks to the Senses, brings the Wonders of another World more home to us, and so makes the Passions which it raises the greater.

The fundamental Rule then that we pretend to lay down, for the succeeding or excelling in the greater Poetry, is, That the Constitution of the Poem be religious, that it may be throughout pathetick.

And we pretend to prove undeniably, that not only the Gentlemen, whose Works we design to examine, have succeeded and excell'd no further than their Poems have been so constituted; but that never any Poets of any Nation, or any Age, ever did or can excel without it. I have already prov'd in the Advancement of modern Poetry, beyond all manner of doubt, to those who have Capacity enough to comprehend the Arguments, that the antient Poets excell'd the Moderns in the Greatness of Poetry, for no other reason, but because their Subjects were religious in their Constitution: And therefore all that I shall say of it here, is, That Poetry is the natural Language of Religion, and that Religion at first produc'd it, as a Cause produces its Effect. In the first Ages of writing among the *Grecians,* there was nothing writ but Verse, because they wrote of nothing but Religion, which was necessary for the cementing the Societies which in those times were but just united; and Nature had taught them, that Poetry was the only Language in which they could worthily treat of the most important Parts of Religion, or worthily perform its most important Duties. But as soon as Religion was sufficiently imprinted in the Minds of Men, and they had leisure to treat of human things in their Writings, they invented Prose, and invented it in imitation of Verse, as *Strabo* tells us in the first Book of his Geography; but after that Prose was invented by them, never any of them treated of their Gods or their religious Matters in Prose, before the Age of *Socrates,* because they found that that way of Writing was by no means proper for it. For the Wonders of Religion naturally threw them upon great Passions, and great Passions naturally threw them upon Harmony and figurative Language, as they must of necessity do any Poet, as long as he continues Master of them. Which is known by Experience to all who are Poets; for never any one, while he was wrapt with Enthusiasm, or with ordinary Passion, wanted either Words or Harmony; and therefore Poetry is more harmonious than Prose, because it is more pathetick: Even in Prose your Orators, and all who pretend to move the Passions, have more harmonious Periods than they who barely speak to the Reason. And in Poetry, they who write with a great deal of Passion, are generally very harmonious; whereas those who write with but little, are not so musical. *Horace* is an illustrious Example of this: No Man, who has read his Odes, can doubt of the Fineness and the Delicacy of his Ear; and therefore his Satires are often harsh and rugged, because the Spirit in them is mean and little. No Man can believe that *Juvenal* had a finer Ear than *Horace*, but yet his Satires are more musical, because they have a greater Spirit in them. At the same time 'tis a little odd to consider, that Passion, which disturbs the Soul, should occasion it to produce Harmony, which seems to imply the Order and Composure of it. Whether this proceeds from the secret Effort that the Soul makes to compose it self, or whatever the Cause is, the Effect is certain. But as Passion, which is the Disorder of the Soul, produces Harmony, which is Agreement; so Harmony, which is Concord, augments and propagates Passion, which is Discord. All who are acquainted with Poetry or Musick; must be as sensible of this, as Mr. *Waller* was fully convinc'd of it.

> Well sounding Verses are the Charm we use,
> Heroick Thoughts and Virtue to infuse;
> Things of deep Sense we may in Prose unfold,
> But they move more in lofty Numbers told;

By the loud Trumpet which our Courage aids,
We learn that Sound as well as Sense persuades.

Thus we may see by Mr. *Waller,* that Numbers are proper to move Passion, and for that reason are inseparable from Poetry, which has no other Design. But we shall have occasion to treat of Harmony more at large, when we come to the particular sorts of Poems; in the meantime let us return to the Business from which we may seem to have digress'd.

As we have formerly undeniably prov'd, in the Advancement of modern Poetry, that the antient Poets deriv'd that Advantage which they have over the Moderns, to the constituting their Subjects after a religious manner; so I shall make it appear, in the Sequel of this Discourse, that it was owing to the same thing that the antient Poets very often excell'd themselves.

And I have reason to believe, that one of the principal Reasons that has made the modern Poetry so contemptible, is, That by divesting it self of Religion, it is fallen from its Dignity, and its original Nature and Excellence; and from the greatest Production of the Mind of Man, is dwindled to an extravagant and a vain Amusement. For the modern Poetry being for the most part profane, has either very little Spirit; or if it has a great one, that Spirit is out of Nature, because it bears no manner of Proportion to the Ideas from which it is forcibly deriv'd, nor the Ideas very often to the Objects from which they are taken: for as Mr. *Waller* says,

In boundless Verse the Fancy soars too high
For any Object but the Deity:
What Mortal can with Heav'n pretend to share
In the Superlatives of Wise and Fair?

A meaner Object when with these we grace,
A Giant Habit on a Dwarf we place.

But that the modern Poetry, as miserably as it is fallen from the Dignity of its original Nature, might gloriously arise and lift up its Head, surpassing even that of the Antients, if the Poets would but constitute their Subjects religious, I have formerly clearly shewn, in the second Part of the *Advancement of modern Poetry*; by shewing that the Design of the Christian Religion is the very same with that of Poetry, which can be said of no other Religion; that the Business of both is to delight and reform Mankind, by exciting the Passions in such a manner, as to reconcile them to Reason, and restore the Harmony of the human Faculties. And therefore that I may repeat nothing at present that I have formerly said there, I shall only add, that if 'tis Religion that gives the Warmth and the Passion to Poetry, it follows that the less mixture that Religion has of any thing profane and human in it, the greater Warmth and Passion it must give to Poetry; for that which moves us in effect in a false Religion, must be the Imagination of that which is true. As for example, in the above-mention'd Passage of the Wrath of *Neptune,* the Anger of *Neptune* is Fiction, and so is the Stroke of his Trident; but that which moves us at the bottom of this Fiction is true, which is, that the Anger of a Deity, and the Effects of it are very terrible. The Reason why Religion moves the Soul so extremely, is because the Soul was created by God, to find its Happiness in him; and all Happiness consists in Pleasure, and all Pleasure in Passion. Now the less mixture Religion has of any thing of human Invention in it, the more divine it is, and the nearer it brings us to God.

But that this may still appear the more clearly, we shall endeavour to prove it by two very signal Examples, and shall produce two Passages from Scripture; the one from the *Psalms,* and the other from *Habbakuk*: which we shall set against the two foremention'd Passages, which *Longinus* has cited from *Homer*; the one of the Wrath, and the other of the Power of *Neptune,* and his awful March thro his own Element. And in setting these Passages against one another, we make no doubt to shew, that not only the Subjects are exactly the same, but that the Advantage is clearly ours.

Let us begin with that Passage concerning the Might of *Neptune,* and his driving his Chariot thro the Sea.

> As from the shaggy Mountain he descends,
> The Mountain trembles, and the Forest bends.

And anon,

> His golden Chariot *Neptune* now ascends,
> And as he drives along the watry Plain,
> Huge Whales, and all the Monsters of the Main,
> Tempest the Ocean, to salute their King;
> Ocean rejoicing, yawns before his March,
> And lets him thro a dreadful Chasm——

Now to this Passage let us oppose that of the Prophet *Habbakuk,* exactly upon the same Occasion, only the Prophet says of the True God what *Homer* says of *Neptune.*

> When the Almighty from Mount *Paran* came,
> The Brightness of his Glory, with its Blaze
> Expanding, fill'd the vast Abyss of Heaven,
> And the whole Earth resounded with his Praise;

The burning Pestilence before him march'd,
And from his Feet a fiery Whirlwind flew:
He stood and measur'd the extended Earth,
Scattering the trembling Nations with a Look,
At which the everlasting Mountains fled,
And shaking the perpetual Hills did bow.
Against the Floods was thy fierce Anger then;
Against the Sea the burning of thy Wrath;
That thou didst thro it with thy flaming Steeds,
And with thy Chariots of Salvation drive.
The Rocks their Summits beetled o'er their Base,
To view the Terrors of thy wondrous March;
Then shivering shrunk from the amazing Sight.
The Floods dividing shew'd a fearful Chasm;
And as thy sounding Horses, all on fire,
Thro Heaps of congregated Waters flew,
The Deep his roaring Voice at all his Mouths
Utter'd, and lifted all his Arms on high.

But now let us come to the Wrath of *Neptune,* and the
Effects of it, in the Battel of the 20th of the *Iliads,* in
which the Gods were engag'd.

Jove flung his dreadful Thunder from on high,
Mean while Majestick *Neptune* from below,
The reeling Globe with his huge Trident strook,
Shook its vast Plains, and made its Mountains smoke.
Mount *Ida* trembled from his hoary Top,
And from his nethermost Foundations shook,
Troubling a thousand Springs that from him flow.
Pluto, from lowest Hell, both heard and felt,
And shivering, started from his burning Throne;
Then striking his infernal Breast, cry'd out,
Lest wrathful *Neptune,* with another Stroke

Of his dread Trident, should the Globe divide,
Should to the gaping Center let in Light
To Mortals, and Immortals should display,
The dreadful Secrets of his dire Domain,
At the bare Thought of which ev'n Gods are wont to
    shake.

As the Necessity of the Subject has obliged us to
repeat these Verses, so we have the same Excuse for
repeating the Reflection of *Longinus.* Behold here, says
Longinus, the Earth laid open to the very Center, and
Hell about to be expos'd to view, and all the vast Machine
of the World demolish'd and overturn'd; to shew that
in that important Conflict, both Heaven and Hell, both
mortal and immortal things, everything in Nature was
engaged with the Gods, and nothing was free from
Danger. Now let us see the Psalmist introducing the
true God, actually demolishing and overturning the
Machine of the World, only with a Word and with a
Look.

    In my Distress I call'd upon the Lord,
And to my God I cry'd; he from his Height,
Above all Heights, strait heard my mournful Voice,
And to my loud Complaint inclin'd his Ear.
Strait the Earth trembled, and her Entrails shook,
As conscious of her great Creator's Wrath:
The Mountains from their fix'd Foundations ran,
And frighted from their inmost Caverns roar'd.
From out his Nostrils a tempestuous Cloud
Of pitchy Smoke in spiry Volumes flew,
And from his Mouth there ran a raging Flood
Of torrent Fire, devouring as it ran:
And then he bow'd the very Heaven of Heavens,

And arm'd with fearful Majesty came down.
Under his feet he plac'd substantial Night,
Which aw'd the Nations with its dreadful Gloom:
Upon the flaming Cherubim he rode,
And on the Wings of all the Winds he flew;
Still Darkness usher'd his mysterious Way,
And a black Night of congregated Clouds
Became the dark Pavilion of his Throne.
The Clouds his Brightness could no longer bear,
But vanishing rever'd the sacred Source of Light;
And as the congregated Clouds dispers'd,
A Storm of monstrous Hail came pouring down,
Down the red Lightning wing'd its slanting way;
But when his wrathful Voice was heard on high,
Strait both the Poles rebellow'd to the Sound,
In thicker Sheets the rattling Hail came down,
Down came the Lightning with repeated Flames,
And Thunder bellowing through the boundless Space,
Astonish'd Nature with redoubled Roars:
Earth could no longer bear the mortal Fright,
But shook it self from its perpetual Hinge
At thy Rebuke, O Lord, and at the Blast,
The dreadful Blast of thy revenging Breath;
Then upwards from the gaping Center cleav'd,
With a prodigious Wound.
The fix'd Foundations of the World display'd,
Display'd the ghastful Caverns of the Deep,
A Sight that blasted ev'n the World's great Eye,
And made the starting Sun recoil
From his eternal Way.

But here it will be necessary to answer an Objection: for it may be urg'd perhaps that common Experience will destroy these new Speculations. For several of the

Moderns have attempted Divine Poetry, and yet some of them have been contemptible to the last degree, and not one of them has excell'd the Antients.

To which we answer, That *Milton* has clearly the advantage of the Antients in several points, as shall be shewn in its proper place: and if the rest of the Moderns, who have attempted Sacred Poetry, have faln so very much short of them, it has been either for want of Genius, or for want of Art to know how to make use of Religion. For Sacred Poetry apparently requires a greater Capacity than the Profane does; because the greater the Ideas are, the greater must the Capacity be that receives them. But Sacred Ideas are greater than the Profane, as hath been shewn above. And therefore if the Rule of *Horace* be true, that a Poet ought to proportion his Subject to his Strength, it follows, that a Man may succeed pretty well in Human Poetry, and yet be despicable in the Divine. Besides, as Religion supplies us with greater Ideas than any thing Human can do; so it requires greater Enthusiasm, and a greater Spirit to attend them, as has been shewn above too. So that Sacred Poetry requires not only a very great Capacity, but a very warm and strong Imagination; which is a happy Mixture that is to be met with in a very few, and even of those few not one in a thousand perhaps applies himself to Sacred Poetry. And even of those rare ones who have apply'd themselves, hardly one of the Moderns has known the true use that ought to be made of Religion in Poetry. *Milton* indeed happen'd upon it, in his *Paradise Lost*; I say, happen'd upon it, because he has err'd very widely from it in his *Paradise Regain'd,* as shall be shewn in its proper place. The Rules for employing Religion in Poetry, are principally these which follow.

1. The first is, That the Religion ought to be one, that the Poet may be mov'd by it, and that he may appear to be in earnest. And the not observing of this Rule, was one Reason why *Spencer* miscarry'd, as we shall shew anon.

2. The second Rule, That the Religion which the Poet employs, ought to be the reigning one, that both the Poet and the Readers may be mov'd the more by a Religion in which they were bred. And this Rule may acquaint us with one of the Reasons why all who have translated *Homer* and *Virgil,* have succeeded so very indifferently.

3. The third is, That it may run through and be incorporated with the Action of the Poem, and consequently that it may always be a part of Action, and productive of Action; for from the Neglect of this third Rule, strange Inequalities would follow in a Poem, as shall be shewn more at large, when we treat of *Spencer* and *Cowley.*

4. The fourth Rule is, That the Religion may be managed so as to promote the Violence of the Enthusiastick Passions, and their Change and Variety; and the constituting his Subject contrary to this Rule, was one great Reason why *Milton* did not succeed in his *Paradise Regain'd.*

5. That it may not hinder the Violence of the ordinary Passions, nor the Change and Variety of them; and the not constituting his Subject according to this Rule, is the chief Reason why *Homer* in his *Odysses* fell so far short of his *Iliads*; and *Milton* of his *Paradise Lost,* in his *Paradise Regain'd.*

6. That the Religion be managed so as not to obstruct the Violence of Action, which is always attended by the Violence of ordinary Passion; and the not observing of

this, was one great Reason of the Miscarriage of *Homer* and *Milton*, in the fore-mention'd Poems.

7. That the divine and human Persons, if there be any, may have Inclinations and Affections; which *Tasso*'s celestial Persons have not, nor as I remember *Cowley*'s.

8. That they be fairly distinguish'd from one another by those Inclinations and Affections. And this is the great advantage that the *Grecian* Machines have, for the most part, over those in our Religion. Yet *Milton* has pretty well distinguish'd his celestial Persons from one another, and his infernal ones admirably.

9. That they be fairly distinguish'd from the human Persons by the same Inclinations and Affections. And here *Milton*, in his infernal Persons, has undeniably the advantage both of Antients and Moderns. The Passions and Inclinations of the *Grecian* Gods are downright human Inclinations and Affections. The Passions of *Milton*'s Devils have enough of Humanity in them to make them delightful, but then they have a great deal more to make them admirable, and may be said to be the true Passions of Devils: but the time to speak more largely of this, will be when we come to the Epick Poets.

But now, as we have shewn that the Religion reveal'd in the Old and New Testament is proper, nay necessary, to give the last Force and Elevation to Poetry; we shall now endeavour to convince the Reader, that Poetry is proper, if not necessary, to give Force to that Religion. For indeed there are Duties in this Religion, which cannot be worthily perform'd without the assistance of Poetry: as the offering up Praise and Thanksgiving, and several sorts of Prayer to God, and the celebrating the Wonders of his Might. Because if the Ideas which these Subjects afford, are express'd with Passion equal to their

Greatness, that which expresses them is Poetry: for that which makes Poetry to be what it is, is only because it has more Passion than any other way of writing.

It is ridiculous to imagine that there can be a more proper way to express some Parts and Duties of a Religion which we believe to be divinely inspired, than the very way in which they were at first deliver'd. Now the most important Part of the Old Testament was deliver'd not only in a Poetical Style, but in Poetical Numbers. The most important Parts of the Old Testament to us, are the Prophecies; because without them we could never be satisfy'd that *Jesus* is the Messiah. For the Prophets were Poets by the Institution of their Order, and Poetry was one of the Prophetick Functions, which were chiefly three: 1. Predicting or foretelling things to come. 2. Declaring the Will of God to the People. And, 3. Praising God with Songs of the Prophets composing, accompany'd with the Harp and other Instrumental Musick. From whence it came to pass, that praising God upon such kind of Instruments, is often in the Scriptures call'd Prophesying, as Mr. *Mede* has observ'd in his *Diatribæ*; and has prov'd it from several Passages of the Old Testament, and more particularly from the three first Verses of the 25th Chapter of the *Chronicles,* which are as follow.

Ver. 1. *Moreover* David *and the Captains of the Host separated to the Service of the Sons of* Asaph, *and of* Heman, *and of* Jeduthun, *such as should prophesy with Harps, with Psalteries, and with Cymbals*; *and the Number of the Workmen according to their Service was,*

Ver. 2. *Of the Sons of* Asaph; Zaccar, *and* Joseph, *and* Nethaniah *and* Asarelah, *the Sons of* Asaph; *under the hands of* Asaph, *which prophesy'd according to the Order of the King.*

Ver. 3. *Of* Jeduthun, *the Sons of* Jeduthun, Gedaliah, *and* Zeri, *and* Jeshaiah, Hashabiah, *and* Metithiah *six, under the hands of their Father* Jeduthun, *who prophesied with a Harp, to give thanks and to praise the Lord.*

Nor was the Poetical Talent confin'd to their Praise and Thanksgiving, but is to be seen in their Predictions too, as we said before, and in their declaring the Will of God to the People.

As the Prophets were Poets by their Institution, so when the Son of God himself came down from Heaven in order to reform the Earth, he who was a Prophet as well as a Priest and a King, did by consequence discharge the three Prophetical Functions, of which the Poetical has been shewn to be one. And consequently tho our Saviour did not make use of a Style that was Figurative and Enthusiastick, because he instructed the World as God, and as God he could not feel either Admiration or Terror, or the rest of the Enthusiastick Passions; yet we find that he not only prais'd God with spiritual Songs, but that the Method of his Instruction was intirely Poetical: that is, by Fables or Parables, contriv'd, and plac'd, and adapted to work very strongly upon human Passions.

Thus the Prophets among the *Jews* were Poets; and the Divine Institutor of the Christian Religion being a Prophet, by a Poetical Method instructed and reform'd the World: And even the *Grecian* Poets pretending to discharge the three Prophetical Functions, were not only vulgarly reputed Prophets, but were stil'd so by St. *Paul* himself, who quoting a Verse out of *Epimenides,* in the Epistle which he wrote to *Titus,* calls that *Cretensian* Poet a Prophet: *As one of their own Prophets has said.*

Thus we have made it very plain, that not only the Predictions, but the Praise and Thanksgiving in the inspir'd Writers, were written in Verse; as were likewise several of the Prayers, and the Instructions, and in short the noblest and most important part of the Old Testament. Now if they were written in Poetry, it could be for no other reason, but because they who wrote them, believ'd that the figurative passionate Style, and the Poetical Numbers, did by Right of Nature belong to them, and consequently were requisite to inforce them upon the Minds of Men. And here we cannot as it were help observing, that for the Scriptures to make all the Impression that they are capable of making upon Men of very good Parts, and perhaps too upon others, all those Parts of them that were written in Verse, ought to be translated in Verse, and by Persons who are the most qualify'd to do it with Force and Harmony. For if the Passion and Harmony were thought requisite by the Original Writers, who were divinely inspir'd, to give Force to the *Hebrew*; why should not Spirit and Passion, and Numbers in a Translation, give a proportionable Force to that? For if Harmony of it self is of force to lift up our Thoughts to Heaven, as our Clergy seem to imply by the use of it in our Churches; and may be gather'd from what happen'd to *Elisha* in the second of *Kings,* when they would have had him prophesy at a time when the Spirit of Prophesy was not upon him, *Ch.* 3. *ver.* 15. where the Prophet says, *Now bring me a Minstrel, and it came to pass as the Minstrel plaid, that the Hand of the Lord came upon him:* If Harmony, I say, is of it self so efficacious, what must it not be, when incorporated with a Religious Sense, and a Poetical Style? There can certainly be no better way to reform the World, than the reading of those Writings which we believe to be divinely inspir'd: But this is as certain, that the greater the Pleasure is with which we read them, we shall the more frequently discharge that Duty; but to make us read them with more Pleasure than we do, they must have more of the Agreeableness of their Originals, that is, more Perspicuity, more Force, and more Harmony. This would more particularly attract the Gentry, and particularly those of the most extraordinary Parts among them, whose Examples would influence the rest, as the rest would influence the People. For they of extraordinary Parts for the most part being extremely delighted with Poetry, and finding the greatest and most exalted Poetry upon Religious Subjects, would by degrees become more us'd to be mov'd by Sacred Ideas, than they would by Profane; that is, would by degrees become reform'd. That this is by no means a Chimera, Experience may serve to convince us: For I know several Gentlemen of very good Sense, who are extremely mov'd by *Milton*'s Hymn, in the fifth Book of *Paradise Lost,* and hardly at all stir'd with the Translation of the 148th Psalm, from whence that Hymn is taken. But if Men of very good Parts are more mov'd by the Hymn, it follows that they ought to be more mov'd by it; because Men of very good Sense are only mov'd to that degree by things by which they ought to be mov'd. So that we may conclude, that the Passion or Enthusiasm in that Hymn is exactly in Nature; that is, that the Enthusiasm, or Passion, or Spirit, call it what you will, flows from the Ideas, and bears a just Proportion to them.

But from hence at the same time it follows, that since those Persons, who are so much mov'd by the Hymn, are not equally stir'd by the translated Psalm, the Passion or Spirit is less in the latter, and does not come up to the Ideas; and therefore we may conclude, that *Milton,* by his Genius and Harmony, has restor'd that Spirit in composing the Hymn, which had been lost by the Weakness of the Translation, and the Want of Poetical Numbers: which last, as we have said before, contribute very much to the raising of Passion.

What *Milton* has done in relation to the 148th Psalm, others may do in a less proportion to other parts of the Old Testament, till the Favour of the Prince and publick Encouragement causes another *Milton* to arise, and apply himself to so necessary and so noble a Work. For this is certain, that there are not wanting great Genius's to every Age: But they do not equally appear in every Age, sometimes for want of knowing themselves, and sometimes for want of Encouragement and Leisure to exert themselves. The Business of the Treatise intended is to shew them how they may try, and know, and form themselves, which is all that I am capable of attempting towards the restoring so useful and so noble an Art. If I were in a Condition to give them Encouragement too, they should not be long without it. If they who so much exceed me in Power, did but equal me in Will, we should soon see Poetry raise up its dejected Head, and our own might come to emulate the happiest of *Grecian* and *Roman* Ages.

And thus much may suffice to shew the Nature of Poetry, but chiefly of the greater Poetry, and the Importance of this Design. For since Poetry has been thought not only by Heathens, but by the Writers of the Old Testament, and consequently by God himself who inspir'd them, to be the fittest Method for the enforcing Religion upon the Minds of Men; and since Religion is the only solid Foundation of all Civil Society, it follows, that whoever endeavours to re-establish Poetry, makes a generous Attempt to restore an Art, that may be highly advantageous to the Publick, and beneficial to Mankind.

III. REFLECTIONS CRITICAL AND SATYRICAL,
UPON A LATE RHAPSODY, CALL'D,
AN *ESSAY UPON CRITICISM*

1711

'Tis now almost seven Years, since I happen'd to say one Morning to a certain Person distinguish'd by Merit and Quality, that wherever the Italian Opera *had come, it had driven out Poetry from that Nation, and not only Poetry, but the very Tast of Poetry, and of all the politer Arts; and that if the same Protection and Encouragement were continued to the* Opera, *by which it was then supported, the same Calamity would befal* Great Britain *which had happen'd to the Neighbouring Nations. As 'tis hard to find a Man more quick or more penetrating, than the Person to whom I spoke this; he immediately enter'd into that Sentiment, and soon after withdrew that Encouragement which he had given to the* Italians. *All that I foretold, and more than all hath happen'd. For such Things, such monstrous Things have been lately writ, and such monstrous Judgments pass'd, that what has been formerly said has been sufficiently confirm'd, that 'tis impossible an Author can be so very foolish, but he will find more stupid Admirers.*

A most notorious Instance of this Depravity of Genius and Tast, is the Essay upon which the following Reflections are writ, and the Approbation which it has met with. I will not deny but that there are two or three

Passages in it with which I am not displeas'd; but what are two or three Passages as to the whole?

Fit Chærilus ille
Quem bis terq; bonum cum risu miror.

The approving two or Three Passages amongst a multitude of bad ones, is by no means advantageous to an Author. That little that is good in him does but set off its contrary, and make it appear more extravagant. The Thoughts, Expressions, and Numbers of this Essay are for the most part but very indifferent, and indifferent and execrable in Poetry are all one. But what is worse than all the rest, we find throughout the whole a deplorable want of that very Quality, which ought principally to appear in it, which is Judgment; and I have no Notion that where there is so great a want of Judgment, there can be any Genius.

However, I had not publish'd the following Letter, but had suffer'd his Readers to have hugg'd themselves in the Approbation of a Pamphlet so very undeserving, if I had not found things in it that have provok'd my Scorn, tho' not my Indignation. For I not only found my self attack'd without any manner of Provocation on my side, and attack'd in my Person, instead of my Writings, by one who is wholly a Stranger to me, and at a time when all the World knew that I was persecuted by Fortune; I not only saw that this was attempted in a clandestine manner with the utmost Falshood and Calumny, but found that all this was done by a little affected Hypocrite, who had nothing in his mouth at the same time but Truth, Candor, Friendship, good Nature, Humanity, *and* Magnanimity.

'Tis for this Reason that I have publish'd the following Letter, in which if I have not treated the Author of the

Essay with my usual Candor, he may thank himself and this good-natur'd Town. For having observ'd with no little Astonishment, that Persons have been censur'd for ill Nature, who have attempted to display the Errors of Authors undeservedly successful; tho' they have done this with all imaginable Candor, and with the best and noblest Designs, which are the doing Justice, the Discovery of Truth, and the Improvement of Arts; while Writers of Lampoons and infamous Libels, whose Anonymous Authors have lain lurking in the dark, sometimes in Clubs, and sometimes solitary, like so many common Rogues and Footpads, to ruin the Fortunes, and murder the Reputations of others; have been caress'd and hugg'd by their thoughtless Applauders, and treated as if they had been the most vertuous and the best natur'd Men in the World; having observ'd all this with no little astonishment, I at last found out the reason of it, which is, because the Attempts of Libellers and Lampooners hurt only those whom they attack, and delight the rest of the Readers; whereas they who expose by a just Criticism the Absurdities of foolish fortunate Authors, attack all those who commend and admire those Authors, and disturb perhaps by opening their Eyes, no fewer than a thousand Fops in the good Opinion which they have conceiv'd of themselves. 'Tis for this Reason that I have endeavour'd to comply with this wise and good natur'd general Disposition of Minds, and to make amends for the Ill-nature of my Criticism, by the Allurements of my Satyr.

To Mr. - - - - - *at* Sunning-Hill,
Berks.

SIR,

I Here send you my Answer to the two Questions which I lately received from you, which are whether the Essay upon Criticism, which I lately sent you is like to take in Town, and who is the Author of that anonymous Rhapsody.

In answer to the first Question, my Opinion is that it will take very well. For the same thing is true of great Bodies of Men, which has been observ'd of particular Persons; and that is, that when Genius thinks fit to depart from among them, good Taste never cares to be very long after it. When the *Italian* Opera drove Poetry from out this Island, Criticism thought it a very great Impertinence for her to stay long behind. Besides that the elegant Translations of the *Italian* Opera's which Mr. *Tonson* has published by the most eminent Hands, have prepared People to like any thing that is of an equal Merit with those Translations, and with *Tom Sternhold*'s Version.

For the second *Quære,* Mr. —— is of Opinion that this Essay was writ by some experienced judicious Person, who knows what Quantity of base Alloy is at this Juncture requisite to debase the Coin of *Parnassus,* and reduce it to the current Standard. But I am inclin'd to believe that it was writ by some young, or some raw Author, for the following Reasons.

First, He discovers in every Page a Sufficiency that is far beyond his little Ability; and hath rashly undertaken a Task which is infinitely above his Force; a Task that is only fit for the Author, with the just Encomium of whose Essay my Lord *Roscommon* begins his own.

> *Happy that Author whose correct Essay*
> *Repairs so well our old* Horatian *way.*

There is nothing more wrong, more low, or more incorrect than this Rhapsody upon Criticism. The Author all along taxes others with Faults of which he is more guilty himself. He tells us in the very two first Lines, that

> *'Tis hard to say if greater want of Skill*
> *Appear in writing, or in judging ill.*

Now whereas others have been at some Pains and Thought to shew each of these wants of Skill separately and distinctly, his comprehensive Soul hath most ingeniously contriv'd to shew them both in a supreme Degree together.

Secondly, While this little Author struts and affects the Dictatorian Air, he plainly shews that at the same time he is under the Rod; and that while he pretends to give Laws to others, he is himself a pedantick Slave to Authority and Opinion, of which I shall give some Instances.

In the beginning of his Essay he lays down this Maxim:

> *Let such teach others who themselves excel,*
> *And censure others who have written well.*

Where he would insinuate, that they alone are fit to be Criticks who have shewn themselves great Poets. And he brings in *Pliny* to confirm by his Authority the Truth of a Precept, which is denied by matter of Fact, and by the Experience of above Two thousand Years.

De Pictore, Sculptore, Fictore nisi Artifex judicare non potest.

It has been observed by Writers of Politicks, That they who have succeeded best in these kind of Writings, have never been either Governours of Provinces, or Ministers of State, as *Plato* and *Aristotle* in *Greece, Machiavel* in *Italy,* and in this Island *Harrington.* I will not say that this may be applied to Criticks. There are and have been very good ones who have been great Poets, as *Horace* in *Italy, Boileau* in *France,* and in *Great Britain* my Lord *Roscommon,* and a living noble Author. Nay I am fully convinc'd, that there never was an admirable Poet, but he was a great Critick. For what can be more absurd than to imagine, that any man can excel in any Art, or Business, or Profession, who does not understand that Profession, Art, or Business. Now he who understands the Art of Poetry is a Critick in Poetry. But this is undeniable at the same time, that there have been Criticks, who have been approv'd of by all the World, who never meddled with Poetry. Was *Aristotle* himself, the very Father of *Criticks,* a Poet? Why yes, 'tis pretended that there is a Fragment of an Ode, which was writ by him, remaining in *Athenæus.* But is that sufficient to denominate him a Poet? Did he ever write either Tragedy or Epick Poem? And yet how freely did he censure both Tragick and Epick Poets? *Dionysius Halicarnassæus,* and *Dionysius Longinus* among the *Greeks,* and *Quintilian* among the *Romans* were free Censurers, yet no Poets. And so are *Bossu* and *Dacier* at present among the *French.* And what is still more remarkable, is, that this young Author forgets himself to that degree, as to commend *Longinus* and *Quintilian* for accomplish'd Criticks contrary to his own Precept.

Another Instance which I shall give of his being a Slave to Authority and Opinion, is the servile Deference which he pays to the Ancients.

> *Still Green with Bays each ancient Altar stands*
> *Above the reach of sacrilegious Hands,*
> *Secure from Flames, from Envy's fiercer Rage,*
> *Destructive War, and all devouring Age.*
> *See from each Clime the Learn'd their Incense bring,*
> *Hear in all Tongues triumphant Pæans ring!*
> *In Praise so just let ev'ry Voice be join'd,*
> *And fill the general Chorus of Mankind.*

Which is just the opposite Extravagance and Extreme to that of Monsieur *Perrault.*

For the *French*-man with an insolent Stupidity contemn'd and blasphem'd, even those Hero's of Antiquity, whose Writings are admirable and Divine: This Essayer deifies Authors, whose Writings are but tolerable and indifferent. *Boileau,* as a reasonable Man, took the Path that lay in the middle of the two Extremes, as we shall see by what follows:

"For what remains, says he, I would not have any one "think, that in this number of ancient Writers approv'd "of by all Ages, 'tis my Intention to comprehend some "Authors, who indeed are ancient, but who have only "acquir'd a moderate Esteem, as *Lycophron, Nonnus,* "*Silius Italicus,* and the Author of the Tragedies which "are attributed to *Seneca,* to whom in my mind we may "not only boldly compare, but justly prefer several of "the modern Writers. I only admit into that exalted "Rank that small number of admirable Writers, whose "Name alone is their Panegyrick, as *Homer, Plato,*

"*Cicero, Virgil, &c.* And I do not regulate the Esteem
"which I have for them, by that length of Time which
"their Works have lasted, but by the number of Years
"which they have been admir'd; of which 'tis convenient
"to advertise a great many People, who otherwise perhaps
"might indiscreetly believe, what Monsieur *Perrault* has
"a mind to insinuate, that we commend the Ancients for
"no other Reason, but because they are Ancients; and
"blame the Moderns for no other Reason, but because
"they are Moderns; which is utterly false; since there
"are several among the Ancients whom we do not admire,
"and several among the Moderns whom all the World
"extols. The Antiquity of a Writer is no certain proof
"of his Merit; but the ancient and constant Admiration
"which all the World has had for his Writings, is a
"certain and infallible proof that we ought to admire
"them. *Boileau* Reflect. the 7th on *Longinus.*

Thus hath *Boileau* determin'd this matter like a
dextrous Distinguisher, and a most rightful Judge. If
I may be allow'd to speak my Sentiments after so great
a Master, I must freely declare my Opinion, that of all
the Poets among the *Græcians,* I only admire *Homer,
Sophocles, Pindar,* and *Euripides,* tho' I am very much
pleas'd with some of the rest; and of all the Poets among
the *Romans,* I admire only *Virgil* and *Horace,* and some
parts of *Lucretius;* tho' I am very much pleas'd with
Catullus, Tibullus, Terence, and others. For as for
*Lycophron, Nonnus, Apollonius Rhodius, Valerius
Flaccus, Silius Italicus, Statius,* I prefer the *Paradise
lost* of *Milton* before them all together: Nay I will go
yet farther, and declare, that tho' I must freely own,
that *Virgil* has infinitely the Advantage of *Milton,* in the
wonderful Contrivance of his Poem, in the Harmony of
his Versification, and in the constant Tenor of his

Majesty, and his Elevation; yet that *Milton* in some particular parts of his Poem has the Advantage of *Virgil,* and of Mankind. And tho' I can by no means believe *Shakespear* to be of equal Merit with *Sophocles* or *Euripides,* for which I shall give my Reasons in another place; yet this I can say for the Honour of my Countryman, and of *Great Britain,* that there are several single Scenes in *Shakespear,* which I prefer to all the Tragedies put together of which *Seneca* is accounted the Author.

I shall give one more Instance, by which it will appear that while this Youngster is pretending to give Laws, he behaves himself like one who is still in awe of the Rod; that he admires the Ancients, because his Master tells him that they must be admir'd; and that if the Ancients were his Contemporaries, and produc'd the same Writings now which they did formerly, he would use them with the same Insolence with which he treats his Contemporaries. In the 8th Page of this Essay, he gives a verbose and indigested Encomium of the first *Græcian* Criticks, but forgets and contradicts himself before he comes to the bottom of that very Page. For, says he,

> *The gen'rous Critick fann'd the Poet's Fire,*
> *And taught the World with Reason to admire;*
> *Then Criticism, the Muses Handmaid, proud*
> *To dress her Charms, and make her more belov'd:*
> *But following Wits from that Intention stray'd,*
> *Who could not win the Mistress, woo'd the Maid,*
> *Set up themselves, and drove a sep'rate Trade.*

Never was any thing more obscure and confus'd than the foregoing Rhimes; but if there is any meaning in them, it must be that which follows.

At first Poets and Criticks were all one; and these Poets made use of their Criticism only to make their Poetry more charming, and more accomplish'd. But the Wits who immediately follow'd after them, deviated from the Design of their Predecessors; and not being able to attain to Poetry, took up a Resolution to drive a separate Trade, and to set up only for Criticks. If this is not his meaning, I should be glad to hear in Prose, and in plain *English* what his meaning is; for Rhime has always been a wicked Abettor and Concealer of Nonsense. But if this is his meaning, then I desire to make these two Remarks, First, that the ancientest Criticks among the *Græcians* were not Poets, as we observ'd before; and Secondly, that if *Aristotle* and *Dionysius Halicarnassæus,* and others were now alive, and their excellent Criticisms were now first to appear, it would be objected to those great Men, in order to disqualify them for Criticks, that they were no Versi-fyers. And it is plain from the 2^d Page that another Objection would be made to them: For when he comes there to speak of the Moderns, he tells us,

> *Some dryly plain, without Invention's Aid,*
> *Write dull Receipts how Poems may be made.*

Now it being evident, that the Criticisms of *Aristotle* and of *Dionysius Halicarnassæus* are writ with a great deal of Simplicity, 'tis manifest that if those two Criticks had writ but yesterday, they would be accus'd to day of being drily plain, and of writing dull Receipts.

But a third infallible mark of a young Author, is, that he hath done in this Essay what School-boys do by their Exercises, he hath borrow'd both from Living and Dead, and particularly from the Authors of the two famous

Essays upon Poetry and Translated Verse; but so borrow'd, that he seems to have the very Reverse of *Midas*'s noble Faculty. For as the coursest and the dullest Metals, were upon the touch of that *Lydian* Monarch immediately chang'd into fine Gold; so the finest Gold upon this Author's handling it, in a moment loses both its lustre and its weight, and is immediately turn'd to Lead.

A fourth thing that shews him a young man, is the not knowing his own mind, and his frequent Contradictions of himself. His Title seems to promise an Essay upon Criticism in general, which afterwards dwindles to an Essay upon Criticism in Poetry. And after all, he is all along giving Rules, such as they are, for Writing rather than Judging. In the beginning of the 8th Page the Rules are nothing but Nature.

> *These Rules of old discover'd, not devis'd,*
> *Are Nature still, but Nature methodiz'd.*

But no sooner is he come to the 10th Page, but the Rules and Nature are two different things.

> *When first great* Maro, *in his boundless mind.*
> *A Work t'outlast immortal* Rome *design'd,*
> *Perhaps he seem'd above the Critick's Law,*
> *And but from Nature's Fountains scorn'd to draw.*

But in the last Line of this very Paragraph they are the same things again.

> *Learn hence for ancient Rules and just Esteem,*
> *To copy Nature is to copy them.*

But to this he will answer, That he is guilty of no Contradiction, that he is only shewing that *Virgil* was guilty of Error and Ignorance; who first absurdly began to write his *Æneis,* and afterwards sate down to learn the Rules of Writing; which when he began to write that Poem, he took to be things distinct from Nature; but that after he had wrote part of it, he fell to the reading of *Homer,* and that undeceiv'd him. That while he is talking of *Virgil*'s Error and Ignorance, he is making a Parade of his own incomparable Wisdom and Knowledge; and not contradicting himself, but *Virgil,* or rather making him appear inconsistent with and contradicting himself: for that tho' *Virgil* took the Rules and Nature to be distinct from each other, for his own part he is wiser, and knows better things. Now is not this a very modest and a very judicious Gentleman?

A fifth Sign of his being a young Author is his being almost perpetually in the wrong. And here in relation to the foregoing passage, I might desire to ask him one or two civil Questions. First, who acquainted him with that noble Particularity of *Virgil*'s Life, that he designed to write his *Æneis* without Art? Had he it from ancient or modern Authors, or does he owe it to a noble Effort of his own sagacious Soul? If *Virgil* had so little Knowledge of the Rules of his own Art, and so very little true Judgment within him, as to be capable of such an Extravagance, an Extravagance which, says this Essayer, nothing but the reading of *Homer* was able to correct, how comes he so far to have surpassed his Master in the admirable Contrivance of his Poem. But secondly, what does he mean by *Maro*'s designing a Work to outlast immortal *Rome*? Does he pretend to put that Figure, call'd a Bull upon *Virgil*? Or would he ambitiously have it pass for his own? 'Tis no wonder that one who is capable of imputing so great an Extravagance to *Virgil,* should be capable of writing himself without any manner of meaning.

Whenever we find a Simile, the first Line of it is like a Warning-piece, to give us notice that something extraordinary false or foolish is to follow. We have one in the 6th Page, where the former and the latter part have not the least relation, and bear not the least proportion to one another.

> *As on the Land while here the Ocean gains,*
> *In other Parts it leaves wide sandy Plains:*
> *Thus in the Soul while Memory prevails,*
> *The solid Power of Understanding fails;*
> *Where Beams of warm Imagination play,*
> *The Memory's soft Figures melt away.*

Here the Soul in the third Verse is made to answer to Land in the first, and Memory to Ocean, which in the fourth Verse is chang'd for Understanding; tho' in this Simile the Author shews neither Memory nor Understanding; for there are as many Absurdities in it as there are Lines. At this rate a man may make a thousand Similes in an hour! Any thing may become like to any thing. *Jungentur jam Gryphes Equis.* But what a thoughtless Creature is this Essayer, to deny in these very Rhimes, by which he pretends to shew both Poetry and Criticism, the co-existence of those Qualities, without which 'tis impossible to be both Poet and Critick? Besides, how wrong is this; and how many Persons have I known who have had all these Qualities at the same time in a very great degree? What follows is more wrong and more absurd:

> *One Science only will one Genius fit*
> *So vast is Art, so narrow Human Wit.*

Is not this a rare Pretender to Poetry and Criticism, who talks at this rate, when all the World knows that 'tis impossible for a Man with only one Science to be either Poet or Critick? Which is so much the more unlucky, because the very Fathers of Poetry and Criticism *Homer* and *Aristotle,* whom he mentions so often in this Essay, are believed to have had all the Sciences. 'Tis now between Two and three thousand Years since *Aristotle* wrote his Morals, his Politicks, his Rhetorick, and his Poetick; and three of these are the very best in their kinds to this very day, and have infinitely the Advantage of all those several thousand Treatises that have been writ since. What follows is still more false and more abominable.

> *Not only bounded to peculiar Arts,*
> *But ev'n in those confin'd to single Parts.*

What a wretched narrow Soul hath this Essayer? And what a thoughtless one—when *Homer,* whom he mentions so often in this Essay, had as admirable a Talent for Pleasantry, as he had a Genius equal to the most exalted Poetry? To come to the *Romans, Horace* is famous both for Eleva[t]ion and Pleasantry. *Virgil* succeeded in his *Bucolicks* and *Georgicks,* as well as he did in his *Æneis.* To descend to the Moderns, *Shakespear* had a very good Genius for Tragedy, and a very good Talent for Comedy. And since him *Otway* had likewise a Talent for both.

But in the next Page there is likewise a Simile; and therefore we may be sure, as we observ'd above, that most of that Page is one continued Absurdity.

> *First follow Nature, and your Judgment frame*
> *By her just Standard, which is still the same;*

> *Unerring Nature still divinely bright,*
> *One clear, unchang'd, and universal Light,*
> *Life, Force and Beauty next to all impart,*
> *At once the Source, and End, and Test of Art:*

Now here wou'd I fain ask one or two Questions? Is he giving Rules here for Judging or for Writing? And is he prescribing those Rules to the Knowing or the Ignorant? If he says to the Knowing, what is it that he tells them here? That they must judge according to Nature, or write according to Nature. Now does he tell them any thing in this that they did not know before? Well, but he says, he is laying down these Rules for the Ignorant; why then I humbly conceive that he ought to have told them what he means by Nature, and what it is to write or to judge according to Nature. For by expressing himself at the rate that he does, he neither says any thing to the Learned which they did not know before, nor any thing to the Ignorant which they can possibly understand. *Horace* proceeded in a very different Method from this, when he was to acquaint the *Piso*'s what was the principal Source of good Writing, he not only told them that it was moral Philosophy,

> *Scribendi recte, sapere est & principium & Fons,*

But pointed to the very Books where they might find that moral Philosophy.

> *Rem tibi Socraticæ poterant ostendere Chartæ.*

So that in one we have a clear and perspicuous Precept, and in the other an obscure and unintelligible Jargon. But let us go on.

> *That Art is best which most resembles her,*
> *Which still presides, yet never does appear.*

That is, as much as to say, *Artis est celare artem,* the common Subject that Pedants give their Boys to make Themes and Declamations upon. Is not this a noble Discovery? Well but now for the Simile;

> *In some fair Body thus the sprightly Soul*
> *With Spirit feeds, with Vigor fills the whole,*
> *Each motion guides, and ev'ry nerve sustains,*
> *It self unseen but in th' effects remains.*

This Youngster has not memory enough to know what he said six Lines before;

> *Thus in a Soul where memory ne'r prevails,*
> *The solid Power of understanding fails.*

In the fifth Line of this Page it was Nature that

> *Life, force and beauty must to all impart.*

And here in the 10th we are told that 'tis Art that

> *With Spirit feeds, with Vigor fills the whole.*

But how absurdly is Art compar'd to the Soul, to which only Genius can be justly compar'd, according to the Observation in the Essay upon Poetry. But let us go on, and we shall find that as all that went before this Simile is unintelligible, so all is mighty absurd that follows it.

There are whom Heav'n hath bless'd with store of Wit
Yet want as much again to manage it.

By the way what rare Numbers are here? Would not one swear that this Youngster had espous'd some antiquated Muse, who had sued out a Divorce upon the account of Impotence from some superannuated Sinner; and who having been pox'd by her former Spouse, has got the Gout in her decrepit Age, which makes her hobble so damnably— Why, this is more dismal than the *Italian* Opera, both that and the Essay are but sounds; but that is Harmony, and this is Discord.

But now, my dear Friend, if I had young Mr. *Bays* here, I would desire that I might ask him one Question, and he not be angry. And that is, what he means by

There are whom Heav'n has bless'd with store of Wit,
Yet want as much again to manage it.

But let us go on, and see if 'tis possible to find it out without him.

> *For Wit and Judgment ever are at strife*
> *Tho' meant each others, are like Man and Wife.*

That is as much as to say, there are People who have that which they call Wit, without one dram of Judgment. Is not this another wonderful Discovery? But I fancy that Mr. *Bays* has the Misfortune to be wrong in the first Verse of the foresaid Couplet.

> *For Wit and Judgment ever are at strife.*

What a Devil, Mr. *Bays,* they cannot be at strife sure, after they are parted, after Wit has made an Elopement, or has been barbarously forsaken by Judgment, or turn'd to separate maintenance! Much less can they be at strife where they never came together, which is the Case in the Essay. But now we talk of Man and Wife, let us consider the Yoke-fellow to the former Rhime.

> *Tho' meant each others, and like Man and Wife.*

Now cannot I for my Soul conceive the reciprocal Aid that there is between Wit and Judgment. For tho' I can easily conceive how Judgment may keep Wit in her

Senses, yet cannot I possibly understand how Wit can controul, or redress, or be a help to Judgment.

If Mr. *Bays* in that Couplet

There are whom Heav'n has bless'd with store of Wit,
Yet want as much agen to manage it.

Intended to say that People have sometimes store of false Wit without Judgment to manage it, he intended nothing but what all the World knew before. But if he meant to say this of true Wit, nothing can be more mistaken; for I cannot conceive how any one can have store of Wit without Judgment. I believe that Father *Bouheurs* has given a tolerable Description of Wit in his Treatise upon that Subject, *C'est un solide qui brille*: "Tis a shining Solid, like a Diamond, which the more "solid it is, is always the more glittering; and derives its "height of Lustre from its perfect Solidity. Now how any thing in the Works of the Mind can be solid without Judgment, I leave Mr. *Bays* to consider.

But let us pass to the 18th Page, at the bottom of which we shall find another Simile, and consequently another absurdity.

> *Poets, like Painters, thus unskill'd to trace*
> *The naked Nature and the living Grace,*
> *With Gold and Jewels cover ev'ry part,*
> *And hide with Ornament their want of Art.*

Which in Prose and plain *English* runs thus:

> Poets like Painters not having the Skill to draw
>   Nature without Art, hide their want of Art
>   with a super-abundance of Art.

In the 20th Page we have another Simile, and consequently another Absurdity.

> *But true Expression, like th' unchanging Sun,*
> *Clears and improves whate'er it shines upon.*

Which is borrow'd from the Essay on Poetry.

> *True Wit is everlasting like the Sun,*

But awkwardly borrow'd, and utterly spoil'd in the removal. For what can Expression be properly said to shine upon? True Wit, or Genius; for that the noble Author means, as is plain from several parts of his Poem, shines thro' and discovers it self by the Expression; but Expression, at the very best, can but shine with a borrow'd Light, like the Moon and the rest of the Planets, whereas Genius shines and flames with its own Celestial Fire.

His Instructions, his Affections, his Commendations, his Censures, his Advice, wherever they are his own, are either false or trivial, or both. Such is that in the beginning of the twelfth Page,

> *And tho' the Ancients thus their Rules invade,*
> *As Kings dispense with Laws themselves have made.*
> *Moderns beware.*

Thus is this Essayer for a double Dispensing Power in Kings and ancient Authors, and is for making the Moderns doubly Slaves, Slaves in their Actions, and Slaves in their Writings. But as we boldly deny that Kings have either Power to make Laws, or to dispense with them after they are made; so those Laws of Writing were neither made by the Ancients, nor can those Ancients dispense with them. As they are the Laws of Nature, and not of Men, as he has himself hinted in the beginning of the 8th Page.

Those Rules of old discover'd, not devis'd,
Are Nature still, but Nature methodiz'd.

They are eternal and irrevocable, and never to be dis-
pens'd with but by Nature that made them; and the
only Rule for that Dispensation is this, that a less Law
may be violated to avoid the infringing of a greater;
and 'tis equally the Duty both of Ancients and Moderns,
to break thro' a less important Rule, when without that
Infringement a greater must be violated, or the great
End of all the Rules neglected. The great End of all
the Rules is to instruct, and the subordinate End is to
please, by moving of Passion, and particularly that kind
of Passion which ought chiefly to reign in that sort of
Poetry in which the Poet writes. Now 'tis a Rule in
Poetry, that the notorious Events of History are not to
be falsifyed, nor the Periods of Time transpos'd or
confounded. And yet *Virgil* in the fourth of his *Æneis,*
broke thro' this Rule at once by a bold and a judicious
Anachronism, in order to make his Poem more admirable, and the more to exalt the Glory of the *Roman*
Name. Whatever the Ancients justly did, the Moderns
may justly do. 'Tis ridiculous and pedantick to imagine,
that the natural Powers of the Soul were stronger or
more excellent in the Ancients than they are in the
Moderns. And as to Experience we have vastly the
Advantage of them. When we consider Experience,
as my Lord *Bacon* observes, we are properly the
Ancients, who live in the elder Ages of the World, and
have the Advantage of the Knowledge of Three thousand Years over the first Writers. Not but that at the
same time that I assert the Equality of Faculties in the
Moderns, and the Advantage of their Experience, I freely
acknowledge the actual Preheminence that several of the

Ancients have over the Moderns; but I have sufficiently shewn in the *Advancement of Modern Poetry,* that the actual Preheminence proceeded from accidental Causes, and not from any Superiority of Faculties in those ancient Authors.

At the bottom of the same Page 12. there is something asserted that is both false and impudent; where speaking of the Ancients, he tells us,

> *Those are but Stratagems which Errors seem,*
> *Nor is it* Homer *nods but we that dream.*

Which is a presumptuous Contradiction of *Horace,*

> *Aliquando bonus dormitat Homerus.*

And of my Lord *Roscommon.*

> *His reeling Hero's and his wounded Gods*
> *Make some suspect he snores as well as nods.*

And is in effect to declare that *Horace* was a Dreamer, and my Lord *Roscommon* a Dotard, and I, my Masters, only I, am *alerte* and *eveillè,* only I am the man of Importance.

In the beginning of the 21st Page there is something too very wrong.

> *In Words as Fashions the same Rule will hold,*
> *Alike fantastick if too new or old,*
> *Be not the first by whom the new are try'd,*
> *Nor yet the last to lay the old aside.*

This being directed to all without Exception, and deliver'd without Limitation or Restriction, is another flat Contradiction of *Horace.*

Si forte necesse est
Indiciis monstrare recentibus abdita rerum:
Fingere cinctutis non exaudita Cethegis
Continget, dabiturq; licentia sumpta pudenter.
Et nova fictaq; nuper habebunt verba idem, si
Græco fonte cadant parce detorta.

This is likewise a Libel upon the memory of Mr. *Dryden* whom he pretends to admire; for never any one was a greater Coiner than he, and it is directly contrary to the Improvement of Languages; for if *Chaucer* and succeeding Authors had had this Advice given them, and had been weak enough to take it, how could our Language ever have improv'd in Purity, in Force, in Grace, or in Harmony? But if it was allow'd to *Chaucer,* and those who immediately follow'd him, why must it be deny'd to those who have liv'd since.

quid autem
Cæcilio, Plautoq; dabit Romanus ademptum
Virgilio, Varroque? Ego cur acquirere pauca
Si possim, invideor? Quum lingua Catonis & Enni,
Sermonem patrium ditaverit, & nova rerum
Nomina protulerit, licuit semperq; licebit
Signatum præsente nota producere nomen.

I must confess if we speak with relation to the constant and general Practice of a Writer, he ought to take what the *French* call the best Use, for the Mistress of the Language in which he writes; but a great Poet if he writes in the Language which he was born to speak, may be allow'd the Privilege sometimes to coin new words, and sometimes to revive the old, which last succeeded so well to *Milton.*

About the middle of the 22^d Page he gives Advice, which shews him very inconsistent with himself.

And praise the easie Vigor of a Line
Where Denham*'s Strength and* Waller*'s Sweetness join.*

How vastly different is this from what he pretends to advise at the bottom of the 9th Page.

Be Homer*'s Works your Study day and night,*
Read them by day, and meditate by night;
Thence form your Judgment, thence your Notions bring,
And trace the Muses upward to their Spring;
Still with it self compar'd, his Text peruse,
And let your Comment be the Mantuan *Muse.*

Now he who is familiar with *Homer,* and intimate with *Virgil,* will not be extremely affected either with the Sweetness of *Waller,* or the Force of *Denham.* He requires something that is far above the Level of modern Authors, something that is great and wonderful. If I were to recommend a *British* Poet to one who has been habituated to *Homer* and *Virgil,* I would for the Honour of my Country, and of my own Judgment advise him to read *Milton*; who very often equals both the *Græcian* and the *Roman* in their extraordinary Qualities, and sometimes surpasses them, is more lofty, more terrible, more vehement, more astonishing, and has more impetuous and more divine Raptures. I will not deny but that *Waller* has Sweetness, and *Denham* Force; but their good and their shining Qualities are so sophisticated and debauch'd with these modern Vices of Conceit, and Point, and Turn, and Epigram, that 'tis impossible they can affect in an extraordinary manner those who have been long acquainted with the Ancients.

There is in the 38th and the 39th Pages another Inconsistency, which I desire to lay before the Reader. In the 38th Page he speaks of *Horace* thus:

> *He who supreme in Judgment as in Wit,*
> *Might boldly censure as he boldly writ;*
> *Yet judg'd with Coolness, tho' he sung with Fire*
> *His Precepts teach but what his Works inspire.*
> *Our Criticks take a contrary Extreme,*
> *They judge with Fury, but they write with Flegm.*

Before he goes ten Lines farther, he forgets himself, and commends *Longinus* for the very contrary Quality for which he commended *Horace,* and for the very same thing for which he condemns his Contemporaries.

> *The Muses sure* Longinus *did inspire,*
> *And blest their Critick with a Poet's Fire:*
> *An ardent Judge that zealous in his Trust*
> *With warmth gives Judgment, yet is always just;*
> *Whose own Example strengthens all his Laws,*
> *And is himself that great Sublime he draws.*

He commends *Horace* for judging cooly in Verse, and extols *Longinus* for criticizing with Fire in Prose. What a miserable Slave is this Author to Opinion? Can any thing be more plain, than that he condemns his Contemporaries for no other reason but because they are his Contemporaries; and commends *Longinus* for no other reason but because he has been approv'd of by others. For why should not a modern Critick imitate the great Qualities of *Longinus*; and when he treats of a Subject which is sublime, treat of it sublimely? Now he who writes any thing with Sublimity, let it be Prose or Verse, let it be Criticism or Poetry, writes sometimes with Fury, as *Longinus* hath shewn both by his Doctrine and his Example in the first Chapter of his Treatise.

But pray who are these Moderns that judge with Fury, and write with Flegm? Who are they that have writ both Criticism and Poetry, who have not in their Poetry shewn a thousand times this Essayer's Fire? Who is there among them that is not above borrowing so openly and so awkwardly from the most known Authors? For what Reader is so unacquainted with our *English* Poetry, as not to know that he has taken this last Couplet, with a very little variation from the Essay on Translated Verse?

> *Thus make the proper Use of each Extreme*
> *And write with Fury, but correct with Flegm.*

But what is a perspicuous sensible Precept in my Lord *Roscommon,* as soon as this Essayer handles it, becomes a gross Absurdity and a palpable Contradiction.

In the 28th Page there are no less than two or three Absurdities in the compass of four Lines.

> *Now length of Fame our second Life is lost,*
> *And bare Threescore is all ev'n that can boast.*
> *Our Sons their Fathers failing Language see,*
> *And such as* Chaucer *is shall* Dryden *be.*

Now what does young Mr. *Bays* mean by *our second Life,* and by *bare Threescore*? If he speaks of himself, and means threescore Days, he means too much in Reason: But if he speaks of *Chaucer, Spencer,* and *Shakespear,* and means threescore Years, he means too little in Conscience. 'Tis now a hundred Years since *Shakespear* began to write, more since *Spencer* flourished, and above 300 Years since *Chaucer* died. And yet

the Fame of none of these is extinguish'd. The reason
that he gives for this is false too.

Our Sons their Fathers failing Language see,

Mr. *Waller* may suffice to shew the Falsity of this.
'Tis above threescore Years since that Gentleman began
to write, and yet his Language is still good and new.
Thus we find that the Assertion is false here, the
Reason of it false; and we shall find anon that the
Inference is false too.

And such as Chaucer *is shall* Dryden *be;*

That is, shall grow obsolete and neglected, and be either
forgot, or be read but by a few.

Whether the Language of Mr. *Dryden* will ever be
as obsolete as is at present that of *Chaucer,* is what
neither this Author nor any one else can tell. For ev'ry
Language hath its particular period of Time to bring
it to Perfection, I mean to all the Perfection of which
that Language is capable. And they who are alive cannot
possibly tell whether that period hath happen'd or not:
If that period has not yet happen'd; yet 'tis not the
Obsoleteness of Language which makes a Poet fall from
the Reputation which he once enjoy'd, provided the
Language in which that Poet wrote was at the Time
of his Writing come to be capable of Harmony. For
Spencer is obsolete, yet is still renown'd. That which
makes an Author fall from his former Reputation, is,
says *Boileau,* in his seventh Reflection upon *Longinus,*
his not having attain'd to that Point of Solidity and
Perfection, which are necessary to give a never dying
Esteem to his Works. For Example, says he, the Latin
Tongue in which *Cicero* and *Virgil* wrote, was already
very much alter'd in the Time of *Quintilian* and of *Aulus*

Gellius; and yet *Cicero* and *Virgil* were more esteem'd when those Criticks wrote, than they were in their own Age, because they had as it were by their Writings fix'd the *Roman* Language, having attain'd to that Point of Solidity and Perfection which I have mention'd above.

If we reflect upon that miserable Tast which reigns now among our Readers, and that want of Genius which is so deplorable in our present Writers, and that Tast and Genius daily more and more decline, we may without being Prophets foretel, according to the foremention'd Observation of the Solidity and Perfection of Poems, that the Language is not like to alter to the Disadvantage of those Poets, whose Works are the only Remains of them here below. But be that as it will, yet this is certain, that Mr. *Dryden* had one Quality in his Language, which *Chaucer* had not, and which must always remain. For having acquir'd some Justness of Numbers, and some Truth of Harmony and of Versification, to which *Chaucer* thro' the Rudeness of the Language, or want of Ear, or want of Experience, or rather perhaps a mixture of all, could not possibly attain, that Justness of Numbers, and Truth of Harmony and of Versification can never be destroy'd by any alteration of Language; and therefore Mr. *Dryden* whatever alteration happens to the Language, can never be like to *Chaucer*.

Wherever this Gentleman talks of Wit, he is sure to say something that is very foolish, as Page 29.

> *What is this Wit that does our Cares employ,*
> *The Owner's Wife that other Men enjoy?*
> *The more his Trouble as the more admir'd,*
> *Where wanted scorn'd, and envy'd where acquir'd.*

Here again I desire leave to ask two or three Questions. First, how can Wit be scorn'd where it is not? Is not this a Figure frequently employ'd in *Hibernian* Land? The Person who wants this Wit may indeed be scorn'd; but such a Contempt declares the Honour that the Contemner has for Wit. But secondly, what does he mean by acquir'd Wit? Does he mean Genius by the word Wit, or Conceit and Point? If he means Genius, that is certainly never to be acquir'd; and the Person who should pretend to acquire it, would be always secure from Envy. But if by Wit he means Conceit and Point, those are things that ought never to be in Poetry, unless by chance sometimes in the Epigram, or in Comedy, where it is proper to the Character and the Occasion; and ev'n in Comedy it ought always to give place to Humour, and ev'n to be lost and absorp'd in that, according to the Precept of the noble Author of the *Essay on Poetry.*

> *That silly thing Men call sheer Wit avoid,*
> *With which our Age so nauseously is cloy'd;*
> *Humour is all, Wit should be only brought*
> *To turn agreeably some proper Thought.*

In the beginning of the 33ᵈ Page there is a Couplet of Advice, the first line of which is very impertinent, and the second very wrong.

> *Be silent always when you doubt your Sense.*

Now who are the Persons to whom he is giving Advice here? Why, to Poets or Criticks, or both; but the Persons to whom he ought to be speaking are Criticks, that is, People who pretend to instruct others. But can any man of common Sense want to be told, that he ought not to pretend to instruct others, as long as he doubts of the Truth of his own Precepts?

But what can be more wrong or more absurd than the latter Verse of the Couplet?

Speak when you're sure, yet speak with Diffidence.

Now I should think that when a man is sure, 'tis his Duty to speak with a modest Assurance; since in doing otherwise he betrays the Truth, especially when he speaks to those who are guided more by Imagination than they are by Judgment, which is the Case of three parts of the World, and three parts of the other Part.

He is so great a Lover of Falshood, that whenever he has a mind to calumniate his Contemporaries, he upbraids them with some Defect, which is just contrary to some good Quality for which all their Friends and their Acquaintance commend them. As for Example, if a Man is remarkable for the extraordinary Deference which he pays to the Opinions and the Remonstrances of his Friends, him he Libels for his Impatience under Reproof. On the contrary, if he has a mind to extol the Ancients, he passes by either thro' Envy or Ignorance all the great Qualities which they have, and extols them for some peculiar one, the very want of which is known to all the World to be their Infirmity and their Defect. Thus in the 37th Page he takes occasion to commend *Aristotle* for what he wrote in Physicks, a great deal of which is so justly censur'd and condemn'd ev'n by the same learned and judicious Men, who allow his *Æthicks,* his *Politicks,* his *Rhetorick,* and his *Poetick,* to be worthy of the greatest Philosopher. And here as the Commendation which he gives him is false, the manner of giving it is still more false. For, says he,

Not only Nature did his Laws obey,
But Fancy's boundless Empire own'd his Sway.

The Expression in the first Verse is not only absurd, but blasphemous. The Laws of Nature are unalterable and indispensable but by God himself; and the greatest Excellence to which the wisest Philosopher can attain, is not to controul, but to obey Nature.

In the Libel upon King *Charles* the Second, he has not only endeavour'd to brand the Memory of that Prince for something which is utterly false, but for something which if it had been true had been an Excellence in that Prince. For *Wits,* says he, in that Monarch's Reign had Pensions, when all the World knows that it was one of the Faults of that Reign that none of the politer Arts were then encourag'd. For of this we may be sure, that whenever we have a Prince and Ministers, who truly understand either their own Interest, or that of the Publick, Arts and Learning will be then encourag'd; I mean not speciously and pretendedly, but really and sincerely.

The King of *France* pretended to encourage Arts by allowing Pensions to some few Professors of them, whereas at the same time he was and is doing a thing, which has a natural Tendency to the driving them out of *Europe.* For by kindling and prosecuting an unjust War thro' so many different Nations, he has gone a very great way towards the barbarizing the Christian World; and the Arts would have been at a much greater height, than they are now, without any manner of Encouragement from him, if they had been suffer'd to have enjoy'd the Quiet of an universal Peace. In the same manner some Persons of Quality in *Great Britain* have been kind to some particular Professors of Poetry; but at the very same time, by not only introducing the *Italian* Opera among us, but by continuing constant Encouragers of it to this very day, they are doing a thing which will drive the very Art it self out of the Kingdom, as it has been already driven out of every other Nation; and are depriving their Favourite Authors of more than ever they yet bestow'd upon them. Any great Minister would now have a glorious Opportunity of being a true Encourager of Poetry, and ev'ry other generous Art, by representing effectually to her Majesty the Mischief that the *Italians* do both to her Subjects, and to the Arts, and so driving those melodious Ballad-Singers out of the Nation.

But to return to the Reign of King *Charles* the Second, from which I may seem to have in some measure digress'd; there was then indeed a favourable regard shewn to Wit, but no real Encouragement. *Butler* was starv'd at the same time that the King had his Book in his Pocket. Another great Wit lay seven Years in Prison for an inconsiderable Debt, and *Otway* dar'd not to shew his Head for fear of the same Fate. These are some of the Glories of that Reign according to this Author. For if it be a Vice in a Prince to encourage an Art, 'tis a Vertue to neglect it. What a wretched Creature is this Pretender to Criticism and Poetry to keep such a pother about an Art, the Encouragement of which he imputes as Infamy to King *Charles* the Second?

Well! but he tells us that not only

The Wits had Pensions, but young Lords had Wit.

Here in the compass of one poor Line are two devilish Bobs for the Court. But 'tis no easy matter to tell which way the latter squinting Reflection looks. For if he pretends to reflect upon that Prince, for receiving Persons of Quality who had Wit into his Court, can any thing be more impertinent than twice in one Line to libel a Monarch for being favourable to that very thing, which he takes so much pains in this very Book to recommend to the World? If he means that the young Lords of the Court who pretended to Wit had it not, can any thing be more arrogant than to fly in the Face of all Mankind, and to contradict almost the only thing in which all sorts of People agree, ev'n in this divided Age, *Britons* and Foreigners, Protestants and Papists, Whigs and Tories, Churchmen and Dissenters, and to pretend to reflect upon Persons whose very Names are their Panegyricks? The young Lords who had Wit in the Court of King *Charles* the Second, are these: The young former Duke of *Buckingham,* the young Earl of *Mulgrave* now Duke of *Buckingham,* the young Lord *Buckhurst* afterwards Earl of *Dorset* and *Middlesex,* and the young Marquess of *Halifax*; the young Earl of *Rochester,* the young Lord *Vaughan* now Lord *Carbury,* and several others. If the looking favourably upon young Persons of Quality who had Wit, may be imputed as Scandal to the Court of King *Charles* the Second, that Court was certainly the most scandalous one in *Europe.* But if he says on the other side that 'tis dishonourable to a Prince to be mistaken in this Point, and to look with a favourable Eye on Pretenders instead of real Masters; to that all the World with one accord will answer that never Prince had a clearer Reputation in this Point.

Thus are his Assertions, and his Precepts frequently false or trivial, or both, his Thoughts very often crude and abortive, his Expressions absurd, his Numbers often harsh and unmusical, without Cadence and without Variety, his Rhimes trivial and common. He dictates perpetually, and pretends to give Law without any thing of the Simplicity or Majesty of a Legislator, and pronounces Sentence without any thing of the Plainness or

Clearness, or Gravity of a Judge. Instead of Simplicity we have little Conceit and Epigram, and Affectation. Instead of Majesty we have something that is very mean, and instead of Gravity we have something that is very boyish. And instead of Perspicuity and lucid Order, we have but too often Obscurity and Confusion.

But what most shews him a very young Author, is, that with all these Faults and this Weakness he has the Insolence of a Hero, and is a downright Bully of *Parnassus,* who is ev'ry moment thund'ring out Fool, Sot, Fop, Coxcomb, Blockhead, and thinks to hide his want of Sense by his pretended Contempt of others, as a Hector does his want of Courage by his perpetual blustring and roaring; and is sagaciously of Opinion, that he arrogates so much Sense to himself as he imputes Folly to other People.

> *Thus a wild* Tartar *when he spies*
> *A Man that's handsome, valiant, wise,*
> *Thinks if he kills him to inherit*
> *His Wit, his Beauty, and his Spirit,*
> *As if just so much he enjoy'd*
> *As in another he destroy'd.*

By what he says Page the 25th, and his returning to the Charge, Page 34, his particular Pique seems to be at People of Quality, for whom he appears to have a very great Contempt, I mean for the Authors of that Rank; as if a Man were to assert his Title to *Parnassus,* by proving himself a Plebeian in *Great Britain*; or as if an *English* Sovereign by making a Man honourable, made him dull. Good Gods, how absolute would our Princes be at that rate! when they would have the very Understandings of their Subjects at their disposal, and would need only to prefer the Disobedient to chastise them.

I hope, I may without offence, gently put young Mr. *Bays* in mind, that the Subordination which is absolutely necessary to the Government of the World requires that Respect should be paid to Persons of Quality, ev'n where Esteem cannot be paid to them; but that in this case they both may and ought to have our Respect and Esteem together. For I know very few People of Quality who have applied themselves to Poetry, who have not succeeded; on the other side 'tis known to all the World that some of them have been admirable. For nothing is more certain than that supposing equal Talent and equal Application, a Man of Quality has great Advantages over the rest of Men. But can any thing be more stupidly impudent and impertinent, than that this little Gentleman should rail thus at the Writings of People of Quality in this very Essay, the one half of which he has borrow'd from two noble Authors, and appropriated it to himself, by the same Method by which a *Jack pudding* engrosses a Sack-posset, *viz.* by mingling some Beastliness with it, which does not fail to render it nauseous to those who made it. This extraordinary Proceeding of borrowing and railing puts me in mind of a Passage in Mr. Cowley.

> *'Tis now become the frugal Fashion*
> *Rather to hide than pay the Obligation;*
> *Nay Wrongs and Outrages we do,*
> *Lest Men should think we Owe.*

But the Men of Quality, as they want not the Discernment, will have the Satisfaction to see, that as there is a great deal of Venom in this little Gentleman's Temper, Nature has very wisely corrected it with a great deal of Dulness.

His rankest Libels lull asleep his Foes,
As Vipers blood in Treacle makes us dose.

As there is no Creature in Nature so venomous, there is nothing so stupid and so impotent as a hunch-back'd Toad; and a Man must be very quiet and very passive, and stand still to let him fasten his Teeth and his Claws, or be surpriz'd sleeping by him, before that Animal can have any power to hurt him.

Thus in order to find out his outward Person have we taken a Survey of his inward Man, in his several noble Talents and Vertues, his Poetry, his Criticism, his Modesty, his Humility, his Gratitude, and his good Breeding. Let us now take a Survey of his Politicks, and his Religion, not by any means by way of Reflection; for Poetry and Criticism are of no Party, and of no Religion, but only to find who he is.

I find then that in the compass of one Page, which is the thirty first, he has Libell'd two Monarchs and two Nations. The two Monarchs are King *Charles* and King *William*: The two Nations are the *Dutch* and our own. The *Dutch* we are told are a parcel of Sharpers, and we are downright Bubbles and Fools. King *Charles* the Second was too much a Libertine, and too much an Encourager of Wit for him; King *William* the Third was too much a *Socinian*. But tho' he has without Mercy condemn'd the Reigns of the foremention'd Monarchs, he is graciously pleas'd to pass over in silence that which comes between them. In the beginning of the 12th Page, we find what that is which so happily reconcil'd him to it, and that was the Dispensing Pow'r, which was set on foot in order to introduce and to establish Popery, and to make it the National Religion. Now I humbly conceive that he who Libels our Confederates, must be by Politicks a *Jacobite*; and he who Libels all the Protestant Kings that we have had in this Island these threescore Years, and who justifies the Dispensing Pow'r so long after we are free'd from it, a Pow'r which as was hinted above was set on foot on purpose to introduce Popery: He who justifies this when he lyes under the Tye of no Necessity, nor ev'n Conveniency to approve of it, must, I humbly conceive, derive his Religion from St. *Omer*'s, as he seems to have done his Humanity and his Criticism; and is, I suppose, politickly setting up for Poet-Laureat against the coming over of the Pretender, which by his Insolence he seems to believe approaching, as People of his Capacity are generally very sanguine.

Let us now see if we can find any thing in his Rhimes, which may direct us to his Coffee-house, or to his Book-sellers. By his taking three Opportunities to commend Mr. *Dryden*, in so small a compass as p. 23, 27, 28, I fancy we may hear of him at *Shakespear*'s Head, or at *Will*'s, for to revive old Quarrels which have been long out of doors, and to renew the memory of Poetical Wars wag'd formerly between Sir *R. B.* Mr. *L. M.* and Mr. *Dryden*, can be agreeable to none but a very few of the Frequenters of those Places. This is to run counter to his own Direction; for he tells us Page 27. that formerly

Pride, Malice, Folly against Dryden *rose*
In various shapes of Parsons, Criticks, Beaus.

Upon which, Page 28, he gives this grave Advice,

Be thou the first true Merit to befriend,
His Praise is lost who stays till all commend.

The appearing in Mr. *Dryden*'s behalf now is too late. 'Tis like offering a Man's self for a Second, after the Principal has been whipp'd through the Lungs. Now

Mr. *Dryden* is dead, he commends him with the rest of the World. But if this little Gentleman had been his Contemporary thirty Years ago, why then I can tell a very damn'd shape that Pride and Malice, and Folly would have appear'd in against Mr. *Dryden*.

For his Acquaintance he names Mr. *Walsh*. I had the good Fortune to know Mr. *Walsh* very well; who was a learned, candid, judicious Gentleman. But he had by no means the Qualification which this Author reckons absolutely necessary to a Critick; it being certain that Mr. *Walsh* was like this Essayer a very indifferent Poet; but he was a Man of a very good Understanding, in spight of his being a Beau. He lov'd to be well dress'd, as *Dorimant* says, and thought it no Disparagement to his Understanding; and I remember a little young Gentleman, with all the Qualifications which we have found to be in this Author, whom Mr. *Walsh* us'd sometimes to take into his Company as a double Foil to his Person, and his Capacity. It has been observ'd that of late Years a certain Spectre exactly in the shape of that little Gentleman, has haunted a certain ancient Wit, and has been by the People of *Covent-Garden* styl'd his evil Genius. For it hath been extremely remarkable, that while that Spectre hath haunted that ancient Wit, he has never been able to write or talk like himself: Which has by no means happen'd by any Decay of his natural Parts, but by the wonderful Pow'r of Magick. For as soon as the dumb Conjurer has been employ'd to lay the Spectre for three or four months, either in the midst of the *Red Sea,* or the middle of *Windsor-Forest,* the old Gentleman has strait been his own Man as perfectly as ever he was in his Life.

And now if your have a mind to enquire between *Sunning-Hill* and *Ockingham,* for a young, squab, short

Gentleman, with the forementioned Qualifications, an eternal Writer of Amorous Pastoral Madrigals, and the very Bow of the God of Love, you will be soon directed to him. And pray as soon as you have taken a Survey of him, tell me whether he is a proper Author to make personal Reflections on others; and tell him if he does not like my Person, 'tis because he is an ungrateful Creature, since his Conscience tells him, that I have been always infinitely delighted with his: So delighted, that I have lately drawn a very graphical Picture of it; but I believe I shall keep the *Dutch* Piece from ever seeing the Light, as a certain old Gentleman in *Windsor-Forest* would have done by the Original, if he durst have been half as impartial to his own Draught as I have been to mine. This little Author may extol the Ancients as much and as long as he pleases, but he has reason to thank the good Gods that he was born a Modern. For had he been born of *Græcian* Parents, and his Father by consequence had by Law had the absolute Disposal of him, his Life had been no longer than that of one of his Poems, the Life of half a day. Instead of setting his Picture to show, I have taken a keener Revenge, and expos'd his Intellectuals, as duly considering that let the Person of a Gentleman of his Parts be never so contemptible, his inward Man is ten times more ridiculous; it being impossible that his outward Form, tho' it should be that of downright Monkey, should differ so much from human Shape, as his immaterial unthinking part does from human Understanding. How agreeable it is to be in a Libel with so much good Company as I have been, with two great Monarchs, two mighty Nations, and especially the People of Quality of *Great Britain,* and this Libel compos'd by a little Gentleman, who has writ a Panegyrick upon himself! Which Panegyrick if it was not writ with Judgment, yet was it publish'd with Discretion, for it was publish'd in Mr. W——'s Name; so that by this wise Proceeding he had the Benefit of the Encomium, and Mr. W—— had the Scandal of the Poetry; which it brought upon him to such a degree, that 'tis ten to one if ever he recovers the Reputation of a good Versifyer. And thus for the present I take my leave of you and of this little Critick and his Book; a Book throughout which Folly and Ignorance, those Brethren so lame and so impotent, do ridiculously at one and the same time look very big and very dull, and strut, and hobble cheek by jowl with their Arms on Kimbo, being led and supported, and Bully-back'd by that blind Hector Impudence. I am,

Sir,
Your, &c.

Annotations.

1. *First follow Nature,* p. 7.

Horace has giv'n a Precept, which may be quoted by undistinguishing People to keep this in countenance.

> *Respicere exemplar vitæ, morumq; jubebo*
> *Doctum imitatorem & veras hinc Ducere voces.*

For he bids the Person to whom this is directed consult Nature; but then he does three things, which vastly distinguish him from the Writer of the Essay: For first he makes it very plain what sort of Person this is to whom he directs himself, and that is *Doctus Imitator,* one who is both Poet and Critick, Dramatick Poet, and Dramatick Critick; one who writes Plays, and understands the Rules, and knows the Secrets of his Art;

notwithstanding which, he may be ignorant of that important one, which *Horace* is about to discover to him; or in case he does already know it, he may want to be put in mind of it, because his Interest, as we shall find anon, is a strong Temptation to deviate from it. But secondly *Horace* tells us very intelligibly what he means by Nature here, and that is, human Life, and the manners of Men. Thirdly, he makes it as clear as the Sun, what it is to follow Nature in giving a draught of human Life, and of the manners of Men, and that is not to draw after particular Men, who are but Copies and imperfect Copies of the great universal Pattern; but to consult that innate Original, and that universal Idea, which the Creator has fix'd in the minds of ev'ry reasonable Creature, and so to make a true and a just Draught. For as ev'ry Copy deviates from the Original both in Life and Grace, and Resemblance, a Poet who designs to give a true Draught of human Life and Manners, must consult the universal Idea, and not particular Persons. For Example, when a Poet would draw the Character of a covetous or a revengeful person, he is not to draw after *Lucius* or *Caius*; but to consult the universal pattern within him, and there to behold what Revenge or Covetousness would do in such and such Natures, upon such and such Occasions. For if he draws after *Lucius* or *Caius,* the workings of Revenge and Covetousness in these two, being but Copies and imperfect Copies of their workings according to the universal *Idea,* and the Poet degenerating in his Draught ev'n from those faint and imperfect Copies, whenever a just and discerning Judge comes to compare that Draught with the Original within him, he immediately finds that that Draught falls extremely short of the Truth of Nature, and immediately disapproves of it, as a second, ungraceful, faint, unresembling Copy. Agreeable to this is that passage of the most discerning Author of the Essay upon Poetry.

> *If once the Justness of each part is lost,*
> *Well may we laugh, but at the Poet's cost.*

Thus *Horace* here speaks to the Knowing, yet tells them something that several of them want to be taught, and several to be put in mind of. For it has been a Complaint of Two thousand Years standing, that Poets have been us'd to violate their Subjects, and to force their Characters out of complaisance to their Actors, that is, to their Interest. Most of the Writers for the Stage in my time, have not only adapted their Characters to their Actors, but those Actors have as it were sate for them. For which reason the Lustre of the most shining of their Characters must decay with the Actors, while those of *Sophocles, Euripides, Terence* and *Ben Johnson* will eternally remain.

2. *Still green with* Bays *each ancient Altar stands,* p. 13.

If Mr. *Bays* should say here that by each ancient Altar he does not mean ev'ry ancient Poet, but only those few who have been admir'd by all succeeding Ages; to this I answer, that besides that the Expression will by no means bear this Sense, it appears plainly from the two first lines of p. 12. that he speaks of the Ancients in general.

> *And tho' the Ancients thus their Rules invade,*
> *As Kings dispense with Laws themselves have made.*
> *Moderns beware.* p. 12.

I think nothing can be more plain, than that here he prefers all the Ancients before all the Moderns, treating the former as so many Monarchs and Legislators at the same time in the Regions of Sense, and the latter as so many Slaves. Besides that these Verses manifestly relate rather to the indifferent Poets among the Ancients, than to those who are admirable; for the indifferent ones have most and oftnest invaded the Rules, Indeed they have scarce ever observ'd them; as *Homer* and *Virgil* have scarce ever transgress'd them.

FINIS.

GEORGE FARQUHAR

GEORGE FARQUHAR

A DISCOURSE UPON COMEDY, IN REFERENCE TO THE ENGLISH STAGE.

1702

In a Letter to a Friend.

WITH Submission, Sir, my Performance in the Practical Part of Poetry is no sufficient Warrant for your
pressing me in the Speculative; I have no Foundation
for a *Legislator,* and the two or three little *Plays* I have
written, are cast carelesly into the World, without any
Bulk of *Preface,* because I was not so learn'd in the
Laws, as to move in Defence of a bad Case. Why then
shou'd a Compliment go farther with me, than my own
Interest? Don't mistake me, Sir, here is nothing that
cou'd make for my Advantage in either *Preface* or
Dedication; no *Speculative Curiosities,* nor *Critical
Remarks*; only some present Sentiments which Hazard,
not Study, brings into my Head, without any preliminary
Method or *Cogitation.*

Among the many Disadvantages attending Poetry,
none seems to bear a greater Weight, than that so many
set up for Judges, when so very few understand a tittle
of the matter. Most of our other Arts and Sciences
bear an awful Distance in their Prospect, or with a bold
and glittering Varnish dazle the Eyes of the weak-sighted
Vulgar. The *Divine* stands wrapt up in his Cloud of
Mysteries, and the amus'd *Layety* must pay Tyths and

Veneration to be kept in Obscurity, grounding their Hopes of future Knowledge on a Competent Stock of present Ignorance (in the greater part of the Christian World this is plain.) With what Deference and Resignation does the bubbled *Client* commit his Fees and Cause into the Clutches of the *Law,* where Assurance beards Justice by *Prescription,* and the wrong side is never known to make it's *Patron* blush. *Physick* and *Logick* are so strongly fortify'd by their impregnable Terms of Art, and the *Mathematician* lies so cunningly intrench'd within his *Lines* and *Circles,* that none but those of their Party dare peep into their puzling Designs.

Thus the Generality of Mankind is held at a gazing Distance, whose Ignorance not presuming perhaps to an open Applause, is yet satisfy'd to pay a blind Veneration to the very Faults of what they don't understand.

Poetry alone, and chiefly the *Dramma,* lies open to the Insults of all Pretenders; she was one of Nature's eldest Offsprings, whence by her Birthright and plain Simplicity she pleads a genuine Likeness to her Mother; born in the Innocence of Time, she provided not against the Assaults of succeeding Ages; and, depending altogether on the generous End of her Invention, neglected those secret Supports and serpentine Devices us'd by other Arts that wind themselves into Practice for more subtle and politick Designs: Naked she came into the Wo[r]ld, and 'tis to be fear'd, like its Professiors, will go naked out.

'Tis a wonderful thing, that most Men seem to have a great Veneration for *Poetry,* yet will hardly allow a favourable Word to any Piece of it that they meet; like your Virtuoso's in Friendship, that are so ravish'd with the notional Nicety of the Vertue, that they can find no Person worth their intimate Acquaintance. The Favour of being whipt at School for *Martial's Epigrams,* or

Ovid's Epistles, is sufficient Priviledge for turning Pedagogue, and lashing all their Successors; and it wou'd
seem by the fury of their Correction, that the ends of
the Rod were still in their Buttocks. The Scholar calls
upon us for *Decorums* and *Oeconnomy*; the Courtier crys
out for *Wit* and *Purity of Stile*; the Citizen for *Humour*
and *Ridicule*; the Divines threaten us for Immodesty;
and the Ladies will have an Intreague. Now here are a
multitude of Criticks, whereof the twentieth Person only
has read *Quæ Genus,* and yet every one is a Critick after
his own way; that is, Such a Play is best, because I like
it. A very familiar Argument, methinks, to prove the
Excellence of a Play, and to which an Author wou'd be
very unwilling to appeal for his Success: Yet such is the
unfortunate State of Dramatick Poetry, that it must
submit to such Judgments; and by the Censure or Approbation of such variety it must either stand or fall. But
what *Salvo,* what Redress for this Inconvenience? Why,
without all Dispute, an Author must indeavour to
pleasure that Part of the Audience, who can lay the best
claim to a judicious and impartial Reflection: But before
he begins, let him well consider to what Division that
Claim do's most properly belong. The Scholar will be
very angry at me for making that the Subject of a
Question, which is self-evident without any Dispute:
For, says he, who can pretend to understand Poetry
better than we, who have read *Homer, Virgil, Horace,
Ovid,* &c. at the University? What Knowledge can out-
strip ours, that is founded upon the Criticisms of
Aristotle, Scaliger, Vossius, and the like? We are the
better sort, and therefore may claim this as a due Compliment to our Learning; and if a Poet can please us,
who are the nice and severe Criticks, he cannot fail to
bring in the rest of an inferiour Rank.

I shou'd be very proud to own my Veneration for
Learning, and to acknowledge any Complement due to
the better sort upon that Foundation; but I'm afraid the
Learning of the Better Sort is not confin'd to Colledge
Studies, for there is such a thing as Reason without
Silligism, Knowlege without *Aristotle,* and Languages
besides Greek and Latin. We shall likewise find in the
Court and City several Degrees, superiour to those at
Commencements. From all which I must beg the
Scholar's Pardon, for not paying him the Compliment of
the better Sort, (as he calls it) and in the next Place,
inquire into the Validity of his Title from his knowledge
of *Criticism,* and the Course of his Studies.

I must first beg one favour of the Graduate - - - Sir,
here is a Pit full of *Covent-Garden* Gentlemen, a Gallery
full of Citts, a hundred Ladies of Court-Education, and
about two hundred Footmen of nice Morality, who
having been unmercifully teiz'd with a parcel of foolish,
impertinent, irregular Plays all this last Winter, make
it their humble Request, that you wou'd oblige them with
a Comedy of your own making, which they don't
question will give them Entertainment. O, Sir, replies
the *Square Cap,* I have long commiserated the Condition
of the English Audience, that has been forc'd to take up
with such wretched Stuff, as lately has crouded the
Stage; your *Jubilees* and your *Fopingtons,* and such
irregular impertinence, that no Man of Sense cou'd bear
the perusal of 'em: I have long intended, out of pure
pity to the Stage, to write a perfect Piece of this Nature;
and now, since I am honour'd by the Commands of so
many, my Intentions shall immediately be put in Practice.

So to work he goes; old *Aristotle, Scaliger,* with their
Commentators, are lugg'd down from the high Shelf,
and the Moths are dislodg'd from their Tenement of

Years; *Horace, Vossius, Heinsius, Hedelin, Rapin,* with
some half a Dozen more, are thumb'd and toss'd about,
to teach the Gentleman, forsooth, to write a Comedy;
and here is he furnish'd with *Unity of Action, Continuity
of Action, Extent of Time, Preparation of Incidents,
Episodes, Narrations, Deliberations, Didacticks, Pathet-
icks, Monologues, Figures, Intervals, Catastrophes,
Chorusies, Scenes, Machines, Decorations,* &c. a Stock
sufficient to set up any Mountebank in *Christendum*; and
if our new Author wou'd take an Opportunity of reading
a Lecture upon his Play in these Terms, by the help of
a *Zany,* and a Joynt-Stool, his Scenes might go off as
well as the Doctors Packets; but the Misfortu[n]e of it
is, he scorns all Application to the Vulgar, and will please
the better Sort, as he calls his own sort. Pursuant
therefore to his Philosophical Dictates, he first chooses
a single Plot, because most agreeable to the regularity of
Criticism, no matter whether it affords Business enough
for Diversion or Surprise. He wou'd not for the World
introduce a Song or Dance, because his Play must be one
intire Action. We must expect no Variety of Incidents,
because the Exactness of his three Hours wont give him
time for their Preparation. The Unity of Place admits
no variety of Painting and Prospect, by which Mischance
perhaps, we shall loose the only good Scenes in the Play.
But no matter for that, this Play is a regular Play; this
Play has been examin'd and approv'd by such and such
Gentlemen, who are staunch Criticks and Masters of
Art; and this Play I will have acted. Look'ee, Mr. *Rich,*
you may venture to lay out a Hundred and fifty Pound
for dressing this Play, for it was written by a great
Scholar, and Fellow of a College.

Then a grave dogmatical Prologue is spoken, to instruct the Audience what shou'd please them; that this

Play has a new and different Cut from the Farce they
see every Day that this Author writes after the manner
of the *Ancients,* and here is a Piece according to the
Model of the *Athenian Drama.* Very well! This goes
off *Hum drum, So, so.* Then the Players go to work on
a piece of hard, knotty Stuff, where they can no more
show their Art, than a Carpenter can upon a piece of
Steel. Here is the Lamp and the Scholar in every Line,
but not a Syllable of the Poet. Here is elaborate Language, Sounding Epithets, Flights of Words that strike
the Clouds, whilst the poor Sense lags after like the
Lanthorn in the Tail of the Kite, which appears only
like a Star, while the Breath of the Players Lungs has
Strength to bear it up in the Air.

But the Audience, willing perhaps to discover his
ancient Model, and the *Athenian Drama,* are attentive
to the first Act or two; but not finding a true Genius of
Poetry, nor the natural Air of free Conversation; without any Regard to his Regularity, they betake themselves
to other Work; not meeting the Diversion they expected
on the Stage, they shift for themselves in the Pit, every
one turns about to his Neighbour in a Mask, and for
default of Entertainment now, they strike up for more
diverting Scenes when the Play is done; and tho' the
Play be as regular as *Aristotle,* and modest as Mr. *Collier*
cou'd wish, yet it promotes more Lewdness in the Consequence, and procures more effectually for Intreague than
any *Rover, Libertine,* or old *Batchelour* whatsoever. At
last comes the Epilogue, which pleases the Audience very
well, because it sends them away, and terminates the
Fate of the Poet; the *Patentees* rail at him, the Players
Curse him, the Town damns him, and he may bury his
Copy in *Pauls,* for not a Bookseller about it will put it
in Print.

This familiar Account, Sir, I wou'd not have you charge to my Invention, for there are Precedents sufficient in the World to warrant it in every particular; the Town has been often disappointed in those Critical Plays, and some Gentlemen that have been admir'd in their speculative Remarks, have been ridicul'd in the practick. All the Authorities, all the Rules of Antiquity have prov'd too weak to support the Theatre, whilst others who have dispenc'd with the Criticks, and taken a Latitude in the *OEconomy* of their Plays, have been the chief Supporters of the Stage, and the Ornament of the *Drama*; this is so visibly true, that I need bring in no instances to enforce it; but you say, Sir, 'tis a Paradox that has often puzled your Understanding, and you lay your Commands upon me to solve it, if I can.

Lookee, Sir, to add a Value to my Complaisance to you, I must tell you in the first Place, that I run as great a hazard in nibling at this *Paradox* of *Poetry,* as *Luther* did by touching *Transubstantiation,* 'tis a Mistery that the World has sweetly slept in so long, that they take it very ill to be waken'd, especially being disturb'd of their rest, when there is no Business to be done. But I think that *Bellarmin* was once as *Orthodox* as *Aristotle*; and since the *German Doctor* has made a shift to hew down the *Cardinal,* I will have a tug with *ipse dixit,* tho' I dye for't.

But in the first Place, I must beg you, Sir, to lay aside your Superstitious Veneration for Antiquity, and the usual Expressions on that Score; that the present Age is illiterate, or their taste is vitiated; that we live in the decay of Time, and the Dotage of the World is fall'n to our Share - - - - 'Tis a mistake, Sir, the World was never more active or youthful, and true downright Sense was never more Universal than at this very Day; 'tis neither confin'd to one Nation in the World, nor to one part of a City, 'tis remarkable in *England* as well as *France*; and good genuine Reason is nourish'd by the Cold of *Swedeland* as by the Warmth of *Italy,* 'tis neither abdicated the Court with the late Reigns, nor expell'd the City with the Play-house Bills; you may find it in the *Grand-Jury* at *Hick's Hall,* and upon the Bench sometimes among the Justices; then why shou'd we be hamper'd so in our Opinions, as if all the Ruins of Antiquity lay so heavily on the Bones of us, that we cou'd not stir Hand nor Foot: No, no, Sir, *ipse dixit* is remov'd long ago, and all the Rubbish of old Philosophy, that in a manner bury'd the Judgment of Mankind for many Centuries, is now carry'd off; the vast Tomes of *Aristotle* and his Commentatore are all taken to pieces, and their Infallibility is lost with all Persons of a free and unprejudic'd Reason.

Then above all Men living, why shou'd the Poets be hoodwink'd at this rate; and by what Authority shou'd *Aristotle's* Rules of Poetry stand so fixt and immutable? Why, by the Authority of two Thousand Years standing, because thro' this long Revolution of time the World has still continu'd the same ---- By the Authority of their being receiv'd at *Athens,* a City, the very same with *London* in every particular; their Habits the same, their Humours alike, their publick Transactions and private Societies *Alamode France*; in short, so very much the same in every Circumstance, that *Aristotle's* Criticisms may give rules to *Drury Lane*; the *Areopagus* give Judgment upon a Case in the *Kings Bench,* and old *Solon* shall give Laws to the *House of Commons.*

But to examine this Matter a little farther; all Arts and Professions are compounded of these two parts, a Speculative Knowledge, and a practical Use; and from

an excellency in both these any Person is rais'd to Emi-
nence and Authority in his Calling. The Lawyer has
his Years of Student in the Speculative Part of his Business; and, when promoted to Bar, he falls upon the
Practick, which is the Tryal of his Ability; without all
dispute the great *Cook* has had many a tug at the Bar,
before he cou'd raise himself to the Bench; and had
made sufficiently evident his Knowledge of the Laws
in his Pleadings before he was admitted to the Authority
of giving Judgment upon the Case.

The Physician to gain Credit to his Prescriptions, must
labour for a Reputation in the Cure of such and such
Distempers, and before he sets up for a *Galen* or *Hippocrates,* must make many Experiments upon his
Patients. Philosophy it self, which is a Science the most
abstract from Practice, has its own publick Acts and
Disputations; it is rais'd gradually, and its Professour
commences Doctor by degrees; he has the Labour of
maintaining Theses's, Methodising his Arguments, and
clearing Objections; his Memory and Understanding is
often puzled by Oppositions couch'd in Fallacies and
Sophisms, in solving all which he must make himself
remarkable, before he pretends to impose his own
Systems upon the World. Now if the Case be thus in
Philosophy, or in any branch thereof, as in Ethicks,
Physicks, which are call'd Sciences, what must be done
in Poetry, that is denominated an Art, and consequently
implies a Practice in its Perfection?

Is it reasonable that any Person that has never writ a
Distich of Verses in his Life, shou'd set up for a Dictator
in Poetry; and without the least Practice in his own
Performance, must give Laws and Rules to that of
others? Upon what Foundation is Poetry made so very
cheap, and so easy a Task, by these Gentlemen? an ex-

cellent Poet is the single Production of an Age, when we have Crowds of Philosophers, Physicians, Lawyers[,] Divines, every Day, and all of them competently famous in their Callings. In the two learned Commonwealths of *Rome* and *Athens,* there was but one *Virgil,* and one *Homer,* yet have we above a hundred *Philosophers* in each, and most part of 'em, forsooth, must have a touch at Poetry, drawing it into *Divisions, Subdivisions,* &c. when the Wit of 'em all set together, wou'd not amount to one of *Martial*'s *Epigrams.*

Of all these I shall mention only *Aristotle,* the first and great Law-giver, in this Respect, and upon whom all that follow'd him are only Commentators. Among all the vast Tracts of this Voluminous Author, we don't find any Fragment of an Epick Poem, or the least Scene of a Play, to authorise his Skill and Excellence in that Art: Let it not be alledg'd, that for ought we know he was an excellent Poet, but his more serious Studies wou'd not let him enter upon Affairs of this Nature; for every Body knows, that *Aristotle* was no *Cinick,* but liv'd in the Splendour and Air of the Court, that he lov'd Riches as much as others of that Station; and being sufficiently acquainted with his Pupil's Affection to Poetry, and his Complaint that he wanted an *Homer* to aggrandize his Actions, he wou'd never have slipt such an Opportunity of farther ingratiating himself in the King's Favour, had he been conscious of any Abilities in himself for such an Undertaking; and having a more noble and copious Theme in the exploits of *Alexander,* than what inspir'd the blind Bard in his Hero *Achilles.* If his Epistles to *Alexander* were always answer'd with a considerable Present, what might he have expected from a Work like *Homer*'s upon so great a Subject; dedicated to so mighty a Prince, whose greatest Fault was his vain Glory, and that took such Pains to be Deify'd among Men.

It may be objected, that all the Works of *Aristotle* are not recover'd; and among those that are lost, some Essays of this kind might have perish'd. This Supposition is too weakly founded; for altho' the Works themselves might have scap'd us, 'tis more than probable that some Hint or other, either in the Life of the Conquerour, or Philosopher, might appear, to convince us of such a Production: Besides, as 'tis beliv'd, he writ *Philosophy,* because we have his Books; so, I dare swear, he writ no *Poetry,* because none is extant, nor any mention made thereof that ever I cou'd hear of.

But stay - - - - - Without any further enquiry into the Poetry of *Aristotle,* his Ability that way is sufficiently apparent by that excellent Piece he has left behind him upon that Subject - - - By your Favour, Sir, this is *Petitio Principii,* or, in plain English, give me the Sword in my own Hand, and I'll fight with you - - - -Have but a little Patience till I make a Flourish or two, and then, if you are pleas'd to demand it, I'll grant you that and every thing else.

How easy were it for me to take one of Doctor *Tillotson*'s Sermons, and out of the *OEconomy* of one of these Discourses, trump you up a Pamphlet, and call it, *The Art of Preaching.* In the first Place I must take a *Text,* and here I must be very learn'd upon the Etimology of this Word *Text*; then this Text must be divided into such and such *Partitions,* which Partitions must have their hard Names and *Derivations*; then these must be Spun into *Subdivisions*; and these back'd by Proofs of Scripture, *Ratiocinatio Oratoris, Ornamenta Figurarum Rhetoricarum*; and *Authoritas Patrum Ecclesiæ,* with some Rules and Directions how these ought

to be manag'd and apply'd; and closing up this difficult
Pedantry with the *Dimensions of Time* for such an
Occasion; you will pay me the Compliment of an excellent Preacher, and affirm, that any Sermon whatsoever,
either by a *Presbiter* at *Geneva,* or *Jesuit* in *Spain,* that
deviates from these Rules, deserves to be hist, and the
Priest kick'd out of his Pulpit. I must doubt your Complaisance in this point, Sir; for you know the Forms
of Eloquence are divers, and ought to be suited to the
different Humour and Capacities of an Audience; you
are sensible, Sir, that the fiery Cholerick Humour of one
Nation must be entertain'd and mov'd by other Means
than the heavy flegmatick Complexion of another; and
I have observed in my little Travels, that a Sermon of
three quarters of an Hour, that might please the Congre-
gation at St. *James*'s, wou'd never satisfy the Meeting
House in the *City,* where People expect more for their
Money; and having more Temptations of Roguery, must
have a larger Portion of Instruction.

Be pleas'd to hear another Instance of a different kind,
tho' to the same Purpose. I go down to *Woollich,* and
there, upon a Piece of Paper I take the Dimensions of
the *Royal Soveraign,* and from hence I frame a Model
of a *Man of War*; I divide the Ship into three principal
Parts, the *Keel,* the *Hull,* and the *Rigging*; I subdivide
these into their proper Denominations, and by the help
of a Saylor, give you all the Terms belonging to every
Rope, and every Office in the whole Ship: Will you from
hence infer, that I am an excellent Shipwright, and that
this Model is proper for a *Trading Junck* upon the *Volga,*
or a *Venetian Galley* in the *Adriatick* Sea?

But you'll object, perhaps, that this is no parallel
Case; because that *Aristotle*'s *Ars Poetica* was never
drawn from such slight Observations, but was the pure

effect of his immense Reason, thro' a nice Inspection into the very Bottom and Foundation of Nature.

To this I answer, That Verity is eternal, as that the Truth of two and two making four was as ce[r]tain in the Days of *Adam* as it is now; and that, according to his own Position, Nature is the same *apud omnes Gentes.* Now if his Rules of Poetry were drawn from certain and immutable Principles, and fix'd on the Basis of Nature; why shou'd not his *Ars Poetica* be as efficacious now, as it was two Thousand Years ago? And why shou'd not a single Plot, with perfect Unity of Time and Place, do as well at *Lincolns-Inn-Fields,* as at the Play-house in *Athens.* No, no, Sir, I am apt to believe that the Philosopher took no such Pains in Poetry as you imagine. The *Greek* was his Mother Tongue, and *Homer* was read with as much Veneration among the Schoolboys, as we learn our *Catechism*: Then where was the great Business for a Person so expert in Mood and Figure, as *Aristotle* was, to range into some Order a parcel of Terms of Art, drawn from his Observation upon the *Iliads,* and these to call the Model of an *Epick Poem.* Here, Sir, you may imagine, that I am caught; and have all this while been spinning a Thread to strangle my self; one of my main Objections against *Aristotle*'s *Criticism,* is drawn from his Non-performance in Poetry. And now I affirm, that his Rules are extracted from the greatest Poet that ever liv'd, which gives the utmost Validity to the Precept, and that is all we contend for.

Look ye, Sir; I lay it down only for a Supposition, that *Aristotle*'s Rules for an Epick Poem were extracted from *Homer*'s *Iliads*; and if a Supposition has weigh'd me down, I have two or three more of an equal Ballance to turn the Scale.

The great Esteem of *Alexander* the great for the

Works of old *Homer,* is sufficiently testify'd by Antiquity; insomuch that he always slept with the *Iliads* under his Pillow: Of this *Stagirite* to be sure was not ignorant; and what more proper Way of making his Court cou'd a Man of Letters Devise, than by saying something in Commendation of the King's Favourite? A Copy of Commendatory Verses was too mean, and perhaps out of his Element. Then something he wou'd do in his own way; a Book must be made of the Art of Poetry, wherein *Homer* is prov'd a Poet by Mood and Figure, and his Perfection transmitted to Poesterity; and if Prince *Arthur* had been in the Place of the *Iliads,* we shou'd have had other Rules for Epick Poetry, and Docor *B* - - - -*re* had carry'd the *Bays* from *Homer,* in spight of all the Criticks in Christendom; but whether *Aristotle* writ those Rules to Complement his Pupil, or whether he wou'd make a Stoop at Poetry, to show that there was no Knowledge beyond the flight of his Genius, there is no Reason to allow that *Homer* compil'd his Heroick Poem by those very Rules which *Aristotle* has laid down: For granting that *Aristotle* might pick such and such Observations from this Piece; they might be meer Accidents resulting casually from the Composition of the Work, and not any of the essential Principles of the Poem. How usual is it for Criticks to find out Faults, and create Beauties, which the Authors never intended for such; and how frequently do we find Authors run down in those very parts, which they design'd for the greatest Ornament. How natural is it for aspiring ambitious Schoolmen to attempt matters of the highest Reach; the wonderful Creation of the World, (which nothing but the Almighty Power that order'd it, can describe) is brought into Mood and Figure by the arrogance of *Philosophy.* But till I can believe that the

Vertigo's of *Cartesius,* or the Atoms of *Epicurus* can determine the almighty *Fiat,* they must give me leave to question the Infallibility of their Rules in respect of Poetry.

Had *Homer* himself by the same Inspiration that he writ his Poem, left us any Rules for such a Performance, all the World must have own'd it for Authentick. But he was too much a Poet to give Rules to that, whose excellence he knew consisted in a free and unlimited Flight of Imagination; and to describe the Spirit of Poetry, which alone is the *True Art of Poetry,* he knew to be as impossible, as for humane Reason to teach the gift of Prophecy by a Difinition.

Neither is *Aristotle* to be allow'd any farther Knowledge in Dramatick than in *Epick Poetry*; *Euripides,* whom he seems to Compliment by Rules adapted to the Model of his Plays, was either his Contemporary, or liv'd but a little before him; he was not insensible how much this Author was the darling of the City; as appear'd by the prodigious Expence disburs'd by the publick for the Ornament of his Plays: and 'tis probable, he might take this Opportunity of improving his Interest with the People, indulging their Inclination by refining upon the Beauty of what they admir'd. And besides all this, the Severity of *Dramatick* Rage was so fresh in his Memory in the hard Usage that his brother *Soph* not long before met with upon the Stage, that it was convenient to humour the reigning Wit, least a second *Aristophanes* shou'd take him to Task with as little Mercy as poor *Socrates* found at the Hands of the first.

I have talk'd so long to lay a Foundation for these following Conclusions; *Aristotle* was no Poet, and consequently not capable of giving Instructions in the Art of Poetry; his *Ars Poetica* are only some Observations drawn from the Works of *Homer* and *Euripides,* which may be meer Accidents resulting casually from the Composition of the Works, and not any of the essential Principles on which they are compil'd. That without giving himself the Trouble of searching into the Nature of Poetry, he has only complemented the Heroes of Wit and Valour of his Age, by joining with them in their Approbation; with this Difference, that their Applause was plain, and his more Scholastick.

But to leave these only as Suppositions to be relish'd by every Man at his Pleasure, I shall without complementing any Author, either Ancient or Modern, inquire into the first Invention of Comedy; what were the true Designs and honest Intentions of that Art: and from a Knowledge of the *End,* seek out the Means, without one Quotation of *Aristotle,* or Authority of *Euripides.*

In all Productions either Divine or Humane, the final Cause is the first Mover, because the End or Intention of any rational Action must first be consider'd, before the material or efficient Causes are put in Execution. Now to determine the final Cause of Comedy we must run back beyond the material and formal Agents, and take it in its very Infancy, or rather in the very first Act of its Generation, when its primary Parent, by proposing such or such an End of his Labour, laid down the first Scetches or Shadows of the Piece. Now as all Arts and Sciences have their first rise from a final Cause, so 'tis certain that they have grown from very small beginnings, and that the current of time has swell'd 'em to such a Bulk, that no Body can find the Fountain, by any Proportion between the Head and the Body; this, with the Corruption of time, which has debauch'd things from their primitive Innocence, to selfish Designs and

Purposes, renders it difficult to find the Origin of any Offspring so very unlike its Parent.

This is not only the Case of Comedy, as it stands at present, but the Condition also of the ancient Theatres, when great Men made Shows of this Nature a rising Step to their Ambition, mixing many lewd and lascivious Representations to gain the Favour of the Populace, to whose Taste and Entertainment the Plays were chiefly adopted. We must therefore go higher than either *Aristophanes,* or *Menander,* to discover Comedy in its primitive Institution, if we wou'd draw any moral Design of its Invention to warrant and authorise its Continuance.

I have already mention'd the difficulty of discovering the Invention of any Art in the different Figure it makes by Succession of Improvements; but there is something in the Nature of Comedy, even in its present Circumstances, that bears so great a Resemblance to the Philosophical *Mythology* of the Ancients, that old *Æsop* must wear the Bays as the first and original Author; And whatever Alterations or Improvements farther Application may have subjoin'd, his *Fables* gave the first Rise and Occasion.

Comedy is no more at present than a *well-fram'd Tale handsomly told, as an agreeable Vehicle for Counsel or Reproof.* This is all we can say for the Credit of its Institution; and is the Stress of its Charter for Liberty and Toleration. Then where shou'd we seek for a Foundation, but in *Æsop*'s symbolical way of moralizing upon Tales and Fables, with this difference, That his Stories were shorter than ours: He had his Tyrant *Lyon,* his Statesman *Fox,* his Beau *Magpy,* his coward *Hare,* his Bravo *Ass,* and his Buffoon *Ape,* with all the Characters that crowd our Stages every Day, with this Distinction nevertheless, That *Æsop* made his Beasts speak good *Greek,* and our Heroes sometimes can't talk *English.*

But whatever difference time has produc'd in the Form, we must in our own Defence stick to the *End,* and Intention of his *Fables. Utile Dulci* was his Motto, and must be our Business; we have no other Defence against the Presentment of the *Grand Jury,* and for ought I know it might prove a good means to mollify the Rigour of that Persecution, to inform the Inquisitors, that the great *Æsop* was the first Inventor of these poor Comedies that they are prosecu[t]ing with so much Eagerness and Fury, that the first *Laureat* was as just, as prudent, as pious, as reforming, and as ugly as any of themselves. And that the Beasts which are lug'd upon the Stage by the Horns are not caught in the City, as they suppose, but brought out of *Æsop*'s own Forrest. We shou'd inform them besides, that those very Tales and Fables which they apprehend as obstacles to Reformation, were the main Instruments and Machines us'd by the wise *Æsop* for its Propagation; and as he would improve Men by the Policy of Beasts, so we endeavour to reform Brutes with the Examples of Men. *Fondlewife* and his young Spouse are no more than the *Eagle* and *Cockle*; he wanted Teeth to break the Shell himself, so somebody else run away with the Meat, - - - - The Fox in the Play, is the same with the Fox in the Fable, who stuft his Guts so full, that he cou'd not get out at the same Hole he came in; so both *Reynards* being Delinquents alike, come to be truss'd up together. Here are Precepts, Admonitions, and Salutary *Innuendo*'s for the ordering of our Lives and Conversations couch'd in these *Allegories* and *Allusions*. The Wisdom of the Ancients was wrapt up in Veils and Figures; The *Ægiptian Hierogliphicks,* and the History of the Heathen Gods are nothing else; but if these pagan Authorities give Offence to their scrupulous Consciences; let them but consult the Tales and Parables of our *Saviour* in holy Writ, and they may find this way of Instruction to be much more Christian than they imagine; *Nathan's* Fable of the poor Man's Lamb had more Influence on the Conscience of *David,* than any force of downright Admonition. So that by ancient Practice, and modern Example, by the Authority of Pagans, Jews, and Christians, the World is furnish'd with this so sure, so pleasant, and expedient an Art, of schooling Mankind into better Manners. Now here is the primary Design of Comedy, illustrated from its first Institution; and the same end is equally alledg'd for its daily Practice and Continuance - - - - Then without all Dispute, whatever means are most proper and expedient for compassing this End and Intention, they must be the *just Rules of Comedy,* and the *true Art of the Stage.*

We must consider then, in the first place, that our Business lies not with a *French* or a *Spanish* Audience; that our Design is not to hold forth to ancient *Greece,* nor to moralize upon the Vices and Defaults of the *Roman* Commonwealth: No, no, - - - - An English Play is intended for the Use and Instruction of an English Audience, a People not only separated from the rest of the World by Situation, but different also from other Nations as well in the Complexion and Temperament of the Natural Body, as in the Constitution of our Body Politick: As we are a Mixture of many Nations, so we have the most unaccountable Medley of Humours among us of any People upon Earth; these Humours produce Variety of Follies, some of 'um unknown to former Ages; these new Distempers must have new Remedies, which are nothing but new Counsels and Instructions.

Now, Sir, if our *Utile,* which is the End, be different

from the Ancients, pray let our *Dulce,* which is the Means, be so too; for you know that to different Towns there are different ways; or if you wou'd have it more Scholastically, *ad diversos fines non idem conducit medium*; or Mathematically, One and the same Line cannot terminate in two Centers. But waving this manner of concluding by Induction, I shall gain my Point a nearer way, and draw it immediately from the first Principle I set down: *That we have the most unaccountable Medley of Humours among us of any Nation upon Earth*; and this is demonstrable from common Experience: We shall find a *Wildair* in one Corner, and a *Morose* in another; nay, the space of an Hour or two shall create such Vicissitudes of Temper in the same Person, that he can hardly be taken for the same Man. We shall have a Fellow bestir his Stumps from *Chocolate* to *Coffee-House* with all the Joy and Gayety imaginable, tho he want a Shilling to pay for a Hack; whilst another, drawn about in a Coach and Six, is eaten up with the Spleen, and shall loll in State, with as much Melancholy, Vexation, and Discontent, as if he were making the *Tour* of *Tyburn.* Then what sort of a *Dulce,* (which I take for the Pleasantry of the Tale, or the Plot of the Play) must a Man make use of to engage the Attention of so many different Humours and Inclinations: Will a single Plot satisfie every body? Will the Turns and Surprizes that may result naturally from the ancient Limits of Time, be sufficient to rip open the Spleen of some, and Physick the Melancholy of others, screw up the Attention of a Rover, and fix him to the Stage, in spight of his Volatile Temper, and the Temptation of a Mask? To make the Moral Instructive, you must make the Story diverting; the Spleenatick Wit, the Beau Courtier, the heavy Citizen, the fine Lady, and her fine Footman, come all to be instructed, and therefore must all be diverted; and he that can do this best, and with most Applause, writes the best Comedy, let him do it by what Rules he pleases, so they be not offensive to Religion and good Manners.

But *hic labor, hoc opus,* How must this Secret of pleasing so many different Tastes be discovered? Not by tumbling over Volumes of the Ancients, but by studying the Humour of the Moderns: The Rules of English Comedy don't lie in the Compass of *Aristotle,* or his Followers, but in the Pit, Box, and Galleries. And to examine into the Humour of an English Audience, let us see by what means our own English Poets have succeeded in this Point. To determine a Suit at Law we don't look into the Archives of *Greece* or *Rome,* but inspect the Reports of our own Lawyers, and the Acts and Statutes of our *Parliaments*; and by the same Rule we have nothing to do with the Models of *Menander* or *Plautus,* but must consult *Shakespear, Johnson, Fletcher,* and others, who by Methods much different from the Ancients, have supported the English Stage, and made themselves famous to Posterity: We shall find that these Gentlemen have fairly dispenc'd with the greatest part of Critical Formalities; the Decorums of Time and Place, so much cry'd up of late, had no force of Decorum with them; the Æconomy of their Plays was *ad libitum,* and the Extent of their Plots only limited by the Convenience of Action. I wou'd willingly understand the Regularities of *Hamlet, Mackbeth, Harry the fourth,* and of *Fletcher*'s Plays; and yet these have long been the Darlings of the English Audience, and are like to continue with the same Applause, in Defiance of all the Criticisms that ever were publish'd in *Greek,* and *Latin.*

But are there no Rules, no Decorums to be observ'd in

Comedy? Must we make the Condition of the English
Stage a State of Anarchy? No, Sir ---- For there are
Extreams in Irregularity, as dangerous to an Author, as
too scrupulous a Deference to Criticism; and as I have
given you an Instance of one; so I shall present you an
Example of the t'other.

There are a sort of Gentlemen that have had the
Jaunty Education of Dancing, French, and a Fiddle, who
coming to Age before they arrive at Years of Discretion,
make a shift to spend a handsom Patrimony of two or
three Thousand Pound, by soaking in the Tavern all
Night, lolling A-bed all the Morning, and sauntering
away all the Evening between the two Play-houses with
their Hands in their Pockets; you shall have a Gentleman
of this size upon his knowledge of *Covent-Garden,* and a
knack of witticising in his Cups, set up immediately for
a Playwright. But besides the Gentleman's Wit and
Experience, here is another Motive: There are a parcel
of saucy impudent Fellows about the Play-house, call'd
Doorkeepers, that can't let a Gentleman see a Play in
Peace, without jogging, and nudging him every Minute.
Sir, will you please to pay ----- *Sir, the Act's done,
will you please to pay, Sir.* I have broke their Heads all
round two or three times, yet the Puppies will still be
troublesom. Before gad, I'll be plagued with 'em no
longer; I'll e'en write a Play my self; by which means,
my Character of Wit shall be establish'd, I shall enjoy
the Freedom of the House, and to pin up the Basket,
pretty Miss ------ shall have the Profits of my third
Night for her Maidenhead. Thus we see, what a great
Blessing is a Coming Girl to a Play-house: Here is a Poet
sprung from the Tail of an Actress, like *Minerva* from
Jupiter's Head. But my Spark proceeds ----- My own
Intreagues are sufficient to found the Plot, and the

Devil's in't, if I can't make my Character talk as wittily as those in the *Trip to the Jubilee* - - - - But stay - - - - what shall I call it first? Let me see - - - - *The Rival Theatres* - - - - Very good, by gad, because I reckon the Two Houses will have a Contest about this very Play - - - Thus having found a Name for his Play, in the next place he makes a Play to his name, and thus he begins.

ACT I. Scene *Covent-Garden. Enter* Portico, Piaza *and* Turnstile.

Here you must note, that *Portico* being a compound of Practical Rake, and Speculative Gentleman, is ten to one the Author's own Character, and the leading Card in the Pack. *Piaza* is his Mistress, who lives in the Square, and is Daughter to old *Pillariso,* an odd out-o' the-way Gentleman, something between the Character of *Alexander* the Great, and *Solon,* which must please, because it is new.

Turnstile is Maid and Confident to *Piaza,* who for a Bribe of ten Pieces, lets *Portico* in at the Back-door; so the first Act concludes.

In the second Enter *Spigotoso,* who was Butler perhaps to the *Czar of Muscovy,* and *Fossetana* his Wife; after these Characters are run dry, he brings you in at the third Act, *Whinewell,* and *Charmarillis* for a Scene of Love to please the Ladies; and so he goes on without Fear or Wit, till he comes to a Marriage or two, and then he writes - - - - - *Finis.*

'Tis then whisper'd among his Friends at *Will*'s and *Hippolito*'s, That Mr. *such a one* has writ a very pretty Comedy; and some of 'em to encourage the young Author, equip him presently with *Prologue* and *Epilogue*; then the Play is sent to Mr. *Rich* or Mr. *Betterton* in a

fair legible Hand, with the Recommendation of some
Gentleman that passes for a Man of Parts, and a Critick;
In short, the Gentleman's Interest has the Play acted,
and the Gentleman's Interest makes a Present to pretty
Miss - - - - - she's made his Whore, and the Stage his
Cully, that for the loss of a Month in Rehearsing, and
a Hundred Pound in Dressing a confounded Play, must
give the Liberty of the House to him and his Friends
for ever after.

Now such a Play may be written with all the Exactness imaginable in respect of Unity in Time and Place;
but if you inquire its Character of any Person, tho of
the meanest Understanding of the whole Audience, he
will tell you 'tis intollerable Stuff; and upon your de-
manding his Reasons, his Answer is, *I don't like it.* His
Humour is the only Rule that he can Judge a Comedy
by; but you find that meer Nature is offended with some
Irregularities; and tho' he be not so learned in the
Dramma, to give you an Inventory of the Faults, yet I
can tell you, that one part of the Plot had no Dependance upon another, which made this simple Man drop
his Attention and Concern for the Event, and so disin-
gaging his Thoughts from the Business of the Action,
he sat there very uneasy, thought the time very tedious,
because he had nothing to do. The Characters were so
unchoherent in themselves, and compos'd of such Variety
of Absurdities, that in his Knowledge of Nature he
cou'd find no Original for such a Copy; and being therefore unacquainted with any Folly they reprov'd, or any
Vertue that they recommended; their Business was as
flat and tiresome to him, as if the Actors had talk'd
Arabick.

Now these are the material Irregularities of a Play,
and these are the Faults, which downright Mother-Sense

can censure and be offended at, as much as the most
learn'd Critick in the Pit. And altho' the one cannot
give me the Reasons of his Approbation or Dislike, yet
I will take his Word for the Credit or Disrepute of a
Comedy, sooner perhaps than the Opinion of some
Virtuoso's; for there are some Gentlemen that have
fortify'd their Spleen so impregnably with Criticism, and
hold out so stifly against all Attacks of Plesantry, that
the most powerful Efforts of Wit and Humour cannot
make the least Impression. What a Misfortune is it to
these Gentlemen to be Natives of such an ignorant, self
will'd impertinent Island, where let a Critick and a
Scholar find never so many Irregularities in a Play, yet
five hundred saucy People will give him the Lie to his
Face, and come to see this wicked Play Forty or Fifty
times in a Year. But this *Vox Populi* is the Devil tho'
in a Place of more Authority than *Aristotle,* it is call'd
Vox Dei. Here is a Play with a Vengeance, (says a
Critick) to bring the Transaction of a Years time into
the Compass of three Hours; to carry the whole Audience
with him from one Kingdom to another, by the changing
of a Scene: Where's the Probability, nay the Possibility
of all this; the Devl's in the Poet sure, he don't think
to put Contradictions upon us?

Lookee, Sir, don't be in a Passion, the Poet does not
impose Contradictions upon you, because he has told
you no Lie; for that only is a Lie which is related with
some fallacious Intention that you should belive it for
a Truth; now the Poet expects no more that you should
believe the Plot of his Play, than old *Æsop* design'd the
World shou'd think his *Eagle* and *Lyon* talk'd like you
and I; which I think was every Jot as improbable, as
what you quarrel with; and yet the Fables took, and I'll
be hang'd if you your self don't like 'em. But besides,

Sir, if you are so inveterate against improbabilities, you must never come near the Play-House at all; for there are several Improbabilities, nay, Impossibilities, that all the Criticisms in Nature cannot correct; as for instance; In the part of *Alexander* the Great, to be affected with the Transactions of the Play, we must suppose that we see that great Conquerour, after all his Triumphs, shunn'd by the Woman he loves, and importun'd by her he hates; cross'd in his Cups and Jollity by his own Subjects, and at last miserably ending his Life in a raging Madness; we must suppose that we see the very *Alexander,* the son of *Philip,* in all these unhappy Circumstances, else we are not touch'd by the Moral, which represents to us the uneasiness of Humane Life in the greatest State, and the Instability of Fortune in respect of worldly Pomp. Yet the whole Audience at the same time knows that this is Mr. *Betterton,* who is strutting upon the Stage, and tearing his Lungs for a Livelihood. And that the same Person shou'd be Mr. *Betterton,* and *Alexander* the Great, at the same time, is somewhat like an Impossibility, in my Mind. Yet you must grant this Impossibility in spight of your Teeth, if you han't Power to raise the old Heroe from the Grave to act his own Part.

Now for another Impossibility; the less rigid Criticks allow to a Comedy the space of an artificial Day, or Twenty Four Hours; but those of the thorough Reformation, will confine it to the natural or Solar Day, which is but half the time. Now admitting this for a Decorum absolutely requisite: This Play begins when it is exactly Six by your Watch, and ends precisely at Nine, which is the usual time of the Representation. Now is it feazible in *rerum Natura,* that the same Space or Extent of Time can be three Hours, by your Watch, and twelve Hours upon the Stage, admitting the same Number of

Minutes, or the same Measure of Sand to both. I'm afraid, Sir, you must allow this for an Impossibility too; and you may with as much Reason allow the Play the Extent of a whole Year; and if you grant me a Year, you may give me Seven, and so to a Thousand. For that a Thousand Years shou'd come within the Compass of three Hours is no more an Impossibility, than that two Minutes shou'd be contain'd in one. *Nullum minus continet in se majus,* is equally applicable to both.

So much for the Decorum of *Time*; now for the Regularity of *Place*. I might make the one a Consequence of t'other, and alledge, That by allowing me any Extent of Time, you must grant me any Change of Place; for the one depends upon t'other; and having five or six Years for the Action of a Play, I may travel from *Constantinople* to *Denmark,* so to *France,* and home to *England,* and rest long enough in each Country besides: But you'll say, How can you carry us with you? Very easily, Sir, if you be willing to go? As for Example: Here is a New Play, the House is throng'd, the Prologue's spoken, and the Curtain drawn represents you the Scene of *Grand Cairo*. Whereabouts are you now, Sir? Were not you the very Minute before in the Pit in the English Play-house talking to a Wench, and now *Presto pass,* you are spirited away to the Banks of the River *Nile*. Surely, Sir, this is a most intolerable Improbability; yet this you must allow me, or else you destroy the very Constitution of Representation: Then in the second Act, with a Flourish of the Fiddles, I change the Scene to *Astrachan*. *O this is intolerable!* Look'ee Sir, 'tis not a Jot more intolerable than the other; for you'll find that 'tis much about the same distance between *Egypt* and *Astrachan,* as it is between *Drury-Lane* and *Grand Cairo*; and if you please to let your Fancy take Post, it will perform the Journey in the same moment of Time, without any Disturbance in the World to your Person. You can follow *Quintus Curtius* all over *Asia* in the Train of *Alexander*; and trudge after *Hannibal* like a *Cadet* through all *Italy, Spain,* and *Africk,* in the space of Four or Five Hours; yet the Devil a one of you will stir a Step over the Threshold for the best Poet in Christendom, tho he make it his Business to make Heroes more amiable, and to surprize you with more wonderful Accidents and Events.

I am as little a Friend to those rambling Plays as any body, nor have I ever espous'd their Party by my own Practice; yet I cou'd not forbear saying something in Vindication of the great *Shakespear,* whom every little Fellow that can form an *Aristus primus* will presume to condemn for Indecorums and Absurdities; Sparks that are so spruce upon their Greek and Latin, that, like our Fops in Travel, they can relish nothing but what is Foreign, to let the World know, they have been abroad forsooth: but it must be so, because *Aristotle* said it; now I say it must be otherwise because *Shakespear* said it, and I'm sure that *Shakespear* was the greater Poet of the two. But you'll say that *Aristotle* was the greater Critick - - - - - - That's a mistake, Sir, for Criticism in Poetry, is no more than Judgment in Poetry; which you will find in your Lexicon. Now if *Shakespear* was the better Poet, he must have the most Judgment in his Art; for every Body knows, that Judgment is an Essential part of Poetry, and without it no Writer is worth a Farthing. But to stoop to the Authority of either, without consulting the Reason of the Consequence, is an Abuse to a Man's Understanding; and neither the Precept of the Philosopher, nor Example of the Poet, shou'd go down with me, without examining the Weight of their Assertions. We can expect no more Decorum or Regularity in any Business, than the Nature of the thing will bear; now if the Stage cannot subsist without the Strength of Supposition, and Force of Fancy in the Audience; why shou'd a Poet fetter the Business of his Plot, and starve his Action, for the nicety of an Hour, or the Change of a Scene; since the Thought of Man can fly over a thousand Years with the same Ease, and in the same Instant of Time, that your Eye glances from the Figure of Six, to Seven, on the Dial-Plate; and can glide from the *Cape of Good-Hope* to the *Bay of St. Nicholas,* which is quite cross the World, with the same Quickness and Activity, as between *Covent-Garden Church,* and *Will's Coffee-House.* Then I must beg of these Gentlemen to let our old English Authors alone - - - - If they have left Vice unpunish'd, Vertue unrewarded, Folly unexpos'd, or Prudence unsuccessful, the Contrary of which is the *Utile* of Comedy, let them be lash'd to some purpose; if any part of their Plots have been independant of the rest; or any of their Characters forc'd or unnatural; which destroys the *Dulce* of Plays, let them be hiss'd off the Stage: But if by a true Decorum in these material Points, they have writ successfully, and answer'd the end of Dramatick Poetry in every Respect, let them rest in Peace, and their Memories enjoy the Encomiums due to their Merit, without any Reflection for waving those Niceties, which are neither instructive to the World, nor diverting to Mankind; but are like all the rest of Critical Learning, fit only to set People together by the Ears in rediculous Controversies, that are not one Jot material to the Good of the Publick, whether they be true or false.

And thus you see, Sir, I have concluded a very unnecessary Piece of Work, which is much too long, if you don't like it; but let it happen any way, be assur'd, that I intended to please you, which shou'd partly excuse,

SIR,

Your most humble Servant.

RICHARD STEELE

RICHARD STEELE

I. FROM THE *TATLER,* NUMBER LXVIII

1709

From *Tuesday September* 13. to *Thursday September* 15.

I have often reflected, that there is a great Similitude
in the Motions of the Heart in Mirth and in Sorrow;
and I think the usual Occasion of the latter, as well as
the former, is something which is sudden and unexpected. The Mind has not a sufficient Time to recollect
its Force, and immediately gushes into Tears before we
can utter our selves by Speech or Complaint. The most
notorious Causes of these Drops from our Eyes, are
Pity, Sorrow, Joy, and Reconciliation.

The Fair Sex, who are made of Man, and not of
Earth, have a more delicate Humanity than we have,
and Pity is the most common Cause of their Tears: For
as we are inwardly composed of an Aptitude to every
Circumstance of Life, and every Thing that befals any
one Person, might have happened to any other of humane
Race; Self-Love, and a Sense of the Pain we our selves
should suffer in the Circumstances of any whom we pity,
is the Cause of that Compassion. Such a Reflection in
the Breast of a Woman, immediately inclines her to
Tears; but in a Man, it makes him think how such a
one ought to act on that Occasion, suitably to the Dignity
of his Nature. Thus a Woman is ever moved for those
whom she hears lament, and a Man for those whom he

observes to suffer in Silence. It is a Man's own Behaviour in the Circumstances he is under which procures him the Esteem of others, and not merely the Affliction it self which demands our Pity: For we never give a Man that Passion which he falls into for himself. He that commends himself, never purchases our Applause; nor he who bewails himself, our Pity.

Going through an Alley the other Day, I observ'd a noisy impudent Beggar bawl out, That he was wounded in a Merchant-Man, That he had lost his poor Limbs, and showed a Leg clouted up. All that passed by, made what Haste they could out of his Sight and Hearing; but a poor Fellow at the End of the Passage, with a rusty Coat, a melancholy Air, and a soft Voice, desired them to look upon a Man not used to beg. The latter received the Charity of almost every one that went by. The Strings of the Heart, which are to be touched to give us Compassion, are not so played on but by the finest Hand. We see in Tragical Representations, it is not the Pomp of Language, or Magnificence of Dress, in which the Passion is wrought that touches sensible Spirits, but something of a plain and simple Nature which breaks in upon our Souls, by that Sympathy which is given us for our mutual Good-will and Service.

In the Tragedy of *Mackbeth,* where *Wilks* acts the Part of a Man whose Family has been murdered in his Absence, the Wildness of his Passion, which is run over in a Torrent of calamitous Circumstances, does but raise my Spirits and give me the Alarm; but when he skilfully seems to be out of Breath, and is brought too low to say more; and upon a second Reflection, cry, only wiping his Eyes, *What both Children! Both, both my Children gone!*—There is no resisting a Sorrow which seems to have cast about for all the Reasons possible for its

Consolation, but has no Recourse. *There is not one left,
but both, both are murdered!* Such sudden Starts from
the Thread of the Discourse, and a plain Sentiment
expressed in an artless Way, are the irresistible Strokes
of Eloquence and Poetry. The same great Master,
Shakespeare, can afford us Instances of all the Places
where our Souls are accessible, and ever commands our
Tears: But it is to be observed, that he draws them
from some unexpected Source, which seems not wholly
of a Piece with the Discourse. Thus, when *Brutus* and
Cassius had a Debate in the Tragedy of *Cæsar,* and rose
to warm Language against each other, insomuch that it
had almost come to something that might be fatal, till
they recollected themselves; *Brutus* does more than
make an Apology for the Heat he had been in, by saying,
Porcia is dead—Here *Cassius* is all Tenderness, and
ready to dissolve, when he considers, that the Mind of
his Friend had been employed on the greatest Affliction
imaginable, when he had been adding to it by a Debate
on Trifles; which makes him in the Anguish of his
Heart cry out, *How scaped I killing when I thus provoked you?* This is an Incident which moves the Soul
in all its Sentiments; and *Cassius*'s Heart was at once
touch'd with all the soft Pangs of Pity, Remorse, and
Reconciliation. It is said indeed by *Horace, If you
would have me weep, you must first weep your self.*
This is not literally true, for it would have been as rightly
said, if we observe Nature, That I shall certainly weep,
if you do not: But what is intended by that Expression,
is, That it is not possible to give Passion, except you
show that you suffer your self. Therefore the true Art
seems to be, that when you would have the Person you
represent pitied, you must show him at once, in the
highest Grief and Struggling, to bear it with Decency

and Patience. In this Case we sigh for him, and give him every Groan he suppresses.

I remember, when I was young enough to follow the Sports of the Field, I have more than once rode off at the Death of a Deer, when I have seen the Animal in an Affliction which appeared humane without the least Noise, let fall Tears when he was reduced to Extremity; and I have thought of the Sorrow I saw him in when his Haunch came to the Table. But our Tears are not given only to Objects of Pity, but the Mind has Recourse to that Relief in all Occasions which give us much Emotion. Thus, to be apt to shed Tears, is a Sign of a great as well as little Spirit. I have heard say, the present Pope never passes through the People, who always kneel in Crowds and ask his Benediction, but the Tears are seen to flow from his Eyes. This must proceed from an Imagination, that he is the Father of all those People, and that he is touch'd with so extensive a Benevolence, that it breaks out into a Passion of Tears. You see, Friends, who have been long absent, transported in the same Manner: A Thousand little Images crowd upon them at their Meeting, as all the Joys and Griefs they have known during their Separation; and in one Hurry of Thought, they conceive how they should have participated in those Occasions; and weep, because their Minds are too full to wait the slow Expression of Words.

His Lacrymis Vitam damus, & miserescimus ultro.

II. THE *GUARDIAN*, NUMBER XII

1714

Wednesday, March 25.

Vel quia nil rectum, nisi quod placuit sibi, ducunt:
Vel quia turpe putant parere minoribus — — Hor.

WHEN a Poem makes its first Appearance in the World, I have always observed, that it gives Employment to a greater number of Criticks, than any other kind of Writing. Whether it be that most Men, at some time of their Lives, have try'd their Talent that way, and thereby think they have a right to judge; or whether they imagine, that their making shrewd Observations upon the Polite Arts, gives them a pretty figure; or whether there may not be some Jealousie and Caution in bestowing Applause upon those who write chiefly for Fame. Whatever the Reasons be, we find few discouraged by the Delicacy and Danger of such an Undertaking.

I think it certain, that most Men are naturally not only capable of being pleased with that which raises agreeable Pictures in the Fancy, but willing also to own it. But then there are many, who, by false Applications of some Rules ill understood, or out of Deference to Men whose Opinions they value, have formed to themselves certain Schemes and Systems of Satisfaction, and will not be pleased out of their own way. These are not Criticks themselves, but Readers of Criticks, who, without the Labour of perusing Authors, are able to give their Characters in general; and know just as much of the several Species of Poetry, as those who read Books of Geography do of the Genius of this or that People or Nation. These Gentlemen deliver their Opinions sententiously, and in general Terms; to which it being impossible readily to frame compleat Answers, they have often the Satisfaction of leaving the Board in Triumph. As young Persons, and particularly the Ladies, are liable to be led aside by these Tyrants in Wit, I shall examine two or three of the many Stratagems they use, and subjoin such Precautions as may hinder candid Readers from being deceived thereby.

THE first I shall take Notice of is an Objection commonly offered, *viz. That such a Poem hath indeed some good Lines in it, but it is not a regular Piece.* This for the most part is urged by those whose Knowledge is drawn from some famous *French* Criticks, who have written upon the Epic Poem, the Drama, and the great kinds of Poetry, which cannot subsist without great Regularity; but ought by no means to be required in Odes, Epistles, Panegyricks, and the like, which naturally admit of greater Liberties. The Enthusiasm in Odes, and the Freedom of Epistles, is rarely disputed; But I have often heard the Poems upon Publick Occasions written in Heroic Verse, which I chuse to call Panegyricks, severely censured upon this Account; the Reason whereof I cannot guess, unless it be, that because they are written in the same kind of Numbers and Spirit as an Epic Poem, they ought therefore to have the same Regularity. Now an Epic Poem, consisting chiefly in Narration, it is necessary that the Incidents should be related in the same Order that they are supposed to have been transacted. But in Works of the above-mentioned kind, there is no more Reason that such Order should be observed, than that an Oration should be as methodical as an History. I think it sufficient that the great Hints, suggested from the Subject, be so disposed, that the first may naturally prepare the Reader for what follows, and so on; and that their Places cannot be changed without Disadvantage to the whole. I will add further, that sometimes gentle Deviations, sometimes bold and even abrupt Digressions, where the Dignity of the Subject seems to give the Impulse, are Proofs of a noble Genius; as winding about, and returning artfully to the main Design, are Marks of Address and Dexterity.

ANOTHER Artifice made use of by Pretenders to Criticism, is an Insinuation, *That all that is good is borrowed from the Ancients.* This is very common in the Mouths of Pedants, and perhaps in their Hearts too; but is often urged by Men of no great Learning, for Reasons very obvious. Now Nature being still the same, it is impossible for any Modern Writer to paint her otherwise than the Ancients have done. If, for Example, I were to describe the General's Horse at the Battel of *Blenheim,* as my Fancy represented such a noble Beast, and that Description should resemble what *Virgil* hath drawn for the Horse of his Hero, it would be almost as ill-natured to urge that I had stolen my Description from *Virgil,* as to reproach the Duke of *Marlborough* for fighting only like *Æneas.* All that the most exquisite Judgment can perform is, out of that great Variety of Circumstances, wherein natural Objects may be considered, to select the most beautiful; and to place Images in such Views and Lights, as will affect the Fancy after the most delightful manner. But over and above a just Painting of Nature, a learned Reader will find a new Beauty superadded in a happy Imitation of some famous Ancient, as it revives in his Mind the Pleasure he took in his first reading such an Author. Such Copyings as these give that double Delight which we perceive when we look upon the Children of a beautiful Couple; where the Eye is not more charm'd with the Symmetry of the Parts, than the Mind by observing the Resemblance transmitted from Parents to their Offspring, and the mingled Features of the Father and the Mother. The Phrases of Holy Writ, and Allusions to several Passages in the Inspired Writings, (though not produced as Proofs of Doctrine) add Majesty and Authority to the noblest Discourses of the Pulpit: In like manner an Imitation of the Air of *Homer* and *Virgil* raises the Dignity of modern Poetry, and makes it appear stately and venerable.

THE last Observation I shall make at present is upon the Disgust taken by those Criticks, who put on their Cloaths prettily, and dislike every thing that is not written *with Ease*. I hereby therefore give the genteel part of the learned World to understand, that every Thought which is agreeable to Nature, and exprest in Language suitable to it, is written with Ease. There are some Things which must be written with Strength, which nevertheless are easie. The Statue of the *Gladiator,* though represented in such a Posture as strains every Muscle, is as easie as that of *Venus*; because the one expresses Strength and Fury as naturally as the other doth Beauty and Softness. The Passions are sometimes to be rouzed, as well as the Fancy to be entertained; and the Soul to be exalted and enlarged, as well as soothed. This often requires a raised and figurative Stile; which Readers of low Apprehensions, or soft and lanquid Dispositions (having heard of the Words *Fustian* and *Bombast*) are apt to reject as stiff and affected Language. But Nature and Reason appoint different Garbs for different Things; and since I write this to the Men of Dress, I will ask them if a Soldier, who is to mount a Breach, should be adorned like a Beau, who is spruced up for a Ball?

JOSEPH ADDISON

JOSEPH ADDISON

I. THE *TATLER,* NUMBER CLXV

1710

From *Thursday April 27,* to *Saturday April* 29

It has always been my Endeavour to distinguish between Realities and Appearances, and to separate true Merit from the Pretence to it. As it shall ever be my Study to make Discoveries of this Nature in Humane Life, and to settle the proper Distinctions between the Virtues and Perfections of Mankind, and those false Colours and Resemblances of them that shine alike in the Eyes of the Vulgar; so I shall be more particularly careful to search into the various Merits and Pretences of the learned World. This is the more necessary, because there seems to be a general Combination among the Pedants to extol one another's Labours, and cry up one another's Parts; while Men of Sense, either through that Modesty which is natural to them, or the Scorn they have for such trifling Commendations, enjoy their Stock of Knowledge like a hidden Treasure with Satisfaction and Silence. Pedantry indeed in Learning is like Hypocrisy in Religion, a Form of Knowledge without the Power of it, that attracts the Eyes of the Common People, breaks out in Noise and Show, and finds its Reward not from any inward Pleasure that attends it, but from the Praises and Approbations which it receives from Men.

Of this shallow Species there is not a more impor-
tunate, empty, and conceited Animal, than that which is
generally known by the Name of a Critick. This, in the
common Acceptation of the Word, is one that, without
entering into the Sense and Soul of an Author, has a
few general Rules, which, like mechanical Instruments,
he applies to the Works of every Writer, and as they
quadrate with them, pronounces the Author perfect or
defective. He is Master of a certain Set of Words, as
Unity, Style, Fire, Flegm, Easie, Natural, Turn, Sentiment, and the like; which he varies, compounds, divides,
and throws together, in every Part of his Discourse,
without any Thought or Meaning. The Marks you may
know him by are, an elevated Eye, and dogmatical Brow,
a positive Voice, and a Contempt for every Thing that
comes out, whether he has read it or not. He dwells
altogether in Generals. He praises or dispraises in the
Lump. He shakes his Head very frequently at the
Pedantry of Universities, and bursts into Laughter when
you mention an Author that is known at *Will*'s. He
hath formed his Judgment upon *Homer, Horace,* and
Virgil, not from their own Works, but from those of
Rapin and *Bossu.* He knows his own Strength so well,
that he never dares praise any Thing in which he has not
a *French* Author for his Voucher.

With these extraordinary Talents and Accomplish-
ments, Sir *Timothy Tittle* puts Men in Vogue, or condemns them to Obscurity, and sits as Judge of Life and
Death upon every Author that appears in Publick. It
is impossible to represent the Pangs, Agonies, and Convulsions, which Sir *Timothy* expresses in every Feature
of his Face, and Muscle of his Body, upon the reading
of a bad Poet.

About a Week ago I was engaged at a Friend's House

of mine in an agreeable Conversation with his Wife and Daughters, when in the Height of our Mirth, Sir *Timothy,* who makes Love to my Friend's eldest Daughter, came in amongst us puffing and blowing, as if he had been very much out of Breath. He immediately called for a Chair, and desired Leave to sit down, without any further Ceremony. I asked him, Where he had been? Whether he was out of Order? He only replied, That he was quite spent, and fell a cursing in Soliloquy. I could hear him cry, *A Wicked Rogue—An Execrable Wretch—Was there ever such a Monster*—The young Ladies upon this began to be affrighted, and asked, Whether any one had hurt him? He answered nothing, but still talked to himself. *To lay the first Scene,* says he, *in St.* James's Park, *and the last in* Northamptonshire! Is that all? says I: Then I suppose you have been at the Rehearsal of a Play this Morning. *Been!* says he; I have been at *Northampton,* in the *Park,* in a Lady's Bed Chamber, in a Dining-Room, every where: The Rogue has led me such a Dance—Though I could scarce forbear laughing at his Discourse, I told him I was glad it was no worse, and that he was only Metaphorically weary. In short, Sir, says he, the Author has not observed a single Unity in his whole Play; the Scene shifts in every Dialogue; the Villain has hurried me up and down at such a Rate, that I am tired off my Legs. I could not but observe with some Pleasure, that the young Lady whom he made Love to, conceived a very just Aversion towards him, upon seeing him so very passionate in Trifles. And as she had that natural Sense which makes her a better Judge than a Thousand Criticks, she began to rally him upon this foolish Humour. For my Part, says she, I never knew a Play take that was written up to your Rules, as you call them.

How Madam! says he, is that your Opinion? I am
sure you have a better Tast. It is a pretty Kind of
Magick, says she, the Poets have to transport an
Audience from Place to Place without the Help of a
Coach and Horses. I could travel round the World at
such a Rate. 'Tis such an Entertainment as an En-
chantress finds when she fancies her self in a Wood,
or upon a Mountain, at a Feast, or a Solemnity; though
at the same Time she has never stirred out of her Cot-
tage. Your Simile, Madam, says Sir *Timothy,* is by no
Means just. Pray, says she, let my Similes pass without
a Criticism. I must confess, continued she, (for I found
she was resolved to exasperate him) I laughed very
heartily at the last New Comedy which you found so
much Fault with. But Madam, says he, you ought not
to have laughed; and I defie any one to show me a single
Rule that you could laugh by. Ought not to laugh!
says she: Pray who should hinder me. Madam, says he,
There are such People in the World as *Rapin, Dacier,*
and several others, that ought to have spoiled your Mirth.
I have heard, says the young Lady, That your great
Criticks are always very bad Poets: I fancy there is as
much Difference between the Works of one and the
other, as there is between the Carriage of a Dancing-
Master and a Gentleman. I must confess, continued
she, I would not be troubled with so fine a Judgment as
yours is; for I find you feel more Vexation in a bad
Comedy than I do in a deep Tragedy. Madam, says Sir
Timothy, That is not my Fault, they should learn the
Art of Writing. For my Part, says the young Lady,
I should think the greatest Art in your Writers of
Comedies is to please. To please! says Sir *Timothy*;
and immediately fell a laughing. Truly, says she, that

is my Opinion. Upon this, he composed his Countenance, looked upon his Watch, and took his Leave.

I hear that Sir *Timothy* has not been at my Friend's House since this notable Conference, to the great Satisfaction of the young Lady, who by this Means has got rid of a very impertinent Fop.

I must confess, I could not but observe, with a great deal of Surprize, how this Gentleman, by his ill Nature, Folly, and Affectation, hath made himself capable of suffering so many imaginary Pains, and looking with such a senseless Severity upon the common Diversions of Life.

II. THE *SPECTATOR,* NUMBER XL

1711

Monday, April 16.

Ac ne forte putes me, quæ facere ipse recusem,
Cum recte tractant alii, laudare maligne;
Ille per extentum funem mihi posse videtur
Ire Poeta, meum qui pectus inaniter angit,
Irritat, mulcet, falsis terroribus implet,
Ut magus; & modo me Thebis, modo ponit Athenis.

Hor.

THE *English* Writers of Tragedy are possessed with
a Notion, that when they represent a virtuous or innocent Person in Distress, they ought not to leave him
till they have delivered him out of his Troubles, or
made him triumph over his Enemies. This Error they
have been led into by a ridiculous Doctrine in Modern
Criticism, that they are obliged to an equal Distribution
of Rewards and Punishments, and an impartial Execution of Poetical Justice. Who were the first that established this Rule I know not; but I am sure it has no
Foundation in Nature, in Reason, or in the Practice of
the Ancients. We find that Good and Evil happen alike
to all Men on this Side the Grave; and as the principal
Design of Tragedy is to raise Commiseration and Terror
in the Minds of the Audience, we shall defeat this great
End, if we always make Virtue and Innocence happy
and successful. Whatever Crosses and Disappointments
a good Man suffers in the Body of the Tragedy, they
will make but small Impression on our Minds, when we
know that in the last Act he is to arrive at the End of

his Wishes and Desires. When we see him engaged in
the Depth of his Afflictions, we are apt to comfort ourselves, because we are sure he will find his Way out of
them; and that his Grief, how great soever it may be
at present, will soon terminate in Gladness. For this
Reason the ancient Writers of Tragedy treated Men in
their Plays, as they are dealt with in the World, by
making Virtue sometimes happy and sometimes miserable, as they found it in the Fable which they made
choice of, or as it might affect their Audience in the
most agreeable Manner. *Aristotle* considers the Tragedies that were written in either of these Kinds, and
observes, That those which ended unhappily, had always
pleased the People, and carried away the Prize in the
publick Disputes of the Stage, from those that ended
happily. Terror and Commiseration leave a pleasing
Anguish in the Mind; and fix the Audience in such a
serious Composure of Thought, as is much more lasting
and delightful than any little transient Starts of Joy and
Satisfaction. Accordingly we find, that more of our
English Tragedies have succeeded, in which the
Favourites of the Audience sink under their Calamities,
than those in which they recover themselves out of them.
The best Plays of this Kind are the *Orphan, Venice
preserved, Alexander the Great, Theodosius, All for
Love, Oedipus, Oroonoko, Othello, &c. King Lear* is
an admirable Tragedy of the same Kind, as *Shakespear*
wrote it; but as it is reformed according to the chymer-
ical Notion of Poetical Justice, in my humble Opinion
it has lost half its Beauty. At the same time I must
allow, that there are very noble Tragedies which have
been framed upon the other Plan, and have ended
happily; as indeed most of the good Tragedies, which
have been written since the starting of the above-

mentioned Criticism, have taken this Turn: As the *Mourning Bride, Tamerlane, Ulysses, Phædra* and *Hyppolitus,* with most of Mr. *Dryden*'s. I must also allow, that many of *Shakespear*'s, and several of the celebrated Tragedies of Antiquity, are cast in the same Form. I do not therefore dispute against this Way of writing Tragedies, but against the Criticism that would establish this as the only Method; and by that Means would very much cramp the *English* Tragedy, and perhaps give a wrong Bent to the Genius of our Writers.

THE Tragi-Comedy, which is the Product of the *English* Theatre, is one of the most monstrous Inventions that ever entered into a Poet's Thoughts. An Author might as well think of weaving the Adventures of *Æneas* and *Hudibras* into one Poem, as of writing such a motly Piece of Mirth and Sorrow. But the Absurdity of these Performances is so very visible, that I shall not insist upon it.

THE same Objections which are made to Tragi-Comedy, may in some Measure be applied to all Tragedies that have a double Plot in them; which are likewise more frequent upon the *English* Stage, than upon any other: For though the Grief of the Audience, in such Performances, be not chang'd into another Passion, as in Tragi-Comedies; it is diverted upon another Object, which weakens their Concern for the principal Action, and breaks the Tide of Sorrow, by throwing it into different Channels. This Inconvenience, however, may in a great Measure be cured, if not wholly removed, by the skilful Choice of an Under-Plot, which may bear such a near Relation to the principal Design, as to contribute towards the Completion of it, and be concluded by the same Catastrophe.

THERE is also another Particular, which may be

reckoned among the Blemishes, or rather the false Beauties, of our *English* Tragedy: I mean those particular Speeches which are commonly known by the Name of *Rants*. The warm and passionate Parts of a Tragedy, are always the most taking with the Audience; for which Reason we often see the Players pronouncing, in all the Violence of Action, several Parts of the Tragedy which the Author writ with great Temper, and design'd that they should have been so acted. I have seen *Powell* very often raise himself a loud Clap by this Artifice. The Poets that were acquainted with this Secret, have given frequent Occasion for such Emotions in the Actor, by adding Vehemence to Words where there was no Passion, or inflaming a real Passion into Fustian. This hath filled the Mouths of our Heroes with Bombast; and given them such Sentiments, as proceed rather from a Swelling than a Greatness of Mind. Unnatural Exclamations, Curses, Vows, Blasphemies, a Defiance of Mankind, and an Outraging of the Gods, frequently pass upon the Audience for tow'ring Thoughts, and have accordingly met with infinite Applause.

I shall here add a Remark, which I am afraid our Tragick Writers may make an ill use of. As our Heroes are generally Lovers, their Swelling and Blustring upon the Stage very much recommends them to the fair Part of their Audience. The Ladies are wonderfully pleased to see a Man insulting Kings, or affronting the Gods, in one Scene, and throwing himself at the Feet of his Mistress in another. Let him behave himself insolently towards the Men, and abjectly towards the Fair One, and it is ten to one but he proves a Favourite of the Boxes. *Dryden* and *Lee,* in several of their Tragedies, have practised this Secret with good Success.

BUT to shew how a *Rant* pleases beyond the most

just and natural Thought that is not pronounced with Vehemence, I would desire the Reader, when he sees the Tragedy of *Oedipus,* to observe how quietly the Hero is dismissed at the End of the third Act, after having pronounced the following Lines, in which the Thought is very natural, and apt to move Compassion.

> *To you, good Gods, I make my last Appeal,*
> *Or clear my Virtues, or my Crimes reveal.*
> *If in the Maze of Fate I blindly run,*
> *And backward trod those Paths I sought to shun;*
> *Impute my Errors to your own Decree:*
> *My Hands are guilty, but my Heart is free.*

Let us then observe with what Thunder-claps of Applause he leaves the Stage, after the Impieties and Execrations at the End of the fourth Act; and you will wonder to see an Audience so cursed and so pleased at the same Time.

> *O that as oft I have at* Athens *seen,*
> [Where, by the way, there was no Stage
> till many Years after *Oedipus.*]
> *The Stage arise, and the big Clouds descend;*
> *So now, in very deed, I might behold*
> *This pond'rous Globe, and all yon marble Roof,*
> *Meet, like the Hands of* Jove, *and crush Mankind.*
> *For all the Elements,* &c.

III. THE *SPECTATOR,* NUMBER CLX

1711

Monday, September 3.

*—Cui mens divinior, atque os
Magna sonaturum, des nominis hujus honorem.* Hor.

THERE is no Character more frequently given to a
Writer, than that of being a Genius. I have heard many
a little Sonneteer called a *fine Genius.* There is not an
Heroick Scribler in the Nation, that has not his Admirers
who think him a *great Genius*; and as for your Smatterers in Tragedy, there is scarce a Man among them who
is not cried up by one or other for a *prodigious Genius.*

MY Design in this Paper is to consider what is properly a great Genius, and to throw some Thoughts
together on so uncommon a Subject.

AMONG great Geniuss, those few draw the Admiration of all the World upon them, and stand up as the
Prodigies of Mankind, who by the meer Strength of
natural Parts, and without any Assistance of Art or
Learning, have produced Works that were the Delight
of their own Times and the Wonder of Posterity.
There appears something nobly wild and extravagant
in these great natural Geniuss, that is infinitely more
beautiful than all the Turn and Polishing of what the
French call a *Bel Esprit,* by which they would express
a Genius refined by Conversation, Reflection, and the
Reading of the most polite Authors. The greatest Genius
which runs through the Arts and Sciences, takes a kind
of Tincture from them, and falls unavoidably into
Imitation.

MANY of these great natural Geniuss that were never disciplined and broken by Rules of Art, are to be found among the Ancients, and in particular among those of the more Eastern Parts of the World. *Homer* has innumerable Flights that *Virgil* was not able to reach, and in the Old Testament we find several Passages more elevated and sublime than any in *Homer*. At the same Time that we allow a greater and more daring Genius to the Ancients, we must own that the greatest of them very much failed in, or, if you will, that they were much above the Nicety and Correctness of the Moderns. In their Similitudes and Allusions, provided there was a Likeness, they did not much trouble themselves about the Decency of the Comparison: Thus *Solomon* resembles the Nose of his Beloved to the Tower of *Libanon* which looketh toward *Damascus*; as the Coming of a Thief in the Night, is a Similitude of the same Kind in the New Testament. It would be endless to make Collections of this Nature: *Homer* illustrates one of his Heroes encompassed with the Enemy, by an Ass in a Field of Corn that has his Sides belaboured by all the Boys of the Village without stirring a Foot for it; and another of them tossing to and fro in his Bed and burning with Resentment, to a Piece of Flesh broiled on the Coals. This particular Failure in the Ancients, opens a large Field of Raillerie to the little Wits, who can laugh at an Indecency but not relish the Sublime in these Sorts of Writings. The present Emperor of *Persia,* conformable to this Eastern way of Thinking, amidst a great many pompous Titles, denominates himself the Sun of Glory and the *Nutmeg of Delight*. In short, to cut off all Cavelling against the Ancients, and particularly those of the warmer Climates, who had most Heat and Life in their Imaginations, we are to consider that the Rule of

observing what the *French* call the *Bienseance* in an
Allusion, has been found out of latter Years and in the
colder Regions of the World; where we would make
some Amends for our want of Force and Spirit, by a
scrupulous Nicety and Exactness in our Compositions.
Our Countryman *Shakespear* was a remarkable Instance
of this first kind of great Geniuss.

I cannot quit this Head without observing that *Pindar*
was a great Genius of the first Class, who was hurried
on by a natural Fire and Impetuosity to vast Conceptions
of things, and noble Sallies of Imagination. At the same
time, can any thing be more ridiculous than for Men of
a sober and moderate Fancy to imitate this Poet's Way
of Writing in those monstrous Compositions which go
among us under the Name of Pindaricks? When I see
People copying Works, which, as *Horace* has represented them, are singular in their Kind and inimitable;
when I see Men following Irregularities by Rule, and
by the little Tricks of Art straining after the most un-
bounded Flights of Nature, I cannot but apply to them
that Passage in *Terence*.

> —*incerta hæc si tu postules*
> *Ratione certa facere, nihilo plus agas,*
> *Quàm si des operam, ut cum ratione insanias.*

IN short a modern pindarick Writer compared with
Pindar, is like a Sister among the *Camisars* compared
with *Virgil*'s Sybil: There is the Distortion, Grimace,
and outward Figure, but nothing of that divine Impulse
which raises the Mind above it self, and makes the
Sounds more than humane.

There is another kind of Great Geniuss which I shall
place in a second Class, not as I think them inferior to
the first, but only for distinction's sake as they are of a

different kind. This second Class of great Genius's are those that have formed themselves by Rules, and submitted the Greatness of their natural Talents to the Corrections and Restraints of Art. Such among the *Greeks* were *Plato* and *Aristotle,* among the *Romans Virgil* and *Tully,* among the *English Milton* and Sir *Francis Bacon.*

THE Genius in both these Classes of Authors may be equally great, but shews it self after a different Manner. In the first it is like a rich Soil in a happy Climate, that produces a whole Wilderness of noble Plants rising in a thousand beautiful Landskips without any certain Order or Regularity. In the other it is the same rich Soil under the same happy Climate, that has been laid out in Walks and Parterres, and cut into Shape and Beauty by the Skill of the Gardener.

THE great Danger in these latter kind of Geniuss, is, least they cramp their own Abilities too much by Imitation, and form themselves altogether upon Models, without giving the full Play to their own natural Parts. An Imitation of the best Authors, is not to compare with a good Original; and I believe we may observe that very few Writers make an extraordinary Figure in the World, who have not something in their Way of thinking or expressing themselves that is peculiar to them and entirely their own.

IT is odd to consider what great Geniuss are sometimes thrown away upon Trifles.

I once saw a Shepherd, says a famous *Italian* Author, who used to divert himself in his Solitudes with tossing up Eggs and catching them again without breaking them: In which he had arrived to so great a Degree of Perfection, that he would keep up four at a Time for several Minutes together playing in the Air, and falling into his Hand by Turns. I think, says the Author, I never saw a greater Severity than in this Man's Face; for by his wonderful Perseverance and Application, he had contracted the Seriousness and Gravity of a Privy-Councellour; and I could not but reflect with my self, that the same Assiduity and Attention had they been rightly applied, might have made him a greater Mathematician than *Archimedes*.

IV. THE SPECTATOR, NUMBER DXCII

1714

Friday, September 10.

——Studium sine divite Vena. Hor.

I Look upon the Play-house as a World within it self. They have lately furnished the middle Region of it with a new Sett of Meteors, in order to give the Sublime to many modern Tragedies. I was there last Winter at the first Rehearsal of the new Thunder, which is much more deep and sonorous than any hitherto made use of. They have a *Salmoneus* behind the Scenes, who plays it off with great Success. Their Lightnings are made to flash more briskly than heretofore; their Clouds are also better furbelow'd, and more voluminous; not to mention a violent Storm locked up in a great Chest that is designed for the *Tempest*. They are also provided with above a Dozen Showers of Snow, which, as I am informed, are the Plays of many unsuccessful Poets artificially cut and shreaded for that Use. Mr. *Rimer*'s *Edgar* is to fall in Snow at the next acting of King *Lear,* in order to heighten, or rather to alleviate, the Distress of that unfortunate Prince; and to serve by way of Decoration to a Piece which that great Critick has written against.

I do not indeed wonder that the Actors should be such professed Enemies to those among our Nation who are commonly known by the Name of Criticks, since it is a Rule among these Gentlemen to fall upon a Play, not because it is ill written, but because it takes. Several of them lay it down as a Maxim, That what-ever

Dramatick Performance has a long Run, must of Necessity be good for nothing; as tho' the first Precept in Poetry were *not to please.* Whether this Rule holds good or not, I shall leave to the Determination of those who are better Judges than my self: If it does, I am sure it tends very much to the Honour of those Gentlemen who have established it; few of their Pieces having been disgraced by a Run of three Days, and most of them being so exquisitely written, that the Town would never give them more than one Night's Hearing!

I have a great Esteem for a true Critick, such as *Aristotle* and *Longinus* among the *Greeks, Horace* and *Quintilian* among the *Romans, Boileau* and *Dacier* among the *French.* But it is our Misfortune, that some who set up for professed Criticks among us are so stupid, that they do not know how to put ten Words together with Elegance or common Propriety, and withal so illiterate, that they have no Taste of the learned Languages, and therefore criticise upon old Authors only at second Hand. They judge of them by what others have written, and not by any Notions they have of the Authors themselves. The Words Unity, Action, Sentiment, and Diction, pronounced with an Air of Authority, give them a Figure among unlearned Readers, who are apt to believe they are very deep, because they are unintelligible. The ancient Criticks are full of the Praises of their Contemporaries; they discover Beauties which escaped the Observation of the Vulgar, and very often find out Reasons for palliating and excusing such little Slips and Over-sights as were committed in the Writings of eminent Authors. On the contrary, most of the Smatterers in Criticism who appear among us, make it their Business to vilify and depreciate every new Production that gains Applause, to descry imaginary Blemishes, and to prove by far-fetched Arguments, that what pass for Beauties in any celebrated Piece are Faults and Errors: In short, the Writings of these Criticks compared with those of the Ancients, are like the Works of the Sophists compared with those of the old Philosophers.

ENVY and Cavil are the natural Fruits of Laziness and Ignorance; which was probably the Reason, that in the Heathen Mythology *Momus* is said to be the Son of *Nox* and *Somnus,* of Darkness and Sleep. Idle Men, who have not been at the Pains to accomplish or distinguish themselves, are very apt to detract from others; as ignorant Men are very subject to decry those Beauties in a celebrated Work which they have not Eyes to discover. Many of our Sons of *Momus,* who dignify themselves by the Name of Criticks, are the genuine Descendants of these two illustrious Ancestors. They are often led into those numerous Absurdities, in which they daily instruct the People, by not considering that, 1*st*, There is sometimes a greater Judgment shewn in deviating from the Rules of Art, than in adhering to them; and, 2*dly,* That there is more Beauty in the Works of a great Genius who is ignorant of all the Rules of Art, than in the Works of a little Genius, who not only knows, but scrupulously observes them.

FIRST, We may often take Notice of Men who are perfectly acquainted with all the Rules of good Writing, and notwithstanding chuse to depart from them on extraordinary Occasions. I could give Instances out of all the Tragick Writers of Antiquity who have shewn their Judgment in this Particular, and purposely receded from an established Rule of the Drama, when it has made way for a much higher Beauty than the Observation of such a Rule would have been. Those who have surveyed the noblest Pieces of Architecture and Statuary both ancient and modern, know very well that there are frequent Deviations from Art in the Works of the greatest Masters, which have produced a much nobler Effect than a more accurate and exact way of Proceeding could have done. This often arises from what the *Italians* call the *Gusto Grande* in these Arts, which is what we call the Sublime in Writing.

IN the next Place, our Criticks do not seem sensible that there is more Beauty in the Works of a great Genius who is ignorant of the Rules of Art, than in those of a little Genius who knows and observes them. It is of the Men of Genius that *Terence* speaks, in Opposition to the little artificial Cavillers of his Time;

> *Quorum æmulari exoptat negligentiam*
> *Potiùs, quàm istorum obscuram diligentiam.*

A Critick may have the same Consolation in the ill Success of his Play, as Dr. *South* tells us a Physician has at the Death of a Patient, That he was killed *secundum artem.* Our inimitable *Shakespear* is a Stumbling-block to the whole Tribe of these rigid Criticks. Who would not rather read one of his Plays, where there is not a single Rule of the Stage observed, than any Production of a modern Critick, where there is not one of them violated? *Shakespear* was indeed born with all the Seeds of Poetry, and may be compared to the Stone in *Pyrrhus*'s Ring, which, as *Pliny* tells us, had the Figure of *Apollo* and the Nine Muses in the Veins of it, produced by the spontaneous Hand of Nature, without any Help from Art.

ALEXANDER POPE

ALEXANDER POPE

PREFACE TO THE TRANSLATION OF THE
ILIAD

1715

HOMER is universally allow'd to have had the greatest
Invention of any Writer whatever. The Praise of
Judgment *Virgil* has justly contested with him, and
others may have their Pretensions as to particular Excellencies; but his Invention remains yet unrival'd. Nor is
it a Wonder if he has ever been acknowledg'd the greatest
of Poets, who most excell'd in That which is the very
Foundation of Poetry. It is the Invention that in different degrees distinguishes all great Genius's: The utmost
Stretch of human Study, Learning, and Industry, which
masters every thing besides, can never attain to this.
It furnishes Art with all her Materials, and without it
Judgment itself can at best but *steal wisely*: For Art
is only like a prudent Steward that lives on managing
the Riches of Nature. Whatever Praises may be given
to Works of Judgment, there is not even a single Beauty
in them but is owing to the Invention: As in the most
regular Gardens, however Art may carry the greatest
Appearance, there is not a Plant or Flower but is the
Gift of Nature. The first can only reduce the Beauties
of the latter into a more obvious Figure, which the
common Eye may better take in, and is therefore more
entertain'd with. And perhaps the reason why most
Criticks are inclin'd to prefer a judicious and methodical

Genius to a great and fruitful one, is, because they find it easier for themselves to pursue their Observations through an uniform and bounded Walk of Art, than to comprehend the vast and various Extent of Nature.

Our Author's Work is a wild Paradise, where if we cannot see all the Beauties so distinctly as in an order'd Garden, it is only because the Number of them is infinitely greater. 'Tis like a copious Nursery which contains the Seeds and first Productions of every kind, out of which those who follow'd him have but selected some particular Plants, each according to his Fancy, to cultivate and beautify. If some things are too luxuriant, it is owing to the Richness of the Soil; and if others are not arriv'd to Perfection or Maturity, it is only because they are over-run and opprest by those of a stronger Nature.

It is to the Strength of this amazing Invention we are to attribute that unequal'd Fire and Rapture, which is so forcible in *Homer*, that no Man of a true Poetical Spirit is Master of himself while he reads him. What he writes is of the most animated Nature imaginable; every thing moves, every thing lives, and is put in Action. If a Council be call'd, or a Battel fought, you are not coldly inform'd of what was said or done as from a third Person; the Reader is hurry'd out of himself by the Force of the Poet's Imagination, and turns in one place to a Hearer, in another to a Spectator. The Course of his Verses resembles that of the Army he describes,

Οἱ δ' ἄρ, ἴσαν, ὡσεί τε πυρὶ χθὼν πᾶσα νέμοιτο.

They pour along like a Fire that sweeps the whole Earth before it. 'Tis however remarkable that his Fancy, which is every where vigorous, is not discover'd immediately at the beginning of his Poem in its fullest

Splendor: It grows in the Progress both upon himself and others, and becomes on Fire like a Chariot-Wheel, by its own Rapidity. Exact Disposition, just Thought, correct Elocution, polish'd Numbers, may have been found in a thousand; but this Poetical *Fire,* this *Vivida vis animi,* in a very few. Even in Works where all those are imperfect or neglected, this can over-power Criticism, and make us admire even while we dis-approve. Nay, where this appears, tho' attended with Absurdities, it brightens all the Rubbish about it, 'till we see nothing but its own Splendor. This *Fire* is discern'd in *Virgil,* but discern'd as through a Glass, reflected, and more shining than warm, but every where equal and constant: In *Lucan* and *Statius,* it bursts out in sudden, short, and interrupted Flashes: In *Milton,* it glows like a Furnace kept up to an uncommon Fierceness by the Force of Art: In *Shakespear,* it strikes before we are aware, like an accidental Fire from Heaven: But in *Homer,* and in him only, it burns every where clearly, and every where irresistibly.

I shall here endeavour to show, how this vast *Invention* exerts itself in a manner superior to that of any Poet, thro' all the main constituent Parts of his Work, as it is the great and peculiar Characteristick which distinguishes him from all other Authors.

This strong and ruling Faculty was like a powerful Planet, which in the Violence of its Course, drew all things within its *Vortex.* It seem'd not enough to have taken in the whole Circle of Arts, and the whole Compass of Nature; all the inward Passions and Affections of Mankind to supply this Characters, and all the outward Forms and Images of Things for his Descriptions; but wanting yet an ampler Sphere to expatiate in, he open'd a new and boundless Walk for his Imagination, and created a World for himself in the Invention of *Fable.* That which *Aristotle* calls the *Soul of Poetry,* was first breath'd into it by *Homer.* I shall begin with considering him in this Part, as it is naturally the first, and I speak of it both as it means the Design of a Poem, and as it is taken for Fiction.

Fable may be divided into the *Probable,* the *Allegorical,* and the *Marvelous.* The *Probable Fable* is the Recital of such Actions as tho' they did not happen, yet might, in the common course of Nature: Or of such as tho' they did, become Fables by the additional Episodes and manner of telling them. Of this sort is the main Story of an Epic Poem, *the Return of* Ulysses, *the Settlement of the* Trojans *in* Italy, or the like. That of the *Iliad* is *the Anger of* Achilles, the most short and single Subject that ever was chosen by any Poet. Yet this he has supplied with a vaster Variety of Incidents and Events, and crouded with a greater Number of Councils, Speeches, Battles, and Episodes of all kinds, than are to be found even in those Poems whose Schemes are of the utmost Latitude and Irregularity. The Action is hurry'd on with the most vehement Spirit, and its whole Duration employs not so much as fifty Days. *Virgil,* for want of so warm a Genius, aided himself by taking in a more extensive Subject, as well as a greater Length of Time, and contracting the Design of both *Homer*'s Poems into one, which is yet but a fourth part as large as his. The other Epic Poets have us'd the same Practice, but generally carry'd it so far as to superinduce a Multiplicity of Fables, destroy the Unity of Action, and lose their Readers in an unreasonable Length of Time. Nor is it only in the main Design that they have been unable to add to his Invention, but they have follow'd him in every Episode and Part of Story. If he has given a regular

Catalogue of an *Army,* they all draw up their Forces in
the same Order. If he has funeral Games for *Patroclus,*
Virgil has the same for *Anchises,* and *Statius* (rather
than omit them) destroys the Unity of his Action for
those of *Archemorus.* If *Ulysses* visit the Shades, the
Æneas of *Virgil* and *Scipio* of *Silius* are sent after him.
If he be detain'd from his Return by the Allurements of
Calypso, so is *Æneas* by *Dido,* and *Rinaldo* by *Armida.*
If *Achilles* be absent from the Army on the Score of a
Quarrel thro' half the Poem, *Rinaldo* must absent himself
just as long, on the like account. If he gives his Heroe
a Suit of celestial Armour, *Virgil* and *Tasso* make the
same Present to theirs. *Virgil* has not only observ'd this
close Imitation of *Homer,* but where he had not led the
way, supply'd the Want from other *Greek* Authors.
Thus the Story of *Sinon* and the *Taking of Troy* was
copied (says *Macrobius*) almost word for word from
Pisander, as the Loves of *Dido* and *Æneas* are taken
from those of *Medæa* and *Jason* in *Apollonius,* and several others in the same manner.

   To proceed to the *Allegorical Fable*: If we reflect upon
those innumerable Knowledges, those Secrets of Nature
and Physical Philosophy which *Homer* is generally
suppos'd to have wrapt up in his *Allegories,* what a new
and ample Scene of Wonder may this Consideration
afford us? How fertile will that Imagination appear,
which was able to cloath all the Properties of Elements,
the Qualifications of the Mind, the Virtues and Vices,
in Forms and Persons; and to introduce them into
Actions agreeable to the Nature of the Things they
shadow'd? This is a Field in which no succeeding Poets
could dispute with *Homer*; and whatever Commendations
have been allow'd them on this Head, are by no means
for their Invention in having enlarg'd his Circle, but for

their Judgment in having contracted it. For when the Mode of Learning chang'd in following Ages, and Science was deliver'd in a plainer manner, it then became as reasonable in the more modern Poets to lay it aside, as it was in *Homer* to make use of it. And perhaps it was no unhappy Circumstance for *Virgil* that there was not in his Time that Demand upon him of so great an Invention, as might be capable of furnishing all those Allegorical Parts of a Poem.

The *Marvelous Fable* includes whatever is supernatural, and especially the Machines of the Gods. If *Homer* was not the first who introduc'd the Deities (as *Herodotus* imagines) into the Religion of *Greece,* he seems the first who brought them into a System of *Machinery* for Poetry, and such an one as makes its greatest Importance and Dignity. For we find those Authors who have been offended at the literal Notion of the Gods, constantly laying their Accusation against *Homer* as the undoubted Inventor of them. But whatever cause there might be to blame his *Machines* in a Philosophical or Religious View, they are so perfect in the Poetick, that Mankind have been ever since contented to follow them: None have been able to enlarge the Sphere of Poetry beyond the Limits he has set: Every Attempt of this Nature has prov'd unsuccessful; and after all the various Changes of Times and Religions, his Gods continue to this Day the Gods of Poetry.

We come now to the *Characters* of his Persons, and here we shall find no Author has ever drawn so many with so visible and surprizing a Variety, or given us such lively and affecting Impressions of them. Every one has something so singularly his own, that no Painter could have distinguished them more by their Features, than the Poet has by their Manners. Nothing can be more exact then the Distinctions he has observ'd in the different degrees of Virtues and Vices. The single Quality of *Courage* is wonderfully diversify'd in the several Characters of the *Iliad.* That of *Achilles* is furious and intractable; that of *Diomede* forward, yet listening to Advice and subject to Command: We see in *Ajax* an heavy and self-considering Valour, in *Hector* an active and vigilant one: The Courage of *Agamemnon* is inspirited by Love of Empire and Ambition, that of *Menelaus* mix'd with Softness and Tenderness for his People: We find in *Idomeneus* a plain direct Soldier, in *Sarpedon* a gallant and generous one. Nor is this judicious and astonishing Diversity to be found only in the principal Quality which constitutes the Main of each Character, but even in the Under-parts of it, to which he takes care to give a Tincture of that principal one. For Example, the main Characters of *Ulysses* and *Nestor* consist in *Wisdom,* and they are distinct in this; the Wisdom of one is *artificial* and *various,* of the other *natural, open,* and *regular.* But they have, besides, Characters of *Courage*; and this Quality also takes a different Turn in each from the difference of his Prudence: For one in the War depends still upon *Caution,* the other upon *Experience.* It would be endless to produce Instances of these Kinds. The Characters of *Virgil* are far from striking us in this open manner; they lie in a great degree hidden and undistinguish'd, and where they are mark'd most evidently, affect us not in proportion to those of *Homer.* His Characters of Valour are much alike; even that of *Turnus* seems no way peculiar but as it is in a superior degree; and we see nothing that differences the Courage of *Mnestheus* from that of *Sergesthus, Cloanthus,* or the rest. In like manner it may be remark'd of *Statius*'s Heroes, that an Air of

Impetuosity runs thro' them all; the same horrid and
savage Courage appears in his *Capaneus, Tydeus, Hip-
pomedon,* &c. They have a Parity of Character which
makes them seem Brothers of one Family. I believe
when the Reader is led into this Track of Reflection, if
he will pursue it through the *Epic* and *Tragic* Writers,
he will be convinced how infinitely superior in this Point
the Invention of *Homer* was to that of all others.

The *Speeches* are to be consider'd as they flow from
the Characters, being perfect or defective as they agree
or disagree with the Manners of those who utter them.
As there is more variety of Characters in the *Iliad,* so
there is of Speeches, than in any other Poem. *Every
thing in it has Manners* (as *Aristotle* expresses it) that
is, every thing is acted or spoken. It is hardly credible
in a Work of such length, how small a Number of Lines
are employ'd in Narration. In *Virgil* the Dramatic Part
is less in proportion to the Narrative; and the Speeches
often consist of general Reflections or Thoughts, which
might be equally just in any Person's Mouth upon the
same Occasion. As many of his Persons have no apparent Characters, so many of his Speeches escape being
apply'd and judg'd by the Rule of Propriety. We oftner
think of the Author himself when we read *Virgil,* than
when we are engag'd in *Homer*: All which are the
Effects of a colder Invention, that interests us less in
the Action describ'd: *Homer* makes us Hearers, and
Virgil leaves us Readers.

If in the next place we take a View of the *Sentiments,*
the same presiding Faculty is eminent in the Sublimity
and Spirit of his Thoughts. *Longinus* has given his
Opinion, that it was in this Part *Homer* principally
excell'd. What were alone sufficient to prove the
Grandeur and Excellence of his Sentiments in general,

is that they have so remarkable a Parity with those of the Scripture: *Duport,* in his *Gnomologia Homerica,* has collected innumerable Instances of this sort. And it is with Justice an excellent modern Writer allows, that if *Virgil* has not so many Thoughts that are low and vulgar, he has not so many that are sublime and noble; and that the *Roman* Author seldom rises into very astonishing Sentiments where he is not fired by the *Iliad.*

If we observe his *Descriptions, Images,* and *Similes,* we shall find the Invention still predominant. To what else can we ascribe that vast Comprehension of Images of every sort, where we see each Circumstance and Individual of Nature summon'd together by the Extent and Fecundity of his Imagination; to which all things, in their various Views, presented themselves in an Instant, and had their Impressions taken off to Perfection at a Heat? Nay, he not only gives us the full Prospects of Things, but several unexpected Peculiarities and Side-Views, unobserv'd by any Painter but *Homer.* Nothing is so surprizing as the Descriptions of his Battels, which take up no less than half the *Iliad,* and are supply'd with so vast a Variety of Incidents, that no one bears a Likeness to another; such different Kinds of Deaths, that no two Heroes are wounded in the same manner; and such a Profusion of noble Ideas, that every Battel rises above the last in Greatness, Horror, and Confusion. It is certain there is not near that Number of Images and Descriptions in any Epic Poet; tho' every one has assisted himself with a great Quantity out of him: And it is evident of *Virgil* especially, that he has scarce any Comparisons which are not drawn from his Master.

If we descend from hence to the *Expression,* we see the bright Imagination of *Homer* shining out in the most enliven'd Forms of it. We acknowledge him the Father of Poetical Diction, the first who taught that *Language of the Gods* to Men. His Expression is like the colouring of some great Masters, which discovers itself to be laid on boldly, and executed with Rapidity. It is indeed the strongest and most glowing imaginable, and touch'd with the greatest Spirit. *Aristotle* had reason to say, He was the only Poet who had found out *Living Words*; there are in him more daring Figures and Metaphors than in any good Author whatever. An Arrow is *impatient* to be on the Wing, a Weapon *thirst*s to drink the Blood of an Enemy, and the like. Yet his Expression is never too big for the Sense, but justly great in proportion to it: 'Tis the Sentiment that swells and fills out the Diction, which rises with it, and forms itself about it. For in the same degree that a *Thought* is warmer, an *Expression* will be brighter; and as That is more strong, This will become more perspicuous: Like Glass in the Furnace which grows to a greater Magnitude, and refines to a greater Clearness, only as the *Breath* within is more powerful, and the *Heat* more intense.

To throw his Language more out of Prose, *Homer* seems to have affected the *Compound-Epithets*. This was a sort of Composition peculiarly proper to Poetry, not only as it heighten'd the *Diction,* but as it assisted and fill'd the *Numbers* with greater Sound and Pomp, and likewise conduced in some measure to thicken the *Images.* On this last Consideration I cannot but attribute these to the Fruitfulness of his Invention, since (as he has manag'd them) they are a sort of supernumerary Pictures of the Persons or Things they are join'd to. We see the Motion of *Hector*'s Plumes in the Epithet Κορυθαίολος, the Landscape of Mount *Neritus* in that of Εἰνοσίφυλλος, and so of others; which particular Images could not have been insisted upon so long as

to express them in a Description (tho' but of a single
Line) without diverting the Reader too much from the
principal Action or Figure. As a Metaphor is a short
Simile, one of these Epithets is a short Description.

Lastly, if we consider his *Versification,* we shall be
sensible what a Share of Praise is due to his Invention
in that also. He was not satisfy'd with his Language
as he found it settled in any one Part of *Greece,* but
searched thro' its differing *Dialects* with this particular
View, to beautify and perfect his Numbers: He consider'd these as they had a greater Mixture of Vowels or
Consonants, and accordingly employ'd them as the Verse
requir'd either a greater Smoothness or Strength. What
he most affected was the *Ionic,* which has a peculiar
Sweetness from its never using Contractions, and from
its Custom of resolving the Diphthongs into two Syl-
lables; so as to make the Words open themselves with
a more spreading and sonorous Fluency. With this he
mingled the *Attic* Contractions, the broader *Doric,* and
the feebler *Æolic,* which often rejects its Aspirate, or
takes off its Accent; and compleated this Variety by
altering some Letters with the License of Poetry. Thus
his Measures, instead of being Fetters to his Sense, were
always in readiness to run along with the Warmth of
his Rapture; and even to give a farther Representation
of his Notions, in the Correspondence of their Sounds
to what they signify'd. Out of all these he has deriv'd
that Harmony, which makes us confess he had not only
the richest Head, but the finest Ear in the World. This
is so great a Truth, that whoever will but consult the
Tune of his Verses even without understanding them
(with the same sort of Diligence as we daily see practis'd
in the Case of *Italian Opera's*) will find more Sweetness,
Variety, and Majesty of Sound, than in any other Lan-

guage or Poetry. The Beauty of his Numbers is allow'd by the Criticks to be copied but faintly by *Virgil* himself, tho' they are so just to ascribe it to the Nature of the *Latine* Tongue. Indeed the *Greek* has some Advantages both from the natural *Sound* of its *Words,* and the Turn and *Cadence* of its *Verse,* which agree with the Genius of no other Language. *Virgil* was very sensible of this, and used the utmost Diligence in working up a more intractable Language to whatsoever Graces it was capable of, and in particular never fail'd to bring the Sound of his Line to a beautiful Agreement with its Sense. If the *Grecian* Poet has not been so frequently celebrated on this Account as the *Roman,* the only reason is, that fewer Criticks have understood one Language than the other. *Dionysius* of *Halicarnassus* has pointed out many of our Author's Beauties in this kind, in his Treatise of the *Composition of Words,* and others will be taken notice of in the Course of the Notes. It suffices at present to observe of his Numbers, that they flow with so much ease, as to make one imagine *Homer* had no other care than to transcribe as fast as the *Muses* dictated; and at the same time with so much Force and inspiriting Vigour, that they awaken and raise us like the Sound of a Trumpet. They roll along as a plentiful River, always in motion, and always full; while we are born away by a Tide of Verse, the most rapid, and yet the most smooth imaginable.

Thus on whatever side we contemplate *Homer,* what principally strikes us is his *Invention.* It is that which forms the Character of each Part of his Work; and accordingly we find it to have made his Fable more *extensive* and *copious* than any other, his Manners more *lively* and *strongly marked,* his Speeches more *affecting* and *transported,* his Sentiments more *warm* and *sublime,* his Images and Descriptions more *full* and *animated,* his Expression more *rais'd* and *daring,* and his Numbers more *rapid* and *various.* I hope in what has been said of *Virgil* with regard to any of these Heads, I have no way derogated from his Character. Nothing is more absurd or endless, than the common Method of comparing eminent Writers by an Opposition of particular Passages in them, and forming a Judgment from thence of their Merit upon the whole. We ought to have a certain Knowledge of the principal Character and distinguishing Excellence of each: It is in *that* we are to consider him, and in proportion to his Degree in *that* we are to admire him. No Author or Man ever excell'd all the World in more than one Faculty, and as *Homer* has done this in Invention, *Virgil* has in Judgment. Not that we are to think Homer wanted Judgment, because *Virgil* had it in a more eminent degree; or that *Virgil* wanted Invention, because Homer possest a larger share of it: Each of these great Authors had more of both than perhaps any Man besides, and are only said to have less in Comparison with one another. *Homer* was the greater Genius, *Virgil* the better Artist. In one we most admire the *Man,* in the other the *Work.* *Homer* hurries and transports us with a commanding Impetuosity, *Virgil* leads us with an attractive Majesty: *Homer* scatters with a generous Profusion, *Virgil* bestows with a careful Magnificence: *Homer,* like the *Nile,* pours out his Riches with a sudden Overflow; *Virgil* like a River in its Banks, with a gentle and constant Stream. When we behold their Battels, methinks the two Poets resemble the Heroes they celebrate: *Homer,* boundless and irresistible as *Achilles,* bears all before him, and shines more and more as the Tumult increases; *Virgil,* calmly daring like *Æneas,* appears undisturb'd in the midst of the Action, disposes all about him, and conquers with Tranquillity: And when we look upon their Machines, *Homer* seems like his own *Jupiter* in his Terrors, shaking *Olympus,* scattering the Lightnings, and firing the Heavens; *Virgil,* like the same Power in his Benevolence, counselling with the Gods, laying Plans for Empires, and regularly ordering his whole Creation.

But after all, it is with great Parts as with great Virtues, they naturally border on some Imperfection; and it is often hard to distinguish exactly where the Virtue ends, or the Fault begins. As Prudence may sometimes sink to Suspicion, so may a great Judgment decline to Coldness; and as Magnanimity may run up to Profusion or Extravagance, so may a great Invention to Redundancy or Wildness. If we look upon *Homer* in this View, we shall perceive the chief *Objections* against him to proceed from so noble a Cause as the Excess of this Faculty.

Among these we may reckon some of his *Marvellous Fictions,* upon which so much Criticism has been spent as surpassing all the Bounds of Probability. Perhaps it may be with great and superior Souls as with gigantick Bodies, which exerting themselves with unusual Strength, exceed what is commonly thought the due Proportion of Parts, to become Miracles in the whole; and like the old Heroes of that Make, commit something near Extravagance amidst a Series of glorious and inimitable Performances. Thus *Homer* has his *speaking Horses,* and *Virgil* his *Myrtles distilling Blood,* without so much as contriving the easy Intervention of a Deity to save the Probability.

It is owing to the same vast Invention that his *Similes* have been thought too exuberant and full of Circumstances. The Force of this Faculty is seen in nothing more, than its Inability to confine itself to that single Circumstance upon which the Comparison is grounded: It runs out into Embellishments of additional Images, which however are so manag'd as not to overpower the main one. His Similes are like Pictures, where the principal Figure has not only its proportion given agreeable to the Original, but is also set off with occasional Ornaments and Prospects. The same will account for his manner of heaping a Number of Comparisons together in one Breath, when his Fancy suggested to him at once so many various and correspondent Images. The Reader will easily extend this Observation to more Objections of the same kind.

If there are others which seem rather to charge him with a Defect or Narrowness of Genius, than an Excess of it; those seeming Defects will be found upon Examination to proceed wholly from the Nature of the Times he liv'd in. Such are his *grosser Representations* of the *Gods,* and the vicious and *imperfect Manners* of his *Heroes,* which will be treated of in the following **Essay*: But I must here speak a word of the latter, as it is a Point generally carry'd into Extreams both by the Censurers and Defenders of Homer. It must be a strange Partiality to Antiquity to think with Madam *Dacier,* "that †those Times and Manners are so much the more "excellent, as they are more contrary to ours." Who can be so prejudiced in their Favour as to magnify the Felicity of those Ages, when a Spirit of Revenge and Cruelty reign'd thro' the World, when no Mercy was shown but for the sake of Lucre, when the greatest Princes were put to the Sword, and their Wives and

*See the Articles of Theology *and* Morality, *in the third Part of the* Essay.

†*Preface to her* Homer.

Daughters made Slaves and Concubines? On the other side I would not be so delicate as those modern Criticks, who are shock'd at the *servile Offices* and *mean Employments* in which we sometimes see the Heroes of *Homer* engag'd. There is a Pleasure in taking a view of that Simplicity in Opposition to the Luxury of succeeding Ages; in beholding Monarchs without their Guards, Princes tending their Flocks, and Princesses drawing Water from the Springs. When we read *Homer,* we ought to reflect that we are reading the most ancient Author in the Heathen World; and those who consider him in this Light, will double their Pleasure in the Perusal of him. Let them think they are growing acquainted with Nations and People that are now no more; that they are stepping almost three thousand Years backward into the remotest Antiquity, and entertaining themselves with a clear and surprizing Vision of Things no where else to be found, and the only authentick Picture of that ancient World. By this means alone their greatest Obstacles will vanish; and what usually creates their Dislike, will become a Satisfaction.

This Consideration may farther serve to answer for the constant Use of the same *Epithets* to his Gods and Heroes, such as the *far-darting Phœbus,* the *blue-ey'd Pallas,* the *swift-footed Achilles,* &c. which some have censured as impertinent and tediously repeated. Those of the Gods depended upon the Powers and Offices then believ'd to belong to them, and had contracted a Weight and Veneration from the Rites and solemn Devotions in which they were us'd: They were a sort of Attributes that it was a Matter of Religion to salute them with on all Occasions, and an Irreverence to omit. As for the Epithets of great Men, Mons. *Boileau* is of Opinion; that they were in the Nature of *Surnames,* and repeated as such; for the *Greeks* having no Names deriv'd from their Fathers, were oblig'd when they mention'd any one to add some other Distinction; either naming his Parents expressly, or his Place of Birth, Profession, or the like: As *Alexander* Son of *Philip, Herodotus* of *Halicarnassus, Diogenes* the *Cynic, &c.* *Homer* therefore complying with the Custom of his Countrey, us'd such distinctive Additions as better agreed with Poetry. And indeed we have something parallel to these in modern Times, such as the Names of *Harold Harefoot, Edmund Ironside, Edward Long-shanks, Edward* the *black Prince, &c.* If yet this be thought to account better for the Propriety than for the Repetition, I shall add a farther Conjecture. *Hesiod* dividing the World into its Ages, has plac'd a fourth Age between the Brazen and the Iron one, of *Heroes distinct from other Men, a divine Race, who fought at* Thebes *and* Troy, *are called Demi-Gods, and live by the Câre of* Jupiter *in the Islands of the Blessed.** Now among the divine Honours which were paid them, they might have this also in common with the Gods, not to be mention'd without the Solemnity of an Epithet, and such as might be acceptable to them by its celebrating their Families, Actions, or Qualities.

What other Cavils have been rais'd against *Homer* are such as hardly deserve a Reply, but will yet be taken notice of as they occur in the Course of the Work. Many have been occasion'd by an injudicious Endeavour to exalt *Virgil*; which is much the same, as if one should think to praise the Superstructure by undermining the Foundation: One would imagine by the whole Course of their Parallels, that these Criticks never so much as heard of *Homer*'s having written first; a Consideration

*Hesiod, *lib.* I. ν. 155, &c.

which whoever compares these two Poets ought to have always in his Eye. Some accuse him for the same things which they overlook or praise in the other; as when they prefer the Fable and Moral of the *Æneis* to those of the *Iliad,* for the same Reasons which might set the *Odysses* above the *Æneis*: as that the Heroe is a wiser Man; and the Action of the one more beneficial to his Countrey than that of the other: Or else they blame him for not doing what he never design'd; as because *Achilles* is not as good and perfect a Prince as *Æneas,* when the very Moral of his Poem requir'd a contrary Character. It is thus that *Rapin* judges in his Comparison of *Homer* and *Virgil.* Others select those particular Passages of *Homer* which are not so labour'd as some that *Virgil* drew out of them: This is the whole Management of *Scaliger* in his *Poetices.* Others quarrel with what they take for low and mean Expressions, sometimes thro' a false Delicacy and Refinement, oftner from an Ignorance of the Graces of the Original; and then triumph in the Aukwardness of their own Translations. This is the Conduct of *Perault* in his *Parallels.* Lastly, there are others, who pretending to a fairer Proceeding, distinguish between the personal Merit of *Homer,* and that of his *Work*; but when they come to assign the Causes of the great Reputation of the *Iliad,* they found it upon the Ignorance of his Times, and the Prejudice of those that followed. And in pursuance of this Principle, they make those Accidents (such as the Contention of the Cities, *&c.*) to be the Causes of his Fame, which were in Reality the Consequences of his Merit. The same might as well be said of *Virgil,* or any great Author, whose general Character will infallibly raise many casual Additions to their Reputation. This is the Method of Mons. *de la Motte*; who yet confesses upon the whole, that in whatever Age *Homer* had liv'd he must have been the greatest Poet of his Nation, and that he may be said in this Sense to be the Master even of those who surpass'd him.

In all these Objections we see nothing that contradicts his Title to the Honour of the chief *Invention*; and as long as this (which is indeed the Characteristic of Poetry itself) remains unequal'd by his Followers, he still continues superior to them. A cooler Judgment may commit fewer Faults, and be more approv'd in the Eyes of *One Sort* of Cricks: but that Warmth of Fancy will carry the loudest and most universal Applauses which holds the Heart of a Reader under the strongest Enchantment. *Homer* not only appears the Inventor of Poetry, but excells all the Inventors of other Arts in this, that he has swallow'd up the Honour of those who succeeded him. What he has done admitted no Encrease, it only left room for Contraction or Regulation. He shew'd all the Stretch of Fancy at once; and if he has fail'd in some of his Flights, it was but because he attempted every thing. A Work of this kind seems like a mighty Tree which rises from the most vigorous Seed, is improv'd with Industry, flourishes, and produces the finest Fruit; Nature and Art have conspir'd to raise it; Pleasure and Profit join'd to make it valuable: and they who find the justest Faults, have only said, that a few Branches (which run luxuriant thro' a Richness of Nature) might be lopp'd into Form to give it a more regular Appearance.

Having now spoken of the Beauties and Defects of the Original, it remains to treat of the Translation, with the same View to the chief Characteristic. As far as that is seen in the main Parts of the Poem, such as the *Fable, Manners,* and *Sentiments,* no Translator can prejudice it but by wilful Omissions or Contractions. As it also breaks out in every particular *Image, Description,* and *Simile*; whoever lessens or too much softens those, takes off from this chief Character. It is the first grand Duty of an Interpreter to give his Author entire and unmaim'd; and for the rest, the *Diction* and *Versification* only are his proper Province; since these must be his own, but the others he is to take as he finds them.

It should then be consider'd what Methods may afford some Equivalent in our Language for the Graces of these in the *Greek*. It is certain no literal Translation can be just to an excellent Original in a superior Language: but it is a great Mistake to imagine (as many have done) that a rash Paraphrase can make amends for this general Defect; which is no less in danger to lose the Spirit of an Ancient, by deviating into the modern Manners of Expression. If there be sometimes a *Darkness,* there is often a *Light* in Antiquity, which nothing better preserves than a Version almost literal. I know no Liberties one ought to take, but those which are necessary for transfusing the Spirit of the Original, and supporting the Poetical Style of the Translation: and I will venture to say, there have not been more Men misled in former times by a servile dull Adherence to the Letter, than have been deluded in ours by a chimerical insolent Hope of raising and improving their Author. It is not to be doubted that the *Fire* of the Poem is what a Translator should principally regard, as it is most likely to expire in his managing: However it is his safest way to be content with preserving this to his utmost in the Whole, without endeavouring to be more than he finds his Author is, in any particular Place. 'Tis a great Secret in Writing to know when to be plain, and when poetical and figurative; and it is what *Homer* will teach us if we will but

follow modestly in his Footsteps. Where his Diction is
bold and lofty, let us raise ours as high as we can; but
where his is plain and humble, we ought not to be
deterr'd from imitating him by the fear of incurring the
Censure of a meer *English* Critick. Nothing that belongs
to *Homer* seems to have been more commonly mistaken
than the just Pitch of his Style: Some of his Translators
having swell'd into Fustian in a proud Confidence of the
Sublime; others sunk into Flatness in a cold and timorous
Notion of *Simplicity*. Methinks I see these different
Followers of *Homer,* some sweating and straining after
him by violent Leaps and Bounds, (the certain Signs of
false Mettle) others slowly and servilely creeping in his
Train, while the Poet himself is all the time proceeding
with an unaffected and equal Majesty before them.
However of the two Extreams one could sooner pardon
Frenzy than Frigidity: No Author is to be envy'd for
such Commendations as he may gain by that Character
of Style, which his Friends must agree together to call
Simplicity, and the rest of the World will call *Dulness*.
There is a *graceful* and *dignify'd* Simplicity, as well as
a *bald* and *sordid* one, which differ as much from each
other as the Air of a *plain* Man from that of a *Sloven*:
'Tis one thing to be tricked up, and another not to be
dress'd at all. Simplicity is the Mean between Ostentation and Rusticity.

This pure and noble Simplicity is no where in such
Perfection as in the *Scripture* and our Author. One may
affirm with all respect to the inspired Writings, that the
Divine Spirit made use of no other Words but what were
intelligible and common to Men at that Time, and in that
Part of the World; and as *Homer* is the Author nearest
to those, his Style must of course bear a greater Resemblance to the sacred Books than that of any other Writer.

This Consideration (together with what has been observ'd of the Parity of some of his Thoughts) may methinks induce a Translator on the one hand to give into several of those general Phrases and Manners of Expression, which have attain'd a Veneration even in our Language from their use in the *Old Testament*; as on the other, to avoid those which have been appropriated to the Divinity, and in a manner consign'd to Mystery and Religion.

For a farther Preservation of this Air of Simplicity, a particular Care should be taken to express with all Plainness those *Moral Sentences* and *Proverbial Speeches* which are so numerous in this Poet. They have something Venerable, and as I may say *Oracular,* in that unadorn'd Gravity and Shortness with which they are deliver'd: a Grace which would be utterly lost by endeavouring to give them what we call a more ingenious (that is a more modern) Turn in the Paraphrase.

Perhaps the Mixture of some *Grœcisms* and old Words after the manner of *Milton,* if done without too much Affectation, might not have an ill Effect in a Version of this particular Work, which most of any other seems to require a venerable *Antique* Cast. But certainly the use of *modern Terms* of *War* and *Government,* such as *Platoon, Campagne, Junto,* or the like (which some of his Translators have fallen into) cannot be allowable; those only excepted, without which it is impossible to treat the Subjects in any living Language.

There are two Peculiarities in *Homer*'s Diction that are a sort of *Marks* or *Moles,* by which every common Eye distinguishes him at first sight: Those who are not his greatest Admirers look upon them as Defects, and those who are seem pleased with them as Beauties. I speak of his *Compound-Epithets* and of his *Repetitions.* Many of the former cannot be done literally into *English*

without destroying the Purity of our Language. I believe
such should be retain'd as slide easily of themselves into
an *English-Compound,* without Violence to the Ear or
to the receiv'd Rules of Composition; as well as those
which have receiv'd a Sanction from the Authority of
our best Poets, and are become familiar thro' their use
of them; such as the *Cloud-compelling Jove, &c.* As
for the rest, whenever any can be as fully and signifi-
cantly exprest in a single word as in a compounded one,
the Course to be taken is obvious. Some that cannot
be so turn'd as to preserve their full Image by one or
two Words, may have Justice done them by Circum-
locution; as the Epithet εἰνοσίφυλλος to a Mountain
would appear little or ridiculous translated literally *Leaf-
shaking,* but affords a majestic Idea in the *Periphrasis:
The lofty Mountains shakes his waving Woods.* Others
that admit of differing Significations, may receive an
Advantage by a judicious Variation according to the
Occasions on which they are introduc'd. For Example,
the Epithet of *Apollo,* ἐκηβόλος, or *far-shooting,* is
capable of two Explications; one literal in respect of the
Darts and Bow, the Ensigns of that God; the other
allegorical with regard to the Rays of the Sun: Therefore in such Places where *Apollo* is represented as a God
in Person, I would use the former Interpretation, and
where the Effects of the Sun are describ'd, I would make
choice of the latter. Upon the whole, it will be necessary
to avoid that perpetual Repetition of the same Epithets
which we find in *Homer,* and which, tho' it might be
accommodated (as has been already shewn) to the Ear
of those Times, is by no means so to ours: But one may
wait for Opportunities of placing them, where they derive
an additional Beauty from the Occasions on which they

are employed; and in doing this properly, a Translator may at once shew his Fancy and his Judgment.

As for *Homer*'s *Repetitions*; we may divide them into three sorts; of whole Narrations and Speeches, of single Sentences, and of one Verse or Hemistich. I hope it is not impossible to have such a Regard to these, as neither to lose so known a Mark of the Author on the one hand, nor to offend the Reader too much on the other. The Repetition is not ungraceful in those Speeches where the Dignity of the Speaker renders it a sort of Insolence to alter his Words; as in the Messages from Gods to Men, or from higher Powers to Inferiors in Concerns of State, or where the Ceremonial of Religion seems to require it, in the solemn Forms of Prayers, Oaths, or the like. In other Cases, I believe the best Rule is to be guided by the Nearness, or Distance, at which the Repetitions are plac'd in the Original: When they follow too close one may vary the Expression, but it is a Question whether a profess'd Translator be authorized to omit any: If they be tedious, the Author is to answer for it.

It only remains to speak of the *Versification*. *Homer* (as has been said) is perpetually applying the Sound to the Sense, and varying it on every new Subject. This is indeed one of the most exquisite Beauties of Poetry, and attainable by very few: I know only of *Homer* eminent for it in the *Greek,* and *Virgil* in *Latine*. I am sensible it is what may sometimes happen by Chance, when a Writer is warm, and fully possest of his Image: however it may be reasonably believed they design'd this, in whose Verse it so manifestly appears in a superior degree to all others. Few Readers have the Ear to be Judges of it, but those who have will see I have endeavour'd at this Beauty.

Upon the whole, I must confess my self utterly in-

capable of doing Justice to *Homer*. I attempt him in no
other Hope but that which one may entertain without
much Vanity, of giving a more tolerable Copy of him
than any entire Translation in Verse has yet done. We
have only those of *Chapman, Hobbes,* and *Ogilby. Chapman* has taken the Advantage of an immeasurable Length
of Verse, notwithstanding which there is scarce any
Paraphrase more loose and rambling than his. He has
frequent Interpolations of four or six Lines, and I remember one in the thirteenth Book of the *Odysses, ver.*
312. where he has spun twenty Verses out of two. He
is often mistaken in so bold a manner, that one might
think he deviated on purpose, if he did not in other
Places of his Notes insist so much upon Verbal Trifles.
He appears to have had a strong Affectation of extract-
ing new Meanings out of his Author, insomuch as to
promise in his Rhyming Preface, a Poem of the
Mysteries he had revealed in *Homer*; and perhaps he
endeavoured to strain the obvious Sense to this End.
His Expression is involved in Fustian, a Fault for which
he was remarkable in his Original Writings, as in the
Tragedy of *Bussy d'Amboise,* &c. In a word, the Nature
of the Man may account for his whole Performance; for
he appears from his Preface and Remarks to have been
of an arrogant Turn, and an Enthusiast in Poetry. His
own Boast of having finish'd half the *Iliad* in less than
fifteen Weeks, shews with what Negligence his Version
was performed. But that which is to be allowed him,
and which very much contributed to cover his Defects,
is a daring fiery Spirit that animates his Translation,
which is something like what one might imagine *Homer*
himself would have writ before he arriv'd to Years of
Discretion. *Hobbes* has given us a correct Explanation
of the Sense in general, but for Particulars and Circum-

stances he continually lopps them, and often omits the most beautiful. As for its being esteem'd a close Translation, I doubt not many have been led into that Error by the Shortness of it, which proceeds not from his following the Original Line by Line, but from the Contractions above-mentioned. He sometimes omits whole Similes and Sentences, and is now and then guilty of Mistakes which no Writer of his Learning could have fallen into, but thro' Carelessness. His Poetry, as well as *Ogilby*'s, is too mean for Criticism.

It is a great Loss to the Poetical World that Mr. *Dryden* did not live to translate the *Iliad*. He has left us only the first Book and a small Part of the sixth; in which if he has in some Places not truly interpreted the Sense, or preserved the Antiquities, it ought to be exceused on account of the Haste he was obliged to write in. He seems to have had too much Regard to *Chapman,* whose Words he sometimes copies, and has unhappily follow'd him in Passages where he wanders from the Original. However had he translated the whole Work, I would no more have attempted *Homer* after him than *Virgil*, his Version of whom (notwithstanding some human Errors) is the most noble and spirited Translation I know in any Language. But the Fate of great Genius's is like that of great Ministers, tho' they are confessedly the first in the Commonwealth of Letters, they must be envy'd and calumniated only for being at the Head of it.

That which in my Opinion ought to be the Endeavour of any one who translates *Homer,* is above all things to keep alive that Spirit and Fire which makes his chief Character. In particular Places, where the Sense can bear any Doubt, to follow the strongest and most Poetical, as most agreeing with that Character. To copy him in all the Variations of his Style, and the different Modulations of his Numbers. To preserve in the more active or descriptive Parts, a Warmth and Elevation; in the more sedate or narrative, a Plainness and Solemnity; in the Speeches a Fulness and Perspicuity; in the Sentences a Shortness and Gravity. Not to neglect even the little Figures and Turns on the Words, nor sometimes the very Cast of the Periods. Neither to omit or confound any Rites or Customs of Antiquity. Perhaps too he ought to include the whole in a shorter Compass, than has hitherto been done by any Translator who has tolerably preserved either the Sense or Poetry. What I would farther recommend to him, is to study his Author rather from his own Text than from any Commentaries, how learned soever, or whatever Figure they make in the Estimation of the World. To consider him attentively in Comparison with *Virgil* above all the Ancients, and with *Milton* above all the Moderns. Next these the Archbishop of *Cambray*'s *Telemachus* may give him the truest Idea of the Spirit and Turn of our Author, and *Bossu*'s admirable Treatise of the Epic Poem the justest Notion of his Design and Conduct. But after all, with whatever Judgment and Study a Man may proceed, or with whatever Happiness he may perform such a Work; he must hope to please but a few, those only who have at once a Taste of Poetry, and competent Learning. For to satisfy such as want either, is not in the Nature of this Undertaking; since a meer Modern Wit can like nothing that is not *Modern*, and a Pedant nothing that is not *Greek*.

What I have done is submitted to the Publick, from whose Opinions I am prepared to learn; tho' I fear no Judges so little as our best Poets, who are most sensible of the Weight of this Task. As for the worst, whatever they shall please to say, they may give me some Concern as they are unhappy Men, but none as they are malignant Writers. I was guided in this Translation by Judgments very different from theirs, and by Persons for whom they can have no Kindness, if an old Observation be true, that the strongest Antipathy in the World is that of Fools to Men of Wit. Mr. *Addison* was the first whose Advice determin'd me to undertake this Task, who was pleas'd to write to me upon that Occasion in such Terms as I cannot repeat without Vanity. I was obliged to Sir *Richard Steele* for a very early Recommendation of my Undertaking to the Publick. Dr. *Swift* promoted my Interest with that Warmth with which he always serves his Friend. The Humanity and Frankness of Sir *Samuel Garth* are what I never knew wanting on any Occasion. I must also acknowledge with infinite Pleasure the many friendly Offices as well as sincere Criticisms of Mr. *Congreve,* who had led me the way in translating some Parts of *Homer,* as I wish for the sake of the World he had prevented me in the rest. I must add the Names of Mr. *Rowe* and Dr. *Parnell,* tho' I shall take a farther Opportunity of doing Justice to the last, whose Good-nature (to give it a great Panegyrick) is no less extensive than his Learning. The Favour of these Gentlemen is not entirely undeserved by one who bears them so true an Affection. But what can I say of the Honour so many of the *Great* have done me, while the *First Names* of the Age appear as my Subscribers, and the most distinguish'd Patrons and Ornaments of Learning as my chief Encouragers. Among these it is a particular Pleasure to me to find, that my highest Obligations are to such who have done most Honour to the Name of Poet: That his Grace the *Duke* of *Buckingham* was not displeas'd I should undertake the Author to whom he has given (in his excellent *Essay*) the finest Praise he ever yet receiv'd.

> *Read* Homer *once, and you can read no more;*
> *For all things else appear so mean and poor,*
> *Verse will seem Prose: yet* often *on him look,*
> *And you will hardly need another Book.*

That the Earl of *Halifax* was one of the first to favour me, of whom it is hard to say whether the Advancement of the Polite Arts is more owing to his Generosity or his Example. That such a Genius as my Lord *Bolingbroke,* not more distinguished in the great Scenes of Business than in all the useful and entertaining Parts of Learning, has not refus'd to be the Critick of these Sheets, and the Patron of their Writer. And that so excellent an Imitator of *Homer* as the noble Author of the Tragedy of *Heroic Love,* has continu'd his Partiality to me from my writing Pastorals to my attempting the *Iliad.* I cannot deny my self the Pride of confessing, that I have had the Advantage not only of their Advice for the Conduct in general, but their Correction of several Particulars of this Translation.

I could say a great deal of the Pleasure of being distinguish'd by the *Earl* of *Carnarvon,* but it is almost absurd to particularize any one generous Action in a Person whose whole Life is a continued Series of them. The Right Honourable Mr. *Stanhope,* the present Secretary of State, will pardon my Desire of having it known that he was pleas'd to promote this Affair. The particular Zeal of Mr. *Harcourt* (the Son of the late Lord Chancellor) gave me a Proof how much I am honour'd in a Share of his Friendship. I must attribute to the same Motive that of several others of my Friends, to whom all Acknowledgments are render'd unnecessary by the Privileges of a familiar Correspondence: And I am satisfy'd I can no way better oblige Men of their Turn, than by my Silence.

In short, I have found more Patrons than ever *Homer* wanted. He would have thought himself happy to have met the same Favour at *Athens,* that has been shewn me by its learned Rival, the University of *Oxford.* If my Author had the *Wits* of After-Ages for his Defenders, his Translator has had the *Beauties* of the present for his Advocates; a Pleasure too great to be changed for any Fame in Reversion. And I can hardly envy him those pompous Honours he receiv'd after Death, when I reflect on the Enjoyment of so many agreeable Obligations, and easy Friendships which make the Satisfaction of Life. This Distinction is the more to be acknowledg'd, as it is shewn to one whose Pen has never gratify'd the Prejudices of particular *Parties,* or the Vanities of particular *Men.* Whatever the Success may prove, I shall never repent of an Undertaking in which I have experienc'd the Candour and Friendship of so many Persons of Merit; and in which I hope to pass some of those Years of Youth that are generally lost in a Circle of Follies, after a manner neither wholly unuseful to others, nor disagreeable to my self.

LEONARD WELSTED

LEONARD WELSTED

A DISSERTATION CONCERNING THE PER-
FECTION OF THE ENGLISH LANGUAGE,
THE STATE OF POETRY, &c.

1724

TO

His GRACE

THE

Duke of *Newcastle,*
Lord Chamberlain of his Majesty's
Houshold, and Knight of the most Noble
Order of the Garter, &c.

My Lord,

WHATEVER, in the ensuing Volume, has been printed
before, was receiv'd with a very remarkable Candour and
Indulgence by all sorts of Readers; and 'tis this, together
with Your GRACE's experienc'd Care for Arts, that has
principally encourag'd me to address these Writings to
You: No Works of mine should have aspir'd to so great
an Honour, if they could not have brought with them
some Marks of publick Favour; that Favour, whatever
it be, and the Good-Nature of the Town express'd
towards them, gives me, I confess, a very sincere
Pleasure, while it gives me an Argument for introducing
them to the duke of NEWCASTLE; the good Fortune, my

Writings have met with, could never have been boasted of, or even mention'd by me, but that it contributes to make their Way to Your GRACE with more Respect and Dignity.

The Generality of Writers, and what they pretend is, I question not, very unaffected, have recourse to the Sanction of Great Names, as a Charm against Envy, sometimes without being in any Danger of exciting it, and as a Defence from the Attacks of Criticks, an inhospitable Race of People, that are at perpetual Enmity with Poets, as the *Turks* with the *Maltese*. The Poets, my LORD, like those of *Malta,* have but a small Territory to defend; like them, they possess certain Immunities and Honours, and boast the most illustrious of Mankind among the Knights of their Order; they are, in common with the Heroes of that Island, Adventurers for Fame and Glory, and there is in either Institution, but one Preferment or Place of Profit; the Enemies of the one and the other are equally savage, and tho' not very famous for the Arts and Discipline of War, yet much to be fear'd in regard of their Rage, Noise, and Numbers: It is therefore with good Reason, that the Writers of Verse so earnestly sollicite Succours from those who are best able to afford it them; they have great need to be protected from their *Mahometan* Adversaries. This, my LORD, is the Case of most of us; but the following Poems do not, at this Time, wholly pretend this Plea for Favour; they have, in the greater Part of them, already pass'd thro' the Trials and Dangers of the poetical Warfare; and now that the Heat of the Day is over, they humbly throw themselves at Your GRACE's Feet, in hopes of finding there an honourable *Asylum*. Many of them, my LORD, which I must not omit to mention in Justice to my self, were, expressly, written to assert my Zeal for the Protestant Establishment, and to celebrate, what in me lay, those brave *Englishmen,* that had signalized themselves in its Defence: As such, they have an additional Right to Your GRACE's Care, over and above that which the Muses claim to the Favour of Great Men, and may, with uncommon Propriety, apply for Patronage, to the acknowledg'd Patron of Liberty.

I shall say nothing farther at present on the Affair of this particular Work; my own private Interests in Poetry, under the Honour of your GRACE's Protection, are, I doubt not, in a very good way: But when I consider Poets, in their general Cause and Concerns, I own, I cannot affirm, that they prosper exceedingly in this Age, even tho', You, my LORD, the living Ornament of it, have so eminently befriended them; Whether it be, that the inordinate Love of Gain has taken off Men's Attention from this delicate sort of Pleasure, or that other Gratifications, by their Variety and Novelty, have cast a Damp on it for awhile; or that from the reigning Temper of the People, at present, not Poetry it self can be popular, if it be not disaffected, or whatever other Reasons may be assign'd: Notwithstanding this, I flatter my self, there is something in the Situation of publick Affairs at this Time, that gives the Votaries of this Art a Promise of better Days. It is not, unless I mistake, much more than a Century, since *England* first recover'd out of something like Barbarism, with respect to its State of Letters and Politeness: The great rude Writers of our Nation, in early Times, did indeed promise what the *English* Genius would one Day be capable of, when the Refinement of our Language, and other Improvements, might afford favourable Opportunities for the exerting of it; and at the *Restoration* it was, that Poetry and polite Arts began to spring up: In the Reign of *William* the Third, the Founder of *English* Liberty, they acquir'd great Strength and Vigour, and have continued to thrive, gradually, down almost to our Times. Thus have they, surrounded with continual Tempests, and through a Series of dangerous and unsettled Times, kept on in a progressive State; How much more will they, in all likelihood, if not greatly check'd, advance in the present Calm, that is spread over publick Affairs? May it not, my LORD, be reasonably hop'd, that the Peace, the Happiness, the universal Quiet and Tranquillity, which *Great Britain* and all *Europe* enjoys under the Influence of his Majesty's Councils, will have such happy Consequences for all the Studies of *Humanity,* as may, in Time, and under just Encouragements, bring them to that *Standard* or Perfection, which denominates a Classical Age?

Every civilized Nation has, I believe, sooner or later, such an Age; how far we may be in it, or what Approaches we have made towards it, I need not go about to ascertain: However, it seems to me plain, that the *English* Language is not capable of a much greater Perfection, than it has already attain'd: We have traffick'd with every Country for the enriching of it; the Moderns and Antients have both contributed to the giving it Splendor and Magnificence; the fairest Scyons, that could be had from the Gardens of *France* and *Italy,* have been grafted on our old Stocks, to refine the Savageness of the Breed; we have laid aside all our harsh antique Words, and retain'd only those of good Sound and Energy; the most beautiful Polish is at length given to our Tongue, and its *Teutonic* Rust quite worn away: Little or nothing, then, is wanting, in respect of Copiousness and Harmony; some new Acquisitions, 'tis granted, may occasionally be gain'd, and a judicious Writer may

find an Opportunity sometimes of throwing a Jewel into
our Language, a Word or Expression of more Sweetness
or Significancy, than it had before; but all Men have
not the Talent of doing this with Judgment, as all do not
distinguish between hard and elegant Words, or see how
Poetry and Eloquence differ from Pedantry: Nor does
any thing, I conceive, require greater Skill or Delicacy,
than to improve a Language by introducing foreign
Treasures into it; the Words, so introduc'd, ought to be
such, as, in a manner, naturalize Themselves; that is,
they ought to fall into the Idiom, and suit with the
Genius of the Tongue, they are brought into, so luckily,
as almost to seem, originally, of its own Growth; otherwise, the Attempt will end in nothing but an uncouth
unnatural Jargon, like the Phrase and Stile of *Milton,*
which is a second *Babel,* or Confusion of all Languages;
a fault, that can never be enough regretted in that immortal Poet, and which if he had wanted, he had perhaps
wanted a Superior. Upon the whole, there is a Point of
Perfection in general, which when once a Language is
arriv'd to, it cannot exceed, tho' it may degenerate from
it; and thus it happen'd both to *Greece* and *Rome*; they
both gain'd this Point of Perfection, and both declin'd
from it; the Stile of *Plutarch,* and the more modern
Greek Authors, being as impure and corrupt, in comparison of that of *Xenophon* and *Plato,* as is the Stile of
Juvenal, Lucan, and others, compared with that of
Horace, Catullus, Virgil. The vulgar Opinion therefore
is a vulgar Error, *viz.* that our Language will continue
to go on from one Refinement to another, and pass thro'
perpetual Variations and Improvements, till in Time the
English, we now speak, is become as obsolete and unintelligible as that of *Chaucer,* and so on, as long as we are

a People; this is what one of our Poets laid down some Years ago as an undoubted Maxim.

And what now Chaucer *is, shall* Dryden *be.*

But whoever this Writer is, he certainly judg'd the Matter wrong; it is with Languages, as it is with Animals, Vegetables, and all other Things; they have their Rise, their Progress, their Maturity, and their Decay: It cannot indeed be guess'd, in the Infancy of a People, how many Generations may pass, e'er their Language comes to this last Perfection; this depends on unforeseen Circumstances and Events; but when once a Tongue has acquir'd such a Degree of Excellence, it is not difficult to judge of it, and to see it; tho' it is as impossible to declare, how long it will continue in that Purity, as it was before to know, when it would arrive to it: The Beauty of the *Roman* Language began to fade soon after the Subversion of the Commonwealth, and was owing to it, as the Loss of their Liberty made way for that Inundation of barbarous Nations, that afterwards over-ran them; the *English* Language, perhaps, may never share the same Fate from the same Causes; it may remain in its present Lustre for many Centuries, perhaps not decline from it, till the divine Will shall think fit, if ever it thinks fit, to transplant the Seats of Learning from these to some other Parts of the World: That This, indeed, may happen some Time or other, is not unlikely, as far as one may judge of Things to come by those that are past; as far, I say, as the Experience of past Things may enable us to form a Judgment concerning the Rules of Providence, it seems to be one Law in his Dispensations, that Arts and Sciences, with their Train of Blessings, shall visit, in their Turn, all Parts of the Globe, and that every Part, in its Turn, shall lie

sunk in Desolation and Barbarism: The prevailing
Opinion is, that the Elements of Knowledge had their
Rise in *Egypt*; but whether this be true or false, or
wherever they began, 'tis certain that Countries, formerly
barbarous, are now learned, and that the most learned
of former Times are the most barbarous of the present:
The lesser *Asia* was a great while the most civiliz'd Spot
of the Earth, and the most distinguish'd for Trade and
Wealth; Science and Ingenuity, in Process of Time,
transmigrated into *Greece,* from *Greece* into *Italy,* and
from thence spread gradually over almost all the other
countries of *Europe*; and we have lately seen, in the
same Quarter of the World, a Nation, the greatest for
Extent of Territory, emerging, as it were, all of a sudden,
out of the Depth of Savageness, and promising to vye
with the politest of their Neighbours in all the Arts
of Peace and War. Thus has *Learning,* in different
Ages, shifted her Abode, deserting one People to cultivate another: At present, she resides among us in *Europe,*
but some time hereafter may possibly take her flight into
America, settle there, and flourish, in that new-discovered
World, even among Nations as yet unknown to us. But
to return, my LORD, from this Digression; the Notion
I have been endeavouring to lead your GRACE into, is,
that the *English* Language does, at this Day, possess all
the Advantages and Excellencies, which are very many,
that its Nature will admit of, whether they consist in
Softness and Majesty of Sound, or in the Force and
Choice of Words, or in Variety and Beauty of Construc-
tion: And I am satisfy'd, that what I have asserted,
could be more fully made out by other Considerations,
than those already suggested; particularly, by comparing
the Improvements our Language has gain'd, since the
Time of the first Refiners of it, with those it had in their

Time, and received from them, and by making the same Comparison with respect to the *Greek, Latin, French,* and other Tongues, and then by stating, as accurately as may be, the Time when these respective Languages ceas'd improving, visibly and materially, and how long they continu'd in such an unprogressive State. But I shall not give my self the Trouble of doing this, since any Person of Learning and Discernment, if he pleases to think on the Subject, may as well do it for himself. It is sufficient to have given the Hint. I shall only add on this Subject, now I am speaking of the acquir'd Advantages of the *English* Tongue, that its natural Ones are likewise very great, and such as, I believe, other Modern Languages do not possess, or not with equal Happiness; as that it is capable of finely compounding its Words oftentimes, like the *Greek* ; and in Verse, which I chiefly have my Eye upon all along, has many Measures, the *Iambic* and *Troche* for Instance, in common with the *Greek* and *Latin,* an Advantage arising from the Variation of the Accent; and that Rhime is peculiarly natural to it, varying itself to the Ear with excessive Sweetness and Truth; not to mention the *Cæsuras, Pauses, Transpositions,* and numberless other Graces, which our Versification is capable of, and which result wholly from the original Goodness of the Tongue.

Thus much for the natural Excellence and present Perfection of the *English* Language; and as far as this goes, my LORD, are we advanced towards what I have call'd a *Classical* Age: The Materials to work with are good; what we further require is Genius in the Workmen; or, in other Words, the Ingredients, that compose the Colouring, being ripe and lasting, there wants only a fine Imagination and a skilful Hand to direct the Pencil.

Nor will Genius's, equal to the highest Undertakings, be wanting, so I am apt to flatter myself, among other Circumstances, from the agreeable Prospect of publick Affairs, provided proper Incitements, as was notic'd before, be added for raising in Men a noble Emulation and Desire of Excelling: The Force of Encouragement is such, that it has carried Arts to the most envied Height even in enslav'd Countries, as well as in those of Freedom; in a word, 'twas the regard paid to Men of great Talents, and the liberal Distribution of Rewards among them, that gave so great an Eclat to the Reigns of two memorable Princes in different Ages, of whom One came to Power by the most infamous Methods, and the Other exercis'd it with the greatest Cruelty.

Every Thing, my Lord, our Trade, our Peace, our Liberty, the Complexion of our Language and of our Government, and the Disposition and Spirit of the *Britons,* admirably turn'd by Nature for succeeding in Poetry, all would conspire to make this Nation the Rival of the most renown'd among the Ancients for Works of Wit and Genius; could we but once see that amiable Temper of Humanity, and that Love of Learning, which distinguish your Grace, more generally prevail among Persons of your Rank: Give us our *Holles's,* and we shall not be long without our Poets.

I am in no doubt, but your Grace will excuse this Ardour, which my Subject has unwarily work'd me into, and which proceeds purely from the Passion I have for the Glory of my native Country; a Passion, which has made, You, my Lord, the Darling of it, and is the only Quality in which I can hope to resemble You, as well as the best Recommendation I can have to your Favour.

It is not unlikely, it may be expected, that, in an Introduction to a Collection of Poems, of a very various Kind, and while I have the Honour of addressing myself to so good a Judge, I should say something of the Maxims and Rules, in general, of Poetry: Some Authors, I take it, do this by way of Key to the Beauties of their Productions, which Method does not yet always answer their Expectation, or much promote the View they have in it: For my own part, as this Kind of Ostentation is by no means agreeable to me, so I am convinc'd, it would give no Satisfaction to your GRACE, nor be in the least useful to any Man: All that the Ancients, or the Moderns copying after them, have written on this Scheme, is no more than a Sett of very obvious Thoughts and Observations, which every Man of good Sense naturally knows without being taught, and which never made a good Poet, or mended a bad one; nor have they, I may venture to affirm, been of any other Service to Mankind, than to furnish our multitudes of Pretenders in Poetry, that otherwise had never teaz'd the Publick with their spiritless Performances: Those Observations or Rules were primarily form'd upon and design'd to serve only as Comments to the Works of certain great Authors, who compos'd those Works without any such help; the mighty Originals, from whence they were drawn, were produc'd without them; and unluckily for all Rules, it has commonly happen'd since, that those Writers have succeeded the worst, who have pretended to have been most assisted by them. What is here said of the Rules of Poetry, is equally true of those of Rhetorick, and some other Arts: The Art of Poetry, of *Horace,* is, no question, a masterly Piece, if one considers the Stile, Method, and Poetry of it, and yet I cannot but think, there are scatter'd thro' the Odes, the Satyrs, and Epistles of that Author, more elegant Hints concerning Poetry, and that go further into the Truth of it, than are to be met with

in his profest Dissertation on that Subject. As to the
numerous Treatises, Essays, Arts, *&c,* both in Verse and
Prose, that have been written by the Moderns on this
Ground-work, they do but hackney the same Thoughts
over again, making them still more Trite: most of these
Pieces are but a pert insipid Heap of Common-Place;
nor do any, or all of them put together, contribute in any
considerable Degree, if they contribute at all, towards
the raising or finishing a good Genius: The truth is, they
touch only the Externals or Form of the Thing, without
entring into the Spirit of it; they play about the Sur-
face of Poetry, but never dive into its Depths; the Secret,
the Soul of good Writing is not to be come at thro' such
mechanic Laws; the main Graces, and the cardinal
Beauties of this charming Art, lie too retir'd within the
Bosom of Nature, and are of too fine and subtle an
Essence, to fall under the Discussion of Pedants, Commentators, or trading Criticks, whether they be heavy
Prose-drudges, or more sprightly Essayers in Rhime:
These Beauties, in a Word, are rather to be felt, than
describ'd; by what Precepts shall a Writer be taught,
only to think poetically, or to trace out, among the
various Powers of Thought, that particular Vein or
Feature of it, which Poetry loves, and to distinguish
between the good Sense, which may have its Weight and
Justness in Prose, and that which is of the Nature of
Verse? What Instruction shall convey to him that
Flame, which can alone animate a Work, and give it
the Glow of Poetry? And how, or by what Industry
shall be learn'd, among a Thousand other Charms, that
delicate Contexture in Writing, by which the Colours,
as in the Rainbow, grow out of one another, and every
Beauty owes its Lustre to a former, and gives Being to
a succeeding one? Could certain Methods be laid down

for attaining these Excellencies, every one that pleas'd, might be a Poet; as every one that pleases, may be a Geometrician, if he will but have due Patience and Attention: Many of the Graces in Poetry may, I grant, be talk'd of in very intelligible Language, but intelligible only to those who have a natural *Taste* for it, or are born with the Talent of judging: To have what we call *Taste,* is having, one may say, a new Sense or Faculty super-added to the ordinarily ones of the Soul, the Prerogative of fine Spirits! and to go about to pedagogue a Man into this sort of Knowledge, who has not the Seeds of it in himself, is the same thing, as if one should endeavour to teach an Art of seeing without Eyes: True Conceptions of Poetry can no more be communicated to one born without Taste, than adequate Ideas of Colours can be given to one born without Sight; all which is saying no more, than it would be to say, that to judge finely of Musick, it is requisite to have naturally a good Ear for it; Those cælestial Bodies, which through their Distance cannot appear to us but by the help of Glasses, do yet as truly exist, as if they could be seen by the naked Eye; so are the Graces of Poetry, though they come within the reach but of few, as real, as if they were perceptible alike to all; the Difference is, the Telescope, which brings the one to our View, is Artificial; that which shews us the other, is Natural: In fine, the same Arguments, that will convince a sightless Man of the Reality of Light, and another, who has no Idea but of Noise, of the Reality of Harmony, will as conclusively prove to one, wholly void of *Taste,* the Existence of poetical Excellencies: Some of these, I have said, may be discoursed of with Accuracy and Clearness enough; that is, so as to be understood by those who understand them already; but there are others of that exquisite Nicety, that they will not fall under any Descriptions, nor yield to the Torture of Explanation: We are irresistibly captivated by them, wherever we find them in good Authors, without being able to say precisely, what that Power is that captivates us; as, when one views a very beautiful Woman, one is immediately affected with her Beauty, tho' we cannot mechanically explain the Cause that has that Force over us; we feel the Enchantment, and the Eye strikes it into the Heart, but are at a Loss for the Solutions and Reasons of it; we know, we are silently struck by the Power of a certain Proportion or Symmetry, but do not strictly know the Measure of that Symmetry, and the positive Laws by which it is govern'd: Poetry, in this particular View of it, may be said to flow from a Source, which like the *Nile,* it conceals; the Stream is rich and transparent, while the Fountain is hid. Here then, at least, Rules are impracticable; but while I am in this Trace of Thought, I am not to be understood, as if I would throw the Talent of writing in Verse into a lawless Mystery, and make of it a wild ungovern'd Province, where Reason has nothing to do: It is certain, every Thing depends on Reason, and must be guided by it; but it is as certain, that Reason operates differently, when it has different Things for its Object; poetical Reason is not the same as mathematical Reason; there is in good Poetry as rigid Truth, and as essential to the Nature of it, as there is in a Question of *Algebra,* but that Truth is not to be prov'd by the same Process or way of Working; Poetry depends much more on Imagination, than other Arts, but is not on that Account less reasonable than they; for Imagination is as much a Part of Reason, as is Memory or Judgment, or rather a more bright Emanation from it, as to paint and throw Light upon Ideas, is a finer Act of the Understanding, than simply to separate or compare them: The Plays, indeed, and the Flights of Fancy, do not submit to that sort of Discussion, which moral or physical Propositions are capable of, but must nevertheless, to please, have Justness and natural Truth: The Care to be had, in judging of Things of this Nature, is to try them by those Tests that are proper to themselves, and not by such as are proper only to other Knowledges. Thus Poetry is not an irrational Art, but as closely link'd with Reason, exerted in a right Way, as any other Knowledge; what it differs in, as a Science of Reason, from other Sciences, is, that it does not equally with them, lie level to all Capacities, that a Man, rightly to perceive the Reason and the Truth of it, must be born with *Taste* or a Faculty of Judging, and that it cannot be reduc'd to a formal Science, or taught by any set Precepts. I will only add to what I have said on this Head, that in most other Arts, Care and Application are chiefly requir'd, which is not sufficient in Poetry; a Poet often owes more to his good Fortune than to his Industry, and this is what is usually call'd the Felicity of a Writer, that is, when in the Warmth of his Imagination he lights upon a Conception, an Image, or way of turning a Thought or Phrase, with a Beauty, which he could not have attain'd by any Study, and which no Rules could have led him to; and this Happiness it is, which, in Honour to great Poets, is sometimes call'd or believ'd to be Inspiration. Upon the whole therefore, that I may draw to a Conclusion, it should seem likely, that general Maxims and Rules in Poetry, at least as they are ordinarily propounded, are rather for Form and Ostentation than for Use; and I think what *Valerius Maximus* has affirm'd concerning Vertue, may, with equal or better Reason, be applied to them, *Quid enim Doctrina proficit*? *Ut politiora, non ut meliora fiant ingenia; quoniam quidem sola Vertus nascitur magis quam fingitur. Some of these Maxims may possibly serve to polish a Genius, but cannot make it better than Nature made it*; as a rough Diamond is not heightened in Value, but only prepar'd to be set to View by the hands of the Lapidary. The Author, of whose Work I have subjoin'd a Translation to the following Poems, attempted when I was very young, but now revis'd, particularly in the Quotations from the Poets, which are all new-translated, and made as faithful in the whole, as my Health and the Time I had for doing it, would allow of: This Author is, indeed, of Opinion, that Precepts may be laid down of Use for acquiring the Sublime; but he presupposes at the same time a natural Genius for it, an Aptitude of Mind to think greatly and happily; and no one, in his Judgment, can be a sublime Writer, who has not a sublimity and a nobleness of Soul.

Astronomers tell us, that Bodies attract one another in Proportion to their solid Contents or Quantity of Matter; this, they say, they know by Experiments, and Calculations, and that by these Principles they can explain the Motions of the Planets, which compose our System; but they do not pretend to shew the Mechanical Causes of this Gravitation, or Attraction; all they can say about it, is, that this general Law was originally impress'd on Nature by God, who might give what Laws to Nature he thought fit. In like manner, to end this Subject at once, must we speak of Taste, Imagination, and of many Beauties in Poetry; we know from Consciousness and Experience, there are such Faculties of the Mind, and such Results of Genius; we know the Effect they have upon us, and the Pleasures they produce in us; but we cannot physically account for them, any more than we can for the Soul itself, or any of those other Operations of it, which, as they lie more in common, are less liable to be called in question.

I did in earnest design to have ended, here, this Subject; but to prevent, if I can, the possibility of being misunderstood, I will add, that, when I speak of *Rules* in Poetry as useless, I do not mean that Experience, Knowledge, Application, and every Method, by which Excellency is attain'd in other Things, are not necessary for the aiding a good Genius: What I contend against is, the common traditionary Rules; such as, for Example, "*Poetry is an Imitation; It has Nature for its Object; As an Art, it has some End, and consequently Means or Rules to attain that End; An English Verse contains five Feet; A Play ought to consist of neither more nor less than Five Acts; there ought to be a Fable or Design in it,* &c. *the Manners are to be preserv'd, and he that is Valiant in the first Act, must not be a Coward in the Second; Old Men are to talk in the Strain of old Age, young Men in that of Youth, and Masters, Servants,* &c. *suitably to their respective Conditions of Life: A gay Similitude or Description avails nothing, when out of Season; in* Pastorals, *let a Shepherd have the Simplicity of a Shepherd; in* Epics, *a Heroe, the Dignity of a Heroe: be not witty in the wrong Place; correct and alter incessantly, and so on.* If I were to run over all the Rules, I might fill many Pages with Maxims of the same Weight and Importance, but I will only collect a little of the like sort out of the *English* Essayers in Rhime.

> *Remember, that the Diction every where*
> *Be gentle, clean* ——
>
> *No cutting off of Vowels must be found.*

Think not, where shining Thoughts to place,
But what a Man should say in such a Case.

—— Be not fondly your own Slave for this,
But change hereafter whate'er seems amiss.

Songs to a just Perfection should be wrought;
Yet where can we see one without a fault?

Bare Ribaldry, and nauseous Songs, are most unfit.

The Language still must soft and easie run.

Our Lovers talking to themselves, for want
Of others, make the Pit their Confident;
Nor is the Matter mended yet, if thus
They trust a Friend, only to tell it us.

First on a Plot employ thy careful Thought.

—— 'Tis Drudgery to stoop so low;
Yet to the Player your secret Meaning show.

Another Fault, which often does befall,
Is, when the Wit of some great Poet shall,
So overflow, that is, be none at all.

That silly thing, Men call, Sheer-wit, avoid.

You must not say too little, nor too much.

I have here cull'd out the finest Things and the very Flower of all I could meet with in most of our Arts or Essays of Poetry; I will not now dwell on the Depth of these wise Sayings, or the uncommon Elegancy with which they are deliver'd; but shall only inform your GRACE, that these are some of the most material of those sublime Truths, which have been handed down from Age to Age with so great Pomp, Authority, and shew of

Learning; these are those wonderful Discoveries, to the
Observation of which alone, it is affirm'd, and to nothing
else, the Perfection of all good poetical Writings has
been owing: It may be so; I will not absolutely gainsay
it, both as I am an Enemy to Disputation, and by reason
of my great Unworthiness to pronounce in so solemn an
Affair: However, I will venture to propose to your GRACE
one Question, and it is this; Of what Advantage, think
you, my LORD, it would be to a young Painter, if with a
magisterial Air, one should document him in this Manner?
*I will disclose to you the Mysteries of your Art, and the
Laws that preside over it: Attend; Painting is an Imitation; if you do not follow Nature, you had as good do
nothing; when you draw a* Venus, *take great Care not
to give her a* Fish's *Tail, since Persons of consummate
Judgment and extraordinary Abilities will laugh at you,
however you may get the Applause of the Unlearned: It
is not sufficient, that one Feature be regular; the Whole
must be of a piece and uniform: Display not a Crocodile
among a Flock of Sheep, or a Bed of Cloth of Gold in
Landscape: Draw no Smiles in the Face of a* Magdalen,
nor give Tears to a Lais: *By no Means paint a Woman
with a Beard, nor a Man more than six Foot and eight
Inches in Heighth, and for this excellent Reason, because
Portraiture, most especially of all Things, is an Imitation
of Nature: Cast a Veil over the Parts of Modesty, for
fear of offending the Religious and Chast: A* Venus
*without a Nose is a Monster: When your Sketches are
rude and imperfect, provided you know it, alter 'em; and
alter 'em for the better, provided you are able: This is an
admirable Precept. These are the Maxims, which have
been deriv'd to us from Antiquity, and which all the Wit
of Man has not been able to change or improve: You
once, indeed, painted a* Madona, *as fine as ever came*

from the Hand of Titian, *long before I let you into the Knowledge of the great fundamental Laws, but yet your happy Execution of it was wholly owing to the Observation of them: If, upon 'the whole, you succeed and gain Reputation, fail not to cry up these Rules, and to own the Obligation you have to 'em; if not, cry 'em up still more, and insist with double Warmth on their Excellence and the Necessity of them.*

I dare say, Your GRACE will be of Opinion with me, notwithstanding the seeming Plausibility of these Maxims, and the evident Truth there is in them, that yet a great deal more, and of a very different and more essential Kind, must conspire in the forming a *Raphael*; it is the same thing in Poetry: But since the known stated Laws of this Art are, probably, of so little Significancy, how, it will be said, and by what Means shall a Person, born with a very good Genius for it, carry that Gift of Nature up to the utmost Improvements and Perfection it is capable of? Why, by carrying his Enquiries closely and carefully into Men, Manners, human Nature; by frequently viewing Things, as they are in themselves, and under their natural Images, and by growing Intimate with them; by accustoming his Mind to look deeply into, and to judge accurately of all Objects; by being conversant with the Writings of great Poets, and by tracing their Beauties, and striking out of his own Reflections Improvements upon 'em; by studying severely the Language he writes in, and by sifting all the Turns, Graces, and Refinements, it will admit of; by adding to his own Notions whatever he can gather from every Man of good Sense and Taste he meets with; and by labouring all the while, to execute and throw out into Practice that Knowledge and those Seeds of Poetry, which he has treasur'd up; and by many other Ways, Processes, and

Experiences, not easy to be describ'd, and which, together with some of those already mention'd, are the Road to Perfection in other Arts: And thus may a Poet go on to improve himself continually, even to the end of his Life, or till the Fire of Poetry is extinguish'd in him by old Age; his Study is endless: The great general Rules of Poetry, are, *to think justly,* Sapere est & principium & fons; *to imagine beautifully; and to distinguish well what sort of Writing best suits one's Genius*: the particular ones are without Number, and must be come at by the Methods above-mention'd. Thus it is, to set this Matter in the strongest Light it will bear, with the Rules of Logic, or the Art of Reason; the first universal Rule is, *Never to give or deny one's Assent to any Thing, till we evidently see the Truth or Falshood of it*; and that we may preserve that Evidence in all our Reasonings, the general Rules are, *Never to reason of Things, that we have no clear Ideas of; to begin by the simplest and easiest Truths; and to dwell long upon them, before we proceed to those that are more difficult and compounded*: the particular Ones, as in Poetry, are infinite; they are not to be found any where altogether, and in part every where; we must gather 'em out of all well-written Books, out of all the reasonable Men we converse with, out of all we read, all we see, all we hear, all we think of: The Study of Logic therefore, like that of Poetry, has no End, and we may go on for ever to improve our Reason: As for the common School Logic, or Syllogisms, these, like the common Rules of Poetry, I take to be wholly useless; they serve to no purpose but to wrangle and dispute; they rather puzzle and embarrass the Understanding, than enlighten it, and are only the Inventions of Sophisters, to get Reputation and Money by difficult Trifles; thay cannot be put in practice by the greatest

Sticklers for them out of an University Disputation; and, I think, the best thing a Man can do, when he has learn'd these Subtilties, is to unlearn them again, as fast as he conveniently can: As the common Rules of Logic serve only for disputing, so the common Rules of Poetry serve only for Pedantry. I might consider the Rules of Rhetoric with the same View and Application, but I think 'tis needless: What has given something like Authority to these wretched poetical Documents, call'd the Rules, is my Lord *Roscommon*'s translation of *Horace*'s *Ars Poetica,* from which nothing is oftner quoted than these Lines:

> *Why is he honour'd with a Poet's Name,*
> *Who neither knows, nor would observe a Rule?*

It is not likely, that any one, that knew a Rule, which he thought a reasonable one, would not be ruled by it, if he could; the Sense therefore is not very just in its self; much less is it the Sense of *Horace,* whose Words are,

> *Descriptas servare vices, operumq; colores,*
> *Cur ego, si nequeo ignoroq; Poeta salutor.*

that is, *If I want Skill or Judgment to write in Character, and to keep up to Propriety, as the Nature of different Works requires; why do I take upon me the Name of a Poet?* This Sense is right enough, but the Translator has levell'd it down to common Cant: To speak plainly, his Translation is, through the Whole, low and prosaic, and has nothing of that Spirit of Poetry, or Beauty of Language, which alone makes the Original pleasing; its utmost Praise is, that it gives us, in the main, the true meaning of *Horace*; the Merit of this noble Author in other respects is, undoubtedly, very great, and he must

be acknowledg'd to have wrote extremely well for the
Age he liv'd in: Criticism, under his Management, was
in tolerably good Hands; but the Unhappiness is, that
among us, it commonly falls to the Lot of Men, of very
mean and narrow Conceptions, strong in Passion and
Bigotry; and therefore their Writings are, mostly,
illiberal, scurrilous, vindictive, insolent, equally void of
Wit and Knowledge, full of the Jargon of Terms, empty
of Argument: And here I mean Critics of all Denominations, whether they plod in modern or ancient Writing.
True Criticism is the truest Friend of Poetry; and all
good Poets may naturally wish, that the Knowledge of
it was as extensive and universal, as the Exercise is
unlimited, and that there were as many just Critics or
Judges in Poetry, as there are in any other Art; a fine
Artist, in every Way, has nothing so much to dread as
an ill Judge, and wants only good ones to be esteem'd
and valued; he is sensible, the Reputation and Honour
of his Art will grow, in proportion as the Nature and
Value of it is known, and therefore he is glad of every
Opportunity to put his Work into the Hands of those,
that are curious in it, and can see the Truth and Neatness of it; if he detests and scorns Triflers, that will be
perpetually meddling in the Affairs of his Skill, without
knowing any thing about 'em, he is not therefore an
Enemy to Judgment and the Exercise of it in his Art,
but the greater Friend to it: It is with these Restrictions,
and in this Sense I am to be understood, in whatever I
have spoke concerning Critics, Rules, and the like; and
I hope, after this Explanation, I shall less risque incurring the Displeasure of Persons greatly learned in
the Writings of *Aristotle, Scaliger, Bossu, Vossius,* and
others.

It would come regularly into my Scheme of Thinking

at this Time, as well as serve to illustrate it, after these abstracted Remarks on Poetry, to go into a View, in some sort, of Poets, particularly our own: But Your GRACE is too learned in the Writings of the Ancients, and of your Countrymen to bear me out in this, or to make it becoming for me to direct to You my Sentiments concerning them; and I chuse besides, that Reason apart, to reserve this Enquiry, till an Opportunity is given me of publishing some Thoughts, I have by me, on Dramatic Writing, and the Authors that have made a Figure in it. In the mean time, my LORD, permit me, among other Hints, cursorily to take Notice of the bizarre Fate of divers of our *English* Poets; no Country, certainly, was ever so fruitful of immature Glory, as ours: How many Authors, that were ador'd in the last Age, are sunk into the utmost Contempt in the present! Our Fathers dwelt with Rapture on the Compositions of Men, whom their Sons would blush, in good Company, but to own they had read: On the contrary, it must be acknowledg'd, there are some, that have acquir'd fresh Strength from Time, and whose well grounded Reputation encreases daily. The former, like false Prophets, gain'd Credit for a Day; the latter secur'd a lasting Fame by the Miracles they perform'd.

If one considers the Herd of Writers, in the past and present Times, they have, great Part of them, been servile Copiers after others; and this perhaps is one Cause that the *English* Genius has not gone greater Lengths. Imitation is the Bane of Writing, nor ever was a good Author, that entirely form'd himself on the Model of another; for Poetry, in this respect, resembles Painting; no Performance in it can be valuable, which is not an Original; and the Reason is, that to imitate is purely mechanical, whereas to write is a Work of Nature:

As that Agreeableness which is seen in Persons of a
genteel Air, does not come by Imitation, or the Instructions of a Dancing-Master, but rises from the original
Turn of the Body; it is about 'em, and all over 'em, one
does not know how; so that which truly and lastingly
pleases in Writing, is always the Result of a Man's own
Force, and of that first Cast of Soul, which gives him
a Promptitude to excel; it is his proper Wealth, and
he draws it out of himself, as the Silk-Worm spins out
of her own Bowels that soft ductile Substance, which
is wrought into so great a Variety of Ornaments: In
effect, Works of Imitation differ from Originals, as
Fruits brought to Maturity by artificial Fires, differ from
those that are ripen'd by the natural Heat of the Sun,
and the Indulgence of a kindly Climate. What has been
here said is not only true, as it regards Poets, but it is
likewise applicable to almost all the great Philosophers
that have rose in former or late Ages: These for the
most part have been Men, who have struck out their
Discoveries by the mere Strength of a great Genius,
without treading in the Steps of any who went before
'em, and without being much oblig'd to the Assistance of
Learning; such, among others, were *Des Cartes, Hobbes,*
and *Locke.* But to proceed, what is worst of all, the
Misfortune of most Imitators is, that they imitate the
Faults, not the Beauties of the Writer in their View;
whatever remarkable Vice or Defect he has, they will
try hard to resemble him in it; whatever Excellence,
they take Care not so much as to endeavour after it.

I will detain You, My LORD, but very little longer on
this Topick of the *English* Poets: Great Part of 'em, as
I just now observ'd, have been Imitators; another Body
of them, yet more numerous and more despicable than
these, consists of such as have learnt from the Rules

the Measure of a Verse, and a few other Things of not much more Consequence; and certainly of all the Causes that have help'd to swell the Throng of ill Writers, none have more contributed to it, than those Essays on Poetry before-mention'd: Hence it is, that we have so many mechanical Poets, and that People daily set themselves to versify, who were never design'd for it by Nature; 'tis this that has turn'd into a Trick, what, in a noble sense, is an Art, *viz.* an Art of Genius. A late eminent Writer of our Nation somewhere says, I know not for what Reason, but it was his Way to say every Thing that came into his Head, and only for the Sake of saying it, which makes his Critical Discourses a pretty amusing Mixture of Wit and Ribaldry, good Sense and Impropriety, and Vanity and Modesty odly jumbl'd together; there is a Liveliness in them that never tires one, but they want Solidity and Justness to give full Satisfaction: This Author, somewhere tells us, that he had by him what I do not remember, whether he calls an *English* Art, Essay, or Prosodia, in which were contain'd all the mechanical Rules of Versification, and wherin he had treated with Exactness, of the Feet, the Quantities, and the Pauses; but he adds, that for fear he should instruct some Poets to make well-running Verses, who wanted Genius to give 'em Strength, he was resolv'd not to publish it: I am heartily glad he did not, for we have enough already of those Books, and in Consequence of them, of a much worse sort of Writing, something, which to speak properly, is neither Prose nor Poetry, a sort of low Sense made yet lower by being put into Metre and Jingle, and that differs from uninform'd Prose, as a country Parson in a Dance differs from himself out of it: Those Compositions, that are thoroughly ridiculous thro' some Extravagancy, have their proper Merit by

making one merry; but those that neither have this
Effect, nor give Delight by their Excellence, are of all
others the least to be born: Who can endure what is like
Wit, in such a Way, as to be worse than the entire want
of it? For my part, I acknowledge, the sprightly Nonsense of some Writers has far more Charms for me,
than the dull Sense of others; there is in Fustian and in
Impertinency, when they are alert, something that
awakens one; but this sober, tastless, I know not what
to call it, raises no Passion, nor of Laughter, nor Joy,
nor Admiration: It is the Plenty of Compositions of
this Strain, which has brought Poetry itself into dis-
grace with the Ignorant, and even made some Persons,
that do not want Shrewdness in other respects, treat it
as a Trifle, and at the best but a plausible Folly.

If I could prevail with your GRACE to go along with
me into any further Detail of these Things, it should
be to examine into that very prevailing but unjust
Opinion, that Poetry is of no Use, that is, of no Consequence or Benefit to Mankind; and the rather, because
Poets themselves have sometimes been so weak as to
prefer all other Knowledges to it in this Regard, and to
keep so disadvantageous a Notion of it in Countenance
by the Authority of their Concessions: There is, in
Reality, nothing in the whole Compass of Literature of
greater Use than Poetry; however, my LORD, I will not
tire You by spending more Words and Time on this
Argument than is worth while: The Knowledges of Law,
Physick, and Divinity, are of too tender a Constitution
to be meddled with; but I may venture to mention some
others; and to begin with Mathematicks; Of what
Advantage has that boasted Part of Science been to
Mankind, excepting what has relation to it in Mechan-
icks? Is the World at all benefitted by the Doctrine of

Fluxions and infinite *Littles*? Or, Does it concern the
Interests of Society, whether the System of *Des Cartes*
be receiv'd, or that other, which is at present in greater
Reputation in *England*? This Branch of Learning may
be said, perhaps, in general, to habit the Mind to Truth,
and give it an Exactitude of Reasoning; which Poetry
may also be said to do, in as fine a Sense, tho' after a
different Manner. With respect to Metaphysical Knowledge, no Body, I am perswaded, will contend much for
the Usefulness of it: Mr. *Cowley*, I think, has said, that
he could never determine certainly, whether there was
any Truth or no in that Science; but he was either too
hasty in this Judgment, or he had not entered into the
finest Parts of it; but however that be, let us add to it
Natural Philosophy, and what do they both together
serve for, further than Curiosity and Amusement?
There are in the former many pleasing Speculations,
and highly delightful to those that take Pleasure in
Abstract Thinking, and that the latter furnishes an agreeable Employment to Men of an inquisitive Turn, is not
denied; but this comes to no more than bare Pleasure,
the Pleasure there is in Knowledge, as such, and in all
Knowledge alike; nor is the Speculative Knowledge of
Poetry less various or delightful than that of any other
Art: To go further; assemble in one View the different
Refinements of Architecture, Painting, Sculpture, Music,
and many others, and what do any or all of them promote,
except the Luxury and the Ornaments of Life? Thus
far, then, Poetry is upon an equal Foot, at least, with
other Arts or Knowledges; and none of these, as yet
mention'd, can be affirm'd to have an Advantage over it,
in regard of their Usefulness. But that I may not seem
to state this Case with Art, by dwelling on those Things,
that are confessedly of least Use, I shall pass to those,

that are acknowledg'd to be of the greatest; and these
are what we call the Learning of *Humanity,* or Books
of Wit, Morality, Good Sense, and the like; the Use
these are of, the very best of them, and set in the most
advantageous View, is, that they convey at once Pleasure
and Instruction: Does not Poetry instruct too, while it
pleases? Does it not instruct much more powerfully,
thro' its superior Charm of pleasing? When a Man of
Good Understanding reads Books of Humanity, he meets
with very little in them, that he did not know before;
he is not, strictly, the wiser for the reading of them; all
his Profit, which is all his Pleasure, is, that he sees his
own natural Sentiments supported sometimes by different
Reasonings, and the Truths, he approv'd in his private
Judgment, authoriz'd by the Judgment of others; he sees
'em plac'd, perhaps, in more clear, in more various, or
in more beautiful Lights: Does not Poetry oblige him
as much? Does it not give him the same Profit and
Pleasure, and that in a livelier and more indirect Way?
Besides that, it impresses more strongly on the Memory,
whatever it inculcates, by the natural Help of Numbers:
Moral Writers recommend Vertue, but Poetry adorns it;
the Moralist gains his Reader, to approve of it; the Poet,
to be in love with it: the one simply proposes Truth and
Vertue to us; the other shews 'em in a Flood of Light,
and enforces 'em, as it were, with the Power of Enchant-
ment: Is it not, Lastly, the Privilege of Poetry, that it
mostly gives us truer Ideas, and always more elegant
ones of the Thing in Question, than any other sort of
Writing? Is there any thing, that so much polishes
Men's Manners, or gives so fine an Edge to their Wit?
Is it not this, which gives the strongest Tincture of good
Nature to the Heart? And does it not keep Men in good
Humour with themselves, and guard 'em from that

Gloominess, which Care and Disappointment are apt to spread over the Soul? There is a great Variety of very fine and just Encomiums on this Art, scatter'd about in good Authors; *Tully* has compos'd a whole Oration in Defence and Honour of it; and I might bring many other Considerations for the strengthening what I have asserted in its Favour; but what has been said is enough to make out, which is all I propos'd, that Poetry has its Usefulness, in an equal Degree, at least, with other Arts: It is, I confess, my LORD, of least Use to those, who have the Merit of it, and propably would be of none at all, did not Providence in every Age raise up Men of your GRACE's godlike Disposition, to be the Protectors of it, and to keep it from languishing under Discouragements. I had forgot, in this comparative View of Poetry and other Arts, to mention History, deservedly esteem'd the most agreeable as well as useful of them all; and it would be, perhaps, to want Candour, and look too much like Pedantry in one's own Profession, if I did not allow, that History is more generally useful than Poetry; but then it must be acknowledg'd on the other hand, that it is less delightful, and that its Usefulness is often the same with that of Poetry, which has something of the Historical in its Nature, and never shines more, than when it alludes to Characters and Things of past times: The Difference is, the one relates Facts in Order; the other produces 'em only for the present Occasion: The one relates them for their own Sake; the other for the sake of something beyond it: Further, if the Historian instructs by truly representing some Circumstance or Facts, the Poet instructs as much by pleasingly feigning others: The Historian profits us by placing in our View great Characters, that were in real Life; the Poet, by displaying greater that never were: To sum up the Account, and state it honourably between 'em, the one and the other is extremely useful and pleasurable; they are both manifest Helps to each other, reciprocally illustrating and illustrated; ancient History, especially, receives great Lights from ancient Poetry, and would be very imperfect without it; we may be very well acquainted with the State of past Ages, by reading the Historians, but shall know it still better, if we read the Poets too. I have not mention'd one great distinguish'd Use of Poetry, because it is mention'd every where by Poets themselves, *viz,* that it transmits more effectually than any thing, the good Deeds of Men to Posterity; and this Advantage it plainly enjoys even above History, and every other sort of Writing; for there is, if I may be allow'd the Hyperbole, something in it, when exquisitely finish'd, of an unperishable Nature, that necessarily, as it were, escapes the Ravage of Time, and triumphs by its own force over all those Wasts, its Sister Arts submit to, which owe to it, that the very Names of those, who have excell'd in them, are preserv'd, after their Labours are long consum'd; and if Writings of another kind, as those of *Thucydides, Demosthenes, Plato,* obtain the same Eternity, it is, because they strongly partake of the same Excellency, and breathe that very poetical Flame, if I may so call it, which will not yield to the common Lot of other Things.

I have hitherto, my Lord, wholly confin'd myself, in these Remarks, to Poetry; and the Tendency of them has led me, here and there, to touch upon some of the Reasons, that have hindred, as I imagine, our making that Progress in it, which might have been hop'd for from the natural Felicity of our Language, and of the Turn of our People: I would now fain, if your Grace will be so good as to humour my Inclination, say a Word or two concerning Prose. In Prose, my Lord, we have

manifestly widen'd our Foundation more than in Poetry,
and we have more good Authors of this Species; a thing
not to be wonder'd at, as this sort of Writing, Prose, is
a much easier Acquisition than the other, and does not
require the same Energy of Genius; besides, there are
infinitely more Men who are able to judge well of it, and
it is generally of greater Service to those, who employ
their Talents in it; but tho' we have advanc'd consider-
ably in this Circumstance of Politeness, and are perhaps
but little inferior to the *French* for Neatness and Perspicuity of Stile, whatever our present Merit is in Prose
Writing, there yet seems, in my humble Judgment, something further wanting to the Perfection of it: A late very
popular Author, has, I own, carried the Essay-Turn of
Writing to a great Height, and left behind him fine
Models of a terse and chast Diction; his Defect, if he has
any, seems to be, that he lies too much in *courte* Sentences, that do not run cleverly into one another, and
are not so connected as to depend naturally enough
together; the Chain is sometimes wanting, and the full
Stop, or Close of the Period, returns too frequently upon
us; which is the Vice also of the *French* Writers, or it
is at least the Opinion of the best Critics of their Nation,
that their Language has suffer'd in this Particular, under
its modern Refinements, and that their ancient Writers
had, not only more of the Vigorous and Masculine, but
were also freer and more disengaged. The *English*
Author, I am speaking of, as he follow'd, or seem'd to
follow very closely in the Traces of *Fontenelle,* and to
have much studied his Manner, so did he succeed extremely well in it; however, he is not without his
Master's Alloy, and there is besides, if I may be allow'd
to speak my impartial Sense of the Matter, something
in his Way, that I may call too *imitable*; that is, one

easily sees thro' his Art; one finds out the Secret Clue, by which he conducts himself: This admir'd Person has lately been succeeded by some others, who have discover'd very good Talents both for the Manner of Writing, and the true Spirit of it; and if their Labours have not had that high Vogue, or been born forward with an amazing *Torrent* of *Success,* the reason is not, that they wanted Merit, but that the Humour of being pleas'd in this Way, and the Inclination, in general, towards such Entertainments, has been long spent and exhausted. In reality, Popularity, or loud Fame, does, the least of all Things, depend on true Excellence, and is commonly attain'd without it; and when not, is owing almost always to somewhat foreign to it, as the Temper and Turn of the Age a Man writes in, or some particular Juncture of Affairs in it, his own Complexion and Quality, and a Thousand other concurring Incidents: Frequently it happens, that the greatest Genius's do not meet the full Recompence of Honour, till after their Death; and those, who have a sudden or violent Run of it in their Life-time, do as often out-live it: Poor old *Settle,* and I might name others, was lately a living Example of this Truth; he was formerly the mighty Rival of *Dryden,* and for many Years bore his Reputation above him; what is he now? and how great is *Dryden?* After having said this with relation to, and for the sake of some amiable Authors, my own Contemporaries, I hope, I shall be forgiven, if I repeat, that it seems, something might still be added of Advantage to Prose Writing, to unfetter it, as it were, and give it a more unconfin'd Air, that it may run out into an easie Extent, bounded, as Nature is, with Mountains and Rivers, at just Distances, but not interrupted with perpetual Stops and Breaks: The Writer, that has made the

most handsome Openings towards this Improvement of
Stile, is Mr. *Philips,* whose Prose-Works, will, I am persuaded, now they are collected into Volumes, grow daily
more and more in the Publick Favour; the sound Knowledge, there is in them, the unwonted Accuracy of Thought
and Expression, and that Liberty of Stile, I have been
speaking of, cannot fail of gaining them the Reputation,
they deserve, with the thinking and unbiass'd Part of
Mankind; and this Praise I could not have refus'd him,
on this Subject, without manifest Partiality, tho' I were
unmindful of the Kindness, he formerly did me, in recom-
mending my Writings to the World with so great Weight
and Authority; nor could I, on the other hand, have paid
this Debt to the Merit of this accomplish'd Writer, more
advantageously for him, than while I am appealing, in
the Cause of Literature, to a Nobleman, known not only
for his delicate Taste of it, but for the largest Heart in
its Support.

Among the various Topics I have fallen into in these
Observations, there is nothing, I have so much endeavour'd to interest your GRACE in the Truth of, as what
I have said concerning the Usefulness, in general, of
Rules in Poetry, and the like: I might produce many
Authorities on this Head, if Authorities were, or ought
to be, of any Weight with Men of Sense; however, I
think it not improper to name two; the first, who, I
believe, will be reckon'd a very good one, is Sir *William
Temple,* and he, to the best of my Remembrance, expressly says, That *Rules never contributed in the least
to the making a Poet*: The other is, *Horace*; the only
one, I shall now quote among the Poets, though both the
Greek and *Latin* are full of the same Sentiments; I have,
my LORD, made some Progress in the Translation of a
considerable and entire Portion of this Author's Works,

and the whole, I hope, might be attempted, not with ill
Success, if suitable Encouragement could possibly be
gain'd, or any Recompence hop'd for so arduous and
painful a Labour: To return, *Horace* has, even in his
Ars Poetica, thrown out several Things, which plainly
shew, he thought, an Art of Poetry was of no sort of
Use, even while he was writing one; but what I have
my Eye upon at this Time is, the Third Ode of his Fourth
Book, and this I shall take leave to lay before your
GRACE at large, and subjoin the Translation of it, not as
a Specimen of the Work I have in Hand, but only to
shew the enthusiastic Notion this Writer had of the
Efficacy of Genius and Nature in Poetry, and how fruit-
less he judg'd all other Aids to be without 'em.

Hor. Ode 3. Lib. 4.

Quem tu, Melpomene, semel
  Nascentem placido lumine videris,

Illum non labor Isthmius
  Clarabit pugilem, non equus impiger

Curru ducet Achaïco
  Victorem, neque res bellica Deliis

Ornatum foliis ducem,
  Quod regum tumidas contuderit minas,

Ostendet Capitolio;
  Sed quæ Tibur aquæ fertile perfluunt,

Et spissæ nemorum comæ,
  Fingent Æolio carmine nobilem:

Romæ, principis urbium,
  Dignatur soboles inter amabiles

Vatum ponere me choros;
　Et jam dente minus mordeor invido.

O testitudinis aureæ
　Dulcem que strepitum, Pieri, temperas;

O mutis quoque piscibus
　Donatura cycni, si libeat, sonum;

Totum numeris hoc tui est,
　Quod monstror digito prætereuntium,

Romanæ fidicen lyræ:
　Quod spiro, & placeo, si placeo, tuum est.

The Commendation given by *Scaliger* to this Ode, is
so extraordinary, that it is known almost to every Body,
viz. that he had rather have been the Writer of it, than
King of *Arragon*: Monsieur *Dacier* is not less sensible
of its Excellence, and adds to other Encomiums of it,
that there is nothing to be met with more finish'd either
among the *Latin* or the *Greek* Poets; it will not, I doubt,
appear to the *English* Reader to be of this Merit from
my Version of it.

Hor. Ode 3. Lib. 4.

Whom thou, O Daughter *chaste of* Jove,
　Didst, at his Birth, with Eyes of Love

Behold; in Isthmian *Games, nor he*
　Fam'd for the Wrestler's Wreath shall be;

Nor his latest Lineage grace,
　By conquering in the Chariot-Race;

Nor him the Toils, to Warriors known,
　The mighty Boasts of Kings *o'erthrown,*

> *In Triumph through the gazing Throng,*
>   *A laurell'd Chief! shall lead along:*
>
> *But fruitful* Tibur's *winding Floods,*
>   *And the silent gloomy Woods,*
>
> *To render famous shall conspire,*
>   *For the* Poem *of the* Lyre.
>
> *Imperial* Rome, *the Nurse of Fame,*
>   *Kindly does enroll my Name*
>
> *Among the* Poets' *charming Choir;*
>   *And Envy now abates her Ire.*
>
> Goddess, *who the Notes dost swell*
>   *So sweetly on my golden Shell;*
>
> *Who can'st give, if such thy Choice,*
>   *To Fishes mute the* Cygnet's *Voice;*
>
> *'Tis to thee, I wholly owe,*
>   *Whispers flying where I go,*
>
> *That to the passing Throng I'm show'd,*
>   *Th' Inventor of the* Roman *Ode!*
>
> *My Life and Fame, if Fame be mine,*
>   *O* Goddess-Muse, *are Gifts of thine.*

After I have mention'd the *French* commentator on *Horace,* I cannot, my LORD, forbear taking Notice, in Justice to his polite Countrymen, that they have taken Criticism out of Pedantry, and made it a delightful Part of Learning by their elegant Way of treating it; the Genius and Capacity they have shewn, thro' the whole Extent of human Knowledge, does, undoubtedly, deserve the Acknowledgments of all Men, particularly of the

English, who have been so much indebted to them; and yet, I know not how, we can never give them a good Word; we are always stealing from them, and always abusing them; Like *Banditti,* we first plunder them of their Wealth, and then do all we can to murther their Reputation. To return, what the same *Dacier* further says of this Ode is spoke extreme prettily, as it is also very just. *Horace, says he, in this Poem, thanks the Muses for the favourable or propitious Eye, which they cast upon him in the Hour of his Nativity; he acknowledges, it was at that first Instant of his Being, that he received from them whatever distinguishes him; and by this Acknowledgment he very evidently shews, he was persuaded, that no Man can be a Poet, unless he received at his Birth from Heaven, by some happy Influence or Impression, that Spirit of Poetry, which Art and Study can never give.* Sir *William Temple,* above-cited, takes a Step yet further, and beyond what he has said of Poetry, asserts concerning Learning in the gross, that *the least Grain of Wit one is born with, is worth all the Improvements one can make afterwards by Study,* or to the same Effect; this would be eminently true, apply'd to Poetry; and tho' it ought perhaps to be receiv'd in a qualified Sense, in regard of Learning in general, yet it is certain, that a great Part of what goes by that Name consists in such Things, as a wise Man, to use *Seneca's* Words, if he knew 'em, would labour to forget.

There is but one Thing more, my Lord, that I shall hint at, before I conclude, and this I shall dispatch with the greater Brevity, as it is not mentioned by me so much for the Sake of the Relation it has to Poetry, as to oblige certain Gentlemen, who seem to have a competent Share of Wit, and to think so themselves, and yet are very frank in professing they don't know what it is; 'tis

possible, it may be so, and they may both think rightly
and profess sincerely, as I once knew a great Poet, highly
valued by your GRACE, who yet could not speak on the
Subject of Poetry with any Address; he felt and possess'd within himself the Power of it, and could, when
he pleas'd, execute it with inimitable Success, but he had
not habited his Mind to think of it in a rational or ex-
plicit Way, nor gone, as far as may be done, into the
Philosophy of his Art: As to *Wit,* the Reason of all the
Puzzle and Contention, that has been about it, and of the
frivolous Definitions that have been given of it is, that
the word *Wit,* in our Language, like that other, *Humour,*
carries in it too vague and indefinite an Idea, and is of
too general a Nature; neither the *French, Greek,* nor
Latin Tongues have any Word, that precisely answers
to it; the Words in those Tongues, that bear an Affinity
to it, are limited and particular, and therefore too plain
to need to be defined: but notwithstanding this, one may
venture, I think, without much Hazard, to declare, that
what commonly is received under the Name of *Wit,* and
pleases as such, is no other than some uncommon Thought
or just Observation, couch'd in Images or Allusions,
which create a sudden Surprize through their Agreeableness, and the Lustre with which they strike the Imagination; that Agreeableness mostly arises from the blend-
ing together different Ideas, which naturally suit with
and illustrate one another; and when this is done happily,
it makes what we call *Wit*; when it is done incongruously,
'tis something else. Now if the Account I have here
given of *Wit,* be true, it may sometimes, far from proceeding from a superior Understanding, be the effect
of Luck, or mere Chance-work; or in other Words, *Wit*
may come from very unwitty Heads; since, where People
think and talk at random, as Persons of a vivacious

Fancy, with little Judgment, commonly do, and where they ignorantly confound a Multitude of different Ideas, it is almost impossible, but that some of them should fall into that Position or Figure of Thought and Language, which may be *Wit,* or not unlike it; it is even possible, that this may frequently happen, and when it does, those, who have the least *Wit,* may be said to have the most: It is, however, in every one's Experience, that a silly Man does sometimes utter a witty Thing; but then it is a witty Thing only with respect to others; with respect to himself, it is no more than a lucky One; he had the good Fortune to say something which he did not deserve to say: It is not true, as certain wise Men imagine, that all *Wits* are Fools, but it is very true, that some Fools are *Wits: Afranius* was of this sort of Men; he never thought justly or consequentially on any Subject; he could not go through the easiest Chain of Reasoning: and yet, by I know not what fortunate Infatuation, he every now and then blundered into good Things; what he said was sometimes witty, but much oftner absurd; so that, taken altogether, he got the name of a *Wit,* and pass'd for such with the Generality; but all thinking Men knew him for what he truly was: The Writings of several Moderns have been much in the Turn and Character of *Afranius's* ordinary Discourse; so they had the Luck to please for a Time; but, like the Children of fond Parents, were too witty to live long.

By this time, I am sensible, tho', I know, your GRACE delights in reading whatever is in the finer Cast of Speculation, that I have extended myself beyond the Bounds, indulg'd to Addresses of this Nature, and beyond, perhaps, the Patience of any one, who has the Opportunities of varying his Pleasures with that Agreeableness and Beauty, which your Rank and Turn of

Mind, my LORD, enable You to do: this was not in my first Intention, but my Argument, and the Matter of it, grew insensibly upon me, as I wrote, and swell'd gradually to a Length I was not aware of; however, your GRACE is at length come within Sight of Land; all that remains, is to add a Word or two more to what has already been slightly spoken, concerning the following Poems themselves; The first, and most considerable of them, entitled, a *Love-Tale,* and which was originally publish'd, together with some others, in the *Free-Thinker,* was form'd upon an Idea, that *Ovid*'s manner, in general, would furnish out a more beautiful Model of Writing, than had yet been practised among us, provided it could be so chastned, as to retain only the Wit and Turn of that Author, without his Puerilities, Indelicacy of Language, and other Vices: These Vices, my LORD, I cannot more luckily describe than in the words of *Quintilian,* where he is giving the Character of an old *Greek* Poet; he might as truly have given it of his own countryman; *Ac si tenuisset modum,* he goes on speaking of *Stesichorus, Videtur æmulari proximus Homerum potuisse, sed redundat atque effunditur, quod ut est reprehendendum, ita copiæ vitium est*; that is, *had he but known, when he had said enough, he might, I think, have come the nearest of any Man towards a Rivalship with* Homer, *but he has too great a Redundancy, and dwells too long on the same Thing, which tho' it must be acknowledged to be a Fault, is yet a Fault arising from Fertility of Imagination.* This was *Ovid*'s great Defect; his Stile of Verse is, otherwise, wonderfully pleasing, and would not fail to shine in the Hands of a Writer, turn'd happily by Nature for it, as he was, with more Judgment and Purity: The *Love-Tale,* among others, was designed after this Idea, and, as it is the first, in Order, in this Collection, so is it my first Attempt in Poetry, of those which I now give the Publick, if I except only a short Copy of Verses, address'd to your GRACE, and one more, call'd *Apple-Pie*, written, while I was at School or very soon after, and which is not inserted here out of any Fondness for that trivial sort of Poetry, but merely because it had the Fortune to be liked, and has by mistake been attributed to another Person; a piece of good Luck I never much envied him: All the rest, like this *Tale* of *Lavinia*, both those before publish'd, and those new to the Reader, have been the Productions of a few Days out of a very few Years last past: I did not therefore think it necessary, in the Printing them, to have any regard to the Order of Time, in which they were written, but sent them to the Press, as they fell into my Hands from among my Papers, and as I could get them out of the Works of Authors, that had publish'd them for me: Such as they are I humbly beg your GRACE's kind Acceptance of them, and that You will please to continue to regard me with the same Favour and Goodness, you have graciously express'd towards me on all Occasions. I am,

With the most profound Respect,

My LORD,

Your GRACE's most obedient,
and most humble Servant,

LEONARD WELSTED.

ALLAN RAMSAY

ALLAN RAMSAY

PREFACE TO THE *EVER GREEN*

1724

I Have observed that *Readers* of the best and most
exquisite Discernment frequently complain of our
modern Writings, as filled with affected Delicacies and
studied Refinements, which they would gladly exchange
for that natural Strength of Thought and Simplicity of
Stile our Forefathers practised: To such, I hope, the
following *Collection of Poems* will not be displeasing.

When these good old *Bards* wrote, we had not yet
made Use of imported Trimming upon our Cloaths, nor
of foreign Embroidery in our Writings. Their *Poetry*
is the Product of their own Country, not pilfered and
spoiled in the Transportation from abroad: Their *Images*
are native, and their *Landskips* domestick; copied from
those Fields and Meadows we every Day behold.

The *Morning* rises (in the Poets Description) as she
does in the *Scottish* Horizon. We are not carried to
Greece or *Italy* for a Shade, a Stream or a Breeze. The
Groves rise in our own Valleys; the *Rivers* flow from
our own Fountains, and the *Winds* blow upon our own
Hills. I find not Fault with those Things, as they are
in *Greece* or *Italy*: But with a *Northern Poet* for fetch-
ing his Materials from these Places, in a Poem, of which
his own Country is the Scene; as our *Hymners* to the
Spring and *Makers* of *Pastorals* frequently do.

This *Miscellany* will likewise recommend itself, by the

Diversity of Subjects and Humour it contains. The grave Description and the wanton Story, the moral Saying and the mirthful Jest, will illustrate and alternately relieve each other.

The *Reader* whose Temper is spleen'd with the *Vices* and *Follies* now in Fashion, may gratifie his Humour with the *Satyres* he will here find upon the *Follies* and *Vices* that were uppermost two or three Hundred Years ago. The Man, whose Inclinations are turned to *Mirth,* will be pleased to know how the good Fellow of a former Age told his jovial Tale; and the *Lover* may divert himself with the old fashioned *Sonnet* of an amorous Poet in Q. *Margaret* and Q. *Mary*'s Days. In a word, the following *Collection* will be such another Prospect to the Eye of the Mind, as to the outward Eye is the various Meadow, where Flowers of different Hue and Smell are mingled together in a beautiful Irregularity.

I hope also the *Reader,* when he dips into these *Poems,* will not be displeased with this Reflection, That he is stepping back into the Times that are past, and that exist no more. Thus the *Manners* and *Customs* then in Vogue, as he will find them here described, will have all the Air and Charm of *Novelty*; and that seldom fails of exciting Attention and pleasing the Mind. Besides, the *Numbers,* in which these *Images* are conveyed, as they are not now commonly practised, will appear new and amusing.

The different *Stanza* and varied *Cadence* will likewise much sooth and engage the Ear, which in *Poetry* especially must be always flattered. However, I do not expect that these *Poems* should please every Body, nay the critical *Reader* must needs find several Faults; for I own that there will be found in these *Volumes* two or three Pieces, whose *Antiquity* is their greatest Value; yet still I am perswaded there are many more that shall merit *Approbation* and *Applause* than *Censure* and *Blame.* The best Works are but a Kind of *Miscellany,* and the cleanest Corn is not without some Chaff, no not after often Winnowing: Besides, *Dispraise* is the easiest Part of *Learning,* and but at best the Offspring of *uncharitable Wit.* Every Clown can see that the Furrow is crooked, but where is the Man that will plow me one straight?

There is nothing can be heard more silly than one's expressing his *Ignorance* of his *native Language*; yet such there are, who can vaunt of acquiring a tolerable Perfection in the *French* or *Italian* Tongues, if they have been a Forthnight in *Paris* or a Month in *Rome*: But shew them the most elegant Thoughts in a *Scots* Dress, they as disdainfully as stupidly condemn it as barbarous. But the true Reason is obvious: Every one that is born never so little superior to the *Vulgar,* would fain distinguish themselves from them by some Manner or other, and such, it would appear, cannot arrive at a better *Method.* But this affected Class of Fops give no uneasiness, not being numerous; for the most part of our Gentlemen, who are generally Masters of the most useful and politest *Languages,* can take Pleasure (for a Change) to speak and read their own.

It was intended that an Account of the *Authors* of the following *Collection* should be given; but not being furnished with such distinct Information as could be wished for that End at present, the *Design* is delayed, until the publishing of a *Third* or *Fourth* succeeding Volume, wherein the *Curious* shall be satisfied, in as far as can be gathered, with Relation to their *Lives* and *Characters,* and the Time wherein they flourished. The Names of the *Authors,* as we find them in our *Copies,* are marked before or after their *Poems.*

I cannot finish this *Preface,* without grateful Acknowl-
edgements to the Honourable Mr. WILLIAM CARMICHAEL
Advocate, Brother to the Earl of *Hyndford,* who, with
an easy Beneficence that is inseparable from a superior
Mind, assisted me in this Undertaking with a valuable
Number of *Poems,* in a large *Manuscript-Book* in *Folio,*
collected and wrote by Mr. *George Bannyntine* in *Anno
1568*; from which MS. the most of the following are
gathered: And if they prove acceptable to the World,
they may have the Pleasure of expecting a great many
more, and shall very soon be gratified.

NOTES

NOTES

CHARLES GILDON (1665-1724)

I. The volume entitled *Miscellaneous Letters and Essays On several Subjects.* Philosophical, Moral, Historical, Critical, Amorous, &c. in Prose and Verse. . . By several Gentlemen and Ladies, is dated 1694. An advertisement in the *London Gazette* for February 19-22, 1694, shows that the book had been published before then. Gildon's contributions, which make up a large part of the work, are signed only in part. The two letters reprinted, which occupy pp. 209-224 of the volume, are certainly his, the second being signed, the first unquestionably from the same pen.

II. The character and scope of the *Art of Poetry* are set forth in the title, which runs as follows:

THE COMPLETE ART OF POETRY. In Six Parts.

I. Of the Nature, Use, Excellence, Rise and Progress of Poetry, &c.

II. Of the Use and Necessity of Rules in Poetry.

III. Of the Manner, Rules, and Art of Composing Epigrams, Pastorals, Odes, &c.

IV. Of Tragedy and Comedy; how to draw the Plot, and form the Characters of both.

V. The Rules of the Epic or Narrative Poem. Of the Poetic Diction or Language, and of *English* Numbers.

VI. A Collection of the most beautiful Descriptions, Similes, Allusions, &c., from *Spenser,* and our best *English* Poets, as well Ancient as Modern, with above Ten Thousand Verses, not to be found in any Performance of this Kind. *Shakespeariana*; or the most beautiful Topicks, Descriptions, and Similes that occur throughout all *Shakespear*'s Plays.

It is advertised as 'Just Published' in the *Daily Courant* for June 25, 1718. No second edition was demanded.

Page 3. *Letters and Poems, Amorous and Gallant* [by William Walsh (1663-1708)] first appeared in 1692. It was later included in the fourth volume of Tonson's *Miscellany* (1716).

Page 4. *my unhappy Circumstances.* Having wasted the inheritance he received from his father, Gildon, with a wife to support, was at this time barely making a living as a literary hack.

Page 5. *its Funeral Elegy.* Ovid, *Amores, 2. 6.*

—*Verses to the . . . Sparrow.* The lyric beginning "Passer, deliciæ meæ puellæ," commonly printed as the second of Catullus' poems.

—*deplores its Death.* The third, beginning "Lugete, et Veneresque Cupidinesque."

—*ad Amicam Navigantem.* Ovid, *Amores, 2. 11.*

—*toss'd in another Storm.* Propertius, *Elegies, 3. 24.* The storm is a metaphorical one.

Page 6. *ad Amicam quam verberaverat.* Ovid, *Amores, 1. 7.*

Page 7. *Then like some wealthy Island.* From the poem entitled *The Enjoyment.*

Page 8. *Un sot . . . de Choisir.* Boileau, Satire II, *A Molière.*

Page 9. *Ovid urges his Fame. Amores,* 1. 3.

Page 10. *Mr. Lock remarks.* Cf. the *Essay concerning Human Understanding,* Book II, Chap. 1, Sect. 11, "I grant that the soul, in a waking man, is never without thought."

Page 11. *Jean Le Clerc* (1657-1736), French Protestant theologian. The *Ontologia* was published in 1692.

Page 12. *Tibullus, when he says.* The poem cannot be certainly ascribed to Tibullus. In editions of his works it is sometimes numbered 3. 19, sometimes 4. 13.

—*Petrarch tells us.* In the sonnet beginning "Come 'l candido piè per l' erba fresca." It is numbered 165 in Scherillo's edition.

Page 13. *Cowley.* In the poem in the *Mistress* entitled *My Diet.*

—*Sir Courtly.* The hero of Crowne's comedy *Sir Courtly Nice, or It Cannot Be* (1685). In the third act Sir Courtly says: "fine Language belongs to Pedants and poor Fellows that live by their Wits. Men of Quality are above Wit. 'Tis true, for our diversion sometimes we write, but we ne'er regard Wit. I write, but I never write any Wit."

Page 14. *Mr. Harrington.* Conceivably James Harrington,

who died November 23, 1693, a date almost certainly later than that of the completion of this letter. He was a lawyer and a poet. He published several works of a controversial character, and wrote the preface for the first edition of *Athenæ Oxonienses*. If Gildon's friend was not this Mr. Harrington, the person referred to was not widely known.

—*Monsieur Perault.* The *Parallèle des Anciens et des Modernes* (1688-1692) by Charles Perrault was the first important work in defense of the moderns issued during the controversy afterwards immortalized in the *Battle of the Books*.

—*Rapin.* The Reverend René Rapin expressed his opinions on the matter in his *Réflexions sur la Poëtique d' Aristote et sur les ouvrages des poëtes anciens et modernes* (1674) ; Rymer, in the preface to his translation of this work (1674). Rymer's preface is reprinted in Spingarn's *Critical Essays of the Seventeenth Century*, 2. 163-181.

Page 15. *Rapin extols their Variety. Op. cit.*, 84-85. Cf. also his *Comparaison des poëmes d'Homère et de Virgile* (1664), especially p. 102 of John Davies' translation (1672).

—*Gemitus dedere Cavernæ.* Virgil, *Æneid*, 2. 53.

—*præruptus aquæ Mons. Ib.* 1. 105.

Page 16. *The Mountains seem to Nod.* Dryden, *The Indian Emperor*, 3. 2.

—*St. Euremont's Opinion.* St. Evremond, *Du merveilleux qui se trouve dans les poëmes des anciens, (Oeuvres Mêlées* ed. Paris, 1865, 2. 508).

Page 17. *Mr. Congreve's Song.* In the *Old Bachelor*, 2. 2.

Page 19. *Bishe's.* Edward Bysshe, *The Art of English Poetry* containing

> I   Rules for making Verses
> II   A Collection of . . . Thoughts . . . in . . .
> English Poets
> III   A Dictionary of Rhymes.

First published in 1702, this compilation went through a number of editions.

Page 20. *Newton's Discoveries.* Notably the method of fluxions.

—*Gusto.* The now obsolete use of this word as equivalent to "aesthetic perception" is specially associated with Shaftesbury. Cf. the *Characteristics*, ed. Robertson, 2. 430.

Page 21. *Why is he . . . Rule.* From the translation of Horace's *Ars Poetica* by Wentworth Dillon, Earl of Roscommon (1633-1685), 108-109. It is not an accurate rendering of the original (*Ars Poetica,* 86-87) :

> Descriptas servare vices operumque colores
> Cur ego si nequeo ignoroque poeta salutor.

Cf. *infra,* p. 375.

—*Messrs. of the Port-Royal.* Cf. *Quatre Traitez de poesies, Latine, Françoise, Italienne, et Espagnole* (1663) [by Le Sieur D. T., *i.e.,* De Trigny, a pseudonym of Claude Lancelot]. The books emanating from this famous school were seldom attributed to individual authors.

—*Crambo.* "A game in which one player gives a word or line of verse to which each of the others has to find a rime." *NED.*

Page 22. *Will's.* Once the favored coffee-house of literary men, and so the stock reference, although it was at this time much less visited.

—*Some think . . . others Aid.* Roscommon, translation of Horace, *Ars Poetica,* 408-411.

Page 27. *Sir Philip Sidney.* In the *Defense of Poesy.*

Page 28. *Horace . . . in his Epistle. Epist.* 2. 1. 114 sq.

Page 29. *Mr. Fontinelle. Entretiens sur la Pluralité des Mondes,* by Bernard Bovier de Fontenelle (1686).

Page 30. *Grimaldi.* Nicolino Grimaldi, or Nicolino Grimaldi Nicolini, one of the most popular of contemporary opera-singers. He came to England in 1708. Cf. the *Spectator,* No. 13, and, on operas in two languages, No. 18.

Page 31. *Harry Purcel.* Henry Purcell (1658?-1695). His operas are in general rather what we should call incidental music —songs and intermezzi. The 'frost-scene' was done for *King Arthur* (1691), written in collaboration with Dryden.

Page 32. *Wits . . . against Opera's.* Cf. Rapin, *Reflections on Aristotle,* Rymer's translation, ed. Kennet, 2. 217; Dacier, *La Poëtique d'Aristote,* 85 (Rem. 12 sur Chap. 6) ; St. Evremond, *Sur les Opéras* (*Oeuvres Mêlées,* ed. Paris, 1865, 2. 389).

—*Lullie, Louigi.* Jean Baptiste Lully (1633?-1687), Italian by birth, famous as a composer of French operas and ballets. Luigi Rossi (d. 1653), whose opera *Orfeo* is criticised by St. Evremond, *op. cit.*

—*Madam Dacier.* Anne Lefevre Dacier, *Des Causes de la Corruption du Goust* (1714), 27-28.

Page 33. *Horace was angry.* Cf. .*Epist.* 2. 1. 187 sq.

—*The Spectator . . . in his Censure.* No. 18.

—*He laughs at.* The *Spectator,* No. 29.

Page 35. *the Arthurs.* Sir Richard Blackmore's *Prince Arthur* (1695) and *King Arthur* (1697).

Page 36. *Duke of Buckingham.* In the *Essay upon Poetry* (1682), by John Sheffield, Earl of Mulgrave and Duke of Buckinghamshire (1648-1721).

Page 37. *Author of the Creation.* Sir Richard Blackmore (d. 1729).

—*Madam Dunois.* The *Ingenious and diverting Letters of the Lady*—[the Countess d'Aulnoy], *Travels into Spain,* &c. The account of the shoemaker-critic is found on p. 177 of the English edition of 1708.

Page 38. *Mamamouche.* Edward Ravenscroft's (fl. 1671-1697) *Mamamouchi, or the Citizen turned Gentleman* (1671).

—*the Orphan,* a tragedy by Thomas Otway; the *Empress of Morocco,* a tragedy by Elkanah Settle; the *Plain-dealer,* a comedy by Wycherly; the *Comical History of Don Quixote,* in three parts, by Thomas D'Urfey.

Page 42. *his own Countryman,* &c. See Dacier's *La Poëtique d'Aristote,* e.g., Rem. 8 on Chap. 6 (pp. 80-83). For the opinion of the Academy, see J. Chapelain's *Sentiments de l'Académie française sur la tragi-comédie du Cid* and Georges de Scudéry's *Observations sur le Cid.* Corneille's ideas are expressed in his *Excuse à Ariste,* in his three *Discours,* and in the *Examens* of his plays.

—*Piccolomini, Casselvetro,* &c. Alessandro Piccolomini, *Il Libro della poetica d'Aristotile* (1572); Lodovico Castelvetro, *Poetica d' Aristotile* (1570); Rapin, *Réflexions sur la Poëtique d' Aristote* (1674); Dacier, *La Poëtique d' Aristote.*

Page 43. *Tatler.* No. 29.

Page 44. *Mr. Isaac,* i.e., Bickerstaff.

—*has played the Critic.* The eighth and ninth numbers of the *Tatler* contain criticisms of *London Cuckolds* and the *Old Bachelor.*

—*Spectators, and Tatlers . . . Censure.* Cf. *Tatler,* No. 165; *Spectator,* No. 291.

Page 45. *When France . . . Pains.* Roscommon's *Essay on Translated Verse,* 29-36.

—*Bossu.* René le Bossu (1631-1680). His *Traité du poëme épique* (1675) was published in an English translation in 1695.

—*Vossius.* The various works of G. J. Vossius were collected by his son Isaac in 1695-1701. They are frequently cited in the criticism of this and the preceding century.

—*Scaliger.* J. C. Scaliger's *Poetices* (1561), another widely used source of critical dicta.

Page 47. *Essay upon Poetry,* by Sir William Temple (Spingarn, *op. cit.,* 3. 83-84).

Page 48. *very same Essay.* *Ib.* 3. 80.

Page 51. *Sir William . . . appeals.* *On Ancient and Modern Learning,* by Sir William Temple (Spingarn, *op. cit.,* 3. 33-34).

Page 53. *Audrands,* &c. The Audrans, a celebrated family of French engravers, the earliest of whom was Charles Audran (1594-1674); the Edelincks, especially Gerard Edelinck (1640-1707); the Simoneau family, especially Charles (1645-1728) and Louis (1654-1727).

—*Mr. Wycherly's Lover.* Lord Plausible, in the *Plain-dealer,* 2. 1.

Page 54. *the Tatler.* No. 29.

Page 58. *Gerhard Vossius.* In the address to the Benigne Lector prefaced to his *Poeticarum Institutionum Libri Tres,* Amsterdam, 1647.

—*Lilius Giraldus.* In his *Historiæ Poetarum tam Græcarum quam Latinorum Dialogi Decem,* &c., ed. Basil, 1580, p. 27.

Page 60. *Yet without Writing,* &c. Trans. of Horace, *Ars Poetica,* 306-308.

Page 61. *Horace complains.* In the *Epistle to Augustus, Epist.* 2. 1, 20 sq.

—*Examination of Milton.* The *Spectator,* Nos. 273, 279, and so on, once a week, up to and including No. 369.

Page 62. *says Xenophon.* Possibly the reference is to the *Memorabilia,* 1. 4. 13, or 4. 3. 13-14, but the resemblance is not close.

—*urge from . . . Dacier.* The long quotation which follows is taken from the beginning of the preface to Dacier's *La Poëtique d'Aristote.* An English translation of this work was published in 1705, but the version in the text seems to be an independent one.

Page 68. *Hypocrates says.* *On Ancient Medicine* (*Works,* trans. Adams, 1. 162).

—*Tragedy is,* &c. By no means a literal translation of Aristotle's famous definition (*Poetics,* 6. 2), which reads, in Butcher's translation, "Tragedy is an imitation of an action that is serious, complete, and of a certain magnitude . . . through pity and fear effecting the proper *katharsis,* or purgation, of these emotions."

Page 71. *according to Aristotle.* Cf. the *Politics,* 3. 11.

JOHN HUGHES (1677-1720)

I. The essay *On Style* has been reprinted from the posthumous volumes entitled *Poems on Several Occasions. With some Select Essays in Prose.* In Two Volumes, London, 1735. This work was edited by Hughes' brother-in-law, William Duncombe, and in it this essay is dated 1698. I have found no trace of its previous publication.

II. The essay *On Allegorical Poetry,* as well as the one following, forms part of the Introduction to Hughes' edition of the Fairy Queen, which was advertised as "This day published" in the *Daily Courant* for August 22, 1715.

III. These *Remarks* are printed without excisions, but the later pages are omitted because they discuss details of Spenser's work in a way which throws little or no light upon Hughes' general critical theories.

Page 79. *Sir William Temple observes.* In the essay *On Ancient and Modern Learning* (Spingarn, *op. cit.,* 3. 62).

Page 80. *Dr. Sprat.* Thomas Sprat (1635-1713), Bishop of Rochester and Dean of Westminster. His best-known piece of prose is the *History of the Royal Society of London* (1667), but no one example completely shows his powers.

—*Dr. Tillotson* (1630-1694), Archbishop of Canterbury. His best writing is found in his sermons.

Page 81. *Multa renascentur,* &c. Horace, *Ars Poetica,* 70-72.

—*his Shield . . . fill'd.* The translation of the Æneid, 9. 1093.

Page 83. *Sir Roger L'Estrange* (1616-1704), Tory journalist and pamphleteer. He is seen at his best in the *Observator,* which he began in 1681.

Page 85. *ut sibi . . . laboret.* Horace, *Ars Poetica,* 240-241.

—*Le Clerc says.* In *Parrhasiana,* done into English by—, 1700, Chap. 2, Of True and False Eloquence, p. 80.

Page 86. *Mr. Waller observes. Of English Verse,* 5-6.

Page 87. *Cowley . . . tells us. Of Myself (Works,* ed. 1721, 2. 719).

—*Dryden assures us.* Preface to the *Fables (Essays,* ed. Ker, 2. 247).

—*frequent Commendations.* Cf. *Essays,* ed. Ker, 1. 178 sq., 268; 2. 28, 29, 109, 165, 212, 223.

Page 88. *Milton's Paradise Lost,* 2. 648 sq.

—*one of his Odes.* Horace, *Carmina,* 1. 14.

Page 89. *of the Luxemburg.* Now in the Louvre.

—*used by Spenser. Shepherd's Calendar,* April 19: "And hath he skill to *make* so excellent."

Page 90. *one of his Discourses.* Plutarch, *How a Young Man Ought to Hear Poems, Moralia,* tráns. Goodwin, 2. 45-46.

—*in another place. Ib.* 2. 74.

Page 98. *Sir William Temple observes. Of Poetry* (Spingarn, *op. cit.,* 3. 84).

Page 99. *Dolphins in a Wood.* Horace, *Ars Poetica,* 30.

Page 100. *the Golden Bough. Æneid,* 6. 185 sq.

Page 101. *Metrodorus Lampsacenus.* Cf. Diogenes Laertius, Life of Anaxagoras (*De Vitis,* 2. 11).

Page 102. *Sir William Temple . . . censures. Of Poetry* (Spingarn, *op. cit.,* 3. 99).

Page 103. *in his Travels.* Chardin, *Journal du Voyage en Perse,* Londres, 1686.

—*Choice of Hercules.* Xenophon, *Memorabilia,* 2. 1. 21. Cf. Addison's paper in the *Tatler,* No. 97.

Page 104. *Boccalini.* Trajano Boccalini, *Advices from Parnassus, in two Centuries* . . . revised and corrected by Mr. Hughes, 1706.

—*Visions in the Tatler,* &c. Cf. *Tatler* 81, 100, 102, 120, 123; *Spectator* 159; *Guardian* 152.

JOHN DENNIS (1657-1734)

I. The *Large Account,* under the caption of *The Epistle Dedicatory,* served as preface to Dennis' version of the *Merry Wives of Windsor,* published under the following title: The *Comical Gallant;* or the Amours of Sir John Falstaffe. A Comedy As it is Acted at the Theatre Royal in Drury Lane. By His Majesty's Servants. By Mr. Dennis. To Which is added A large Account of the Taste in Poetry and the Causes of the Degeneracy of it. It was advertised in the *Post-Man* for May 16-19, 1702. In the present text the original arrangement of type has been reversed, Roman being substituted for Italic, and vice versa.

II. On May 27, 1704, the *Daily Courant* announced as 'this day published' *The Grounds of Criticism in Poetry,* contain'd In some New Discoveries never made before, requisite for the Writing and Judging of Poems surely. Being a Preliminary to a larger Work design'd to be publish'd in Folio, and Entitul'd, A Criticism upon our Most Celebrated English Poets Deceas'd. This was reprinted in the second volume of the *Select Works* of Mr. John Dennis, 1718, where it occupies pages 415-479. The original edition contains a preface, "specimen", etc. Otherwise the variations between the two texts are practically confined to matters of spelling and punctuation, in which the second edition is the more logical and consistent. Since this was published under Dennis' supervision, it has been made the basis of the present text.

III. The *Reflections, Critical and Satyrical, upon a late Rhapsody call'd an Essay upon Criticism,* a pamphlet of thirty-two octavo pages, appeared, according to the *Daily Courant,* on June 20, 1711. It has never been reprinted.

Page 113. *George Granville,* Lord Lansdowne (1667-1735), author of several plays, a number of lyrics, and a poem called *Upon Unnatural Flights in Poetry.*

Page 120. *A fault . . . Poets cost.* Mulgrave's *Essay upon Poetry,* 262-268.

—*That silly thing . . . thought. Ib.* 269-272.

Page 121. *a Master-piece.* Presumably the *Plain-dealer.*

Page 123. *Madam de Montausier.* Julie-Lucine d'Angennes,

Duchesse de Montausier (1607-1671), daughter of the Marquise de Rambouillet, and herself a 'precieuse'.

Page 127. *a Modern Critick.* St. Evremond, *Observations sur le Gout et le Discernement des François* (*Oeuvres Mêlées,* ed. Paris, 1865, 2. 470).

Page 130. *Ainsi qu'en sots Auteurs,* &c. Boileau, *L'Art Poétique,* 1. 225-232.

Page 131. *The only Play.* Cowley's *Cutter of Coleman Street.*

Page 132. *She wou'd if she cou'd* (1668), a comedy by Sir George Etherege.

Page 134. *Aimez . . . leur prix.* Boileau, *L'Art Poétique,* 1. 37-38.

Page 137. *Idem rex . . . natum.* Horace, *Epist.* 2. 1. 237-244.

Page 142. *advice of Horace. Ars Poetica,* 129.

—*known subject.* Granville's tragedy, *Heroic Love* (1698), has for its theme the love of Achilles for Briseïs.

Page 143. *The Design.* Owing to lack of encouragement, this was never completed.

Page 144. *Milton's Expression.* In the treatise *On Education* (Milton's Prose, ed. Garnett, 56).

—*Milton says. Ib.* 56-57.

Page 152. *Aristotle might prefer. Poetics,* XXVI.

Page 156. *Longinus says. On the Sublime,* VII.

Page 158. *Oh by what Name,* &c. Milton, *Paradise Lost,* 8. 357 sq.

Page 161. *The next they sang,* &c. *Ib.* 3. 383 sq.

Page 162. *Boundless the Deep,* &c. *Ib.* 7. 168-173.

Page 164. *Fairfax.* Edward Fairfax (d. 1635) published in 1600 his translation of Tasso's *Gerusalemme Liberata.*

Page 166. *Down thither prone,* &c. *Paradise Lost,* 5. 266 sq.

Page 167. *the Apostle says. Romans,* 1. 20.

—*Above them all,* &c. *Paradise Lost,* 3. 571 sq.

Page 168. *O thou,* &c. *Ib.* 4. 32-35. Dennis' reference is a slip.

—*If unforbid,* &c. *Ib.* 7. 94 sq.

—*Sol . . . lustras. Æneid,* 4. 607.

Page 169. *Hesperus, that led,* &c. *Paradise Lost,* 4. 605-609.

—*Where'er at utmost Stretch,* &c. The concluding lines of the paraphrase by Dennis, originally published in the *Advance-*

ment and Reformation of Modern Poetry (1701), and included in the *Select Works*, 1. 18.

Page 170. *And for the Heavens*, &c. *Paradise Lost*, 8. 100-106.

Page 171. *When I behold*, &c. *Ib.* 8. 15-22.

Page 172. *On Adam last*, &c. *Ib.* 10. 197 sq.

Page 173. *Mr. Dryden.* In *A Discourse concerning the Original and Progress of Satire (Essays*, ed. Ker, 2. 29).

—*These are thy glorious Works*, &c. *Paradise Lost*, 5. 153 sq.

Page 176. *Go then*, &c. *Ib.* 6. 710-713.

—*Mr. Cowley.* The *Davideis*, Note 31 upon the first book.

—*Argument of Monsieur Paschal.* An expansion of the Thought: "A Mechanic speaking of Riches; a Solicitor speaking of War; or of Regal State, &c. But the Rich discourse well of Riches; a King speaks coldly of a vast Present which he is about to make; and God discourseth well of God." See Paschal's *Thoughts on Religion*, trans. Kennet (1704), Preface, xxv.

Page 177. *Latius regnes*, &c. Horace, *Carmina*, 2. 2. 9-12.

Page 178. *Non me . . . hostis.* Virgil, *Æneid*, 12. 894-895.

Page 179. *What tho the Field*, &c. *Paradise Lost*, 1. 105-108.

Page 181. *Passage of Homer. Iliad*, 20. 56-65.

Page 183. *as this. Ib.* 5. 770-772.

—*concerning Neptune. Ib.* 13. 18-19 and 26-29.

Page 188. *Doctrine of Aristotle. Nicom. Ethics*, 10. 5.

Page 196. *Well sounding Verses*, &c. Waller, *Upon the Earl of Roscommon's Translation of Horace*, 23-28.

Page 197. *Mr. Waller says. Of Divine Poesy*, 1. 21-26.

Page 199. *When the Almighty*, &c. A paraphrase by Dennis of *Habakkuk*, 3. 3-10.

Page 201. *In my Distress*, &c. A paraphrase of *Psalm* 18. 6-15.

Page 203. *Rule of Horace. Ars Poetica*, 38-40.

Page 206. *Mr. Mede.* Joseph Mede, *Diatribæ. Discourses on divers Texts of Scripture* (1642).

Page 207. *Epistle . . . to Titus*, 1. 12.

Page 212. *Italian Opera.* Such attacks upon opera are common during this period. Cf. pp. 30-34; the *Spectator*, Nos. 5, 13, etc.

—*the Essay.* Pope's *Essay on Criticism* was first published in 1711, being advertised in the *Spectator* for May 15. It was written probably not earlier than 1709, though Pope is said to have placed it in 1708, in 1707, and even in 1706.

—*the Approbation which it has met with.* The *Essay* met with little success at first, the original edition of one thousand copies not being disposed of within a year. It was, however, much discussed. The author's name first appeared on the title-page of the second edition, that of 1713.

Page 213. *Fit Chærilus . . . miror.* Horace, *Ars Poetica,* 357-358.

—*my self attack'd.* The passage in the *Essay* which specially roused Dennis' anger is that beginning with line 585. This 'attack'—if it may be called such—was probably provoked by Dennis' disapproval of Pope's *Pastorals,* and marks the beginning of the long war between the two men.

Page 215. *To Mr.——.* This seems to be a letter by convention only, and is really addressed to no one in particular—certainly to no well-known man of letters, the point of the address being that Sunning Hill is not far from Binfield, Pope's home.

—*Sternhold's Version.* Sternhold's version of the *Psalms* was published not earlier that 1547. Sternhold, with the assistance of Hopkins, turned the *Psalms* into that ballad metre of which *Chevy Chase* is a well-known example.

Page 216. *Roscommon begins. Essay on Translated Verse,* 1-2.

—*Let such teach others,* &c. Pope, *Essay on Criticism,* 15-16. Here and elsewhere Dennis, or his printer, quotes inaccurately. I have reproduced Dennis' text, calling attention to important variants, but letting inaccuracies speak for themselves.

Page 217. *Pliny.* Epist. 1. 10. 4. This is Pope's note on the passage just quoted.

—*A living noble Author.* The Earl of Mulgrave, Duke of Buckinghamshire.

Page 218. *Still Green with Bays,* &c. *Essay on Criticism,* 181-188. For 'all devouring' Pope substituted 'all-involving'.

—*Monsieur Perrault.* See note to page 14.

Page 220. *in another place.* The *Essay on the Genius and Writings of Shakespear; with Some Letters of Criticism to the Spectator* (1712).

—*The gen'rous Critick,* &c. *Essay on Criticism,* 100-105. The last line of the quotation was omitted in later editions of the *Essay.*

Page 221. *Some dryly plain,* &c. *Ib.* 114-115.

Page 222. *These Rules . . . methodiz'd.* *Ib.* 88-89.

—*When first great Maro,* &c. *Ib.* 130-133. Pope altered the first couplet because of this criticism, but later restored it, substituting 'young' for 'great.'

—*Learn hence . . . them.* *Ib.* 139-140.

Page 224. *As on the Land,* &c. *Ib.* 54-59.

—*Jungentur jam Gryphes Equis.* Virgil, Æneid, 8. 27.

—*One Science . . . Wit.* *Essay on Criticism,* 60-61.

Page 225. *Not only . . . Parts.* *Ib.* 62-63. The later reading is, "But oft in those confined to single parts."

—*First follow Nature,* &c. *Ib.* 68-73. In 1. 72 we have 'must' instead of 'next'.

Page 226. *Scribendi . . . Fons.* Horace, *Ars Poetica,* 309.

—*Rem . . . Chartæ.* *Ib.* 310.

—*That Art . . . appear.* *Essay on Criticism,* 74-75. For this Pope substituted:

> " Art from that fund each just supply provides;
> Works without show, and without pomp presides."

Page 227. *In some fair Body,* &c. *Ib.* 76-79. Instead of 'sprightly' we now have 'informing.'

—*Thus . . . fails.* *Ib.* 56-57. The accepted reading is "Thus in the soul while memory prevails."

—*Life . . . impart.* *Ib.* 72.

—*according to the Observation.* Mulgrave, *Essay upon Poetry,* 20.

—*There are . . . it.* *Essay on Criticism,* 80-81. In the edition of 1743 and thereafter this reads:

> " Some, to whom heav'n in wit has been profuse,
> Want as much more, to turn it to its use."

Page 228. *For Wit . . . Wife.* *Ib.* 82-83. 'Often' was substituted for 'ever.'

Page 229. *Description of Wit.* Apparently from *La Manière de bien penser dans les ouvrages d'esprit* by Dominique Bouhours (1628-1702), although the closest parallel to the text is the following (p. 392 of the edition of 1687) : "Les pensées ingenieuses sont comme les diamans, qui tirent leur prix de ce qu'ils ont encore plus de solidité que d'éclat."

—*Poets . . . Art.* *Essay on Criticism,* 293-296.

Page 230. *But true Expression,* &c. *Ib.* 315-316.

—*True Wit . . . Sun.* Mulgrave, *Essay upon Poetry,* 12.

—*And tho' the Ancients,* &c. *Essay on Criticism,* 161-163.

Page 231. *Those Rules of old,* &c. *Ib.* 88-89.

—*Lord Bacon observes.* *Novum Organum,* 1. 84. Cf. also the *Advancement of Learning,* 1. 5. 1.

Page 232. *Those . . . dream. Ib.* 179-180. For 'are but' Pope substituted 'oft are.'

—*Aliquando . . . Homerus.* *Ars Poetica,* 359.

—*His reeling Hero's,* &c. Roscommon, *Essay on Translated Verse,* 139-140.

—*In Words . . . aside.* *Essay on Criticism,* 333-336.

Page 233. *Si forte . . . detorta.* *Ars Poetica,* 48-53.

—*quid autem . . . nomen. Ib.* 53-59.

Page 234. *And praise . . . join.* *Essay on Criticism,* 360-361.

—*Be Homer's Works,* &c. *Ib.* 124-129. 'Notions' was replaced by 'maxims.'

Page 235. *He who supreme,* &c. *Ib.* 657-662.

—*The Muses . . . draws. Ib.* 675-680. The only important change is in the first line, which now reads: "Thee bold Longinus! all the Nine inspire."

Page 236. *Thus make . . . Flegm.* Roscommon, *Essay on Translated Verse,* 301-302.

—*Now length of Fame,* &c. *Essay on Criticism,* 480-483.

Page 237. *says Boileau. Réflexions Critiques sur quelques passages du Rhéteur Longin,* Réflexion VII (*Oeuvres,* ed. Amar, 3. 242).

Page 238. *What is this Wit,* &c. *Essay on Criticism,* 500-503. In a letter to Carryl, June 25, 1711, Pope admitted that he had made a bull here. He altered the couplet twice, leaving it finally :

> " Then most our trouble still when most admired,
> And still the more we give, the more required."

Page 239. *That silly thing,* &c. Mulgrave, *Essay upon Poetry,* 269-272.

—a Couplet of Advice. *Essay on Criticism,* 566-567. As a result of Dennis' criticism, the line was made to read:

> "And speak, though sure, with seeming diffidence."

Page 240. *Libels for his Impatience.* Dennis obviously means himself, for the passage referred to (584 sq.) in the first edition mentioned him by name, D————.

—*Not only . . . Sway.* This couplet followed what is now 1. 648. It was removed entirely.

Page 241. *Libel upon King Charles. Ib.* 534-543.

Page 244. *Thus a wild Tartar,* &c. Butler, *Hudibras,* 2. 23-28.

—*what he says. Essay on Criticism,* 420-423.

—*returning to the Charge. Ib.* 588-591.

Page 245. *'Tis now . . . Owe.* Inaccurately quoted from Cowley's Imitation of the *Second Olympic Ode* of Pindar, §11.

Page 246. *His rankest Libels,* &c. I have been unable to place this couplet.

—*King William.* The couplet referring to William was deleted. It ran as follows:

> " Then first the Belgian morals were extolled,
> We their religion had, and they our gold."

The remaining lines of the reference to William are 544-553.

—*the 12th Page. Essay on Criticism,* 162.

Page 247. *St. Omer's,* a Jesuit seminary.

—*three Opportunities. Essay on Criticism,* 374-383, 458, 483.

—*Shakespear's Head.* Many of the books of Tonson, Dryden's printer, are announced on the title-page as "printed for Jacob Tonson at Shakespear's Head over against Katharine-Street in the Strand." Pope's *Pastorals* had already appeared in Tonson's Sixth *Miscellany.*

Will's. See note to page 22.

—*Sir R. B.* Sir Richard Blackmore.

—*Mr. L. M.* Luke Milbourne (1649-1720), who started a bitter war with Dryden by his strictures on the latter's *Virgil.*

—*Be thou . . . commend. Essay on Criticism,* 474-475.

Page 248. *he names Mr. Walsh. Ib.* 729 sq.

—*Dorimant,* a character in Etherege's *Man of Mode.*

—*ancient Wit.* Wycherly (1640?-1716), whose work Pope 'edited.'

—*Covent-Garden.* Many favorite coffee-houses were in or near Covent Garden.

—*Red Sea.* Cf. the *Spectator,* No. 12, for this phrase; and for a suggested explanation, see *Notes and Queries,* 3. 12. 56.

—*Sunning-Hill and Ockingham.*   I.e., at Binfield.

Page 249. *Dutch Piece.* Possibly *A True Character of Mr. Pope* (1716). This is not, however, certainly by Dennis, though the evidence on the whole favors this ascription. Cf. Paul, *John Dennis,* 90 and note.

—*a Panegyrick.* The verses referred to are those by Wycherly entitled *To my friend Mr. Pope, on his Pastorals.* They were originally published in the volume of Tonson's *Miscellany* containing the *Pastorals.* It is commonly believed to-day that Wycherly wrote the verses and that Pope revised them.

Page 250. *First follow Nature. Essay on Criticism,* 68.

—*Respicere . . . voces. Ars Poetica,* 317-318.

Page 252. *If once the Justness,* &c. Mulgrave, *Essay upon Poetry,* 267-268.

—*Still green with Bays. Essay on Criticism,* 181.

—*And tho' the Ancients,* &c. *Ib.* 161-163.

GEORGE FARQUHAR (1677-1707)

This essay was printed in a volume entitled: *Love and Business: in a Collection of Occasionary Verse, and Epistolary Prose, Not hitherto Publish'd. A Discourse likewise upon Comedy in Reference to the English Stage. In a Familiar Letter. By Mr. George Farquhar.* The volume is advertised as 'this day published' in the *Post-Man* for February 26-28, 1702. Many of the ideas of the essay appear in the prologue to *Sir Harry Wildair* (1701).

Page 259. *Divines threaten us.* Especially the Reverend Jeremy Collier, whose *Short View of the Immorality and Profaneness of the English Stage* (1698) excited a furious controversy.

—*Quæ genus.* Early in their university course, students were required to master the *Isagoge* of Porphyry, which begins: "Cum sit necessarium, Chrysaori, et ad eam quæ est apud Aristotelem prædicamentorum doctrinam nosse, quid genus sit," &c. The first section is headed, *De Genere.*

Page 260. *Jubilees . . . Fopingtons.* Farquhar's *The Constant Couple,* or a *Trip to the Jubilee* (1699 or 1700). Sir Novelty Fashion, who is a character in Cibber's *Love's Last Shift,* figures under the title of Lord Fopington in Vanbrugh's *Relapse* (1696). In the prologue to *Love's Contrivance,* Mrs. Centlivre says: "I believe Mr. Rich will own he got more by the *Trip to the Jubilee* with all its irregularities, than by the most uniform piece the stage could boast of ever since."

Page 261. *Heinsius. De Tragœdiæ Constitutione* (1611).

—*Hédelin,* Francois, Abbé d'Aubignac, *La Pratique du Théatre* (1657).

—*Zany.* For an account of the methods of such peripatetic quacks, see the *Spectator,* No. 572.

—*Mr. Rich.* At this time manager of the Theatre Royal in Drury Lane.

Page 262. *Mr. Collier.* See note on page 259.

—*Rover, Libertine, or old Batchelour.* Comedies by Mrs. Aphra Behn, Thomas Shadwell, and William Congreve.

—*Patentees.* The stockholders of the Drury Lane theatre, called patentees because they owned collectively the patent which gave this theatre for a time the monopoly.

Page 263. *German Doctor.* The reference is to Gerhard's attack on Bellarmine in his *Bellarminus Orthodoxiæ Testis* (Jena, 1631-1633).

Page 264. *Hick's Hall* stood at the bottom of St. John Street. It was built for the county magistracy by Sir Baptist Hicks in the second decade of the seventeenth century.

—*King's Bench.* One of the superior courts of common law.

Page 265. *great Cook.* Sir Edward Coke (1552-1634), one of the greatest of English judges and writers on law.

Page 267. *Doctor Tillotson.* See note to page 80.

Page 268. *Woollich.* One of the chief navy-yards of England from the sixteenth century to the appearance of iron men-of-war.

Page 269. *Lincolns-Inn-Fields.* The theatre which was the important rival of Drury Lane, especially before the opening of the Haymarket in 1705.

Page 270. *Prince Arthur,* by Sir Richard Blackmore.

Page 271. *Soph,* i.e., Socrates.

Page 274. *Utile Dulci.* Horace, *Ars Poetica,* 343.

—*Fondlewife.* Character in Congreve's *Old Bachelor.*

Page 275. *Nathan's Fable.* II *Samuel,* 12. 1-14.

Page 276. *Wildair . . . Morose.* Wildair appears both in the *Trip to the Jubilee* and in the sequel, *Sir Harry Wildair.* As a typical fine gentleman he is contrasted with Morose, a character in Jonson's *Epicœne,* who loathed all society.

Page 279. *Hippolito's.* I can find no trace of a coffee-house called Hippolito's. Either the establishment was more commonly known by another name, or it was one of the three thousand said to have existed in the eighteenth century, most of which were unknown to fame.

Page 282. *Alexander the Great.* Hero of Lee's tragedy *The Rival Queens.*

—*Mr. Betterton.* Thomas Betterton (1635-1710), the most famous actor of his day and manager of the theatre in Lincoln's Inn Fields from 1700-1705.

RICHARD STEELE (1672-1729)

All the selections from the periodicals are printed from the first collected edition in octavo. Addison, at least, made some revisions in his work before it appeared in this format. In respect also to spelling and punctuation, this is a somewhat better text. All the papers are given in full except *Tatler* LXVIII, the earlier part of which has nothing to do with criticism.

Page 290. *Wilks.* Robert Wilks (1665?-1732). His first appearance as Macduff was made at the Haymarket on December 27, 1707.

Page 291. *said . . . by Horace. Ars Poetica,* 102-103.

Page 292. *His Lacrymis . . . ultro.* Virgil, *Æneid,* 2. 145.

Page 293. *Motto.* Horace, *Epist.* 2. 1. 83-84.

Page 295. *Virgil hath drawn.* Cf. *Georgics,* 3. 72-94, and *Æneid,* 8. 551-553.

JOSEPH ADDISON (1672-1719)

Page 306. *Motto.* Horace, *Epist.* 2. 1. 208-213.

—*Poetical Justice.* One of the strongest supporters of the doctrine in England was Dennis. Before him it had been maintained, among others, by Rymer, *Tragedies of the Last Age* (Spingarn, *op. cit.*, 2. 188, 200). One of the many French exponents was Hédelin, *La Pratique du Théatre*, 5.

Page 307. *Aristotle . . . observes. Poetics*, 13. 6.

—*Orphan*, &c. The *Orphan* and *Venice Preserved* are by Otway; the *Rival Queens*, or the *Death of Alexander the Great*, and *Theodosius*, by Lee; *All for Love*, by Dryden; *Oedipus*, by Dryden and Lee; *Oronooko*, by Southerne.

Page 308. *Mourning Bride*, &c. The *Mourning Bride* is by Congreve; *Tamerlane* and *Ulysses*, by Rowe; *Phædra and Hyppolitus*, by Edmund Smith.

Page 309. *Powell.* George Powell (1658?-1714), a well-known actor who was the original Portius in Addison's *Cato*.

Page 311. *Motto.* Horace, *Sat.* 1. 4. 43-44.

Page 312. *Solomon resembles. Canticles*, 7. 4.

—*Coming of a Thief.* I *Thess.* 5. 2; II *Pet.* 3. 10.

—*one of his Heroes.* Homer, *Iliad*, 11. 558-562.

—*another of them.* Homer, *Odyssey*, 20. 24-27.

Page 313. *Horace has represented them. Carmina* 4. 2. 1-4.

—*Passage in Terence. Eunuch*, 61-63.

—*Camisars.* The Camisards were French Protestants, some of whom had taken refuge in London, where they were known as 'French prophets'. Their ecstatic fits in which they uttered pseudo-prophecies were often ridiculed. Cf. the *Tatler*, No. 11, and Shaftesbury, *A Letter concerning Enthusiasm.*

Page 316. *Motto.* Horace, *Ars Poetica*, 409.

—*Salmoneus.* Cf. Virgil, *Æneid*, 6. 585.

Page 319. *Terence speaks. Andria*, 20-21.

—*Dr. South tells us.* In a sermon preached at Westminster Abbey, February 22, 1685 (*Sermons*, ed. 1842, 1. 168).

—*Pliny tells us. Nat. Hist.* 37. 3.

ALEXANDER POPE (1688-1744)

An advertisement in the *Daily Courant* announces for June 6, 1715, the delivery to the subscribers of the first volume of the *Iliad*. It was advertised as 'this day published' in the *London Gazette* for June 28-July 2.

Page 326. *Aristotle calls. Poetics*, 6. 14.

Page 327. *says Macrobius. Saturnalia*, 5. 2.

Page 328. *Herodotus imagines. History*, 2. 53.

Page 330. *Aristotle expresses it. Poetics*, 24. 7.

—*Longinus has given. On the Sublime*, VIII, IX.

Page 331. *Duport*. James Duport, *Homeri Gnomologia*, Cambridge, 1660.

Page 332. *Aristotle had reason*. A somewhat exaggerated version of the *Rhetoric*, 3. 11. 3.

Page 337. *Madam Dacier*. The *Iliad . . . with Notes. To which are prefixed a large preface, and the life of Homer*, by Madam Dacier. 1712.

Page 338. *Boileau is of opinion. Réflexions Critiques sur Longin*, Réfl. IX (*Oeuvres*, ed. Amar, 3. 262-263).

Page 340. *Rapin judges. Comparaison des poëmes d' Homère et de Virgile* (1664), Réfl. III, IV, V.

—*Scaliger in his Poetices*. V. 3.

—*Perrault. Parallèle des Anciens et des Modernes* (1693), 2. 42-43.

—*de la Motte*. Houdart de la Motte, *Discours sur Homère, Du Merite Personel d'Homère* (*Oeuvres*, ed. 1754, 3. 95 sq.).

Page 351. *Read Homer once*, &c. Mulgrave, *Essay upon Poetry*, 325-328.

—*Author of the Tragedy*. George Granville, Lord Lansdowne.

LEONARD WELSTED (1688-1747)

The volume for which the essay here reprinted serves as an introduction was announced as 'this day published' in the *Daily Post* for March 25, 1724. The title-page reads: *Epistles, Odes,*

&c., Written on Several Subjects: with a Dissertation Concerning the Perfection of the English Language, the State of Poetry, &c. By Mr. Welsted.

Page 355. *Duke of Newcastle.* Thomas Pelham-Holles, Duke of Newcastle (1693-1768), was a prominent but undistinguished figure in politics who incidentally patronized some men of letters without being specially interested in literature. Later in the *Dissertation* he is referred to as Holles.

Page 360. *And what . . . be.* Pope, *Essay on Criticism,* 483.

Page 363. *two memorable Princes.* Augustus Cæsar and Cosimo dei Medici (?).

Page 368. *Valerius Maximus has affirmed. De Dictis,* 5. 4, Ext. 5.

Page 369. *a Translation.* Of Longinus, *On the Sublime.* For the opinion referred to, see this treatise, Section II.

Page 370. *Essayers in Rhime.* With the exception of the first two, these quotations are all from Mulgrave, *Essay upon Poetry,* as follows: 246-247, 244-245, 73-74, 81-82, 126, 185-188, 229, 248-249, 262-264, 269, 346. The first two are quoted from *A Grammar of the English Tongue, with the Arts of Logick, Rhetorick Poetry, &c.* (1711), pp. 145 and 146.

Page 374. *Sapere . . . fons.* Horace, *Ars Poetica,* 309.

Page 375. *Descriptas . . . salutor. Ib.* 86-87.

Page 379. *This Author . . . tells us.* Dryden, *Dedication of the Æneis* (*Essays,* ed. Ker, 2. 217).

Page 381. *that other.* I.e., Newton's.

—*Mr. Cowley . . . has said.* I cannot find precisely this. Possibly Welsted had in mind Cowley's interest in experimental as opposed to theoretical science as set forth in the preface to *A Proposition for the Advancement of Experimental Philosophy.*

Page 383. *a whole Oration.* Cicero, *Pro Archia.*

Page 385. *A late very popular Author.* Addison.

Page 387. *Mr. Philips.* Ambrose Philips (1675?-1749). For the recommendation of Welsted's poems, see the *Freethinker,* Nos. 98, 99, 112. This periodical was edited and chiefly written by Philips. It ran from March 24, 1718, to September 28, 1719.

—*Sir William Temple . . . says.* Cf. pages 47-48 and note.

Page 389. *Commendation . . . by Scaliger. Poetices* 6. 7 (ed. 1651, p. 339a).

—*Dacier is not less sensible. Oeuvres d'Horace,* 4. 84. The quotation on page 391 directly follows this.

Page 391. *Sir William Temple . . . takes a Step.* Essentially the point of a passage in the *Essay on Ancient and Modern Learning* (Spingarn, *op. cit.,* 3. 47-48).

—*Seneca's Words. Epist. Moral.* 13. 3. 37.

Page 393. *Afranius.* This conceivably applies to L. Afranius (fl.c. 94 B. C.), the writer of comedies; but, more probably, to an unidentified writer nearly contemporary with Welsted.

Page 394. *words of Quintilian. Oratoriæ Institutiones,* 10. 1. 62.

ALLAN RAMSAY (1686-1758)

This preface is taken from *The Ever Green,* being a selection of Scots Poems, wrote by the Ingenious before 1600. Edinburgh, 1724. The original is printed in italics.

Page 399. *our . . . Makers of Pastorals.* Cf., e.g., Pope, *Pastorals,* 2. 66, 3. 79.

BIBLIOGRAPHY

BIBLIOGRAPHY

The following list of critical writings published between 1700 and 1725 has been compiled largely from contemporary newspapers and periodicals. Only a portion of the material dealing with individual writers or works has been included. Practically no mention is made of works containing only isolated sentences of a critical character.

Anonymous. *A New Session of the Poets, occasion'd by the Death of Mr. Dryden.* 1700.

An Epistle to Sir Richard Blackmore, occasion'd by the New Session of the Poets. 1700.

A Pacquet from Parnassus: Or, a Collection of Papers, viz . . . On the Advancement of Poetry. Vol. I. Numb. II. 1702.

A Short Defence of the Comparison of the two Stages. By "Henry Ramble." 1702.

Satira in Poetastros O — — C — — ensis. 1702.

The Parliament of Criticks, the Menippæan Satyr of Justus Lipsius In a Dream, Paraphras'd in a Banter upon the Criticks of the Age. 1702.

Religio Poetæ, or, a Satyr upon our English Poets. 1703.

The Tryal of Skill; or a new Session of the Poets, calculated for the Meridian of Parnassus in the Year 1704.

A Panegyrick Epistle (Wherein is given An Impartial Character of the Present English Poets) To Sir R — B — On his most Incomparable Incomprehensible Poem, call'd Advice to the Poets. 1706.

The Muses Mercury, or the Monthly Miscellany. January, 1707, to January, 1708. [ed. Oldmixon?]

The Scrutiny . . . with . . . Reflections upon Cyder, Censura Temporum, and poor Bays. 1708.

Milton's Sublimity asserted, in a Poem occasion'd by a late Celebrated Piece, entituled, Cyder . . . By Philo-Milton. 1709.

Essays upon Nothing . . . 9. The Description of a genius Truly Sublime. 1709.

A Comment on the History of Tom Thumb, ridiculing Addison on Chevy Chase. 1711. [Dr. William Wagstaffe? Swift?]

A Grammar of the English Tongue, with the Arts of Logick, Rhetorick, Poetry, &c. 1711. [Attributed on insufficient evidence to Steele.]

A modest Survey of that Celebrated Tragedy The Distrest Mother. 1712.

On the Death of Mr. Edmund Smith . . . a Poem in Miltonick Verse, with a Preface containing some Remarks upon Milton. 1712.

Cato Examin'd. 1713.

Bibliotheca: A Poem. Occasion'd by the sight of a Modern Library. 1713.

A Collection of the Occasional Papers For the Years 1716-1719. Especially the *Essay on Genius,* 1718.

An Essay on the Poets. 1717.

Congratulatory Verses to Edward Biddle . . . with some Remarks, Critical . . . By the Old Three. 1718.

The Critick. January 6 to June 22, 1718.

A Vindication of the Press; Or, An Essay on the Usefulness of Writing, Criticism, and the Qualification of Authors. 1718.

The Scriblers Lash'd. 1718.

Critical Remarks on the Four Taking Plays Of this Season; viz. Sir Walter Raleigh, The Masquerade, Chit-Chat, *and* Busiris, King of Egypt . . . By Corinna. 1719.

The Creation. A Pindarick Illustration of a Poem, Originally written by Moses. With a Preface to Mr. Pope, concerning the Sublimity of the Ancient Hebrew Poetry. 1720.

Homer Travestie: Being a new Translation . . . with a critical Preface. [after Marivaux] 1720.

The Present State of Poetry; a Satire; address'd to a Friend. To which are added, 1. Advice to a young Author. 1721.

Modern Poetasters [by "Isaac Bickerstaff, Jr."]. 1721.

The Oxford Criticks; a Satire. 1721.

The Eagle, a Fable on the Times. With an Essay on Fable in Verse. 1722.

The Censor Censured; or, The Conscious Lovers *examin'd: in a dialogue . . . into which Mr. Dennis is introduced.* 1723.

An Essay upon Kings, Poets, Stoics, Sceptics . . . and for defining the Term Barbarous. 1723.

The many Advantages of a good Language to any Nation: With an Examination of the present State of our own: As also, an Essay towards correcting some Things that are wrong in it. 1725.

A letter to my Lord — — — on the present Diversions of the Town. With the true Reason of the Decay of our Dramatic Entertainments. 1725.

The Authors of the Town; a Satire: inscrib'd to the Author of the Universal Passion. 1725.

Addison, Joseph. *Poems on Several Occasions, with a Dissertation upon the Roman Poets.* 1719.
See also the *Guardian, Spectator,* &c.

Aristotle. *The Art of Poetry. Translated from the Original Greek, according to Mr. Theodore Goulston's Edition. Together with Mr. D'Acier's Notes Translated from the French.* 1705.

Barker, Henry. *The Polite Gentleman; or, Reflections upon the several kinds of Wit . . . Done from the French.* 1700.

Blackmore, Sir Richard. *Satyr against Wit.* 1700.
Essays upon Several Subjects. 1716.

Blackwell, Anthony. *An Introduction to the Classicks, containing a short Discourse upon their Excellencies.* 1717.
The Sacred Classicks defended and illustrated. 1725.

Boileau, Nicolas. *The Works of . . . made English by several Hands.* 1712.

Bouhours, Dominique. *The Art of Criticism . . . Translated . . . by a Person of Quality.* 1705.

Brown, Thomas. *Works.* 1707.

Bysshe, Edward. *The Art of English Poetry.* 1702.

Callières, F. de. *Characters and Criticisms upon the Ancient and Modern Authors. Written originally in French.* 1705.

Cobb, Samuel. *Poems on Several Occasions . . . To which is prefix'd A Discourse on Criticism, and the Liberty of Writing.* 1700.

Cooke, T. *The Battle of the Poets.* 1725.

Coppinger, Matthew. *A Session of the Poets.* 1705.

Coward, W. *Licentia Poetica discuss'd; or, The True Test of Poetry.* 1709.

Cowper, John. *Bag-Pipes no Musick. A Satire. Upon the Scotch Poetry.* 1720.

Dart, John. *The Works of Tibullus . . . With some Observations on . . . Elegiack Verse; with Characters of the most celebrated Greek, Latin, and English Elegiack Poets.* 1720.
A Poem on Chaucer and his Writings. 1722.

Dennis, John. *The Advancement and Reformation of Modern Poetry.* 1701.
The Comical Gallant . . . To Which is Added a Large Account of the Taste in Poetry and the Causes of the Degeneracy of it. 1702.
The Person of Quality's Answer to Mr. Collier's Letter, being a Dissuasive from the Play-house. 1704.
The Grounds of Criticism in Poetry. 1704.
Britannia Triumphans [containing a preface upon the use of rime]. 1704.
An Essay upon the Operas after the Italian Manner. 1706.
Reflections . . . upon a late Rhapsody called An Essay upon Criticism. 1711.
An Essay on the Genius and Writings of Shakespear: with Some Letters of Criticism to the Spectator. 1712.
Remarks upon Cato. 1713.
A True Character of Mr. Pope [?]. 1716.
Remarks upon Mr. Pope's Translation of Homer; with Two Letters concerning Windsor Forest, *and the* Temple of Fame. 1717.

Proposals for printing by Subscription . . . *Miscellaneous Tracts* [contains a letter concerning Addison on *Paradise Lost*]. 1721.

Original Letters, Familiar, Moral, and Critical. 1721.

A Defence of Sir Fopling Flutter. 1722.

A Short Essay toward an English Prosody [in Greenwood's *An Essay towards a Practical English Grammar,* 2d ed.]. 1722.

Remarks on a Play, call'd The Conscious Lovers. 1723.

Farquhar, George. *Love and Business* . . . *A Discourse likewise upon Comedy in Reference to the English Stage.* 1702.

Felton, Henry. *A Dissertation On Reading the Classics, And Forming a Just Style.* 1713.

Fénelon, François de Salignac de la Mothe. *Reflections upon the Art of Writing with Propriety, Elegance and Accuracy* . . . *with a Discourse upon Poetry in General* . . . *translated from the French.* 1717.

Dialogues concerning Eloquence in General . . . *translated* . . . *by* William Stevenson. 1722.

Fiddes, Richard. *A prefatory Epistle concerning some Remarks to be publish'd on Homer's* Iliad. 1714.

Gay, John. *The Present State of Wit.* 1711.

Gildon, Charles. *A Comparison between the two Stages.* 1702.

An Essay on the Art, Rise, and Progress of the Stage [in the *Works of Mr. William Shakespeare,* ed. Rowe, Vol. 7]. 1709.

A New Rehearsal, or Bays the Younger . . . *To which is prefix'd, an Essay upon Criticism in General.* 1714.

Some Remarks on Mr. Rowe's Tragedy of the Lady Jane Grey. 1715.

The Art of Poetry. 1718.

The Laws of Poetry . . . *Explain'd and illustrated.* 1721.

Gordon, Thomas. *The Humourist: Being Essays upon several Subjects* . . . *On Criticism.* 1720.

Guardian, The [by Addison, Steele, &c.]. March 12 to October 1, 1713.

Hardouin, J. *An Apology for Homer* [translated from the French]. 1716.

Horace. *Satires and Epistles of Horace . . . To which is now added* [2d ed.], *His* Art of Poetry. 1712.

Hughes, John. *The Works of Mr. Edmund Spenser.* 1715.

Hutcheson, F. *An Inquiry into the Original of our Ideas of Beauty and Virtue.* 1725.

Jacob, Giles. *The Poetical Register.* 1719-1720.

Killigrew, Thomas, the younger. *Chit-Chat, a Comedy.* 1719.

Morrice, Bezaleel. *An Epistle to Mr. Welsted, and a Satire on the English Translations of Homer.* 1721.
An Essay on the Poets. 1721.

Oldmixon, John. *A Pastoral Poem on the Victories of Schellenburgh and Bleinheim . . . With a large Preface, shewing the antiquity and dignity of Pastoral Poetry.* 1705.

Pack, Richardson. *Miscellanies in Prose and Verse.* 1719.

Parnell, Thomas. *An Essay on the Different Stiles of Poetry.* 1713.

Philips, Ambrose. *The Free-Thinker.* March 24, 1718, to September 28, 1719 [edited and for the most part written by A. P.].
A Criticism on Song-Writing [in *The Hive,* 2d ed.]. 1723.
A Collection of old Ballads . . . with Introductions, Historical, Critical, or Humourous [?]. 1723-1725.

Pope, Alexander. *An Essay on Criticism.* 1711.
Preface to the *Translation of the* Iliad *of Homer.* 1715.
Preface to *The Works of Mr. William Shakespear.* 1725.

Prior, Matthew. Preface to *An Ode Humbly Inscribed to the Queen.* 1706.
Poems on Several Occasions [preface to *Solomon*]. 1718.

Ramsay, Allan. *The Ever Green.* 1724.

Roche, Michael de la, editor. *Memoirs of Literature.* Irregularly from March 13, 1710, to April, 1717.

Rowe, Nicholas. *Some Account of the Life, &c., of Mr. William Shakespear* [in *The Works of Mr. William Shakespear,* Vol. 1]. 1709.

Sewell, George. *The Life and Character of Mr. John Philips.* 1712.

   Observations upon Cato. 1713.

   A Vindication of the English Stage, exemplified in the Cato *of Addison.* 1716.

   Preface to the seventh volume of the *Works of Mr. William Shakespear* [ed. Pope]. 1725.

Shaftesbury, Anthony Ashley Cooper, 3d Earl of. *Sensus Communis: An Essay on the Freedom of Wit and Humor.* 1709.

   Soliloquy: or, Advice to an Author. 1710.

   Characteristicks of Men, Manners, &c. [Vol. 3, *Miscellaneous Reflections on . . . other Critical Subjects*]. 1711.

Spectator, The [by Addison, Steele, &c.]. March 1, 1711, to December 6, 1712; June 18 to December 20, 1714.

Steele, Sir Richard. *The Theatre.* January 2 to April 5, 1720.
   See also the *Spectator, Tatler,* &c.

Swift, Jonathan. *The Battel . . . Between the Antient and Modern Books in St. James's Library.* 1704.

   A Proposal for Correcting, Improving and Ascertaining the English Tongue. 1712.

   A Letter of Advice to a Young Poet. 1721.

Tate, Nahum. *The Muses Memorial . . . with an Account of the Present State of Poetry.* 1707.

Tatler, The [by Steele, Addison, &c.]. April 12, 1709, to January 2, 1711.

Terrasson, Jean. *A Discourse of Ancient and Modern Learning* [trans.]. 1716.

   A Critical Dissertation upon Homer's Iliad *. . . translated from the French* by F. Brerewood. 1722.

Theobald, Lewis. *The Censor.* April 11 to June 17, 1715; January 1 to June 1, 1717.

Trapp, Joseph. *Prælectiones Poeticæ.* 1711.

Victor, B. *An Epistle to Sir Richard Steele, on his play, call'd,* The Conscious Lovers. 1722.

Vida, G. *The Art of Poetry. Translated . . . by* Christopher Pitt. 1725.

Webster, —. *The Stage: a Poem.* 1713.

Welsted, Leonard. *The Works of Dionysius Longinus . . . translated . . . with some Remarks on . . . the English Poets.* 1712.

    Epistles, Odes, &c. . . . To which is prefix'd A Dissertation concerning the Perfection of the English Language, the State of Poetry, &c. 1724.

Wesley, Samuel. *An Epistle to a Friend concerning Poetry.* 1700.

Wotton, William. *A Defense of the* Reflections upon Ancient and Modern Learning . . . *With Observations upon the* Tale of a Tub. 1705.

Young, R. *An Essay upon the Writings of Mr. Addison.* 3d ed. 1720.

INDEX

INDEX